Fortress Church

For my mother

Fortress Church

The English Roman Catholic Bishops and Politics 1903–63

Kester Aspden

GRACEWING

First published in 2002

Gracewing
2 Southern Avenue, Leominster
Herefordshire HR6 0QF

ISBN 0 85244 203 3

Typeset by Action Publishing Technology Ltd,
Gloucester, GL1 5SR

Printed in England by
Antony Rowe Ltd, Eastbourne BN23 6QT

Contents

Abbreviations

A.C.T.U.	Association of Catholic Trade Unionists
C.B.C.R.	Committee of British Catholics for Reconciliation between Great Britain and Ireland
C.E.C.	Catholic Education Council
C.E.G.	Catholic Evidence Guild
C.L.A.	Catholic Land Association
C.O.P.E.C.	Conference on Christian Politics, Economics and Citizenship
C.S.G.	Catholic Social Guild
C.S.S.	Catholic Socialist Society
C.S.U.	Christian Social Union
C.R.A.	Catholic Representation Association
C.T.F.	Catholic Teachers' Federation
C.T.S.	Catholic Truth Society
C.T.U.	Catholic Trade Unionists
C.U.G.B.	Catholic Union of Great Britain
C.W.C.	Catholic Workers' College
C.W.L.	Catholic Women's League
C.W.S.S.	Catholic Women's Suffrage Society
I.C.C.J.	International Council of Christians and Jews
I.L.P.	Independent Labour Party
I.P.C.	International Peace Campaign
I.P.P.	Irish Parliamentary Party
I.R.A.	Irish Republican Army
I.S.D.L.	Irish Self-Determination League
L.N.U.	League of Nations Union
N.C.C.J.	National Council of Christians and Jews
N.C.C.T.U.	National Conference of Catholic Trade Unionists
N.C.W.C.	National Catholic Welfare Council (USA)
P.D.C.	Pro-Deo Commission
Sword	Sword of the Spirit
T.U.C.	Trades Union Congress
U.I.L.	United Irish League
Y.C.W.	Young Christian Workers

Acknowledgements

This book started life long ago in October 1994 as a doctoral dissertation. Warm thanks are due to my supervisor, the Revd Dr David M. Thompson of Fitzwilliam College, Cambridge, for his encouragement, patience and constant help, both during the course of my degree and in the months after.

A special mention must go to Revd Dr F. P. McHugh of St Edmund's College, Cambridge, whose friendship, expertise, guidance and linguistic skills, have been of especial help to me.

Dr Mary Heimann was generous with her advice at key stages. I would like to thank my doctoral examiners, Dr Eamon Duffy and the late Professor Adrian Hastings, for all their useful and generous comments at my viva. In addition, their help in the months following was gratefully received. Professor Hastings was particularly generous with his comments on later drafts; it is a great personal regret that I never had the opportunity to present him with this book.

The help of the diocesan archivists has been invaluable during the course of this research. I must give special mentions to Fr David Lannon, who received me with warmth and hospitality, putting his excellent archives and library at my disposal, both at Burnley and earlier at Derker, Oldham; Fr Christopher Smith of Dartmouth; Fr Aidan Bellenger, O.S.B. and the monks of Downside Abbey, and Fr Ian Dickie of the Westminster archives. I am grateful also to Fr Michael Clifton, archivist of the archdiocese of Southwark; Fr Stewart Foster, archivist of Brentwood diocese; Revd Dr John Harding, archivist of the Clifton diocese; Dr John Cashman, also at Clifton; Fr John Sharp, archivist of the Birmingham archdiocese; the former archivist at Birmingham, Fr Petroc Howell; Margaret Osborne, archivist of the diocese of Northampton; Canon Marmion, archivist of the Shrewsbury diocese; Fr Dominique Minskip, former archivist of the Middlesbrough diocese; Mgr George Bradley and Mr Robert Finnigan, archivists of the Leeds diocese; Mr Robin Gard, archivist of the Hexham and Newcastle diocese; Fr Francis Isherwood, archivist of the Porstmouth diocese and Fr A. P. Dolan, archivist of the Nottingham diocese. I would like to record my gratitude to Fr Anthony McCaffery, Chancellor of the archdiocese of Liverpool, for arranging access to archival material then held in the Curial Offices; the Duke of Norfolk and John Robinson, librarian to the Duke of Norfolk, for access to the archives of Arundel Castle; Mrs Sara Rodger, assistant librarian of Arundel Castle; Dr Judith Champ, archivist of Oscott College; Michael Blades, Principal of Plater College, Oxford; the Keeper of the archives of Churchill College, Cambridge; Fr Thomas McCoog and Fr Holt of the English Province of the Society of Jesus; David Murphy of the Catholic Truth Society; David Sheehy, archivist of the archdiocese of Dublin; Fr Seán Clyne, archivist of the Armagh archdiocesan archives; Mgr Charles Burns, formerly of the Vatican Library; David Potter and Richard Whinder, archivists of the Venerable English College, Rome. Last but by no means least, I would like to pay a special tribute to Dr Meg Whittle, archivist of the Liverpool archdiocese: her labours in taking the Liverpool archives from chaos into its current high standard were nothing short of Herculean. The sections on Archbishop Keating were greatly improved after her work on this material; unfortunately time constraints meant I could not make use of all the Downey material.

I would like to thank Joan Bond and all the staff of the Catholic Central Library, London; this has proved an invaluable research resource and I hope it is eventually put on a secure and permanent footing. I would also like to thank the staff of the Talbot Library, Preston; Cambridge University Library; House of Lords Record Office; National Library of Ireland; Lambeth Palace Library, Public Record Office; Fawcett Library, Guildhall University; Colindale Newspaper Library, Talbot Library, Preston; Brynmor Jones Library, University of Hull; the Record Offices of Warwickshire, Northamptonshire, Liverpool and Lancashire; Secret Vatican Archives and the Congregation for the Evangelization of Peoples, Rome.

Warm thanks to the Master and Fellows of Fitzwilliam College, Cambridge, for assisting with research costs; the trustees of the Andrew C. Duncan Catholic History Trust; the trustees of the Lightfoot Fund; the trustees of the Prince Consort and Thirlwall Fund; the British Academy. I would like to thank the Master and Fellows of St Edmund's College, Cambridge, for all their kindness and hospitality.

For assistance, friendship and encouragement during the course of my research I would like to mention James and Lucia Aitken, Lucy Collins, Sister Gemma Simmonds, I.B.V.M., Heather Davidson and family, Calum Murray, Elaine Conroy, Andrew Savage and Jane Brookfield, Ulrike Ehret, Anne Henry, Keith Hayward, Frank Palser, Andrew Brons and Harro Höpfl. Professor V. A. McClelland, Michael Hornsby-Smith and Michael Walsh were generous with their advice. Participants at the Church History seminar at Cambridge have provided helpful comments. Emma Worsfold – a true original – is greatly missed.

Tom Longford and Jo Ashworth at Gracewing have been extremely patient and helpful in seeing this book through to publication.

Without the help of my family, all of them conveniently placed near the Catholic archives of northern England, I would not have managed the research. I would like to thank Maureen Greenwood for all her support and interest. Special thanks to my grandmother for all her support through the years. Her gift of a computer was a great help. I am immeasurably grateful to my father for his support in this and earlier academic ventures.

Without the patient love and support of Sarah the going would have been much tougher. Nobody will be more pleased to see the back of the bishops than Sarah (I hope she will now return from Russia!).

My greatest debt is owed to my mother. Without her support, belief and encouragement, the book would not have been possible. The book is rightfully dedicated to her.

Illustrations

1.   Peter Amigo and William Brown, courtesy of Salford Diocesan Archives.

2. & 3. Francis Bourne, courtesy of Westminster Diocesan Archives.

4. & 5. Arthur Hinsley, courtesy of Westminster Diocesan Archives.

6.   Richard Downey, courtesy of the Archives of the Archdiocese of Liverpool.

7.   John Heenan, courtesy of Westminster Diocesan Archives.

8.   William Godfrey, courtesy of Westminster Diocesan Archives.

Introduction

... for all the pomp that surrounds him in his life and death, a bishop is apt to be one of the most isolated of men. In the ecclesiastical household, he enjoys neither the prerogative of 'the first born' nor the special predilection of 'the Benjamin'. The Pope, as the 'Holy Father', is in everybody's loving prayers, while the parish priest is united to multitudes of souls by a thousand and one ties arising out of his sacred ministry. But the bishop is often an unknown, if not a negligible quality. He lives in seclusion. His public appearances are ceremonious. Out of pontifical attire, he is likely to pass unrecognized. His visits to the parishes are comparatively rare; his pastoral addresses formal, his intervention in parochial affairs not always welcomed! He removes a popular priest, or issues some irksome mandate: he refuses dispensations, or imposes severe penalties. Hence he is respected rather than loved. He is valued as the spokesman and figure-head of the local Catholic body. He is acclaimed, on occasion, as their official standard bearer. He is prayed for when he is sick or dying. At other times, he is likely to be forgotten.[1]

My concern with those now mostly forgotten men at the top end of the Church goes somewhat against the grain of recent approaches to the history of the Catholic community. Two recent studies of aspects of nineteenth-century English Catholicism, Dermot Quinn's *Patronage and Piety* and Mary Heimann's *Catholic Devotion in Victorian England*, set themselves against a tradition of Catholic historiography which has tended to focus exclusively on the ideas and public actions of those few men at the top.[2] 'Lamentably nearly every English Catholic history has been beguiled by the swish of the purple and ended up as a cardinals' portrait gallery', Daniel Rees observed in a critique of Edward Norman's history of the nineteenth-century Church.[3] However, whilst recognizing that the history of the Church should be viewed from perspectives other than those which encourage an overly clerical understanding of the Church's past, it would be equally misleading given the importance attached to the episcopal office and the great stress on hierarchical direction throughout the period of this study (1903–63), to minimize the role and importance of the bishops. This book is concerned with one aspect of episcopal activity: the attitudes and responses of the English Roman Catholic bishops to a range of social and political questions.

Despite the increasing accessibility of diocesan archives the twentieth century is a neglected period in English Catholic history. The gap is beginning to be addressed,[4] but to those who have ventured into this area it can appear a somewhat arid field to plough.[5] As Buchanan notes, 'the dramatic achievements and charismatic personalities associated with Catholicism in the later nineteenth century gave way to an administrative blandness and greater insularity after 1900.'[6] The Church during this period is frequently characterized as a ghetto or a fortress,[7] inward-looking and defensive in its priorities. There is need of a reassessment.

*   *   *

The greatest achievement of Pope Pius X (1903–14) was undoubtedly bringing together the very scattered sources which constituted the mystery that was the canon law of the Latin Church into one uniform codification.[8] Promulgated on 27 May 1917 during the reign of Pope Benedict XV (1914–22), the Code of Canon Law – 'arguably the most important event in the history of the Catholic Church in the modern era', John Cornwell has gone so far as to assert[9] – sanctioned the centralization of the Church in the papacy that was already under way in the nineteenth century. It said much on the rights and duties of the bishops, and its effect was to strengthen their position over the local church. Again, this process was already under way in the nineteenth century: in England the restoration of the ecclesiastical hierarchy in 1850 had reinforced the increasing authority of the episcopate over the clergy and laity.[10] Canon 329 of the revised Code affirmed that the 'Bishops are the successors of the Apostles and by divine institution are in command of particular churches which they rule with ordinary power, but subject to the Roman Pontiff'.[11] A bishop has the right and duty of governing the diocese in both spiritual and temporal matters with legislative, judicial and coercive power; he is the chief teacher of doctrine in the diocese, and possesses the legal right to direct all administrative acts (canon 335. 1). He has the duty to see to the observance of the laws of the Church, prevent abuses, safeguard the purity of faith and morals, and promote Catholic education (canon 335, 336). No priest was allowed to publish a book, to edit or contribute to journals or newspapers, without the permission of the local bishop (canon 1393. 1). But the most important feature of the Code was that it marked the culmination of the process of increasing centralization of power in the papacy. Papal power had been inflated by the dogmas of papal primacy and infallibility promulgated at the First Vatican Council of 1869–70; now the scope of papal responsibility was extended by canon 329. 2 to include the right of nominating all bishops, a momentous innovation since throughout most of the history of the Church the popes had claimed no such right.[12]

The logic of Roman centralization was that national hierarchies came ever more to reflect papal concerns and priorities. As part of the Pope's drive to restructure the Roman Curia on a more rational and efficient basis, the constitution of June 1908, *Sapienti Consilio*, removed the English Church from the jurisdiction of Propaganda Fide and placed it under the *Sacred Consistorial Congregation* and the general law of the Church. It meant that England was no longer considered missionary territory, and as such was welcomed by the English Catholic Church as a sign that it had finally come of age. Yet it was in effect a centralizing measure: as Chadwick notes, 'Propaganda had allowed them [the bishops] more local decision than they were now to get under the Consistorial'.[13] Increasingly it was considered desirable that the best students, the future bishops, received their training in Rome's educational institutions, the assumption being that this would imbue a greater sense of devotion to the papacy. In England this meant that the Venerabile (the English College, Rome) would come to assume an increasing importance as a breeding-ground for bishops. Stricter enforcement of *ad Limina* visits, when bishops were expected to provide detailed accounts of the conditions of their diocese, and a greater degree of scrutiny to ensure conformity to Roman discipline, were features of the pontificate of Pius X.[14]

During the period of this study there were five popes: Pius X, Benedict XV, Pius XI (1922–39), Pius XII (1939–58) and John XXIII (1958–63). The pontificate of John XXIII, which laid the ground for the Second Vatican Council (1962–5), had only a minimal impact on the English bishops at the time – their mindset had been formed in the more defensive atmosphere of the first half of the century. Whilst differences between the popes during this age of intransigence can be discerned, these were mainly differences of emphases. For instance, whilst Benedict XV's encyclical letter *Ad Beatissimi Apostolorum* (1914) renewed the condemnation of Modernism, his pontificate really marked an end to the worst excesses of the modernist witch-hunt inaugurated by Pius X.[15] But whilst each pope left his own particular stamp on the office it is the continuity in their outlook which is more impressive. The early twentieth-century popes promoted a vision of the Church which would brook no compromise with the modern world. The papal assault on the most dangerous tendencies of modern society which began during the reign of Pius IX (1846–78) and culminated in the encyclical *Quanta Cura* (1864) and the attached *Syllabus of Errors*, was continued with unabated vigour during the pontificate of Pius X. Liberal Catholics who sought to build bridges between the Church and modern culture were now in retreat. Pius's decree *Lamentabili* and the encyclical *Pascendi*, both issued in 1907, were the decisive hammer-blows: these condemned the errors of Modernism, a term used to anathematize scholars who were striving to bring modern scientific and historical methods to bear on Catholic doctrines. Though the so-called Modernists – the French biblical scholar and priest Alfred Loisy, and an Irish-born priest in England, the Jesuit William Tyrrell, were those more prominent in the firing-line – repudiated the notion that they formed a 'school' of thought, the common element was a reforming impulse, the desire to bring Church theology and structures into a positive dialogue with modernity; a commitment which could not be furthered, it was maintained, through the rigidities of the prevailing neo-scholastic version of Catholicism.[16] The Modernist crisis had grave and long-lasting consequences for freedom of thought and discussion within the Church: a strict anti-modernist oath was imposed on all the clergy to be policed by a diocesan committee,[17] and the seminaries and theological faculties were purged. But it was not just in the realm of thought that the atmosphere became oppressive. Social Catholicism – the movement of organizations which emerged in the late nineteenth century and early twentieth century to bring a Catholic view to bear on social questions – was particularly vulnerable to integralist (anti-Modernist) attacks. McSweeney has asserted that by 1910, the year in which one such group, the Sillon movement in France, was banned, 'theological and social innovation in the Church had died'.[18]

The benchmark of all areas of human behaviour and activity, as Pius X constantly asserted, was ecclesiastical authority, by which he meant papal authority. Lay people were urged to be docile and submissive, like lambs, in the face of this authority. Although he made Catholic Action a central feature of his encyclical letters, which was defined as the organized activity of lay people to bring about the reign of Christ on earth, to reChristianize society, the role envisaged for the laity was in fact little more than that of foot-soldiers: independent initiative was not an option. As he tersely put it, 'The Church is by its nature an unequal society: it comprises two categories of person, the pastors and the flocks ... The duty of the multitude is to suffer itself to be governed and to carry out in a submissive spirit the orders of those in control'.[19] His encyclical of 1905, *Il Fermo Propisito*, laid down strict guidelines for Catholic Action groups which left no scope for independent initiative. This restricted understanding of lay action was taken up by Pius's successors, and indeed was the dominant view right up until the Second Vatican Council.

Pius X's strictures against independent lay action had been rehearsed by the English bishops a few years earlier in a joint pastoral letter, *The Church and Liberal Catholicism*, issued on 29 December 1900. This was the year in which the scientist and convert George St Mivart, a typical liberal Catholic in his attempt to demonstrate the 'compatibility' between 'advanced science and the most orthodox Christianity', fell foul of ecclesiastical authority. In several articles he challenged Church teaching on hell and eternal punishment, and for this he was condemned by the Holy Office. In 1900 he was denied the sacraments; when he died later that year he was buried without Catholic rites. This was the immediate context of *The Church and Liberal Catholicism*.[20] It was ominous in tone, emphasizing the dangers to faith arising from 'various forms of rationalism and pride'. The tendency of the age 'has been to substitute the principle of private judgement for the principle of obedience to religious authority, and to persuade the people that they are the ultimate judge of what is true and proper in conduct and religion'. The discussion rested on a firm distinction between *ecclesia docens* (teaching church), identified in the pope and bishops, and *ecclesia discens* (learning church), consisting of the entire body of the faithful (including bishops in their private capacity). The *ecclesia discens* owed a duty of obedience to the teaching authority of the Church, which included the pastoral letters of bishops and the decisions of Roman Congregations. Those who had difficulties with Church teaching were exhorted to adopt a 'docile spirit'.

The guiding hand behind the pastoral letter was the fierce ultramontane Merry del Val (1865–1930), a member of the Vatican Curia and Secretary of State to Pius X from 1903 (the first non-Italian to hold the office). Although of Spanish-Irish descent he was born in England and saw himself as 'English to all intents and purposes'.[21] He was even a front-runner to succeed Herbert Vaughan as Archbishop of Westminster in 1903, but powerful lay interests believed he was not quite English enough. As Hastings notes, if he had been appointed the 'anti-modernist purge might have been less thorough-going in Rome, but it would have been a great deal fiercer in England'. Still, for much of the early twentieth century he was a powerful influence on the English scene. If, as George Tyrrell put it, 'authority fever' was in the air,[22] then this was in no small measure down to Merry del Val.

Bishops were increasingly being urged to demonstrate vigilance in protecting and warning the simple faithful against threats from within and outside the Church – Modernism and socialism being the main suspects. Papal expectations of the episcopal task were set out in *Communium Rerum*, an encyclical of 1909. It provided a bleak survey of the age, heavy with imagery of storms and shipwreck. The Church was assailed from outside and within. It referred to the recent separation of Church and State in France, which was only part of a larger campaign 'to deprive the Church of her rights, to treat her as though she were not by nature and by right the perfect society that she is ... to supplant the kingdom of God by a reign of licence under the lying name of liberty. And to bring about by the rule of vices and lusts the triumph of the worst of all slaveries and bring the people headlong to their ruin ...' Within the Church, the encyclical went on, there were many in the grip of 'false philosophy' who 'are being tossed about miserably on the waves of doubt, knowing not themselves at what port they must land ...';[23] misguided persons 'who are trying by their cunning systems to overthrow from the foundations the very constitution and essence of the Church, to stain the purity of her doctrine, and destroy her entire discipline'.[24] This kind of imagery would be a conspicuous feature of contemporary episcopal statements on social and political action. Political activity was viewed mostly in negative terms; at the very best it was seen as a necessary evil. It was considered a perilous pursuit fraught with dangers to the faith, encouraging contention and divisiveness, a spiritually damaging concern with this world at the expense of the next. Even the most socially-concerned bishops of the time did not dispute this interpretation. It might be expected, therefore, that the bishops' social and political role would be primarily negative, consisting of dampening and restraining lay initiative.

Yet while papal hostility to lay initiative and innovation clearly shaped episcopal attitudes, it was not all negativity. Indeed, within certain limits politics allowed scope for initiative and legitimate differences of opinion. Benedict XV, in *Ad Beatissimi Apostolorum*, expressed it thus: 'As regards matters in which without harm to faith and discipline – in the absence of any authoritative intervention of the Apostolic See – where there is room for divergent opinions, it is clearly the right of everyone to express and defend his own opinion.'[25] Whilst Hastings is right to state that the 'fears and counterfears engendered by the Modernist movement and its repression undoubtedly produced in this country as elsewhere a somewhat arid piece of intellectual history in the twenty years subsequent to *Pascendi*',[26] there were still signs of vitality in some areas. Creativity and innovative thought post-*Pascendi* may have been squeezed out of the theological colleges,[27] but social and political questions to a certain extent still offered an outlet for free expression. There was, as this study will demonstrate, the possibility for a wide range of views on social questions to flourish.

Historians have also pointed to a tradition within English Catholicism of lay independence in political matters. 'In comparison with the situation in many other countries, in England the Catholic Church was led to a remarkable extent in its wider, more secular life by the laity, not the clergy', Hastings has written.[28] Despite the victory of ultramontanism over traditional English Catholicism or 'Cisalpinism', Edward Norman has argued that a vigorous English patriotism characterized the Church, at least at the top end.[29] This attachment to a set of values – fair play, tolerance, freedom – which were tied up with the idea of Englishness, mitigated the harshest aspects of the ultramontane ideal.[30] J. H. Whyte has argued that an 'open Catholicism' was the dominant characteristic of the English Church, with the clergy interfering very rarely in politics, neither giving advice, nor taking a share in the running of lay organizations.[31] In a recent essay, Jeffrey von Arx has made the most emphatic case for identifying English Catholic politics with an 'open' as opposed to 'closed' model. The 'closed' model which took hold in continental Europe during the early twentieth century included the development of specifically Catholic political parties with a strong clerical element guiding their activities, but these were not, von Arx maintains, features of the English scene, rather, since Cardinal Manning's time Catholics had been encouraged to take a full, constructive part in liberal democratic, pluralist politics, collaborating with others of different or no religious affiliation.[32] Von Arx offers us a new criterion for assessing Catholic political activity: rather than testing it (as he asserts that previous historians have done) against a model of Catholic Action drawn from continental European experience, we should consider the extent to which it contributed in a constructive, yet critical way to existing liberal democratic, pluralist politics. This book will consider the extent to which the English hierarchy facilitated or participated in this constructive engagement, and will question whether this was indeed the dominant characteristic of English social and political Catholicism.

Von Arx may be right to question whether the Catholic Action model conveyed the experience of early twentieth-century English Catholicism, but one must also ask whether the smooth integration with the surrounding society was ever achieved. His essay crucially ignores those factors which were encouraging the Church's separation from the wider society. Foremost among these factors were the denominational schools, to which the Church was passionately committed. Denominational divisions were also exacerbated by the *Ne Temere* decree of 1908, which ended the situation whereby Catholics could validly marry in a Protestant church. There was a deep anxiety about mixed marriages. The attitude taken by one Manchester priest was typical: 'The man wants to get married as soon as may be. I stormed at him strongly for going with a Protestant woman. But he could hardly be expected to do better, seeing that his father married a Wesleyan choirsinger not long ago.'[33] The ban on joint prayer (*communicatio in sacris*) put a major obstacle in the way of inter-church initiatives. The possibility of making connections and having meaningful dialogue with those of 'other religious affiliations or none' was not helped by the antipathy which many of the bishops felt towards the universities, an awkward fact which von Arx fails to mention in his assessment of Manning's role.[34] Although a product of Oxford, the antipathy of Cardinal Henry Edward Manning (1808–92) to the universities was notorious,[35] and although the ban on Catholics entering such institutions was lifted in the last decade of the nineteenth century, traces of this negative attitude would persist well into the next century.

How far was Manning's interest in social and political questions shared by his contemporaries? Until the great papal social encyclical of 1891 *Rerum Novarum* put questions of social justice on the agenda,[36] interest amongst the bishops in social and political questions was slight.[37] Apart from Manning, only Edward Bagshawe (1829–1915), Bishop of Nottingham between 1874 to 1901, displayed any sustained commitment to social reform, and for this he drew much opprobrium from Conservative Catholics.[38] Yet the charge frequently made in the late nineteenth century, that Catholics put 'the service of an exceptional institution, or the saving of an individual soul, in opposition to loyal service to society',[39] began to touch nerves.[40] Herbert Vaughan (1832–1903), Archbishop of Westminster between 1892 and 1903, the archetypal Tory prelate, famously attributed Manning's interest in social questions to the onset of senile decay,[41] but even from this unlikely source there were signs of a more positive response to the new emphasis on social questions. In his Advent pastoral letter of 1894, Vaughan urged his flock not to remain 'idle spectators of the great social movement which is ... being legally and constitutionally directed, and to mix freely with and 'bear witness' to their fellow countrymen'.[42] In his foreword to the English edition of Count Edward Soderini's *Socialism and Catholicism* (1896), he stated that the 'Social Question has taken so firm a possession of the modern mind that no educated Catholic can afford to neglect it. The future of the world depends upon its solution.'[43] Vaughan differed from Manning in that he viewed as dangerous too close an involvement with 'worldly' concerns, and certainly he did not see it as any part of the duty of a bishop to entangle himself, as Manning famously did, in industrial disputes.[44] But it was the generation of bishops after Vaughan, those appointed in the first decades of the twentieth century, who to varying degrees recognized the urgency of the social question. Although none would ever attain the public stature of Manning, the episcopate was made up of individuals far closer to the people than the gentry-dominated, Tory-leaning bench of the late nineteenth century. Furthermore, whilst insularity and parochialism were certainly features of the early twentieth-century Church, other currents were pushing Catholics towards greater assimilation to the mainstream of national life. The First World War accelerated public toleration of Catholicism, putting any vestigial suspicions of Catholic disloyalty to rest,[45] and with this heightened sense of being part of the national community came a greater confidence and assertiveness on the part of its leaders, and an increasing willingness to engage with public issues. Links with other churches in the work of social reconstruction were explored which would have been inconceivable beforehand. The Second World War would have a similarly broadening effect on Church life.

A helpful way, it seems, of understanding the politics of the English Catholic community in this period, is to avoid labelling it as either 'open' or 'closed' – for there were, as J. H. Whyte states, elements of both – and rather see it as a product of the tensions between conflicting sets of demand, some drawing the Church away from, some pushing it towards the wider society. The purpose of this book is to show how the bishops negotiated this paradoxical situation.

*   *   *

It should be stressed that although social and political questions were beginning to arouse interest, with one or two exceptions these were by no means a major preoccupation of the bishops and must, therefore, be kept in their proper perspective. The bishops' primary concern was the spiritual welfare of their flock: above all providing priests and churches, although perhaps even more of a concern than building churches in this period was the need to provide Catholic schools; indeed, as this book will show, with some bishops the 'struggle for the schools' bordered on the obsessional, for without this early indoctrination it was feared that many Catholics would lapse on entering adulthood.

Hastings has remarked of the Church in this period that it was 'led by Englishmen and mostly pretty local ones'. Many of the bishops of the period were native sons;[46] a great number had previous administrative experience in the dioceses as curial administrators or private secretaries to their bishop. Indeed, the greater stress placed by Rome on pastoral abilities in weighing the merits of episcopal candidates advantaged those with prior knowledge and experience of the conditions of that diocese. The negative effect of this was a tendency to parochialism. The impression of the Church that has persisted, therefore, was that it was absorbed with improving its pastoral machinery, presided over by 'men of efficiency, duty and devotion' rather than 'inventiveness'.[47] 'It was not to be expected that leaders of such high qualities as Wiseman, Newman, Manning and Ullathorne would be followed by a similar group of outstanding personalities', E. B. Reynolds commented.[48] David Mathew (1902–75), who wrote his history of English Catholicism shortly before his appointment as Auxiliary Bishop of Westminster, remarked that Church's preoccupations of the early part of the century were 'of a domestic character far removed from court or government. They were interested in development and in conversions and in the affairs of their own body.'[49] This was particularly true of the first quarter of the century. Several new dioceses were carved out: Brentwood in 1917 and Lancaster in 1924. A key change came in 1911 with the papal constitution *Si Qua Est*, which established Westminster, Liverpool and Birmingham as metropolitan provinces; Cardiff was added in 1916. By 1924 the diocesan structure was as follows: Westminster as a province with Northampton, Brentwood, Nottingham, Portsmouth and Southwark as suffragan sees; Liverpool with Lancaster, Hexham and Newcastle, Leeds, Middlesborough and Salford; Birmingham with Clifton, Plymouth and Shrewsbury; Cardiff with Menevia as the suffragan see. Such major structural changes absorbed the attention of the bishops during much of the early twentieth century.

Political involvement was generally eschewed as a derogation of episcopal duty. Pius X's encyclical *Il Fermo Proposito* had warned against 'attaching an excessive importance to the material interests of the people, forgetting the much more serious ones of their sacred ministry'. To enable the priest to fulfil his mission it was vital that he was not seen as a 'party man'.[50] Political neutrality was stressed by Archbishop Bourne of Westminster (1861–1935) in *ad clerum* from 1905: 'It is no part of the pastoral duty of the Bishops to interfere in what are generally called politics'.[51] This tradition was for the most part observed even where one might have expected challenges. When William F. Brown (1862–1951), a leading figure in various social movements and the Apostolic Visitor of the Church in Scotland, was being talked about in connection with a vacant see, he told Cardinal Gasquet that 'To be a Bishop would be in some ways an embarrassment to me. I should have to consider episcopal dignity and could not take part as freely as I now do in various works.'[52] Even when social and political questions did assume a greater prominence during this period, it was accepted that a bishop's duty was to state the principles of the Church's social teaching, but not to deal explicitly with the question of their practical application. Political neutrality was regarded as essential to the discharge of the pastoral role. Social and ethnic divisions within the community meant that neutrality was a prudent course to follow, although the education question, particularly in the first decade of the century, forced a number of bishops into a more partisan stance. The majority of Catholics of Irish origin remained resolutely Liberal until the Irish settlement of 1922, although in 1918 some observers recognized that the Labour Party's time would come. At the opposite end of the spectrum, the forty or so Catholic peers were emphatically Conservative, and their tradition of vigorous patriotism included hostility to home rule. Although the episcopate of the early twentieth century has been portrayed as a Conservative plot,[53] it was really because of the schools question, *faut de mieux*, that they inclined to the Conservative Party; as we shall see there was little sympathy between the majority of the bishops and the Catholic peers on other political issues, notably Ireland and the social question.

The extent to which the bishops were involved in social questions and politics has, however, been underestimated in the secondary works. David Mathew stated of the 1918–35 period that 'Politics play little part in the Catholic community as such'.[54] Hastings found that the 'bishops expected loyalty on the schools question and they got it, otherwise they hardly tampered with politics'.[55] While there have been several studies of lay involvement in social questions,[56] and an excellent survey by Buchanan of the political concerns of British Catholics in the period between 1918 and 1965,[57] there has been nothing specifically on the bishops.[58] This book aims to fill the gap in the historiography.

The tendency to treat the history of the Catholic community as having 'little or no life apart . . . little significance, except as a backdrop to the drama of episcopal politics',[59] is of course a special danger for one whose primary focus is the ideas, attitudes and actions of bishops. Such an approach can often create the impression that lay people and clergy responded passively to policies and decisions handed down from above. Of course, it should not be assumed that the pronouncements of bishops were always received reverentially. In 1924 *The Tablet*, probably at the behest of Cardinal Bourne complained about the lack of respect with which pastoral letters were greeted:

> Surely the public reading of a Bishop's letter should be attended with something of the respect which would be shown to the Bishop himself. Unhappily this is not the case with most of our Catholic congregations. As the priest stands up in the pulpit, folding back the paper covers of the pastoral, far too many of the faithful become glum and look at one another as if to say: 'Oh, dear! Another of those long letters'.
>
> In certain parishes the priest, fondly imagining that the flock will be much less attentive to the words of their Bishop than to one of their own sermons, reads far too quickly; with the result that his hearers lose the thread of the argument and sit listlessly, hoping for the end.[60]

In a similar vein, Thomas Henshaw (1873–1938), Bishop of Salford between 1925 and 1938, wrote:

> Regarding my recent message in the Pastoral I learn with sorrow that in some places the parish priest has stood between me and my people inasmuch as my message has not been read or not read verbatim. Not to read a Pastoral ordered to be read is, besides being a lack of due loyalty and obedience, a source of scandal to the laity.
>
> The May and Advent Pastorals are supplied *gratis* for distribution. The Lenten Pastoral is the only one which the clergy may sell, and the proceeds of the sale help me pay the printing bill. Looking over this year's orders for it I must remark upon the general slackness in circulating the Bishop's printed word, and the absurd disproportion in the orders: whilst some large parishes take 10, 12, or 16 dozen, other parishes of the same size have 1 or 2 dozen.[61]

As these quotations illustrate, the sometimes inflated self-understanding of bishops did not in practice guarantee an automatic entrée into the hearts and minds of the faithful. As Archbishop Keating recognized in the quotation with which I began, the local bishop was 'often an unknown, if not a negligible quality' in the lives of ordinary Catholics.

* * *

The chronological period of this book, 1903 to 1963, spans the period of office of four Archbishops of Westminster. 1903 was the year in which Francis Bourne, a neglected and much maligned figure, was translated from Southwark to become the fourth Archbishop of Westminster. 1963 was the year in which William Godfrey, seventh

Archbishop of Westminster, died. By taking the period of these archiepiscopates I do not intend to give the impression that Westminster possessed an authority over the other bishops which, in theory and in practice, it did not actually have, or to imply that the rest of the episcopate were subservient to Westminster. Moloney states in his study of the public ministry of Arthur Hinsley (1865–1943), fifth Archbishop of Westminster, that 'his fellow bishops comprised an independent and forthright bench', and this book confirms such a view.[62] However, there are good reasons for taking Westminster as a starting point. The Archbishop of Westminster was uniquely placed to determine priorities and set the agenda. He was termed by the apostolic constitution *Si Qua Est* (1911), *coetus episcopalis totius Angliae et Cambriae praeses perpetuus*, permanent president of the bishops' conference of England and Wales and chairman of the annual meeting. It was to the Archbishop of Westminster that all dealings with the civil authorities on behalf of the bishops fell. This position of pre-eminence – though he did not possess primatial authority – gave the Archbishop of Westminster a strategic advantage over his fellow bishops in determining the line the ecclesiastical hierarchy should take on issues. Despite persistently voiced concerns amongst the episcopate about Westminster's autocratic tendencies, it was invariably to the Archbishop of Westminster that the other bishops looked for a lead. The dates I have chosen also correspond to key dates in papal history: 1903 was the year Giuseppe Sarto became Pope; 1963, with the Second Vatican Council only just under way, saw the death of Pope John XXIII.

As for the geographical field of this book, excluding Wales is unfortunate – it is after all the ecclesiastical hierarchy of England and Wales and not just England – but given that the most important archive, that of the archdiocese of Cardiff, is closed to researchers, I felt that it was appropriate to restrict the scope of the present study rather than provide what would inevitably have been an imbalanced account.[63]

This book is based mainly on the private papers of the bishops, as well as the more formal utterances of pastoral letters, *ad clera* and the *acta* of the meeting of the bishops. Because of the relative neglect of twentieth-century English Catholic history, I have been able to draw upon a wealth of previously unresearched archival material. Unfortunately, Vatican archives were not accessible after 1922, the end of Pope Benedict's reign. The Catholic press (*The Tablet, The Universe, Catholic Times* and *The Catholic Herald*) and monthly journals such as the *Dublin Review* and *The Month*, together attracted a huge readership and give an idea of the issues that concerned Catholics. Diocesan journals were also of some value. The papers of the Catholic Social Guild (CSG) have proved a rich source of information on the development of social Catholicism in England.

The approach I have adopted is mainly chronological, although some overlap has been unavoidable, and certain themes have been isolated to help the story flow. Chapter one deals with the bishops' social and political attitudes and involvement between 1903 and 1918. I have not discussed at any great length the Church's attitudes and involvement in the First World War, other than emphasizing the wholehearted support they gave to the nation's cause. One historian has commented: 'Whereas Anglicans and Free Churchmen wrote frequently to the newspapers, Roman Catholic participation in public political debate about the war was rare'.[64] Those who did speak surpassed other sections of the Christian community in bellicosity.[65] Chapter two examines the Irish question from 1918 until the truce that marked the end of the Anglo-Irish War in 1921. Chapter three goes back to 1918 to discuss the Church's response to social and political questions through to 1924. This was the year of the Catholic withdrawal from the Conference on Christian Politics, Economics and Citizenship, the great post-war inter-church contribution to social reconstruction. It marked the beginning of a period of growing conservatism among Catholic leaders, which forms the subject of chapter four, and a reaction to some of the post-war enthusiasm for social change, culminating in Cardinal Bourne's condemnation of the General Strike of 1926. Chapters five and six examine the impact of Arthur Hinsley's archiepiscopate (1935 to 1943). For these chapters I have been able to draw upon many previously unresearched sources. The final chapter takes a broad view of the period running from Bernard Griffin's appointment as Archbishop of Westminster through to 1963, the year in which his successor, William Godfrey, died.

Notes

1. Archbishop F. W. Keating, 'The Catholic Episcopate', *The Messenger: Organ of the Apostleship of Prayer* (October 1922), 311.
2. D. Quinn, *Patronage and Piety: The Politics of English Roman Catholicism, 1850–1900* (Stanford: Stanford University Press, 1993), pp. xi–xii, 1; M. Heimann, *Catholic Devotion in Victorian England* (Oxford: Clarendon Press, 1995).
3. Daniel Rees's review of E. Norman, *The English Catholic Church in the Nineteenth Century* (Oxford: Clarendon Press, 1984) in *The Downside Review*, 103 (April 1985), 159. A similar point is made in G. P. Connolly, 'The Transubstantiation of Myth: Towards a New Popular History of Nineteenth-Century Catholicism in England', *Journal of Ecclesiastical History*, 35 (January 1984), 78.

4. See the essays in V. A. McClelland and M. Hodgetts (eds), *From Without the Flaminian Gate: 150 years of Roman Catholicism in England and Wales 1850–2000* (London: Darton, Longman and Todd, 1999), esp. S. Gilley, 'The Years of Equipoise, 1892–1943', pp. 21–61; M. P. Hornsby-Smith, *Catholics in England 1950–2000: Historical and Sociological Perspectives* (London: Cassell, 2000), esp. S. Gilley, 'A Tradition and Culture Lost, To be Regained?', pp. 29–45. Useful for the second half of the twentieth century is C. Longley, *The Worlock Archive* (London and New York: Geoffrey Chapman, 2000). D. A. Bellenger and S. Fletcher, *Princes of the Church: A History of the English Cardinals* (Stroud: Sutton Publishing, 2001), ch. 6, provides a useful historical overview.

5. Gilley said little about the English Church post-*Pascendi* in 'The Roman Catholic Church, 1780–1940', in S. W. Gilley and W. J. Sheils (eds), *A History of Religion in Britain: Practice and Belief from Pre-Roman Times to the Present* (Oxford: Blackwells, 1984), pp. 346–62. The sections on Catholicism in A. Hastings, *A History of English Christianity 1920–1985* (London: Collins; Fount Paperbacks, 1987 edn), provide a valuable survey of the main events and personalities. See also E. Norman, *Roman Catholicism in England from the Elizabethan Settlement to the Second Vatican Council* (Oxford: Oxford University Press, 1985), ch. 6.

6. T. Buchanan, 'Great Britain', in T. Buchanan and M. Conway (eds), *Political Catholicism in Europe* (Oxford: Clarendon Press, 1996), p. 249.

7. M. P. Hornsby-Smith, *Roman Catholic Beliefs in England: Customary Catholicism and Transformations of Religious Authority* (Cambridge: Cambridge University Press, 1991), pp. 226–7.

8. H. Jedin and J. Dolan, *The History of the Church*, vol. 10 (New York: Crossroads, 1981), p. 151; O. Chadwick, *A History of the Popes 1830–1914* (Oxford: Clarendon Press, 1998), pp. 359–60.

9. J. Cornwell, *Hitler's Pope: The Secret History of Pius XII* (London: Viking, 1999), p. 41.

10. J. Bossy, *The English Catholic Community 1570–1850* (London: Darton, Longman and Todd, 1979 edn), p. 361; J. Derek Holmes, *More Roman than Rome: English Catholicism in the Nineteenth Century* (London: Burns and Oates; Sheperdstown: Patmos Press, 1978), p. 86.

11. For the text of the canons see *Codex Iuris Canonica: Piu X Pontificis Maximi Iussu Digestus Benedicti Papae XV Auctoritate Promulgatus* (Rome, 1918).

12. For the historical background to canon 329 see G. Sweeney, 'The 'wound in the right foot': unhealed?', in A. Hastings (ed.), *Bishops and Writers: Aspects of the Evolution of Modern English Catholicism* (Wheathampstead: Anthony Clarke Books, 1977), pp. 207–34.

13. Chadwick, *History of the Popes*, pp. 369–70.

14. E. Duffy, *Saints and Sinners: A History of the Popes* (New Haven, CT: Yale University Press, 1997), p. 248. For discussions on Roman central-

ization in the context of America see G. P. Fogarty, *The Vatican and the American Hierarchy from 1870 to 1965* (Wilmington, Delaware: Michael Glazier, 1985 edn), esp. pp. 177–207; idem. 'Cardinal William O'Connell', in J. von Arx (ed.), *Varieties of Ultramontanism* (Washington: the Catholic University of America Press, 1998), pp. 118–46.

15. A point made in Duffy, *Saints and Sinners*, p. 251. For the papal encyclicals I have mainly used the English translations in C. Carlen, *The Papal Encyclicals 1903–1939*, vol. 3 (Washington: McGrath, 1981), providing the section number and page reference(s) within that volume. Where different sources are used this has been indicated in the notes. For a trenchant assessment of the papacy of Benedict XV, see J. F. Pollard, *The Unknown Pope: Benedict XV (1914–1922) and the Pursuit of Peace* (London and New York: Geoffrey Chapman, 1999).

16. D. Jodock, 'Introduction I: The Modernist crisis', in D. Jodock (ed.), *Catholicism Contending with Modernity: Roman Catholic Modernism and Anti-Modernism in Historical Context* (Cambridge: Cambridge University Press, 2000), pp. 2–3. See also G. Daly, 'Theological and Philosophical' in ibid., pp. 88–112.

17. This was not abolished until 1967.

18. B. McSweeney, *Roman Catholicism: The Search for Relevance* (Oxford: Basil Blackwell, 1980), pp. 85–6.

19. Quoted in Duffy, *Saints and Sinners*, p. 249.

20. Reprinted in *The Tablet*, 5 January 1901 and 12 January 1901. For a discussion of this pastoral letter, see M. J. Weaver, 'George Tyrrell and the Joint Pastoral Letter', *The Downside Review*, 99 (January 1981), 18–39; W. J. Schoenl, *The Intellectual Crisis in English Catholicism: Liberal Catholics, Modernists, and the Vatican in the Late Nineteenth and Early Twentieth Centuries* (New York and London: Garland Publishing Inc., 1982), ch. 3; E. M. Leonard, 'English Catholicism and Modernism', in Jodock (ed.), *Catholicism Contending with Modernity*, pp. 264–6.

21. Hastings, *English Christianity*, p. 145.

22. Weaver, 'George Tyrrell and the Joint Pastoral Letter', p. 36.

23. *Communium Rerum*, 175, p. 103.

24. Ibid., p. 109.

25. *Ad Beatissimi Apostlorum*, 180, p. 148.

26. A. Hastings, 'Some Reflexions on the English Catholicism of the Late 1930s', in Hastings (ed.), *Bishops and Writers*, p. 108.

27. In 1934 Thomas Flynn, then editor of *The Clergy Review* (later Bishop of Lancaster), lamented the lack of any scholastic philosophy of note, remarking to the Archbishop of Birmingham, 'most of our people unless applying it to social issues ... don't seem to be able to get it across': Flynn to Williams, 21 November 1934, Birmingham, Birmingham Archdiocesan Archives (B.A.A.), Archbishops' Papers 1929–65.

28. Hastings, *English Christianity*, pp. 139, 140.

29. Norman, *Roman Catholicism in England*, p. 2.

30. See the discussion in Hastings, *English Christianity*, pp. 139–40, 151; Norman, *Roman Catholicism in England*, p. 116.

31. J. H. Whyte, *Catholics in Western Democracies* (Dublin: Gill and Macmillan, 1981), pp. 7–8.

32. J. von Arx, 'Catholics and Politics', in McClelland and Hodgetts (eds), *From Without the Flaminian Gate*, pp. 245–71.

33. Fr H. Roche to Canon Boulaye, u/d, Burnley, Salford Diocesan Archives (Sal.D.A.), Vicar General Papers, File 168.

34. Though this is recognized as a problem in J. Pereiro, *Cardinal Manning: An Intellectual Biography* (Oxford: Clarendon Press, 1998), p. 240.

35. For attitudes to the universities see esp. J. G. Snead-Cox, *The Life of Cardinal Vaughan* (2 vols., London: Herbert and Daniel, 1912) II, ch. 3.; A. McCormack, *Cardinal Vaughan* (London: Burns and Oates, 1966), pp. 261–5; V. A. McClelland, *English Roman Catholics and Higher Education, 1830–1903* (Oxford: Clarendon Press, 1973); Norman, *English Catholic Church*, pp. 287–301; V. A. McClelland, 'St. Edmund's College, Ware and St. Edmund's College, Cambridge: Historical Connections and Early Tribulations', *Recusant History*, 23 (May 1997), 470–82; E. Duffy, 'The Thinking Church: a Recent History', *Priests and People*, 14 (October 2000), 374–9.

36. K. S. Inglis, *Churches and the Working Classes in Victorian England* (London: Routledge and Kegan Paul; Toronto: University of Toronto Press, 1963), p. 317, maintains that the response to *Rerum Novarum* in England was somewhat mute. For a different view see B. Aspinwall, 'Rerum Novarum in the Transatlantic World', in P. Boury (ed), *Rerum Novarum: Écriture, Contenu et Réception d'une Encyclique: Actes du Colloque International Organisé par L'École Française de Rome et le Greco Nº 2 du CNRS, Rome, 18–20 Avril 1991* (École Française de Rome: Palais Farnèse, 1997), pp. 465–95. See also idem, 'Towards an English Catholic Social Conscience, 1829–1920', *Recusant History*, 25 (May 2000), 106–19.

37. However, as Bernard Aspinwall points out, English Catholic social concern did not begin with Manning: 'Before Manning: Some Aspects of British Social Concern before 1865', *New Blackfriars*, 61 (March 1980), 113–26. See also J. L. Altholz, 'Social Catholicism in England in the Age of the Devotional Revolution', in S. J. Brown and D. W. Miller (eds), *Piety and Power in Ireland 1760–1960: Essays in Honour of Emmet Larkin* (Notre Dame, Indiana: University of Notre Dame Press, 2000), pp. 209–19.

38. Bagshawe's social radicalism is exemplified in the two pastoral letters published as *Mercy and Justice to the Poor: The True Political Economy* (London: Kegan Paul and Co., 1885). This publication elicited a hostile rejoinder from a prominent layman in his diocese, Edwin de Lisle, *Pastoral Politics: A Reply to Dr. Bagshawe, Catholic Bishop of Nottingham* (London: Simpkin, Marshall and Co.; Loughborough: H. Wills, 1885). For Bagshawe see G. Roberts, 'English Catholics and Politics in the Late Nineteenth Century', *Studies*, 74 (Winter 1985), 455–63. The literature on Manning's involvement in public issues is

extensive: V. A. McClelland, *Cardinal Manning: His Public Life and Influence* (London: Oxford University Press, 1962) is the authoritative study. See also J. von Arx, 'Manning's Ultramontanism and the Catholic Church in British Politics', *Recusant History* 19 (May 1989), 332–47; D. Quinn, 'Manning as Politician', *Recusant History*, 21 (October 1992), 267–86. See Norman, *English Catholic Church*, pp. 196–200, for a discussion of late nineteenth-century episcopal attitudes to social reform.

39. T. H. Green's comment on hearing of the reception of Gerard Manley Hopkins into the Church: quoted in D. M. Thompson, 'The Christian Socialist Revival in Britain: A Reappraisal', in J. Garnett and C. Matthew (eds), *Revival and Religion since 1700: Essays for John Walsh* (London: Hambledon, 1993), p. 290. One sympathetic to Christian socialist developments, Mandall Creighton, Anglican Bishop of London, insisted that to be a Roman Catholic was to 'stand on one side and cut yourself off from your part in striving to do your duty for the religious future of the country': quoted in J. Kent, 'Late-Nineteenth-Century Nonconformist Renaissance', in D. Baker (ed.), *Renaissance and Renewal in Christian History* (Studies in Church History, 14; Oxford: Blackwell, 1977), p. 351.

40. W. S. Lilley to the Duke of Norfolk, 11 Sept. 1895, Arundel, Arundel Castle Archives (A.C.A.), Norfolk Papers, C/597.

41. McClelland, *Cardinal Manning*, p. 146; McCormack, *Cardinal Vaughan*, pp. 223–4.

42. *The Tablet*, 8 December 1894.

43. Count Edward Soderini, *Socialism and Catholicism* (London: Longman, Green and Co., 1896), p. v.

44. McCormack, *Cardinal Vaughan*, p. 223.

45. See E. R. Norman, *Anti-Catholicism in Victorian England* (London: George Allen and Unwin, 1968), esp. pp. 1–22.

46. Hastings, *English Christianity*, p. 138.

47. Norman, *Roman Catholicism in England*, p. 109.

48. E. B. Reynolds, *The Roman Catholic Church in England and Wales: A Short History* (Wheathampstead: Anthony Clarke, 1973), p. 351.

49. D. Mathew, *Catholicism in England 1535–1935* (London: Catholic Book Club, 1938 edn), p. 247.

50. *Il Fermo Proposito*, in *The Pope and the People*, p. 199.

51. *Ad Clerum*, Bourne on behalf of the Bishops, 19 December 1905, A.A.W., Bourne Papers.

52. Mgr Brown to Gasquet, 10 March 1918, Stratton-on-the-Fosse, Downside Abbey Archives (D.A.A.), Gasquet Papers, File 917a.

53. Buchanan, 'Great Britain', p. 254.

54. Mathew, *Catholicism in England*, p. 259.

55. Hastings, *English Christianity*, p. 143.

56. G. P. Macentee, *The Social Catholic Movement in Great Britain* (New York: Macmillan Co., 1927); J. Keating, 'Roman Catholics, Christian Democracy and the British Labour Movement 1910–1960' (unpublished Ph.D. dissertation, Manchester University, 1989); B. Wraith, 'A Pre-

Modern Interpretation of the Modern: The English Catholic Church and the 'Social Question' in the Early Twentieth Century', in R. N. Swanson (ed.), *The Church Retrospective* (Studies in Church History, 33; Woodbridge: The Boydell Press, 1997), pp. 529-45. See also R. H. Butterworth, 'The Structure and Organisation of some Catholic Lay Organisations in Australia and Great Britain: A Comparative Study with Special Reference to the Function of the Organisations as Social and Political Pressure Groups' (unpublished D.Phil. dissertation, Oxford University, 1959).

57. Buchanan, 'Great Britain', see p. 255 for comments on the ecclesiastical hierarchy

58. Whyte, *Catholics in Western Democracies*, p. 125, comments on the lack of studies of the political involvement of national ecclesiastical hierarchies (and clergy).

59. G. P. Connolly, 'The Transubstantiation of Myth: Towards a New Popular History of Nineteenth-Century Catholicism in England', *Journal of Ecclesiastical History*, 35 (January 1984), 78.

60. *The Tablet*, 1 March 1924.

61. Henshaw to Mr Dean [Catholic Education Council], 1 March 1936, Sal.D.A., Dean's Meetings/Reports, Box 203, Folder 3.

62. T. Moloney, *Westminster, Whitehall and the Vatican: The Role of Cardinal Hinsley 1935-43* (London: Burns and Oates, 1985), p. 15.

63. A valuable study of Welsh Catholicism has appeared recently: T. O. Hughes, *Winds of Change: The Roman Catholic Church and Society in Wales, 1918-62* (Cardiff: University of Wales Press, 1999). See also C. Daniel, 'Wales', in A. Hastings (ed.), *The Church and the Nations* (London and New York: Sheed and Ward, 1959), pp. 116-32; D. J. Mullins, 'The Catholic Church in Wales', in McClelland and Hodgetts (eds), *From Without the Flaminian Gate*, pp. 272-94.

64. A. Wilkinson, *The Church of England and the First World War* (London: SPCK, 1978), p. 2. There is an interesting discussion of Catholic attitudes and responses in S. Mews, 'Religion and Society in the First World War' (unpublished Ph.D. dissertation, University of Cambridge, 1973).

65. M. Ceadel, 'Christian Pacifism in the Era of Two World Wars', in W. J. Sheils (ed.), *The Church and War* (Studies in Church History, 20; Oxford: Blackwell, 1983), p. 404. Roman Catholic pacifism receives no more than a footnote in M. Ceadel, *Pacifism in Britain 1914-1945: The Defining of a Faith* (Oxford: Clarendon Press, 1980), p. 163.

1

'Docile, Loving Children': Social and Political Action 1903–1918

As the English Catholic Church entered the twentieth century the outward signs were of expansive confidence. Whereas the other main churches were in numerical decline, the Catholic Church in England continued to grow at a steady pace.[1] According to figures received by Propaganda Fide in Rome, whilst in 1850 there had been 826 priests and 597 churches, in 1905 there were 3,273 priests and 1,673 churches.[2] Westminster Cathedral, completed during the latter years of the archiepiscopate of Vaughan, stood as a symbol of Catholic resurgence, 'a monument to ultramontanism'.[3] The foundations for future growth seemed further secured by the Education Act of 1902, which went most of the way to meeting the Church's demands for denominational education. It seemed that Francis Bourne had arrived at Westminster at a propitious moment.

But despite the sanguinary confidence the new Archbishop of Westminster could hardly have been more low-key. Diminutive, bespectacled and clerkish, Bourne cut a far less impressive figure than his dashing, bucolic predecessor, Vaughan.[4] He would never capture the public imagination in his long, thirty-two year period of office (1903–35) in the way that, for instance, his successor Arthur Hinsley would do in a quarter of that time. However, at the turn of the century English Catholicism was not looking for an inspirational figure with a high public profile, but rather for someone who would consolidate and build on the expansion of the previous half century. Bourne was an entirely fitting appointment. His outlook was that of a diocesan bishop rather than a national Church leader: he recorded in 1932 that his main tasks on arriving at Westminster had been 'the proper organization of the Cathedral, Archbishop's House, Clergy House, and Curia; the reconstruction of St. Edmund's College with the philosophical and theological studies: the

Cathedral Choir School: the foundation of a secondary day-school'.[5]

Bourne embodied many of the characteristics of the early twentieth-century English Church as it has been described by historians. If administrative blandness was the order of the day, then that is also the abiding impression of Bourne. Indeed, David Mathew's chapter on the Bourne era in his *Catholicism in England* is appropriately entitled 'Administration'. Most assessments of Bourne's contributions, contemporary and historical, have tended to minimize his influence within the Church and society.[6] Cosmo Lang, Archbishop of Canterbury from 1928 to 1942, observed that Bourne did not occupy a 'place of very distinguished leadership in the national life compared with Cardinal Manning, or in the sphere of learning compared with Cardinal Gasquet, or in the sphere of international life like Cardinal Mercier. He is more in the position of Cardinal Vaughan though not even as prominent as he was in general social life.'[7] He was described by Lady Kenmare as the 'efficient postman', perhaps an allusion to his father's occupation.[8] With memoirs of contemporaries thin on the ground, most of what we know of Bourne is derived from Oldmeadow's biography.[9] It is an unsatisfactory account and was seen as such by contemporaries, mainly because Oldmeadow was writing as Bourne's 'convinced apologist'.[10] Only nine years after its publication, Fr G. Wheeler was lamenting the 'very sad lack of a comprehensive and understanding biography of this great priest',[11] whilst an Anglican prelate dismissed it as a 'dull and narrow account of a humourless and rigid man. Absurd adulation mingled with spitefulness against all non-Roman Catholic Christians. Political Romanism at its worst.'[12] To be fair to Bourne, it has been rightly said that Oldmeadow's *Bourne* reveals as much about the narrowness of the author's attitudes as it does of its subject's.[13]

Born on 23 March 1861, Bourne's early years were spent in shabby genteel Clapham, an unremarkable part of South London populated by unremarkable clerks. Henry Bourne, Francis's father, was one such man. A clerk in the Receiver General's branch of the Post Office, Henry converted to Catholicism along with his brother, Edward, in 1845, soon after the reception into the Church of the Tractarian, Frederick Oakeley, under whose influence the two boys fell whilst regular attenders at the Margaret Street chapel;[14] several years later he married Ellen Byrne, the deeply pious daughter of a Dublin merchant. At the age of eight Francis was sent to Ushaw College, of which his memories would be mostly be sad and unpleasant: 'It was a hard school for young boys so very far from home', he later recalled.[15] His first Christmas away, in 1869, 'was very lonely and sorrowful';[16] a feeble boy, he suffered during the unforgiving Durham winters, but this winter would be the worst of all. In February 1870 he heard that his father had died of dysentery (later he confided that he could hardly recall his father's face);[17] his mother was left in near-poverty and was forced to sell the family home. Francis remained at Ushaw with his elder brother, Henry, whilst his mother took up work as a governess in France. Never a brilliant student, hard work ensured that he was always near the top of the class; he was remembered as quiet and restrained but possessing a stubborn streak.[18] His health continued to suffer from the ravages of the Durham climate and he proved too weak to participate in team sports; an older student was appointed to 'take him for walks in the country, whilst his more robust schoolfellows played games'.[19] Perhaps Bourne's sense of detachment from his fellow man, that inscrutable elusiveness, began on Ushaw Moor. His isolation was complete when his brother, who had remained at Ushaw until poor health forced his departure in May 1874, died of consumption at the age of nineteen later that year. Bourne left Ushaw soon after when it was feared that he might go the same way as his brother.[20]

Without parental guidance, Bourne was thrown back on his own resources. Regular travel to and from France to visit his mother increased his self-reliance, and he became highly fluent in the language. When, in 1881, he failed to secure a place at the Venerabile (he would have no great love for that institution in later years) it was to St Sulpice, Paris, that he went to train for the priesthood. He would remember his time there as the 'foundation and abiding inspiration of my life'.[21] The frugality and austere discipline clearly left a strong imprint; close friendships were discouraged and he became accustomed to loneliness, a condition which he came to accept as the lot of the priest.[22] This outwardly cold and aloof manner, which extended even towards his mother, found an emotional release in an intensely passionate and warm spiritual life centred on devotion to Our Lady.[23]

A figure of some influence in Bourne's life at this time was his tutor, the liberal theologian Professor J. B. Hogan.[24] Oldmeadow notes that although the seminary of St Sulpice was a 'home of unimpeachable orthodoxy', Hogan ensured that 'it was also a place where one learnt what were *necessaria* in which there must be a solid and absolute *unitas* of faith and what were the *dubia* concerning which there is temperate *libertas*'.[25] Another liberalizing influence that Bourne encountered at St Sulpice was Eudoxe-Irénée Mignot, a disciple of Hogan who became a close friend of Alfred Loisy and Friedrich Von Hügel, and who, as a bishop, endorsed historical criticism of scripture.[26] Bourne's anger at Vaughan's treatment of George Mivart, the scientist whose articles on evolution and the doctrine of hell led to his condemnation for heresy, indicated a mind and temper disinclined to stifle free inquiry.[27] However, Bourne was not himself a scholar; a spell at Louvain in 1884 where he had intended to pursue his studies further was cut short due to his continuing ill-health and that brought to an end any thoughts of a scholarly life.

Bourne moved swiftly up the ecclesiastical ladder: after curacies at Blackheath, Mortlake and West Grinstead, he took up an appointment as the Rector of the Southwark diocesan seminary at Wonersh at the age of only twenty-eight. In 1896 he was appointed coadjutor to Bishop Butt of Southwark with the titular see of *Epiphania* and the right of succession. On Butt's retirement in 1897 he became Bishop of Southwark. During his time there he was invested with the responsibility for the hierarchy's dealings with the War Office during the Boer War.

When the see of Westminster fell vacant after the death of Vaughan in 1903, Bourne did not initially appear on the *terna* of the Westminster Chapter. The list comprised Bishop Hedley of Newport and Menevia (1837–1915), Abbot Francis Aiden Gasquet (1846–1929), a distinguished historian and President of the English Benedictine Congregation (in 1914 he was made a cardinal), and Merry del Val. As Shane Leslie puts it, 'The good Canons were in a mood for an experiment'.[28] It was widely believed that Gasquet was the front-runner.[29] However, before the *terna* was sent to the bishops for their approval objections were raised. As the most prominent layman in the English Church and the message-boy of the British Establishment in Rome, Henry FitzAlan Howard (1847–1917), fifteenth Duke of Norfolk, was traditionally consulted on the matter of senior ecclesiastical appointments, and now sought to apply his veto to Merry del Val. In a letter to Antonio Gotti, Prefect of Propaganda, he said that Merry del Val was 'not sufficiently English to make it wise to appoint him . . . I feel that everything he did would be mistrusted and that on many public questions . . . our difficulties would be increased and any position jeopardized'. Whilst Norfolk recognized that 'a great deal of this would arise from the stupid side of our insular character', he insisted 'that we have to take facts as we find them and this sort of stupidity as one of our great obstacles'. Norfolk also raised objections to the other two: Gasquet because of his relative youth (he was fifty-six): 'If any experiment fails the result is more disastrous if the cause of the disaster is a young man': Hedley because he was too old (he was sixty-six) and infirm, and because he doubted whether his scholarly cast of mind was suitable for 'the energetic control and development of an important diocese'.[30] Soon after this letter was sent the bishops met to consider the *terna*, which had placed Hedley first, followed by Gasquet, then Merry del Val. The bishops expressed reservations about all three candidates. Hedley was unsuitable for two reasons: first, he was a Benedictine, 'and it was felt that with a Regular for Archbishop there might arise difficulties'; secondly, because he 'has been for many years Bishop of a small diocese where there are only thirty-six secular priests and where there is no seminary'. Gasquet was objected to because he was without 'any experience in secular ecclesiastical affairs', and because he was a Benedictine. Most of the bishops shared Norfolk's view of Merry del Val.[31] It was at this meeting that Bourne emerged as a candidate, put forward by Bishop Riddell of Northampton (1836–1907), the senior bishop of the Westminster province.[32] Bourne's name was added to the *terna* at this stage because it was felt that the Holy See should not be bound to a choice from one religious order.[33] Bishop Cahill of Portsmouth (1841–1910) was Bourne's most vigorous advocate and the case he put to Gotti is worth quoting at length:

The three Archbishops who have ruled Westminster since the establishment of the hierarchy in England have been very distinguished men. They have been very much before the public: Cardinal Wiseman as a learned and most capable writer and lecturer; Cardinal Manning as a writer and politician, and Cardinal Vaughan as an energetic man always planning great schemes and enterprises. The great prominence of these men hardly permitted a detailed attention to the more ordinary duties of a Bishop; and, in each case it was said of them, and probably with truth, that they had no personal knowledge of the priests of the diocese, or of the conditions and circumstances of the several parishes (or as we call them missions) in the diocese, such as would be gained by regular canonical visitation.

There are many who think that while this excellent work is very useful, some interval should be allowed, during which the internal organisation of the diocese might be perfected, and that this is the serious need of the present time. In other words the Church in England is sufficiently well known to the outside public, and that for efficiency of action attention should in preference be given to putting the machinery of the diocese on a more certain basis, and that the Archbishop should be rather a good organiser than a brilliant public man.

I stated to the Bishops that the chief qualification of the Bishop of Southwark was his great power of organisation, with a thorough grasp of details, that the diocese of Southwark was completely and perfectly organised, but most especially his seminary was a triumph of order, method, and careful thought, and that the whole merit of this was due to Monsignor Bourne for he had commenced his work as Rector until he was made Bishop, and that the whole scheme was his.[34]

Cahill's views would undoubtedly have struck chords in the Vatican where there was now a greater stress placed on pastoral and administrative abilities in weighing the qualities of candidates. There are interesting parallels between Bourne and Giuseppe Sarto, who was elected Pope in 1903 taking the name Pius X. Duffy has noted that Sarto was very different in style and temperament to his predecessor, Leo XIII. Whereas Leo was remote, austere and regal, Sarto was from a peasant background; unlike nineteenth-century popes Sarto had had parochial experience; he had been an effective diocesan administrator; he was concerned about priestly formation and recognized the priority of pastoral issues.[35] Bourne's social background was not quite as humble – although it was certainly more humble than Vaughan's – nor was he warm and approachable like Sarto, nevertheless they shared a pastoral orientation and both placed great stress on the priority of priestly formation.[36] (The only book Bourne wrote was called *Ecclesiastical Training* (1926)) But what was more important in securing Bourne's appointment was the negative intervention of Cardinal Moran of Sydney, who sat on the Propaganda committee responsible for selecting bishops. He was a fierce opponent of Benedictine influence and appears to have swayed the vote narrowly in Bourne's favour.[37] Hedley gained two votes, Gasquet four and Bourne five. The announcement of Bourne's elevation to Westminster was made on 28 August, and on 20 September 1903 he took formal possession of the see.

* * *

Whilst the quiet administrator was preferable to the 'brilliant public man', it was not entirely possible for the leading Catholic bishop to remain aloof from politics. First, there were the Catholic schools to defend: throughout this period it was the issue which above all others drew Catholics *qua* Catholics into the political arena. Secondly, the upsurge of interest in social and political questions did not leave Catholics unaffected, and therefore the attitude the Church should adopt towards social reform and socialism was firmly on the agenda. Beneath the surface confidence it was, therefore, to be an anxious first decade for Bourne and English Catholicism. The Church appeared vulnerable on several fronts. A political climate inimical to its interests in the educational sphere was created as a result of the Liberal Party's landslide victory at the 1906 general election. This brought into parliament a solid phalanx of Nonconformist MPs determined on ending 'Rome on the Rates'. There were deeper anxieties, however, which could not be removed by shifts in electoral fortunes. Significantly, the English bishops had chosen to mark the new century with a joint pastoral letter, *The Church and Liberal Catholicism*, which, whilst noting 'the peaceful growth and expansion of the Catholic faith in England', emphasized the dangers to faith arising from 'various forms of rationalism and pride'. The tendency of the age, it stated, 'has been to substitute the principle of private judgement for the principle of obedience to religious authority, and to persuade the people that they are the ultimate judge of what is true and proper in conduct and religion'.[38] It was a foretaste of what was to follow later in the decade. Pius X's assault on Modernism from 1907 was the apogee of the Church's increasingly hardened stance against modern secular thought and science. Ecclesiastical authority, the Pope insisted, was to be the benchmark of all human activity.

The political activities of Catholic organizations would also be governed by this principle. One of Pius X's early encyclical letters, *Il Fermo Proposito*, insisted that Catholic Action organizations must 'in every least thing be subordinated to the authority of the Church and also to the authority of the Bishops placed by the Holy See to rule the Church of God in the dioceses assigned to them'.[39] It urged on Catholics the duty to 'submit as docile, loving children to this maternal vigilance'.[40] Movements which appeared not to exemplify the virtues of docility and obedience were dealt with as ruthlessly as the doctrinal Modernists. In 1910 the French Sillon movement was condemned by the Pope after disquietude spread amongst the French episcopate and in Rome about its activities – it was accused of weakening the spirit of absolute submission to the hierarchy.[41] McSweeney has asserted that 1910 was the year in which social innovation in the Church died.[42]

How do the attitudes and actions of the English bishops measure up against such assessments? It is the purpose of this chapter to consider the emergence of social Catholicism in England against this background of apparent hostility to the idea of 'the freedom of the individual to act and think independently of clerical supervision and control'.[43] To what extent was it possible for the social Catholic movement in England to pursue objectives independently of episcopal control? How far did the bishops seek to exercise such control over its activities? These issues would also emerge in the context of the schools question.

More than any other issue in the early twentieth century it was the 'struggle for the schools' which absorbed the attention of the bishops and pushed them into the political arena. Liberal assaults on the 1902 educational settlement provoked an intense agitation in defence of the schools. A consideration of the attempt to mobilize an opposition to Liberal education policy in these fraught years enables an assessment of the extent and limits of the episcopate's political influence.

Catholic opposition to the Education Bill of 1906, a serious attack on the favourable 1902 settlement, has been well described.[44] Augustine Birrell's Bill proposed to abolish the dual system of education and bring all state funded schools under public control. Local authorities could opt to take over voluntary schools, and all religious tests for teachers would end. Clause three of the Bill allowed for some denominational teaching, but this had to be given outside school hours and was restricted to two days a week. As a concession to Church interests, clause four offered 'extended facilities' for denominational teaching if four-fifths of the parents of the children at the school requested it, and provided the school was located in an area which had a population of at least 5,000. There were estimates that half of England's Catholic schools could be wiped-out as a result.[45]

The Church's opposition to the Bill was not straightforward. It was directed at the political party to which the vast majority of Irish Catholics in England inclined because of its support for home rule – the Liberal Party. Furthermore, there were political divisions which reflected the social and ethnic divide in the Catholic community and which raised barriers to unity. What seemed an impressive display of Catholic unity, exemplified by monster demonstrations such as that held at the Albert Hall when Birrell's Bill was before the House of Commons in April 1906, belied these divisions. As McClelland has shown, Catholics in parliament were split between those set on wrecking the Bill, and those seeking concessions to render it less objectionable. The first course was urged by the bulk of the forty Catholic peers, a not insignificant body led by the fifteenth Duke of Norfolk (hereafter 'Norfolk'), who also fronted the Catholic Education Council (CEC), the body set up by the hierarchy to safeguard educational interests. On the other side were members of the Irish Parliamentary Party (IPP) who mainly urged a conciliatory approach. McClelland has argued that Bourne was far-sighted enough to recognize that an alliance with hardline Tory opposition was fraught with dangers; that if the Bill was wrecked, a conflict between the Commons and the Lords would be precipitated with potentially harmful consequences for Catholic educational interests. Bourne instead lent the weight of his influence to the strategy adopted by the IPP, which rejected the Lords' wrecking amendments whilst at the same time pursuing concessions within the four corners of the Bill. Concessions satisfactory to Bourne and the majority of the bishops were obtained: first, Birrell indicated to John Redmond, the IPP's leader, that a parents' committee would have a consultative role in the appointment of teachers to denominational schools; secondly, instead of the initial requirement that four-fifths of the parents in an area had to request 'extended facilities' for religion, Birrell was prepared to accept three-quarters. The second point was rejected by Norfolk who would accept nothing less than a simple majority. Overwhelmingly the IPP voted with the government to reject the Lords' amendments, leaving Norfolk 'furious that the new leader of the Catholic community [Bourne] should be prepared to compromise with a Liberal government and, above all, that he had followed the advice of the Irish members rather than that of the hereditary lay leaders of the Catholic community'.[46] On 19 December, Lord Landsdowne, leader of the Conservative opposition to the Bill, moved a motion that the Lords 'do insist upon their amendments'. The Lords' unwillingness to compromise made a collision between the Commons and Lords unavoidable. Landsdowne's motion was carried and the Bill was killed,[47] though after it had been mangled by the Lords few mourned its passing.

Outside Parliament the attempt to mobilize Catholics to the cause of the schools opened up political divisions. Between 1906 and the first general election of 1910, lay people were directed to place the education question above all other issues at the ballot box. For a bishop to highlight the issues which should be at the front of the voter's mind was regarded as a legitimate exercise of his teaching authority: education was seen as a moral not a political question, so when the bishops taught the laity were obliged to follow. But it was considered highly inappropriate for the clergy to go beyond general statements of guidance and direct voters to support a particular electoral candidate. In practice, however, there were numerous cases in this period when the most explicit directions were given and the crudest forms of pressure brought to bear on the laity. Invariably the Conservative Party were the beneficiaries of the hierarchy's opposition to the Liberal Party. McClelland's assessment that Bourne put his political trust in IPP influence was not the perception of contemporaries: T. P. O'Connor, the redoubtable Liverpool Irish Nationalist leader, told Lloyd George in 1909 that 'Archbishop Bourne has declared war against us in England; and I gather from other quarters that he and the Tories are probably already in secret alliance. This will make it a very bitter fight [the 1910 general election] – especially in Lancashire.'[48] Yorkshire Catholicism was especially vehement in defence of the schools. It was the Bishop of Leeds, William Gordon (1831–1911), who set the political tone, describing Liberal ministers in the run-up to a by-election in 1908 as 'blackguards' and 'thieves'.[49] It was hardly surprising given Gordon's robust and uncompromising lead that senior clergymen of the diocese were equally immoderate. During the West Riding municipal elections of 1906, Canon Dolan of Huddersfield went so far as to inform his parishioners that he intended to vote for the Conservative Party candidate, Foster Fraser.[50] At the Dewsbury by-election of 1908 precipitated by the Liberal Walter Runciman's appointment as Minister of Education, Gordon did little to restrain the exercise of clerical pressure. Canon Mulcahy surpassed even Gordon in his vituperation. At one public meeting he declared that any Catholic who voted for Runciman was a 'renegade who would have no luck and would meet with an early death'. Referring to Runciman's Irish sympathies, Mulcahy dismissed home rule as a 'red-herring', castigating Nationalists as a 'black-livered set', '5 or 6 who met in a tap-room ... and in the name of all the people in Ireland passed a resolution on behalf of Catholics'.[51] However, despite such intense clerical pressure, perhaps even because of it, the Irish vote remained solidly Liberal and Runciman was re-elected with only a slightly reduced majority.

Another combative opponent of the Liberals was Louis Casartelli, Bishop of Salford (1852–1925). With his preference for noisy forms of political protest and intransigent opposition to any attempts to reverse the 1902 education settlement, Casartelli emerged as a Catholic counterpart to E. A. Knox, Anglican Bishop of Manchester. There was nothing smooth about this son of an Italian optical instrument manufacturer: his forthright political views often set him on a collision course with his more cautious episcopal colleagues. But he was also distinguished academically, unlike most of his brother bishops. After Ushaw he took his external degree from London University, and from there went on to study oriental languages at Louvain, achieving his doctorate in 1884. His expertise lay mainly in the fields of Sanskrit and Zoroastrianism – although he also published a book of ecclesiastical history[52] – and in 1889 he was elected to the Royal Asiatic Society in recognition of his scholarly accomplishments. In May 1903, then Rector of St Bede's College, Manchester, he was appointed to lecture at the new University of Manchester on Iranian languages and literature.[53] It was a role he continued to perform until 1923. This background explains why he was convinced of the need for more university-trained priests.[54] His was not a 'closed' mentality, even if his political outlook was to prove far from 'open'.

On 21 September 1903, Casartelli was consecrated Bishop of Salford. His episcopate was notable for its encouragement of the idea of the lay apostolate. His first pastoral letter, entitled the *Sign of the Times* (1903), called for the laity to engage in public life, insisting that there were 'vast fields of action for the general good' beyond 'mere party politics'. In particular, he urged the laity to organize themselves for the protection of the schools – the level of vulnerability this implies is interesting considering that it was only a year after the 'success' of 1902.[55] In 1906 he launched the Catholic Federation (hereafter the 'Federation'), which was conceived as an organization for the defence of Catholic interests. Casartelli's encouragement to lay activity was not singular: in the first half of the decade the Catholic Truth Society (CTS) published a number of pamphlets on this theme.[56] Bourne was to claim at the first National Catholic Congress in 1910 that he had envisaged something like the Federation soon after arriving at Westminster, although he later stated that without the threat to the schools it would not have come into existence.[57] In some respects the Federation showed continuities with organizations founded in the nineteenth century like the Catholic Registration Association, whose purpose was to ensure that Catholics who were entitled to vote were registered as voters, and to ascertain the attitudes of electoral candidates to denominational education. But there were also novel features. With the Birrell Bill before parliament, Casartelli expressed the hope that the Federation would not prove to be ephemeral but that it would become rather a permanent force for the protection and furtherance of Catholic interests.[58] Whilst studying at Louvain he had had the opportunity to gain first-hand knowledge of developments in continental social Catholicism. His ideas for lay organization bore the traces of that experience. Doyle has suggested that Casartelli hoped the Federation would develop into a Catholic political party similar to the German Centre Party or the Belgian Catholic Party,[59] but this was never seriously entertained and was even rejected by the Federation in 1911.[60] However, Casartelli's strong emphasis on distinctively Catholic lay organizations formed to defend confessional interests did owe much to his knowledge of the continental scene. Furthermore, Doyle traces the militancy of Casartelli's anti-socialism to his identification with continental social Catholic experience. In Belgium, for instance, Catholic organizations were founded initially in response to the threat of anti-clerical socialism (and liberalism), and throughout his episcopate Casartelli was unwilling to see socialism as anything but a threat to the Church, even when its English incarnation displayed few traces of anti-clericalism. Organizations of Catholic trade unionists had flourished on the continent since the late nineteenth century – now at Casartelli's behest the Catholic Trade Unionists (CTU) were formed as a sub-committee of the Federation in response to the feeling that the trade union movement had deviated from its original purpose. Casartelli believed that under socialistic influence the trade union movement had intruded into areas of policy they had no business to enter, such as the resolutions at successive congresses committing trade unions to support of secular education.[61] Catholic trade unionists such as James Sexton, the redoubtable docker's MP, received encouragement from Casartelli in his attempts to frustrate the adoption of such a policy.

The Federation did not prove to be the agent of Catholic unity that Casartelli had envisaged, indeed, the Catholic vote was often a 'house divided against itself'.[62] The failure of the Federation was mainly down to resentments created by its ill-judged attempts to influence the Catholic vote against the Liberal Party. In the hard-fought Manchester North-West by-election of 1908, intense pressure was brought to bear against the Liberal candidate. The defection of the Irish vote was cited as one of the reasons for Winston Churchill's defeat by 400 votes at the hands of the Conservative, William Joynson-Hicks.[63] (Ironically, Joynson-Hicks was a vehement anti-papist, although it does not appear that this was an issue at the election.) Casartelli was more scrupulous than Bishop Gordon about the extent to which the clergy should attempt to influence the course of elections. His correspondence around the time of the Manchester North-West by-election reveals anxieties about the possible divisive effects of intervention, and some concern that any statements of clerical guidance be as 'mild and dispassionate as possible'.[64] It was a concern mainly about the degree of pressure that was to be exerted, for he was in no doubt as to where Catholic allegiances should lie – emphatically not with the Liberal Party – and he still encouraged the distribution of handbills directing the vote in the churches of that division.[65] It was an acrimonious contest with the United Irish League (UIL) directing the Irish to vote Liberal, and the Federation, prompted by Casartelli, attempting to bring the Irish to heel. But the desired defeat of the Liberals was not achieved without cost to the harmony of the Catholic community: fierce brawls were common occurrences at Catholic political meetings.[66] Two members of the Salford Chapter, Canons McArthy and Lynch, continued to support the Liberal Party, which Casartelli took to be an act of disloyalty.[67] Soon after the election, Casartelli's charge that the UIL had put their duties as Irishmen before their duties as Catholics did nothing to endear either him or the Federation to the Irish: commenting on Casartelli's complaints about the dismal attendance at the Federation's meeting at the 1909 Manchester CTS conference, *The Catholic Herald* put this down to Casartelli's 'anti-Irish' remarks.[68] In Blackburn also the Federation was seen as an instrument of local Conservative interest. Casartelli's correspondence at the beginning of 1908 reveals his concern that Blackburn's Catholic community was divided between an 'ultra-Irish and anti-English party' led by the Liberal, James Kershaw, and an 'ultra-English and anti-Irish party concentrated around Dr Londsdale, a Conservative councillor, and his brother, Canon Londsdale of St Alban's, Blackburn.[69] Canon Joseph Burke, who Casartelli saw as a potentially emollient influence because of his Irish and English ancestry,[70] was transferred from his Bolton parish to St Mary's, Blackburn, to harmonize the situation. But hostilities reopened at the by-election of October 1908 occasioned by the death of Dr Londsdale. At a public meeting, Kershaw, himself a member of the Federation, alleged that after announcing his candidature the Conservative Party put up another Catholic candidate, W. Almond, and 'certain members of the Federation' began 'stirring up strife to get the Federation to support his opponent'. Casartelli intervened, sending a message to Blackburn Federationists that 'he was not going to have any of this intrigue', insisting that local Catholics should vote for whoever they wished.[71] In the event Almond defeated Kershaw by 673 votes to 531.[72]

Far from facilitating Catholic unity the Federation was threatening to open up a breach between Church and people. Sensing this, the bishops urged a lessening of lay political activity, a difficult position to maintain bearing in mind the premium they placed on the schools question. However, the failure of two Liberal education bills in 1908 helped lower the political temperature. That September the Eucharistic Congress was held in London and, although attended with political controversy,[73] it served to stimulate religious enthusiasm and helped to unify the Catholic community. There were also indications that Casartelli was becoming uncomfortable with the political forces he had unleashed. In 1909 he wrote to Bourne urging that the spiritual, non-political side of the Federation be accentuated.[74] In October of that year, the six northern bishops met at Ushaw College to discuss the impending general election and set out strict guidelines governing the issuing of test questions. It was resolved that questions should be restricted to the issue of religious education; that no direction should be given by either the bishops or the Federation as to how to vote beyond qualifying responses as 'satisfactory or unsatisfactory'.[75] 'Everything should be avoided that may be considered direct *political* action', Casartelli warned Fr Sharrock.[76] In the event his concern was justified. During the general election of January 1910, Canon Lynch, who was hostile to the Federation,[77] was involved in an unseemly public conflict with Casartelli. In the contest for Manchester South-West a member of the Federation, apparently with Casartelli's prior knowledge,[78] placed a poster on the notice board of Lynch's church indicating that C. T. Needham, the Liberal candidate, had not responded to the hierarchy's test questions. Thus provoked, Lynch wrote to the *Manchester Guardian,* which Casartelli regarded as a 'hostile, anti-Catholic Nonconformist organ',[79] accusing the

Federation of threatening the trust that he had built-up with the working men of Hulme over a period thirty-four years: 'They know me . . . and it is common council that we are to decide how we are to vote'. The Federation 'are taking all the power out of our hands, humiliating and degrading us before our people and the outside public, as if we were not able to safeguard the Catholic faith and Catholic interests without their control and advice'.[80] Lynch's letter elicited a sympathetic response from Catholic correspondents in the *Manchester Guardian*.[81] Casartelli admitted in private correspondence that the Federation had made an error of judgement in not putting the full facts before the voters,[82] but his ire was directed mainly at Lynch for 'striking a blow of so serious a character at Catholic Unity'. 'No other incident in my episcopate has caused me such distress', he told Lynch.[83]

Such incidents heightened the mood for a withdrawal from political engagement. After the election of January 1910 there was indeed a recoil from politics as the constitutional, rather than the schools question began to engross attention. Prior to the general election of December 1910 the bishops insisted that as constitutional issues were paramount 'on which Catholics are free to hold any views',[84] no test questions should be put to the candidates.[85] The withdrawal from politics also reflected concerns that the new lay organizations were becoming too independent: there was a feeling that they should be subjected to a greater degree of episcopal control. At the first National Catholic Congress held at Leeds in 1910, with the Manchester controversy fresh in the mind, Fr Thomas Wright of Hull, one of the speakers, declared that 'a total absence of interference in party politics . . . is a necessary condition of the strength and solidarity of the Federation'. Alluding to the Manchester troubles, Wright stressed that the question, 'Does the Irish political policy involve a danger to the religious principles of Catholic education, and, therefore, is there sufficient justification for the Federation to assume an attitude of opposition?', was a matter for 'the Episcopacy to determine, and not for the Federation'. The Federation should not attempt 'to steal a march upon our leaders and press forward in advance of them'.[86] These views were reinforced by Cardinal Bourne in 1911: he told the Westminster Federation that they were an advisory body and could not take 'public executive action' until directed by the hierarchy.[87]

Such assertions of episcopal authority were a response to the impression that a mood of lay dissension was abroad. In 1910 Bishop Gordon, backed by Casartelli, issued a protest against *The Catholic Herald* – which under the proprietorship of Charles Diamond was an organ of Irish nationalism – for fostering a spirit of disloyalty to ecclesiastical authority over the schools question. Other bishops shared this antipathy to Diamond.[88] Bourne had complained two years previously that *The Catholic Herald* was too 'aggressively political'.[89] But Diamond was a stubborn Liberal eager to maintain a Catholic presence in that party, and would not ditch his convictions at the behest of bishops. In Diamond's view it was the Catholic hierarchy who were guilty of politicking.[90] The feeling against Diamond on the bench of bishops was intense. To Casartelli, the 'so-called *Catholic Herald*'[91] was a 'many-headed hydra'[92] which had 'surpassed itself in invective, not only against individual bishops and clergy, but against the very principles of ecclesiastical authority and the rights of the Church in the matters of Schools. The poison is rapidly spreading among our young people, – alas! I fear among some of our youngest clergy.'[93] Casartelli even suspected that Diamond was under the sway of Nonconformist influence.[94] He proposed the following resolution at the Low Week meeting of 1910: 'The Bishops view, with very great concern, the attitude adopted for a considerable period by the Editor of *The Catholic Herald*, as tending to lessen the respect due from all Catholics to ecclesiastical authority and fostering division and dissension among Catholics'.[95] Here was an example of how the stigma of disloyalty was invariably attached to those who gave weight to political issues other than the 'struggle for the schools'.

Such suspicion of lay freedom and initiative, as stated earlier, reached its height during the reign of Pius X. Theological inquiry was not the only casualty of the Modernist crisis; suspicion extended to other attempts 'to adapt the teaching and practice of the Church to ... the requirements of contemporary culture'.[96] Integralists in the Roman Curia began to use the expression 'social modernism' to stigmatize those social Catholics who were prepared to consider collaboration with non-Catholic, even anti-clerical, forces in their quest for social justice and the reChristianization of society.[97] French social Catholics operating in the context of the trauma of the Law of Separation, which cut the ties between Church and State, had to tread particularly carefully. Although the French bishops had to negotiate with the Republican government in the difficult transitional period, Pius X was anxious not to lend any appearance of legitimacy to the matter.[98] Against this background, democratically orientated initiatives such as the *Semaines sociales* (social weeks) and Marc Sangnier's Sillon, which aimed to unite Protestants and non-believers behind a democratic political programme, became targets for the integralists.[99] Critics of these undertakings wanted less stress on social justice, more on charity and the rights of private property; instead of workers' organizations, they favoured a benevolent paternalism of 'mixed associations' of workers and owners to maintain social peace.[100] What really fuelled antipathy, as Misner points out, was the belief that the common denominator of all these modernisms, social and doctrinal, was 'autonomy and intolerance for authority'.[101] The anxiety was that democracy in the political sphere would carry over into the ecclesiastical domain. The response of the Vatican was to insist even more emphatically on the need for Catholic social action to be bound to the ecclesiastical hierarchy. In 1910 the various groups which comprised the Sillon were dissolved and placed under the authority of the bishop in each diocese.[102] In the light of this, it is interesting to consider whether expressions of English social Catholicism post-*Pascendi* could be anything more than a tame reflection of the outlook of ecclesiastical authority.

*   *   *

For a number of reasons English social Catholic organizations never ran into the kind of trouble that bedevilled the Sillon. Most bishops felt there to be little of real consequence in those pamphlets and debates on social questions that were read and heard by a relatively small number of Catholics. This more relaxed approach contrasted, as we have seen, with the vigorous stance on the schools question. The episcopate allowed the Catholic social movement a certain latitude; in turn, its leaders moved cautiously. Organizations like the CSG were not simply the instrument of the hierarchy, but neither did they pose a challenge – they were the accepted channel for the laity's social and political energies.

Yet such was the anxiety about the spread of socialism that an attitude of complete indifference to the development of social Catholic groups was not an option. Certainly the hierarchy came down heavily on Catholics who sought to develop initiatives independently of episcopal control. Consider the case of the Catholic Socialist Society (CSS), a group started in 1908 in Leeds by a young factory worker and member of the Independent Labour Party, Henry Somerville, and presided over by Fr Theodore Evans, a Jesuit and convert from Nonconformity.[103] Taking their lead from a Glasgow society of the same name,[104] the Leeds group was not as radical as it sounded: it was a study club not dissimilar to those that sprang up under the auspices of the CSG; it was not conceived as a political party and its members had little grasp of socialist ideology.[105] Yet it was dealt with in the most ruthless way by the local bishop. Somerville and Evans were unfortunate that their bishop should have been Gordon. He was a severe authoritarian and disciplinarian (he was famous for striking children with his crozier if they did not answer correctly their questions at Confirmation[106]) who regarded the current stress on social questions with nothing but disdain. Even after *Rerum Novarum*, Gordon continued to emphasize in a one-sided fashion those parts of papal social teaching which called on the poor to 'embrace poverty as the position his Heavenly Father allots to him'.[107] In a pastoral letter read out in the churches of the diocese on 20 June 1909 he banned the CSS, admonishing his flock to 'shun it as they would a pestilence': 'They are on a course where many a rock of danger lies hidden, upon which many a soul has been utterly wrecked and brought to destruction. Furthermore, these men are giving scandal to their brethren ... We call on them to lay aside all their Socialist theories, and to make an end of this, so-called, Catholic Socialist Society.'[108] Gordon's shipwreck metaphor was probably derived from *Communium Rerum*, issued by the Pope just two months previously. As for Somerville, having received Gordon's letter as 'unexpectedly as a thunderbolt from a summer sky', he had no desire to court further disfavour and dutifully submitted to Gordon's will. He was to later confess that his 'constant friction with the clergy was giving me a tendency to anti-clericalism',[109] but this was after he had found an acceptable outlet for his interest in social questions in the CSG, after being introduced by Evans to its founder, Fr Charles Plater (1875–1921), at Manchester in 1909.[110]

The other place in which a CSS was formed was the Salford diocese. Anxiety about socialism was far higher in Salford, which was overwhelmingly urban, than in many other dioceses. Visitation returns for 1900 indicate the concerns of parish priests about the inroads socialism was making amongst Catholic working people. Drunkenness was still the main pastoral problem, but socialism was a major concern at St Anne's, Greenacres, Oldham; the Blackburn parishes of St Alban's, St Joseph's, and St Peter's ('When Catholics join them they give up the Mass and the Sacraments', was the recorded observation); Guardian Angels, Elton, Bury; St Mary's, Eccles, and St James', Pendleton.[111] Such anxieties only heightened during the course of the decade. Casartelli was determined to take an uncompromising stand, and in 1908 he banned the Manchester CSS, declaring that 'whilst there may be, and are, many social and economic reforms which can be advocated both by the Catholic Church and the system known as Socialism, the latter itself, as a system, is not consistent with Catholicism. It is therefore as inconsistent to speak of a 'Catholic Socialist Society' as it would be to speak of a 'Catholic Wesleyan Society'.'[112] Casartelli soon acquired a reputation as a hammer of socialists. It is interesting to note that in January 1909 Fr Leo Puissant, who had been engaged in an unsuccessful campaign against

John Wheatley's organization in Glasgow, wrote to Casartelli requesting a 'field to labour on in your diocese'. Casartelli was sympathetic to Puissant's case, commending his 'fine work in Scotland combating the "Catholic Socialist Society"'.[113] The affinity between Casartelli and the Belgian Puissant (also Louvain educated) went beyond mere reactionary anti-socialism. Both were similarly impressed with the network of specifically Catholic organizations which mushroomed in Belgium and Germany during the latter part of the nineteenth century. As Gilley states, Puissant was by no means blind to social problems, rather it was the 'very sharpness' of his 'vision of a populist radical Catholicism which so violently estranged him from any social programme not completely controlled by the Church'.[114] Just as Puissant's vision of a confrontational Catholicism left him very much an isolated figure in the Scottish Church,[115] so Casartelli's intransigent politics would send him too down a lonely path.

As I have stated, the CSG became the acceptable outlet for lay Catholic social concern.[116] Doyle has recognized the caution with which CSG leaders proceeded in its early days,[117] but this is a point which needs further emphasis. The moving spirits of the CSG were the Jesuit Fr Charles Plater and Leslie Toke. Plater's interest in social Catholicism was aroused by a meeting with several French priests in 1904 who opened his eyes to continental developments; in that year he also met Marc Sangnier, President of the Sillon, an event which he thought to be the turning-point of his life.[118] It certainly gave a focus and purpose to his life. He had drifted through his undergraduate years at Oxford (1900–04) feeling very little enthused by the life of scholarship.[119] He appeared a bundle of nervous energy and passion in search of a cause. Francis Urquhart, Fellow of Balliol College, Oxford, said of Plater: 'He's not a bad fellow – though I think a few months silence in the desert would be a good thing. There are some people who always crave to be talking – who 'dilletant' about the place and write verses on odd scraps of paper and read essays 'on style'. They want a good round Cambridge education: hard application to the stern realities of erudition – that's the thing for them.'[120] It would not have surprised Urquhart that Plater pursued his new interest in social questions in breathless and indiscriminate fashion. In April 1909 his diary announces: 'Have purchased about 40 books on Socialism and kindred subjects – my room is stacked with 'em'.[121] The early days of the CSG found Plater almost uncontrollable with excitement. Lucy Gibbs, an original CSG member who had knocked Fr Plater sideways with her good looks (he had pictured her as a frump with 'podgy hands' and a 'shrill falsetto'), scolded him at the inaugural meeting for 'being like an excited child'.[122]

Leslie Toke was the perfect counterpoise to Plater. A 'drooping, melancholy, bearded man', Toke was educated at Balliol College, Oxford, imbibing its strong ethic of public service. During his time at Oxford in the 1890s he became involved with the Workers' Educational Association, which had an important place in the Christian socialist tradition, and joined the Fabians, to which he remained attached even after his conversion to Catholicism.[123] Toke was just one of a number of converts who with great energy and enthusiasm sought to shake English Catholicism from what they saw as its indifference to the wider society. The key figures were Margaret Fletcher, a disciple of Ruskin and an 'ardent feminist'[124] who bemoaned the lack of social concern amongst English Catholics;[125] and Virginia Mary Crawford, a childhood friend of Beatrice Webb who earned early notoriety as a participant in a three-in-the-bed scandal with Sir Charles Dilke and his servant,[126] and who, encouraged by a meeting with Manning soon after her conversion, devoted the rest of her life to social work and politics.

With anxiety about Modernism and socialism at a high pitch, the CSG was bound by its perceptions of what ecclesiastical authority would tolerate. Episcopal concern about the spread of socialism was at its height in 1908 and 1909, and although the CSG was in many ways a positive attempt to apply the Church's teaching to social questions, it was prudent for its leaders to present it as a movement of defence. Indeed, Plater received donations from Catholic industrialists concerned about the spread of socialism; his retreats for workers initiative, a spiritual movement out of which he hoped would emerge a cadre of working men who would diffuse Catholic social principles in their workplaces,[127] relied heavily on such assistance.[128] CSG leaders recognized that their more adventurous designs had to be suppressed until they had attained a respected position within the Church. In September 1909, Toke sent a memorandum to Plater which insisted that an 'ecclesiastic' was needed 'to bring about the safe birth and guard the dangerous boyhood of the movement'. Toke suggested that no converts under ten years standing should be admitted to active membership of the CSG for they would likely 'get in all sorts of ecclesiastical disfavour' if 'young and trying to teach grandmother'. Trust was to be gained by attaching themselves to 'some "cause" that is being started, advocated, and "run" by the ... "great ecclesiastics" i.e. Education, Rescinding of Royal Declaration; The allowing of priests to stand for Parliament ...' Members should 'be assiduous in attending Archdiocesan functions ... to show that we really love obedience and are quick to its lesser as well as its greater occasions'. Toke went on to stress that 'attempts at deeper and broader solidarities with extra-Catholic social and civic movements should be internally worked out and silently realized, but not with too much "speaking", or at any rate, speaking "before the time". We must at all times and in all places and with all persons be careful about the outward and visible form of the society ... '[129] The reference to 'extra-Catholic' movements possibly indicates that the Sillon was a model for the CSG; certainly Toke and Plater had a high regard for the work of Sangnier.[130]

A strong clerical contribution was a vital element in the CSG's quest for respectability and acceptance. Fr Henry Parkinson (1852-1924), who had done much to encourage interest in social questions at Oscott College,[131] became the CSG's guide and censor, whilst Frederick Keating (1859-1927), Bishop of Northampton, became its President. Although Toke had been anxious to secure episcopal support for the CSG, the possibility that innovation would be dampened as a result was also a worry. This was a constant dilemma for social Catholics. Soon after the CSG's formation, Toke told Fr Parkinson that although it was important to receive the approbation of the bishops, he wondered 'whether they will not want to have too many fingers in our pie!', adding 'Better to remain free and unofficially approved!'[132] This was not an option in the current climate – at any rate Toke's worst fears were not realized. Although CSG publications had to secure the *imprimatur* of the particular author's diocesan bishop, examples of episcopal intrusion were unusual enough to be considered noteworthy, this despite the fact that bishops post-*Pascendi* were urged to use 'the utmost severity in granting permission to publish'.[133] Fr T. Wright of Hull submitted a pamphlet for publication which was passed by Plater and Fr Keating, but to his surprise the local Ordinary, Richard Lacy of Middlesbrough (1841-1929), insisted on certain amendments on the advice of his censor. Wright commented to Fr Parkinson that Lacy was 'exceedingly sensitive about his authority. He is out of sympathy with "new ideas" ... being old and running prudence to extremes.'[134] But this kind of intervention was unusual as clerical tutelage obviated the need for episcopal scrutiny. In contrast to the informal, spontaneous nature of Sillon meetings,[135] the CSG kept a tight rein on expression. The attitude taken at Fr Wright's Catholic Academy – out of which a branch of the CSG emerged – was typical. Wright decided that social and political education would take the form of lectures rather than debate: 'In a debating society we would only get a loose handling of principles which are really too sacred to be trifled with'.[136] Within the CSG the scope for individual initiative was limited further when it was decided by the Executive Committee that 'nothing can appear under

the name of the "Catholic Social Guild" except what we be collectively responsible for'.[137] Henry Somerville's suggestion that he
contribute a series of articles in a catechism format on the social question was refused by Fr Parkinson. 'I look on this with some dread',
he told V. M. Crawford, 'Unless he obtains the help of experts, he
may answer ten questions correctly, and in the eleventh get himself
denounced to the ecclesiastical authority.' Parkinson dismissed
Somerville's suggestion as 'preaching in preserves already occupied
by our special committees'.[138]

The overriding concern of Plater and Toke to ensure that the CSG
developed along lines favourable to ecclesiastical authority meant that
however radical the views of individual members may have been,
there was little likelihood that these could be translated into an official programme.[139] On contentious issues such as socialism its leaders
avoided explicit pronouncements. In 1910 B. W. Devas had been
pushing for a conference on the nature of socialism but was blocked
by Plater. Plater explained to V. M. Crawford:

> I don't think the Guild need deal very explicitly just yet with the subject
> of socialism, though it can supply materials. When it does so, it should
> do so as the result of much careful consideration. We don't want to
> damage ourselves by advancing rotten arguments against it. Such a
> commission as Devas suggests would lead to acrimony and division.
> We need education rather than a conference. This is where the guild
> can do much good: and this is why I am so keen to make our commit-
> tees representative even though they might seem thereby to be less
> compact and efficient.[140]

The conviction of CSG leaders that their organization should be representative of divergent political views[141] blunted any radical edge.
After proposing for publication Fr Vincent McNabb's pamphlet on the
housing question, Toke suggested that 'in order to pacify the enemy,
we ought to publish a similar one (at the same time) on "The Rights
of Property", or some such thing'.[142] The leaders' avoidance of political commitment led one member, when considering the reasons why
the CSG held out little appeal for the Catholic working classes, to
question the effectiveness of 'writing around vague or indefinite principles without any clue as to their application'.[143] But apart from the
involvement of some of its leading members on the Royal Commission
on the Poor Laws,[144] such forays into practical politics were unusual.
The industrial unrest of 1911–13 did, however, prompt some questioning of this detached approach. For instance, in 1912 Bishop
Keating told Thomas Burns that 'The C.S.G. is desirous of coming
down from the generalities to details of Social Reform'; although the

emphasis remained on 'systematic study', the questions proposed by Keating – 'Trade Unionism and the Living Wage' – did indicate a growing concern for relevance.[145] The shift in emphasis was shown in the CSG's *Catholic Studies in Social Reform* series which began in 1911 and provided a body of informed comment on pressing contemporary questions: housing, sweated labour, the poor laws and eugenics were subjects treated in this series.[146]

The control exerted by 'responsible clerics', and the emphasis on study and research rather than political action[147] ensured that the CSG's infancy was a safe one. To that extent it fulfilled one of its founders' ambitions. The similarities between the CSG's approach and that of other contemporary organizations, notably the Christian Social Union founded by Anglicans in 1889, are striking. Its leaders were similarly anxious to accommodate as many different political viewpoints as possible, to eschew political partisanship and to focus on study, research and 'conscience-raising'; there was a certain academic flavour and an air of 'middle-class moralism'.[148]

On the face of it the CSG's early years were a period of steady growth and consolidation. New publications were launched to disseminate its ideas, such as the *Catholic Social Yearbook* which first appeared in 1910 and the *Quarterly Bulletin* which began in July 1911. In addition to these *The Month*, under the editorship of Fr Joseph Keating from 1912, carried much social Catholic material. However, the CSG failed to make the major impact it had hoped. Its publications did not sell well,[149] memberships only trickled in,[150] it was weak in the north of England,[151] and although it had set itself, as the first statute of its constitution declared, to 'facilitate intercourse between Catholic social students and workers',[152] it appeared very much a middle-class affair which made few inroads into the class it was intended to reach.[153] Only two years after its formation Toke, lamenting the 'slump in fortunes', asked Parkinson: 'Won't the Bishops help at all?'[154] Despite securing a measure of episcopal support, conservative opinion continued to regard it as suspect: *The Tablet*, for instance, ignored the CSG for many years. 'Our manuals have not even been noticed in their pages', Fr Keating complained to Parkinson.[155] He wondered whether there was 'yet a public for such wares'.[156]

Arguably the most influential CSG publication of this early phase of development was Fr Plater's *The Priest and Social Action* (1914). This was his most significant work: it continued to be read in British and Irish seminaries well into the 1950s.[157] The significance of *The Priest and Social Action* did not lie primarily in its stress on the importance of social questions or in its critique of socio-economic conditions – although these were key elements – rather it was that he introduced generations of seminarians to the notion that they had an obligation to actively involve themselves in movements for social reform,[158] and that this was not an optional extra. The introduction to the book was provided by Bishop Keating, which clearly helped legitimate views which even after *Rerum Novarum* were viewed in some quarters as dangerous.

*   *   *

The tendency of social Catholics to tread warily lest they upset ecclesiastical authority was clearly justified in the contemporary climate, although in examining the attitudes and responses of the bishops to social questions and the nascent social movement it would be misleading to suggest that they were uniformly conservative and hostile to all innovation. Bourne is a case in point.

Cardinal Gasquet predicted soon after Bourne's elevation to Westminster that 'tho' he will never be brilliant, he certainly won't be narrow-minded'.[159] Gasquet was not so far off the mark. Whilst Bourne could appear distant, there is anecdotal evidence to suggest that he was not quite a cold automaton. There are flashes, here and there, of human sympathies and humour, and in particular a concern for the vulnerable. For instance, he banned the use of corporal punishment for junior students at the diocesan seminary: 'this led at St Edmund's [Ware] to ribald remarks about consecrated bottoms!', Cyril Cowderoy, Bishop of Southwark (1949–76), recalled.[160] He could empathize with errant priests. When a young priest of his diocese became involved with a woman, he explained to the Archbishop of Liverpool: 'He has no relatives, and was devoted to his mother, and I have always felt that it was his sense of intense loneliness after her death that was the beginning of the fall'.[161] Bourne knew all about loneliness.

The inflexibility that came to characterize his later episcopate was not so evident in the early stages. A sign of this was in his attitude to the lay apostolate. Bourne's openness to lay initiative was demonstrated by his encouragement of the Catholic Women's League (CWL), one of the many lay apostolate organizations which sprang up in the mid–1900s. Founded by Margaret Fletcher in 1907, its purpose was to encourage Catholic women to recognize their social responsibilities and duties; many became involved in social and political action as a result. It encountered some opposition from priests who were wary of an organization which appeared to be bringing secular concerns right into the midst of parish life. No doubt some were uneasy around articulate, questioning women. Fletcher was understandably anxious that the CWL could appear as a dangerous innovation, so requested a censor 'whose name would be a guarantee of orthodoxy' and who would 'examine our projects in advance and measure them against the mind of the Church'.[162] In a response that typified his dealings with lay people, Bourne told Fletcher that this was unnecessary, although he warned her that there would be a 'wrap over the knuckles' if they went too far.[163] He took the same line with the National Conference of Catholic Trade Unionists (NCCTU): he was reported in *The Tablet* as saying that it was 'his way to interfere as little as possible with my organisations ... At the same time, naturally from the position he held, he reserved to himself the right to tell them when he thought that they were going a little astray'.[164] His style was paternalistic, on occasions patronizing, and he avoided wielding the big stick. Yet at the same time David Mathew observed Bourne's 'desire for centralization' and 'tendency to concentrate authority', and his marked preference for 'Monarchical institutions'.[165] There need be no contradiction: Bourne was impatient with bureaucracy and officialdom, encouraging rather a more immediate sense of respect and duty amongst his 'subjects', and recognized that this could be achieved without the heavy-hand and without recourse to intermediate authorities, censors and the like. At all times aloof and taciturn,[166] Bourne was respected, even a little feared,[167] rather than loved. He kept his distance from the organizations over which he presided, allowed them a considerable degree of freedom and rarely felt the need to intrude in their business.

Bourne was to display these traits in his response to Modernism. Frank Sheed, whilst finding Bourne 'rather cold in manner', was impressed that

> During the Modernist uproar ... he had insisted, against all pressure from heresy hunters in Rome, that there was no Modernism among his clergy. When his successor in Southwark forbade Maud Petre the sacraments for her support of Father Tyrrell, she had only to cross the Thames and receive communion in Westminster. He gave me two rules, 'Don't ask my advice. Just tell me what you're doing. I'll stop you if I think it necessary.' He never did. Another time he put it even more concisely: 'I never start anything. But I never stop anything.' When I was a publisher his censor demanded a number of changes in one of our books. I complained to Cardinal Bourne. He said, 'I won't alter the censor's decision. But I won't mind a bit if you appeal to Rome.' I said, 'To whom should I direct the appeal?' He said, 'I have no idea.' We got along splendidly.[168]

It was this sort of attitude which belied Bourne's stiff, formal image, but which also aroused the suspicion of the Holy See that he was not the safe pair of hands it had been expecting. Bourne's insouciance of Roman structures was not contrived: he was never comfortable in his dealings with the Vatican authorities, and preferred to correspond in French rather than in the lingua franca of Latin. It was to be a cause of great scandal to the Vatican authorities that Bourne sent so few students to study in Rome.[169]

It was eight years after his appointment as Archbishop of Westminster before Bourne was made a cardinal. A rumour circulated that he was out of favour in Rome because of alleged sympathies to 'advanced views' – Modernism in other words.[170] The source of this rumour was thought to be Peter Amigo (1864–1949), Bourne's successor as Bishop of Southwark.[171] Bourne heard that Amigo had written to Cardinal Merry del Val asking advice on the closing of Wonersh Seminary, claiming 'the tone of the young priests who had come from that seminary was quite Modernist, and the priests themselves quite unmanageable'.[172] Amigo vehemently denied this allegation.[173] Neither the rumours of Amigo's agitations nor the allegations of Bourne's Modernism were ever substantiated – but Bourne remained suspect. The affair pained Bourne and sullied his relations with Amigo,[174] whom, ironically, he had recommended for the see of Southwark against the express wishes of the Southwark Chapter and the other bishops. 'The dignity in itself is nothing – but the manifest confidence of the Holy See is of extreme importance', Bourne remarked to Bishop Cahill, adding, 'To me personally such clear absence of confidence would be unspeakably painful.'[175] It is difficult to get behind the intrigue and rumour and establish facts, but what is apparent is that Bourne's tolerance of those deemed Modernists, or his perceived tolerance of Modernists, – indeed one historian has tentatively suggested that Bourne's concern to avoid a witch-hunt in his diocese went beyond mere tolerance and extended to actual sympathy for the Modernists[176] – had highly damaging consequences for his standing and reputation in Rome.

The second half of the decade saw a distinct upsurge of interest amongst Catholics in social questions which the bishops could not ignore. This paralleled the greater stress on social questions in other churches and in the nation as a whole after the general election of 1906,[177] which brought in a Liberal government with reforming ambitions and saw the Labour Party with a significant parliamentary presence for the first time (twenty-nine seats). Social questions began to feature more regularly in the Catholic press and periodicals. In 1908 the CTS published a volume entitled *The Catholic Church and*

Labour, comprised of pamphlets from the Benedictines Francis Gasquet and Abbot Terence Snow, Leslie Toke, as well as a reprint of Cardinal Manning's 'Leo XIII on the Condition of Labour'. It aimed to 'disprove this stupid, and often malignant, lie' that the Church 'will use her influence to support the wealthy and powerful rather than to champion the poor and disinherited'.[178] The appearance of this book seemed to indicate that there were those in the Church who were taking seriously Manning's contention that the progress of the Church was bound up with the fate of the poorest classes.

The extent to which the episcopate itself emphasized social questions should not, however, be overstated. Despite the endorsement of the CSG, the concerns which occupied its activists and theorists still featured only marginally on the bishops' agenda. It is significant that at the Leeds National Catholic Congress, a meeting of the CSG chaired by Edward Ilsley (1837–1926), Bishop of Birmingham, and Casartelli, clashed with a much larger gathering devoted to temperance chaired by Bourne and Bishop Amigo of Southwark. This perhaps suggests that whilst housing, sweated labour, trade unions and the question of the living wage had replaced moral crusades on the agenda of leaders of the Catholic social movement, the bishops on the whole did not yet view these as central to the Church's concern and still prioritized moral campaigns. Social questions were rarely discussed at the annual Low Week meeting; an exception was the interest devoted to the promotion of temperance, an issue where questions of personal moral responsibility seemed more obviously to be involved.[179] Even attendance at CSG meetings did not, in Bishop Ilsley's case, appear to have entailed any commitment to social reform – his pastoral letters contain no references to the social question, although Birmingham's diocesan magazine carried regular, albeit cautious, discussions from the early 1910s. Furthermore, it was not the case that an interest in social questions was always an indicator of progressive social and political attitudes.[180] Anxiety about the rise of socialism was contemporaneous with the formation of the CSG. One of the most anxious, Bishop Casartelli, was a supporter of the CSG in its initial stages. Even before the CSG was formed, Casartelli had promoted the study of social questions in his diocese. The Catholic School for Social Science was set up under the auspices of the Federation and a course of lectures was held at St Bede's College, Manchester, under the tutelage of another Oscott disciple of Parkinson, Fr Joseph Lomax.[181] In 1909 Casartelli commended the Federation as

> perhaps the only efficient means of protecting our intelligent young men of the working classes from grave danger ... Against this danger

the Catholic Federation provides by affording its members opportunities of learning the hollowness of the underlying Socialistic philosophy
and its opposition to Christian doctrine, and of becoming acquainted
with the writings of Catholic authorities on social and economic
topics.[182]

Concerns about the hazards of political activity, and a feeling that
spiritual matters should bulk larger, also served as a brake on episcopal commitment to social reform.[183] In 1910 these concerns surfaced
publicly. After the condemnation of the Sillon movement in that year,
the CTS thought it an opportune moment to publish an English translation of *Il Fermo Proposito*.[184] In the preface, Fr Parkinson drew
attention to passages which emphasized that 'Christian Democracy is
strictly bound to dependence on ecclesiastical authority by complete
submission and obedience to the Bishops and their representatives'.[185]
Submission and obedience were the themes which rang out at the first
National Catholic Congress, held at Leeds between 29 July and 2
August 1910. Although it can be seen as the institutional embodiment
of the upsurge in lay activity, the Congress also provided an opportunity for the bishops to impress their authority on the enthusiastic
gathering. Bishop Keating's inaugural address, for instance, which
was later issued as a pastoral letter and a CSG pamphlet, was a
warning 'to those Catholics . . . who habitually pay too little heed to
the voice of the Church, or even resent her interference in matters
which they consider outside her domain'.

> Crag climbers and other venturesome spirits, knowing the dangers of
> their enterprise, adopt the precaution of roping themselves together.
> Implicit obedience to ecclesiastical guidance is the equivalent safeguard
> for those who attempt the perilous paths of social reform . . . The track
> of history is strewn with the whitened bones of too venturesome battal-
> ions who, breaking the bonds of discipline, have paid away life and true
> glory for barren success.[186]

Keating's preface to the 1911 CTS publication of this pastoral letter
laid heavy stress on the duty of obedience to ecclesiastical authority.
He referred to the example of the Sillon, talented and worthy men
whose 'zeal overran discretion': 'Yet so practical was their piety and
so loyal their submission, that, at the word of the Holy See, they
forthwith dissolved their associations, suppressed their journal, and
offered their services to be employed under other leaders in whom the
authorities had greater confidence – a magnificent example of the
Catholic temper at its best!'[187]
   Elements in the Church hostile to the increasing emphasis on social

questions attempted to exploit the more cautious mood which prevailed after 1910 to reverse the trend. Some of the more hostile could be found within the ranks of the Catholic Union of Great Britain (CUGB), a body of laymen formed by the 15th Duke of Norfolk in 1871, drawn from the landed gentry and upper middle class and over-whelmingly Tory in political sympathy. Their main campaigning issue was the removal of the remaining Catholic disabilities;[188] in 1908 they managed to secure adjustments to the coronation oath which removed some of the features deemed offensive to Catholics. But this concern with securing the passage of Catholics into the mainstream of national life also led the CUGB to oppose Irish home rule and to attempt to disrupt what they perceived as an alliance of the Church with social radicalism.

One of the most vigorous opponents of the tendencies embodied in the CSG was Stuart Coats. Coats had stood three times as a Unionist candidate in parliamentary elections; three times he lost. (He eventually won the Wimbledon seat in 1916.) He was a prominent member of both the CUGB and the CTS Executive. The CTS had been responsible for publishing CSG pamphlets until 1914, but the relationship between those two organizations had never been a comfortable one. Whilst James Britten, President of the CTS, encouraged the discussion of social questions, this interest was not shared by other members of the Executive, some of who began to complain about the dispro-portionate 'output of social stuff'.[189] Coats was among them. Accentuating the difficulties, strains were to develop in the relation-ship of Toke of the CSG and Britten. Toke resented any interference in the CSG's publications by Britten and his Committee, and feared that the CSG was becoming a 'mere sub-committee of the CTS';[190] on the other hand, Britten was not the first to be put off by Toke's abra-sive, whingeing manner,[191] and believed that the already problematic task of promoting the publication of social pamphlets was being made impossible by Toke's constant haranguing.[192]

To Coats, the owner of a Scottish textile firm, the CSG were misguided men fallen amongst Fabians: he saw it as his Christian duty to resist its creeping influence. To add credibility to his campaign it was vital that he did not appear hard-headed. His donation to the CTS towards a reprint of *Rerum Novarum* was designed to give the impres-sion of one concerned to see sound principles observed in social and economic life, key amongst them the right to private property and the elimination of class hatred.[193] Those aspects of the encyclical which attacked unrestrained individualistic capitalism did not unduly disturb him: he was to deny that Leo XIII ever had in mind the social and indus-trial conditions of Britain.[194] At the same time Coats pursued a vituperative campaign against the CSG. At a CTS Executive meeting on 14 November 1910, Coats brought before them Leslie Toke's *Some Methods of Social Study*, which contained references to Fabian tracts and which commended the Sillon. Coats moved a resolution: 'That in view of the Pope's condemnation of *le Sillon* it would be wise to submit at once all publications of the society on Socialism, Social Reform and the study of social questions including Methods of Social Study and recommended books to some competent persons to be selected by the Chairman'. The minutes reveal that the Committee was divided on the resolution. Whilst the majority did not wish to go as far as Coats in submitting all the social output to the scrutiny of ecclesiastical authority, one member, Fr Herbert Thurston, whilst deprecating 'the entire suppression of pamphlets', nevertheless thought 'it would be wise to put ourselves on the safe side' proposing that 'a small sub-committee be appointed to consider the existing pamphlets of the CTS dealing with social questions to make sure that they are in accord with the latest pronouncement of the Holy See'. The resolution was carried.[195]

There were indeed signs of closer censorship after 1910. In 1912, for instance, Fr Vincent McNabb's pamphlet on the housing question was withdrawn.[196] The following year McNabb was casting around, unsuccessfully, for alternative outlets for his progressive social views, even approaching Archbishop McGuire of Glasgow, known for his sympathy to social reform, to request his *imprimatur* on the rejected pamphlet.[197] The squeeze was clearly on those who wished to promote a social interpretation of Christianity. In 1916 Coats led a group of *Universe* shareholders in an attempt to depose its managers and editor, T. Dunbar McConnell, ostensibly because of the paper's espousal of social reform. Previous to his stint at *The Universe*, McConnell had founded and edited the *Local Government Review*, so it was perhaps not surprising that his aims, as set out in a memorandum to Mark Sykes, Unionist MP for Hull Central (1911–19), in 1912, included a 'more complete and capable treatment than has hitherto been given' to social questions. It was a challenge to those 'large numbers who would prefer their Catholic weekly paper to leave politics alone altogether'.[198] Unfortunately for McConnell, the majority of *The Universe*'s shareholders fell into this camp. Norfolk held one of the largest stakes in the paper, but it was leading CUGB figures like Coats and James Hope, a nephew of Norfolk's and Conservative MP for Sheffield Central (1908–29), part of a majority group of shareholders, who most resented the editorial shift and McConnell's support for the CSG. According to McConnell, Coats had complained in 1914 that he had put money into the paper 'on the understanding that it was to attack "socialism and socialistically inclined Catholics at all points" and in his opinion the Guild and its members were socialistic'.[199] Both sides attempted to win the episcopate to their cause after Coats's group put in a requisition to wind-up the company in March 1916.[200] Bourne refused to take sides and handed the matter over to his Secretary, Canon Arthur Jackman, who, according to Casartelli, aligned himself with Coats.[201] Bishop Keating, by contrast, referred to the 'egregious Coats'.[202] Others side-stepped the issue. Casartelli was approached by McConnell for his support and indicated to Bourne that he was sympathetic, but stated: 'I should be very careful not to be drawn into what may prove a disedifying dispute among Catholics ... divided counsels among us would be deplorable'. Although Casartelli had become concerned by the socialist proclivities of some high-profile CSG members, he referred to the organization in his letter to Bourne as 'Well-meaning and so useful'.[203] In 1917 a new manager, Sir Martin Melvin, was in place at *The Universe* with H. S. Dean taking over the editorship. Dean's political views were not, however, those of Coats: a year later he clashed with the CUGB over its stance on the Irish conscription crisis. The impression that the Toryism of Coats was in eclipse is hard to avoid.

It was clear by the early 1910s that an alliance of the episcopate with Conservative reaction was unlikely, despite the shared anxiety about socialism. Indeed, the latest episcopal appointments had very little in common, socially or politically, with that section of the Catholic community. It is worth considering the political attitudes of one of those appointments, Frederick Keating, Bishop of Northampton between 1908 and 1921, and later Archbishop of Liverpool, for his response to social questions illustrates some of the tensions experienced in the Catholic social movement between encouragement to social reform and an awareness of the limits and constraints on social and political action.

* * *

Born in 1859, Keating was a native of Birmingham, the son of an Irish brewery worker and an English mother. In 1872 he was sent to Sedgley Park School (later Cotton College), where he was an exemplary student.[204] In 1874 he went on to Douai, returning to the Birmingham diocese in 1877 to complete his studies at St Bernard's Seminary, Olton. Ordained in October 1882, his early career was in teaching: he taught Classics at Cotton College until 1884; from there he went to Oscott as Professor of Theology,[205] before returning to Olton in 1887. There was a change of direction in 1888 when he was appointed Rector of St Mary's, Wednesbury, Staffordshire. After a fairly closeted upbringing he was thrown into a mission, as he described it in a letter to Propaganda, 'almost entirely composed of the roughest labouring class'.[206]

The mission of St Mary's, Wednesbury, was founded in 1850 by an extraordinary Irish convert, Fr George Montgomery. His flock consisted of a few 'Old Catholic' families and a large contingent of Irish – some 3–4,000 – who had settled near the rapidly developing ironworks. Montgomery had a strong interest in social and political questions, which may have been aroused by the acute distress he witnessed after the slump in the local industry in the mid–1860s. He brought out a publication, *Rev. G. Montgomery's Register*, which discussed political economy and advocated state sponsored overseas settlement for destitute workers. Thinly populated, fertile lands would be occupied by workers, who would live by the fruits of their labour.[207] Although Montgomery was not alone in espousing such solutions to economic distress,[208] he was unusual in his determination to put his ideas into practice. On 3 February 1868 around 300 of his flock left Wednesbury for a remote part of Brazil. The project was a sorry failure. The British government was forced to send a vessel to remove them, and the unhappy Wednesbury pioneers ended up at a steelworks in Pennsylvania. Montgomery was also notable for his robust stand against W. Murphy, a local anti-papist agitator, who held a series of provocative meetings at the nearby Ridding Lane Chapel; emboldened by Montgomery's counterblast from the St Mary's pulpit, his flock went on the rampage outside Murphy's chapel. Montgomery's successor was in sharp contrast. A convert educated at Winchester School and Christ Church, Oxford, Fr Stuart Bathurst directed most of his considerable private wealth to local charitable efforts and to providing two schools and a chapel to the mission. But he was assisted by a priest who, the parish historian notes, was so heated about 'the wrongs of Ireland that he fanned the flames of Irish patriotism among the congregation to an unbalanced pitch till it resulted even in personal antagonism to the Rector'. Bathurst was forced to resign the mission in 1875. Bishop Ullathorne's stern reproof left both assistant and flock 'shaken with tears and shame'.[209] The mission to which Keating ministered for ten years had, therefore, its legacy of priestly social concern and action and a strong sense of being assailed from without by hostile Protestant forces. Possibly Keating's sensitivity to the divisive nature of the Irish question was also a product of Wednesbury.

Keating was a success at Wednesbury. He was immensely popular and respected, an eloquent and scholarly preacher; he consolidated the achievements of his predecessors and proved to be adept in his dealings with the public authorities. Little is known of his political views at this time though ministering to such a mission could not have left him indifferent to the 'social question'. In 1898 Keating left Wednesbury to take up the post of Administrator of St Chad's Cathedral, Birmingham, and in 1900 he was promoted to the Birmingham Chapter. More can be gleaned about Keating's politics here thanks to the existence of a book of notes for sermons covering the period between 1899 and 1901. The drink problem was his greatest concern: it was, he told his congregation at a New Year's Day Midnight Mass, the 'supreme enemy', 'robbing men and women of their senses', 'self-respect' and 'wages'; young girls, once innocent and modest, were transformed by drink into 'blotched and screaming furies'.[210] Keating was not blind to the social deprivation that encouraged drunkenness – during the same sermon he remarked on the 'huge contrast between the eulogies of progress and the dreadful reality of want and sin upon which it is rested' – but it was the 'overwhelming mass of sin' rather than the poverty and want which most upset him.[211] Drink was seen by Keating as primarily a problem of individual self-control and responsibility; he was reluctant to offer explanations which pointed to the social and economic background. The 'condition of the multitude' was the subject of one of his sermons in 1901, in which he discussed, in order to dismiss, fashionable social and political panaceas:

> The Gospel of Jesus Christ – this is the one sole sovereign remedy. Be Christians, be Catholics. Thus and thus only shall you find your salvation. You would originate movements, you would invent new forms of government, you would sweep away old landmarks and start afresh! You want a new Philosophy, a new science of living! See you have it – the Gospel. All for you – Popes and clergy, sacraments and liturgy – Councils and dogmas – all are yours![212]

There is a gap in Keating's papers between 1901 and 1908, by which time he was coming round to a more positive view of social reform. Yet these scattered comments seem to add support to the view of K. S. Inglis, that the positive programme of Christian social reform encouraged by *Rerum Novarum* barely moved English Catholics in the decade following its publication.[213] But it was probably not the whole story. There is a suggestive reference in a sermon from 1899 to 'a recently published life of a great non-conformist minister, who for many years exercized very considerable influence over the mind and conduct of this city'.[214] Although he does not refer to him by name, Keating was talking about the Minister of Carr's Lane Congregational Church, R. W. Dale, who is associated with Birmingham's 'civic gospel', arguing for a positive view of political life and emphasizing the obligation to participate fully in municipal and national politics.[215] Keating, who was always conscious of the public profile and impact of his Church, came to see social concern and work for the common good as the 'passport to goodwill'. At this stage, however, Keating's social activism was channelled mainly through Catholic charitable organizations such as the SVP,[216] rather than through broader social and political movements.

Keating's appointment as Bishop of Northampton in 1908 came as a surprise since the claims of Bernard Ward (1857–1920), a distinguished church historian and Prefect of Studies at St Edmund's College, Ware, were being pushed by Bourne. Whilst Ward had private wealth, Keating had none: on hearing of his nomination Keating wrote to Cardinal Gotti at Propaganda, 'With regard to this particular see of Northampton, it is generally understood that the possession of fairly ample private means is a *sine qua non* for its bishop; not only that he may maintain the dignity of his office, but also for the assistance of the diocesan clergy, who, in many instances, depend upon the bishop for their subsistence'.[217] But since Ward had forcefully indicated his disinterest in episcopal office it was Keating, the second choice on the *terna*, who was appointed on 25 February 1908. It was above all his reputation as a tenacious and industrious cathedral administrator and mission priest which recommended him.[218]

A stranger to Northampton, Keating was very different, in social background and political outlook, to his predecessor, Arthur Riddell (1836–1907). Riddell, noted Phillip Hughes, was 'one of the few bishops of the last hundred years who have come from those Old Catholic families that were in earlier times the sole support of the Church'.[219] His great-uncle, William Riddell, had been Secretary to Cardinal Weld at the Conclave which had elected Gregory XVI, and was appointed Vicar-Apostolic to the Northern District of England in 1847. He died months later whilst ministering to cholera victims in Newcastle.[220] For a short period the author and fantasist Frederick Rolfe resided at the family's estate, Cheeseburn Grange near Newcastle, where he was employed as the tutor to young Arthur. A leading authority attributes Rolfe's adoption of 'certain aristocratic attitudes' to his time spent with the Riddells: 'From his employers he derived his preference, among all Thackeray's works, for *Henry Esmond*, that great novel of English Catholics' misplaced allegiances and lost opportunities. More importantly, Rolfe learned his reverence for the Stuarts and ... acquired Royalist sympathies which he deliberately opposed to democracy.'[221] Riddell moved comfortably amongst the Catholic elite of the Northampton diocese: he was related to the Duchess of Norfolk and the Jerninghams of Costessey, a family claiming descent from three martyrs; he was close to Valentine Cary-Elwes, a convert and prominent layman who was active in local politics through the Northamptonshire Conservative Association, and whose son Dudley would succeed Keating as Bishop.[222] Keating stood very much outside this world.

Although Northampton was the largest diocese in area it had the sparsest Catholic population in England. A later Bishop of Northampton described the diocese as a 'second Cinderella. What little splashes our poverty enables us to indulge in are necessarily small, and when they are over we go back quietly to our back quarters in the kitchen, and get on with our work.'[223] It was not quite Keating to skulk in the back quarters; he was outward-looking and always looking for ways to make an impression on the public mind. During his time at Birmingham, for instance, he launched a mission to Protestants, an idea he probably derived from the Paulist Fathers he encountered on a visit to North America in 1903. Running for ten days, priests, mainly former Anglicans, gave instructions and sermons on various points of Catholic doctrine and practice. Keating's attempts to proselytize irritated the *Birmingham Post*, but he countered that it was both necessary and consistent to 'add this work to the normal work of attending to the needs' of his own people.[224] It was typical of Keating to take a broader view of his responsibilities. In Northampton he linked the expansion of the diocese with conversions – 'among all the dioceses, the diocese of Northampton is a missionary diocese', he stated in a pastoral letter of 1912[225] – and the leakage from the faith was never a pressing concern as it was for those bishops in predominantly urban dioceses. The growth of the Northampton diocese in the late nineteenth century from about 6,000 Catholics in 1875 to the 14,728 cited in his 1912 *ad limina* report was almost entirely due to conversions,[226] so Keating's approach was to continue strengthening the appeal of his Church to those outside the fold. Bold efforts to raise the public profile of Catholicism were a feature of Keating's Northampton episcopate: the erection of St John the Baptist Cathedral at Norwich in 1911 was an impressive if somewhat lugubrious public statement; the same city hosted the National Catholic Congress in 1912. Keating's interest in social and political questions became more pronounced in the early 1910s, and it is evident that he saw this kind of activity as a means of 'bringing the Catholic faith to the attention of the English Protestant Public'.[227]

Despite the constraints under which the diocese of Northampton laboured, Keating was relatively free from the onerous administrative burdens that could exhaust even the more youthful bishops, and this undoubtedly enabled him to develop a broader range of interests than would normally have been expected. His passion for public activity was in part a response to the tedium he frequently experienced at Cathedral House. Urging one friend to drop in on him, the Master of St Edmund's House, Cambridge, he wrote: 'Usually I am quite alone'.[228] For one used to the bustle of Birmingham life, social action was a psychological necessity in this dullest of backwaters. He made many appearances on the platform of CSG and CWL meetings, exhibiting a willingness to go beyond the merely local to address issues of a wider, national interest. He became the first President of the CSG, remarking that he would 'throw over the alleged redness of the Catholic Social Guild a nice shade of episcopal purple'.[229] He was in close accord with Fr Joseph Keating (no relation) who, as editor of *The Month*, earned a reputation – not always welcome – for his progressive treatment of social and political issues.[230] 'Over and above our sharing the same patronymic', he once observed to Fr Keating, 'I am often tempted to think there must be further kinship between us, at least of a psychological sort. In reading the *Month*, I repeatedly find you working at the same themes as myself, in particular, phases of the social question, Feminism, or Religious Intolerance ...'[231] The phrase 'social gospel' entered his vocabulary around this time.[232] Since the mid-1880s this had been a crusading slogan for Nonconformists who diagnosed sin in social structures, and who therefore sought to remodel society – a project which some critics thought detracted from the evangelical emphasis on individual conversion.[233] At this stage in the development of his social thought, Keating saw no fundamental antagonism between the 'social gospel' and the 'individual gospel'.

Also notable was Keating's interest in higher education for the clergy; unlike most of the bishops he did not regard the universities with suspicion and contempt. Whereas his predecessor at Northampton had been an outspoken opponent of Catholic attendance at Cambridge,[234] Keating encouraged the students under his care to take a positive role in the life of the University. St Edmund's House, Cambridge, where Catholic clerical students resided, was to find a valuable ally in Keating,[235] and he was a regular visitor to Fisher House, the Catholic chaplaincy. He came to stress the importance of a university education in instilling a sense of concern for the wider society and as a means of enabling the individual to understand social change. By engaging with a common intellectual culture Catholics would acquire the tools to become more effective actors in public life. He told the students at the annual Fisher House dinner of 1914, that a 'University education is as necessary to frank intercourse with the cultured ruling classes, as our vernacular tongue is necessary for communication with the masses'.[236] Keating was attracted in particular by the Economics Tripos at Cambridge. The creation of Alfred Marshall in 1903, the idea behind the re-modelled curriculum was that economics, far from being a 'dismal science', could be put to the service of society. Students would be trained, in 'a scientific spirit', to get 'to the root of the urgent social issues of the day, and to lay bare the ultimate as well as the immediate results of plausible proposals for social reform'. Marshall suggested that this kind of training would be beneficial to ministers of religion concerned with 'the "condition of the people" question'.[237] This struck chords with Keating; in his preface to Fr Plater's *The Priest and Social Action* (1914) he argued that 'A scholarship in Economics, tenable by Clerics at St. Edmund's House, Cambridge, is an urgent need'. Social action, he insisted, is 'the golden key which opens ears and hearts to his influence. Any interest in the public welfare is a passport to public good will, as many of us can bear witness.'[238] Although in the event it does not appear that any scholarship was established, Keating's willingness to even consider such routes marked him out from his contemporaries; it was unusual for a Catholic bishop at this time to suggest that the Church did not have all the answers, that it could even learn from the secular mind. (It is worth noting that amongst the next generation of Church leaders, Cardinal Hinsley, who shared Keating's concern for social questions, was dismissive of such ideas: to Fr O'Hea's suggestion that a talented young priest should go to Oxford for two years to study for the diploma in economic and social science, Hinsley responded: 'We want Fr. Bernard Goode to become a *practical* worker, who will get into real touch with men: theories are too numerous; the Encyclicals are our best text books'.[239]) Keating's interest in higher education did not, however, stop at social service; in other ways he encouraged Catholicism into closer contact with the universities, notably through the Summer School of Catholic Studies held annually at Cambridge, which began its life at Keating's instigation as the Catholic Bible Congress in 1921,[240] and which did something to revivify English Catholic biblical and theological scholarship in the 1920s and 1930s.

Keating's political ideas were familiar and unremarkable in the context of contemporary Catholic social thought, yet they did mark a departure from the stock episcopal responses. The rejection of political economy and laissez-faire was a marked feature of Christian social comment from the 1880s onwards, and would have been familiar to anyone acquainted with *Rerum Novarum*; so Keating's reference at the

Cardiff National Catholic Congress of 1914 to 'the ignoble method of *Laissez-Faire*' did not alarm his listeners.[241] At the Congress the previous year, his proclamation that the 'economics of the early Victorian days were "dead, buried, and damned"' was received with 'hearty endorsements'.[242] More challengingly, Keating took a more positive view of state action than Catholic contemporaries were usually prepared to allow. He once declared, in an address to the CSG at Manchester, that 'Legislation can make or bar opportunities. We have emancipated the slave, freed the serf, protected the young and women, recognized the right of combination, regulated working mines and factories, made provisions for old age – Which of all these do we wish to go back on? Yet all were met with similar outcries.'[243] This was a very different attitude to the role of the state than that taken by Hilaire Belloc in his influential *The Servile State* (1913), a hostile response to the National Insurance Act of 1911 which had introduced a massive contributory scheme to insure the working population against sickness and, to a lesser extent, unemployment. Another novel element was Keating's insistence, in an address of 1912, that the poverty produced by modern social conditions was 'hopeless, without expectation of the life that is now or of that which is to come' – an implicit criticism of the notion that poverty should be welcomed as a divine blessing. 'It is not to be expected that the Church can remain a passive spectator of such calamities. Her work is spiritual work, but it has to be done in a material world. She can contend with pestilence and famine when such are a visitation from God. But the degradation of our slums is not only a crying injustice which she is bound to voice, but also a barrier which check-mates all her agencies for good.'[244] By contrast, his 1908 Advent pastoral letter had talked very simply of a 'piety that hallowed suffering, and the doggedness that refused to whine under it . . .'[245]

The progressiveness of Keating's response to social questions should not be exaggerated. He was very concerned not to appear as a radical – he wanted to mend not end the industrial system.[246] Against a background of growing industrial unrest and recent papal reaction against social radicalism, Keating submitted a draft of his Advent pastoral letter of 1910 – which had urged nothing more drastic than that working men should study the social question and participate in trade unions – to the scrutiny of Fr Keating. 'Please read it carefully and submit it to the frank and fearless criticism of discreet colleagues. I am in no hurry to be labelled "radical" or even "socialist" . . . But for the sake of the delicate tint I wear, I am anxious to be prudent. If what I have written is likely to make a reasonable Tory squirm, please say so.'[247] This caution reflected the Northampton context: the maintenance of priests and erection of churches and schools in the diocese relied very heavily on the largesse of a small number of generous benefactors such as Valentine Cary-Elwes, Henry Fitzalan-Howard, fifteenth Duke of Norfolk, and Lord Braye, all Conservative in their politics to varying degrees of reasonableness. Keating was also as anxious about socialism as his more conservative brother bishops. At Manchester in 1911 he warned those present of the dangers of the 'cursed lust of gold' which 'may possess the poor' in times of industrial distress:

> The Church opposes Socialism ... because in secular life, individual possession is the only safeguard of individual liberty. A man cannot delegate all his responsibilities. He must safeguard his own soul ... If one thing is certain it is this – that in a Socialistic state there would be tolerated no religion, or a religion so tamed and subdued as to merely preach obedience to the State and submission to the ruling powers.[248]

His fundamental objection to socialism derived from its materialism – it was this philosophical error which vitiated all schemes for social reform. In a pastoral letter of 1908, written at the height of the Modernist crisis, he linked the project to reconcile revealed truths of religion with the insights of modern scientific knowledge and the message of materialistic social philosophies 'that religion is a fable, even a fraud. They exhort him to seek salvation *here*, and to look for it in the daily victories of science and the progress of education. They prophesy to him a golden age in the near future when wealth and comfort shall be universal, and poverty and strife unknown.'[249] A bleaker social vision characterized Keating's war-time pronouncements. His antipathy to materialistic philosophy was thrown into starker relief: he traced its numerous manifestations – rationalism, higher criticism, capitalism and socialism – back to the German spirit.[250] References to social reform were less generous: in a Lenten pastoral letter of 1917 he inveighed against the 'tendency of our social effort to make men moral by Act of Parliament. Certainly, the tendency has been to exaggerate the efficacy of legislation, education and environment; and to belittle the need of individual character and responsibility.'[251] The Bolshevik Revolution at the end of 1917 crystallized Keating's anxieties about the 'Red Terror'.[252]

Ministering to a largely rural diocese such as Northampton, one might have expected Keating to display a certain detachment from industrial realities. The main industry in Northamptonshire was footwear, but this was not subject to the level of strikes seen in the heavy industries. Conciliation, restraint and the avoidance of strikes were urged by a generally moderate leadership of the industry's trade union, the National Union of Boot and Shoe Operatives. The hostility of many manufacturers to trade unions, and the strong degree of paternalism which characterized relations between employer and employee in many of the smaller firms, were among the factors which restrained the emergence of a more militant spirit.[253] Traditional aspects of contemporary Catholic social thought would not have sounded irrelevant in this context. A tendency to shy away from the realities of urban, industrialized England was a weakness of CSG literature; the best example of the genre, Fr Plater's *The Priest and Social Action*, was typical in its nostalgia for the Christian social order of the Middle Ages, which as Doyle states was viewed as 'a balanced society able to cope with poverty through the ministrations of the religious orders and a strong community spirit shared by masters and men'.[254] Many of the social solutions proposed by the CSG were therefore hopelessly irrelevant to modern English society. However, Keating was not as prone as many in the Catholic social movement to this sort of medieval romanticising; he was addressing a rapidly changing social situation not a stable, hierarchical one. Keating's episcopate coincided with a revival in the shoe industry, and booming trade resulted in a sharp rise in membership of the Union. New classes of workers were being organized, the most significant group being the women workers.[255] A more assertive and militant leadership emerged in the early 1910s, reflecting the mood in the country at large. Keating had a difficult balancing act to perform: on the one hand he wished to see Catholics working towards the amelioration of social and industrial conditions, and he recognized, therefore, the central role of trade unions; on the other hand, his task, as emphasized in recent papal social teaching, was to restrain the build up of class antagonism, to preach the unity of all men. In the militant climate of the early 1910s even modest gestures towards labour were prone to misrepresentation, and coupled with the suspicion of trade unions shown by the Vatican under Pius X, it was bold of Keating to even venture into such areas.

*   *   *

Between 1911 and 1913 the country was experiencing severe industrial unrest and strikes.[256] Syndicalist ideas spread among the trade unions that envisaged the rejection of parliamentary action and its replacement by a doctrine of direct industrial action and class warfare with the general strike as its apotheosis. Against this background the questions of trade unions, industrial relations and strikes began to be discussed by the hierarchy. At the Low Week meeting of 1911 the CTU was mentioned for the first time,[257] and the following year it was resolved 'to give the patronage and approval of the Bishops' to their annual conference, the NCCTU.[258] The CTU was seen as essential in insulating the worker from the dangers lurking in the trade union movement: secularism in the educational sphere, socialism and syndicalism. Bishops began to show an interest in the Church's teaching on strikes. In 1912 Casartelli recommended the serialization of Geremia Bonomelli's 'Strikes and Strike Makers' in the *Catholic Federationist*.[259] Bonomelli, an Italian bishop, responding to concerns expressed in his diocese as to the lawfulness or unlawfulness of the sympathetic strike, argued that they were not illegal, providing 'no deceit or violence is used either towards comrades or masters, and when there is a reasonable motive for resistance', but went on to state that 'they constitute a weapon that is always dangerous' for they divide society into 'two camps.'[260] Bourne made two important pronouncements on strikes during this period. Speaking to the CTU at the Norwich National Catholic Congress in 1912, whilst not declaring strikes illegal, he asked intending strikers to consider whether 'the reasons which seemed to call for the exercise of their power were sufficient to justify them in inflicting upon the whole community perhaps tremendous sufferings and dislocation of society'.[261] The following year, at Leicester, he addressed the question of sympathetic and general strikes. Bourne's argument in most respects followed Bonomelli, although it was more tersely worded and clearly less conciliatory:

> I am inclined to think that the sympathetic lock-out or strike of those who are in no way personally interested in the question which has occasioned the dislocation of some other industry can hardly ever be justified; while the idea of the universal strike appears contrary to every principle of justice and charity. I know well that these extreme methods, in this and other political controversies, are being justified on the ground that there is now a real war being waged between capital and labour; and that in war all means, however terrible, may be lawfully employed. The argument, to my judgement, is absolutely fallacious. It is not strictly correct to define the industrial conflict as a state of war. At most, the term can be used analogously, and analogies are to be employed warily and with circumspection. And no such lame and halting analogy can justify in God's sight the criminal acts which sabotage and the universal strike most certainly involve.[262]

Despite the often severe tone of episcopal pronouncements on labour questions, beneath the surface there were signs of flexibility. Bishops for the most part were careful not to present themselves as the stern arbiters of political and economic questions, but rather sought to ensure that Catholic social action moved along a moderate and responsible path. They came to see that too much control was as dangerous as too much freedom. At the 1911 NCCTU, Bourne told the delegates that he 'felt perfectly sure that, as Trade Unionists, they were competent to deal with the economic difficulties'. Bishop Keating, who had opened his address by expressing the wish 'that they would always speak out when occasion demanded ... undeterred by the presence of a member of the Hierarchy', did not take any part in the subsequent debate as it was generally accepted that while the bishops had a duty to speak on 'the Catholic side of the question', it was not their duty to be 'judges of the trade union side of the question'.[263]

That the bishops were prepared to allow social Catholics some latitude was also apparent during a sharp dispute concerning the nature of English socialism. Fr Plater's policy of steering the CSG away from potentially divisive discussions on the nature of socialism succeeded until 1914 when a controversy broke out in the Catholic press and at the Cardiff National Catholic Congress concerning the question of whether certain 'forms of socialism' were compatible with Catholicism. A *Tablet* article of January 1914, 'Towards Social Thinking', by Fr Vincent McNabb, a member of the CSG,[264] sparked the debate. It was written as a rejoinder to the claim that 'absolution could not be given to a Catholic Socialist because the policy of the Socialist party was secularisation'.[265] McNabb noted that socialists were accused of wanting 'to socialise everything and everybody and that it would therefore make slaves of us all', but went on to argue that 'this inhuman programme which Socialism is expected to bring forth is already a great part realized and not by the Socialists'. His analysis drew on Belloc's *Servile State* which was published the previous year: 'One only has to read *The Servile State* to be haunted by the idea that not only existing Socialism but the existing Conservative and Liberal, and Democratic and Republican parties, are committed to the programme of secularized services which rest essentially on a basis of compulsory work, i.e. slavery.' The logical conclusion: 'If a Social thinker refuses absolution to a member of the Socialist Party because the Socialist Party would bring in a state of things, why does he not refuse absolution to the other political parties; for the state of things is already in existence and has been brought about or, at least, is being upheld by them.' McNabb did not espouse socialism in the article, but when challenged to define his position by Thomas Burns, Secretary of the NCCTU and a prominent member of both the Federation and the CSG, he conceded that 'certain forms of socialism were compatible with Catholicism'. In support of this position he cited remarks made by Thomas Whiteside (1857–1921), Archbishop of Liverpool, at the

Plymouth National Catholic Congress of 1913. Whiteside had been impressed by Philip Snowden's recently published *Socialism and Syndicalism*, which had argued for gradual social change against social revolution.[266] Also reassuring to Whiteside were Snowden's comments on the alleged incompatibility of socialism with Christianity: a Nonconformist preacher and advocate of temperance, Snowden interpreted socialism as the attempt to 'establish an industrial and social order based upon the ethical principles upon which the Christian religion is founded'.[267] Against a background of mounting industrial unrest, *Socialism and Syndicalism* did much to reassure moderate opinion that the leaders of English Labour were themselves moderate men. Whiteside became convinced that Labour's socialism was of a very different nature to the atheistic, materialistic variety which had been condemned repeatedly by the popes:

> He had just been reading [the Archbishop added] the book of the hour, Philip Snowden's *Socialism and Syndicalism*. A new Socialism has sprang up in England, and that Socialism, advocated by one who was perhaps the greatest leader of Socialism in England, was going to prevail. Instead of being its enemy, they would not even need to be in a position of armed neutrality, but could clasp hands with it. I think that the Socialism which is going to prevail in England ... will be a Socialism with which we can make friends.– [applause].[268]

Although more reserved in his approbation, Keating endorsed Whiteside's interpretation. His Plymouth speech, as recorded in the *Western Daily Mercury*, stated: 'Whether they admired the personnel of that party or not, he thought that they should be well satisfied that such a large class, and such a suffering class, should be represented in the House of Commons by a substantial party [hear, hear]'. He went on to argue that the 'Working-classes have no monopoly of false prophets ... Catholic Tories have to reckon with the Belfast Orangemen with their hate ... Catholic liberals ... have to reckon with their Nonconformist stalwarts who are radically hostile to our schools, and Catholic women have to reckon with a very evil form of vicious literature called "feminism"'.[269] There was, therefore, enough episcopal encouragement to support the view espoused by McNabb.

Not all CSG members possessed such a nuanced understanding of socialism. Thomas Burns, almost certainly with the backing of Casartelli, attempted to secure a resolution from the CSG repudiating the notion that '"Socialism" is patient of a Catholic interpretation'. The Executive Committee demurred, maintaining that by adopting a resolution of a 'widely condemnatory character' they would run the risk of 'usurping functions which belong to the province of the

Hierarchy'.[270] It was this unwillingness to commit the CSG to an emphatically anti-socialistic line which led to Burns's resignation from the Executive, opening up a rift between the Federation/CTU and the CSG which never healed.

Burns's hopes of a decision on the question now rested with the bishops. But although he could claim the support of Casartelli,[271] he was to be disappointed. This was partly due to the presence of Keating and Whiteside on the bench, but mainly it was because to the majority of the bishops the question was of marginal, academic interest, and there was a reluctance to take sides in the dispute. It was not until the Low Week meeting of 1917 that they broached the subject after an incessant campaign of vituperation waged by Burns in the *Catholic Federationist*. The resolution that emerged from the meeting was an attempt to chart a middle course between the two extremes, rather than to provide any hard-and-fast ruling. Put positively, the resolution reflected something of the more relaxed attitude to freedom of opinion taken during Benedict XV's reign, as exemplified by *Ad Beatissimi Apostolorum* (1914).[272] The bishops thought that as this was a question on which the Holy See had not given authoritative guidance, there was scope therefore for legitimate differences of opinion. The bishops concluded:

> They do not consider that there is anything to pronounce upon. Their Lordships agree that no Catholic can consistently belong to any of the Socialist organisations, and consider it a distinct advantage that Catholic Trade Unionist's have laid down for themselves that excellent prohibition without the intervention of Bishops. The CSG on the other hand claims a certain latitude in discussing economic theories, until those theories have been authoritatively condemned. As the Bishops are not prepared to deal with these theories, the CSG will continue to enjoy the latitude it claims without their telling them so.[273]

It was far from satisfying to Casartelli, who was further piqued when, soon after the Low Week meeting, Bourne indicated his wish to step down as Ecclesiastical Superior of the NCCTU. Casartelli told Bourne that this would appear to the public as a 'formal repudiation of the organisation and the complete triumph of the opposing forces which have antagonised it hitherto'.[274] Casartelli also took issue with the second part of the Low Week resolution, which he thought 'would give a distinct impetus to Socialists among our working class'.[275] Bourne's subsequent agreement to remain as patron of the NCCTU, but not Ecclesiastical Superior, failed to mollify Casartelli.[276] The controversy did not die with that pronouncement. Whilst in 1917 the question of socialism could be dismissed as theoretical, the commitment of the Labour Party at the 1918 general election to an avowedly socialistic programme, and the appeal which they held out to working-class Catholics – many newly enfranchised – forced the issue on the hierarchy in a more concrete and urgent fashion.

The upsurge in political involvement in the first decade of the century was mainly a response to the threats to the schools, but the resulting emphasis on lay organization and commitment gave an impetus to a broader engagement. The initiatives launched in the second half of the decade enjoyed varying fortunes. The Federation's political entanglements were to vitiate Casartelli's vision of lay people welded together in the pursuit of Catholic interests. Political divisions in the community were exacerbated in the drive to ensure unanimity on the education question, and Casartelli was not without responsibility for this. The CSG enjoyed a happier infancy. This was partly because its activities did not raise such conflicts of loyalties: study not political action was its métier. It was a broad church which could both contain and channel enthusiasm for social change, as well as presenting itself as a bulwark against radicalism. The caution with which its leaders proceeded was prudent in the anxious years following *Pascendi*, and the self-censorship they exercised in response to their expectations of what ecclesiastical authority would tolerate ensured that they progressed without undue episcopal interference. Although the bishops were anxious not to give a handle to social radicalism, neither did they wish to stifle all expressions of lay commitment and initiative. Although some may have wished to turn off the tap when the threat to the schools had passed, for the most part the stream of lay commitment was viewed positively. In the episcopate's response to social questions a range of attitudes was represented, but it became clear that there was little desire to ally the Church with a conservative reaction. This was also apparent in their response to the Irish question.

Notes

1. R. Currie, A. Gilbert, and L. Horsley (eds), *Churches and Churchgoers: Patterns of Church Growth in the British Isles since 1700* (Oxford: Clarendon Press, 1977), p. 31.
2. *Relatio Confidentialis de Statu Ecclesiae in Anglicae*, April 1905, Rome, Archives of the Sacred Congregation of Propaganda Fide (S.C.P.F.), 354 (1906) rubr. 102–4, fo. 66695.
3. Norman, *Roman Catholicism in England*, p. 94.
4. Mathew, *Catholicism in England*, p. 219.

5. Quoted in E. Oldmeadow, *Francis Cardinal Bourne* (2 vols., London: Burns Oates and Co., 1944), II, p. 168.
6. C.f. Fr John Baptist Reeves's tribute to Bourne: *The Catholic Herald*, 9 June 1934.
7. Lang to Clive Wigram, 19 January 1934, London, Lambeth Palace Library (L.P.L.), Lang Papers 123, fo. 271.
8. S. Leslie, *The Passing Chapter* (London: Cassell, 1934), p. 205.
9. W. F. Brown, Auxiliary Bishop of Southwark, contributed pen-portraits Manning, Vaughan and Hinsley in his memoirs, *Through Windows of Memory* (London: Sands and Co., 1946), but made only passing references to Bourne, pp. 98, 117.
10. Oldmeadow, *Bourne*, II, p. ix.
11. G. Wheeler, 'The Archdiocese of Westminster' in Beck (ed.), *English Catholics*, p. 180.
12. C. Smyth, *Cyril Foster Garbett* (London: Hodder and Stoughton, 1959), p. 380.
13. R. J. Lahey, 'Cardinal Bourne and the Malines Conversations', in Hastings (ed.), *Bishops and Writers*, pp. 81-105. Gilley has described Oldmeadow's book as 'singularly unctuous and over-defensive', 'Years of Equipoise', p. 34.
14. Bourne to Shane Leslie, 13 November 1913, Dublin, National Library of Ireland (N.L.I.), Shane Leslie Papers, MS 22, 829 acc 3669. See also Oldmeadow, *Bourne*, I, p. 13.
15. Oldmeadow, *Bourne*, I, p. 45.
16. Ibid., p. 48.
17. Ibid., p. 49.
18. *Ushaw Magazine* (March 1935), 2-3. p. 4.
19. Ibid., p. 4.
20. Ibid., p. 3.
21. Oldmeadow, *Bourne*, I, p. 82.
22. F. Bourne, *Ecclesiastical Training* (London: Burns Oates and Co., 1926), p. 47.
23. Oldmeadow, *Bourne*, I, p. 89.
24. Ibid., p. 96.
25. Ibid., p. 97.
26. A. Vidler, *A Variety of Catholic Modernists* (Cambridge: Cambridge University Press, 1970), pp. 94-5.
27. Ibid., p. 176.
28. S. Leslie, *Cardinal Gasquet* (London: Burns and Oates, 1953), p. 80.
29. Ibid., p. 81.
30. Norfolk to Cardinal Gotti, 12 July 1903, Rome, S.C.P.F., 102 (1904), rubr. 32.
31. Bishop Cahill to Cardinal Gotti, u/d, ibid., rubr. 54.
32. P. Hughes, 'The Bishops of the Century', Beck (ed.), *English Catholics*, p. 213.
33. Leslie, *Gasquet*, p. 82.
34. Bishop Cahill to Cardinal Gotti, u/d, S.P.C.F., 102 (1904), rubr. 54.

35. Duffy, *Saints and Sinners*, pp. 245-7.
36. Wheeler, 'Archdiocese of Westminster', pp. 173, 178.
37. Oldmeadow initially rejected Moran's role as a rumour in volume 1 of his biography of Bourne, but subsequently confirmed the story: Oldmeadow, *Bourne*, II, p. viii; see also Hughes, 'Bishops of the Century', p. 213 n.; Leslie, *Gasquet*, pp. 82-3.
38. Reprinted in *The Tablet*, 5 January 1901 and 12 January 1901.
39. *Il Fermo Proposito*, 168, pp. 42-3.
40. Ibid., p. 43.
41. Vidler, *Catholic Modernists*, p. 213.
42. McSweeney, *Search for Relevance*, p. 85.
43. Ibid.
44. J. Cashman, 'The 1906 Education Bill: Catholic Peers and Irish Nationalists', *Recusant History*, 18 (October 1987), 422-39; V. A. McClelland, 'Bourne, Norfolk and the Irish Parliamentarians: Roman Catholics and the Education Bill of 1906', *Recusant History*, 23 (October 1996), 228-56; M. Fanning, 'The 1906 Liberal Education Bill and the Roman Catholic Reaction of the Diocese of Salford' (unpublished undergraduate dissertation, University of Oxford, 1996).
45. M. Cruickshank, *Church and State in English Education* (London: Macmillan and Co., 1964), 94.
46. McClelland, 'Bourne, Norfolk and the Irish Parliamentarians', p. 245.
47. G. K. A. Bell, *Randall Davidson: Archbishop of Canterbury* (2 vols., London: Oxford University Press, 1935), I, p. 530.
48. T. P. O'Connor to Lloyd George, 25 September 1909, House of Lords Record Office (H.L.R.O.), Lloyd George Papers, C/6/10/1.
49. *Yorkshire Daily Observer*, 24 July 1908. At the same meeting Charles Russell, a prominent member of the Catholic Federation, likened the Liberal Nonconformist to a 'child-killing pharaoh'.
50. *The Tablet*, 1 December 1906.
51. *Dewsbury Reporter*, 25 April 1908. Press cuttings relating to municipal elections in this period are held in the Leeds Diocesan Archives.
52. L. Casartelli, *Sketches in History* (New York, Cincinatti and Chicago: Benzinger Brothers, 1906).
53. I am grateful to Joseph Murphy for providing me with a copy of his paper on the life of Casartelli which he presented to the Catholic Record Society conference at Oxford in July 1996, and to Dr James Peters of the University of Manchester Library for information on Casartelli's academic career.
54. See Bishop Casartelli's Lenten *Pastoral Letter* of 1923, Sal.D.A.
55. Bishop Casartelli's Lenten *Pastoral Letter* of 1903, ibid.
56. Bishop Hedley, *The Public Spirit of the Catholic Laity* (London: CTS, 1900); Cardinal Vaughan, *The Work of the Catholic Laity in England* (London: CTS, 1900); Revd J. Norris, *The Help of the Laity* (London: CTS, 1901); Revd W. Barry, *The Layman in the Church* (London: CTS, 1905).
57. *The Tablet*, 13 March 1911.

58. *Ad Clerum*, Whit Sunday 1906, Sal.D.A., *Acta*.
59. P. Doyle, 'The Catholic Federation 1906-1929', in W. J. Sheils and D. Wood (eds), *Voluntary Religion* (Studies in Church History, 23; Oxford: Blackwell, 1986), pp. 461-76.
60. *Catholic Federationist* (September 1911).
61. Casartelli to J. Berril, 9 April 1910 (copy), Sal.D.A., Casartelli Papers, Box 157.
62. P. F. Clarke, *Lancashire and the New Liberalism* (Cambridge: Cambridge University Press, 1971), p. 259.
63. Secretary of the Manchester Liberal Federation to Runciman, 29 April 1908, Newcastle, University of Newcastle Library, Walter Runciman Papers.
64. Casartelli to Canon Tynan, 22 April 1908 (copy), Sal.D.A., Casartelli Papers, Box 157.
65. Casartelli to Canon Tynan, Holy Saturday 1908 (copy), ibid.
66. P. Lane, *The Catenian Association 1908-1983* (London: The Catenian Association, 1982), p. 14. See also J. Hickey, *Urban Catholics: Urban Catholicism in England and Wales from 1829 to the Present Day* (London: Geoffrey Chapman, 1967), p. 149.
67. Casartelli to Canon Tynan, Holy Saturday 1908 (copy), Sal.D.A., Casartelli Papers, Box 157.
68. *The Catholic Herald*, 2 October 1909.
69. Casartelli to Canon Burke, 9 January 1908 (copy), Sal.D.A., Casartelli Papers, Box 157.
70. Ibid.
71. *Northern Daily Telegraph*, 2 October 1908.
72. Ibid., 9 October 1908.
73. G. I. T. Machin, 'The Liberal Government and the Eucharistic Procession of 1908', *Journal of Ecclesiastical History*, 34 (October 1983), 559-83; T. Horwood, 'Public Opinion and the 1908 Eucharistic Congress', *Recusant History*, 25 (May 2000), 120-32.
74. Casartelli to Bourne, 4 October 1909 (copy); Casartelli to Bourne, 14 October 1909 (copy), Sal.D.A., Casartelli Papers, Box 157
75. Casartelli to Bourne, 4 October 1909, 14 October 1909 (copy); Casartelli to Bourne, 14 October 1909 (copy); Casartelli to Bourne, 17 October 1909 (copy), ibid.
76. Casartelli to Fr Sharrock, 29 December 1909 (copy), ibid.
77. Casartelli to Mgr Beesley, 22 June 1909 (copy), ibid.
78. Casartelli to Lady Winifride Elwes, 13 April 1910 (copy), ibid., Box 158.
79. Casartelli to Canon Lynch, 15 January 1910 (copy), ibid.
80. *Manchester Guardian*, 12 January 1910.
81. See ibid., 13, 14, 15 January 1910. Some of the letters are cited in Clarke, *Lancashire and the New Liberalism*, p. 256.
82. Casartelli to Lady Winifride Elwes, 13 April 1910 (copy), Sal.D.A., Casartelli Papers, Box 157.
83. Casartelli to Canon Lynch, 12 January 1910 (copy), ibid.

84. Casartelli to Thomas Burns, 15 November 1910 (copy), ibid., Box 158.
85. Meeting of the Bishops, 6 April 1910, A.A.W., *Acta*.
86. Fr T. Wright, 'The Attitude of the Federation in Regard to Elections', *Official Report of the First National Catholic Congress* (Edinburgh: Sands and Co., 1910), 173-4
87. *Catholic Times*, 10 March 1911.
88. Casartelli to Gordon, 14 February 1910 (copy), Sal.D.A., Casartelli Papers, Box 157. A leading article in *The Catholic Herald*, 1 January 1910, made critical references to the hierarchy's attitude to the Liberal Party.
89. Charles Diamond to Bourne, 18 February 1908, A.A.W., Bourne Papers, Bo. 1/97.
90. Charles Diamond to Walter Runciman, 14 February 1910, University of Newcastle Library, Walter Runciman Papers, WR35. See also Charles Diamond to Walter Runciman, 22 February 1910, ibid.
91. Casartelli to Gordon, 14 February 1910 (copy), Sal.D.A., Casartelli Papers, Box 157.
92. Apart from the main London edition of *The Catholic Herald* there were twenty-nine provincial editions.
93. Casartelli to Bourne, 23 January 1910 (copy), Sal.D.A., Casartelli Papers, Box 157. See also Casartelli to Bourne, 18 January 1910 (copy), ibid.
94. Casartelli to Canon O'Kelly, 24 October 1909 (copy); Casartelli to Fr Sharrock, 29 October 1909 (copy); Casartelli to Fr Sharrock, 31 October 1909 (copy), ibid.
95. Meeting of the Bishops, 6 April 1910, A.A.W., *Acta*.
96. Vidler, *Catholic Modernists*, p. 191.
97. P. Bernardi, 'Social Modernism: the Case of the *Semaine Sociales*', in Jodock (ed.), *Catholicism Contending with Modernity*, pp. 277-307.
98. P. Misner, 'Catholic Anti-Modernism: the Ecclesial Setting', in ibid., pp. 83-4.
99. P. Misner, *Social Catholicism in Europe* (London: Darton Longman and Todd, 1991), pp. 301-6.
100. Bernardi, 'Social Modernism', p. 304.
101. Misner, 'Catholic Anti-Modernism', p. 84.
102. Vidler, *Catholic Modernists*, pp. 215-8; Misner, *Social Catholicism in Europe*, p. 300.
103. Fr Theodore Evans was received into the Church in 1891 and was ordained in 1905: W. Gordon Gorman, *Converts to Rome* (London: Sands and Co., 1910 edn).
104. See I. S. Wood, 'John Wheatley, the Irish, and the Labour Movement in Scotland', *Historical Journal*, 31 (Autumn 1980), 71-85; S. W. Gilley, 'Catholics and Socialists in Glasgow, 1906-1912', in K. Lunn (ed.), *Hosts, Immigrants and Minorities: Historical Responses to Newcomers in British Society 1870-1914* (Folkestone: Dawson, 1980), pp. 160-200; idem, 'Catholics and Socialists in Scotland, 1900-30', in R. Swift and S. W. Gilley (eds), *The Irish in Britain, 1815-1939* (London: Pinter, 1989), pp. 212-38.

105. Anon., 'The Confessions of a Catholic Socialist', *Dublin Review*, 115 (July – October 1914), 101–15. Although this article was published anonymously the author was certainly Somerville.
106. John C. Heenan, *A Crown of Thorns: An Autobiography 1951–1963* (London: Hodder and Stoughton, 1975 edn), p. 24.
107. These words are taken from his Advent pastoral letter of 1894, quoted in J. F. Supple, 'The Catholic Church and the Yorkshire Poor, 1850–1900' in G. T. Bradley (ed.), *Yorkshire Catholics* (Leeds Diocesan Archives Occasional Papers, No. 1), 54.
108. Bishop Gordon's *Pastoral Letter* of 10 June 1909, Leeds Diocesan Archives.
109. Anon., 'Confessions of a Catholic Socialist', p. 106.
110. Fr O'Hea to Frank Bywater, 27 February 1951 (copy), Oxford, Plater College, Catholic Social Guild Archive (C.S.G.A.), File E15.
111. I would like to thank Fr David Lannon for providing a photocopied file of these visitation returns.
112. *Catholic Times*, 18 December 1908.
113. Fr Puissant to Casartelli, 21 January 1909, Sal.D.A., Vicar General Correspondence, Box 166. Nothing came of this application as the *Catholic Directory* of 1910 lists Puissant as the parish priest of St Sophia's, Galston, Ayrshire.
114. Gilley, 'Catholics and Socialists in Glasgow', p. 181.
115. Ibid., pp. 186–8.
116. J. M. Cleary, *Catholic Social Action in Britain 1909–1959* (Oxford: Catholic Social Guild, 1961) remains a useful history. For more recent treatments, see P. Doyle, 'Charles Plater S.J. and the Origins of the Catholic Social Guild', *Recusant History*, 21 (May 1993), 401–17; Keating, 'Roman Catholics, Christian Democracy', passim; Wraith, 'English Catholic Church and the "Social Question"'.
117. Doyle, 'Origins of the Catholic Social Guild', p. 406.
118. C. C. Martindale, *Charles Dominic Plater S.J.* (London: Harding and More, 1922), pp. 67–8.
119. Ibid., p. 71.
120. Francis Urquhart to Francis Devas, 29 August 1902, London, Farm Street, English Province of the Society of Jesus Archives (E.P.S.J.), Francis Devas Papers, MS/3.
121. Fr Plater's Diary, 31 April 1908, E.P.S.J., Charles Plater Papers.
122. Ibid., 21 September 1909.
123. Cleary, *Catholic Social Action*, pp. 31–2.
124. M. G. Segar, *Margaret Fletcher* (London: CTS, 1943).
125. See M. Fletcher, *Light for New Times* (London: Art and Book Company, 1903); idem., *The School of the Heart* (London: Longmans and Co., 1904).
126. For a discussion of Crawford's role in the affair, see D. Nicholls, *The Lost Prime Minister: A Life of Sir Charles Dilke* (London: Hambledon, 1995), pp. 187–93.
127. C. Plater, *Retreats for the People* (London: Sands and Co., 1912).

128. Fr Plater's Diary, 5 March 1908, E.P.S.J., Charles Plater Papers.
129. Confidential memorandum from Leslie Toke to Fr Plater, September 1909, C.S.G.A.
130. Leslie Toke to Fr Parkinson, 9 June 1910, Sutton Coldfield, Oscott College, Oscott College Archives (O.C.A.), Fr Parkinson Papers.
131. Discussed in M. Williams, *Oscott College in the Twentieth Century* (Leominster: Gracewing, 2001), pp. 50-62. This book appeared before I could make use of it.
132. Leslie Toke to Fr Parkinson, 16 November 1909, O.C.A., Fr Parkinson Papers.
133. F. J. Coppa, *The Modern Papacy since 1789* (London: Longman, 1998), p. 145.
134. Fr T. Wright to Fr Parkinson, 19 May 1914, O.C.A., Fr Parkinson Papers.
135. Vidler, *Catholic Modernists*, p. 198.
136. Minute Book of the Hull Catholic Federation, 7 July 1909, Middlesbrough, Middlesbrough Diocesan Archives (M.D.A.).
137. Fr Parkinson to V. M. Crawford, 18 October 1912, C.S.G.A., Misc. Letters 1912-20, File E6 Box 11.
138. Ibid.
139. This was the policy of the CSG throughout the period discussed in this dissertation. In 1935 Fr O'Hea of the CSG told A. J. Smith that 'for various reasons the Guild cannot issue manifestos, nor pledge itself collectively to any opinion on debatable points': Fr O'Hea to A. J. Smith, 22 March 1935, E.P.S.J., Fr O'Hea Papers, 28/2/1/1.
140. Fr Plater to V. M. Crawford, 20 October 1910, Cambridge, Churchill College Archives, V. M. Crawford Papers, REND 12/3.
141. *The Catholic Social Year Book for 1910* (London: CTS, 1910), p. 37.
142. Leslie Toke to Fr Parkinson, 12 June 1911, O.C.A., Fr Parkinson Papers.
143. A. Mooney to Fr Parkinson, u/d but 1911, ibid.
144. B. W. Devas to Fr Parkinson, 28 September 1909, ibid.; Wraith, 'English Catholic Church and the "Social Question"', p. 536.
145. Keating to Thomas Burns, 19 January 1912 (copy), Northampton, Northampton Diocesan Archives (Nrt.D.A.), Keating Papers, FV. 6.
146. MacEntee, *Social Catholic Movement in Great Britain*, p. 186.
147. Fr Parkinson to Thomas Burns, 24 April 1914, O.C.A., Fr Parkinson Papers.
148. J. Oliver, *The Church and Social Order: Social Thought in the Church of England, 1918-1939* (London: Alden and Mowbray, 1968), pp. 5-11; G. Neville, *Radical Churchman: Edward Lee Hicks and the New Liberalism* (Oxford: Clarendon Press, 1998), p. 100.
149. Referring to the poor sales of the Year Book, Fr Keating suggested that 'we have not yet a public for such wares': Fr J. Keating to Fr Parkinson, 17 March 1911, O.C.A., Fr Parkinson Papers.
150. Leslie Toke to Fr Parkinson, 16 October 1910, ibid.
151. Leslie Toke to Fr Parkinson, 25 November 1909, ibid.

152. Quoted in Keating, 'Roman Catholics, Christian Democracy', p. 43.
153. Leslie Toke to James Britten, 3 August 1910, O.C.A., Fr Parkinson Papers; Leslie Toke to Fr Parkinson, 27 September 1910, ibid.
154. Leslie Toke to Fr Parkinson, 24 October 1911, ibid.
155. Fr J. Keating to Fr Parkinson, 23 October 1911, ibid.
156. Fr J. Keating to Fr Parkinson, 17 March 1911, ibid.
157. A point made by Finìn O'Driscoll in 'The Changing Face of Roman Catholic Social Thought in Britain in the 1920s'; a paper given to the Church History Seminar at the Faculty of Divinity, Cambridge, 19 May 1999.
158. C. Plater, *The Priest and Social Action* (London: Longmans, Green and Co., 1914), pp. 33–4.
159. Quoted in Leslie, *Gasquet*, p. 83
160. Memorandum: 'Some suggested improvements concerning the students and system at Mark Cross (1956) ', A.A.W., Griffin Papers, Gr. 2/144b.
161. Bourne to Whiteside, 25 June 1918, Liverpool, Archives of the Archdiocese of Liverpool (A.A.L.), Early Bishops' Collection 1873–1921, Series II Box V.
162. M. Fletcher, *O, Call Back Yesterday* (Oxford: Basil Blackwell, 1939), p. 141.
163. Ibid., p. 138.
164. *The Tablet*, 17 August 1912.
165. Mathew, *Catholicism in England*, p. 241
166. For comments on Bourne's reserve see ibid.; M. Ward, *Insurrection versus Resurrection* (London: Sheed and Ward, 1937), p. 150; idem., *Unfinished Business* (London: Sheed and Ward, 1964), pp. 90–1; Oldmeadow, *Bourne*, II, p. 345; Norman, *Roman Catholicism in England*, p. 109; Hastings, *English Christianity*, p. 145; McClelland, 'Bourne, Norfolk and the Irish Parliamentarians', p. 228.
167. E. Waugh, *Monsignor Ronald Knox* (Boston and Toronto: Little, Brown and Co., 1959), p. 167.
168. Sheed, *Church and I*, pp. 82–3.
169. Hinsley to Amigo, 7 December 1926, London, Southwark, Archives of the Archdiocese of Southwark (A.A.S.), Amigo Papers, Correspondence with Hinsley, C4.
170. Cahill to Amigo, 24 May 1909, Portsmouth, Portsmouth Diocesan Archives (Por.D.A.), Cahill Papers, 6.04.1.
171. A treatment of this issue can be found in Clifton, *Amigo*, pp. 23–36.
172. Cahill to Amigo, 24 May 1909, Por.D.A., Cahill Papers, 6.04.1.
173. Amigo to Cahill, 28 May 1909, ibid.; see also Clifton, *Amigo*, p. 26.
174. Amigo 'once used to consult me but never does so now': Bourne to Whiteside, 1 July 1909, A.A.L., Correspondence 1874–1929 (B).
175. Bourne to Cahill, 16 May 1909, Por.D.A., Cahill Papers, 6.04.1.
176. Vidler, *Catholic Modernists*, pp. 94–5, 176. Holmes, *More Roman than Rome*, pp. 235–8; Norman, *English Catholic Church*, pp. 342–4.
177. E. R. Norman, *Church and Society in England 1770–1970* (Oxford: Clarendon Press, 1976), p. 237; D. Bebbington, *Evangelicalism in*

Modern Britain (London: Unwin Hyman, 1989), pp. 211–4.

178. *The Catholic Church and Labour* (London: CTS, 1908), preface.
179. Bourne brought the issue of temperance before the bishops at the Low Week meetings of 1910, 1911 and 1915: Meeting of the Bishops, A.A.W., *Acta*.
180. See John Kent's criticisms of Edward Norman's approach: *William Temple: Church, State and Society in Britain, 1880–1950* (Cambridge: Cambridge University Press, 1992), p. 119.
181. *Almanac for the Diocese of Salford*, 1909; Leslie Toke to Fr Parkinson, 11 January 1909, O.C.A., Fr Parkinson Papers.
182. Bishop Casartelli's Lenten *Pastoral Letter* of 1909, Sal.D.A.
183. There are parallels here with Nonconformity: D. Bebbington, *The Nonconformist Conscience: Chapel and Politics 1870–1914* (London: Allen and Unwin, 1982), pp. 158–60.
184. Minutes of the CTS Executive Meeting, 21 March 1910, London, Vauxhall Bridge Rd., Archives of the Catholic Truth Society (A.C.T.S.).
185. *Pope Pius on Social Reform, intr. Right Rev. Mgr Parkinson* (London: CTS, 1910), p. xiv.
186. Bishop Keating of Northampton 'The Church and Social Reformers', *Publications of the C.T.S.*, 84 (London: CTS, 1911), p. 1.
187. Ibid., preface, p. 3.
188. A. Goodfellow to Norfolk, 5 March 1901, A.C.A., Norfolk Papers, MD2078; Merry del Val to Norfolk, 10 August 1901, ibid., C610. One of its leading members, W. S. Lilly, had co-written *A Manual of the Law Specially Affecting Catholics* (London: William Clowes, 1893); Sir Francis Fleming, 'Religious Disabilities of Catholics', *The Downside Review*, 28 (July 1909), 100–7.
189. James Britten to Fr Parkinson, 7 October 1910, O.C.A., Fr Parkinson papers; see also Leslie Toke to Fr Parkinson, 18 February 1910, ibid.
190. Leslie Toke to Fr Parkinson, 1 November 1910, ibid; see also Leslie Toke to Fr Parkinson, 6 September 1910, ibid.
191. 'As for Toke, really he is a bit of a baby – lacks sense of humour, or proportion or something'. These were the words of Toke's closest working partner, the CSG's General Secretary: G. C. King to Fr Parkinson, 2 March 1910, ibid.
192. James Britten to Fr Parkinson, 26 November 1910, ibid.
193. Minutes of the CTS Executive Meeting, 21 March 1910, A.C.T.S.
194. Stuart Coats to Keating, 17 December 1919, Nrt.D.A., Keating Papers, FV. 1 (G).
195. Minutes of the CTS Executive Meeting, 14 November 1910, A.C.T.S.
196. Ibid., 15 May 1912.
197. Gilley, 'Catholics and Socialists in Glasgow', pp. 193–4.
198. Memorandum by T. D. McConnell to Mark Sykes, 19 January 1912, Hull, Hull University, Brynmor Jones Library (B.J.L.), Mark Sykes Papers, DDSY (2)/1/18.
199. T. D. McConnell to Fr Parkinson, 24 March 1916, O.C.A., Fr Parkinson Papers.

200. V. M. Durnford to Norfolk, 13 March 1916, A.C.A., Norfolk Papers, MD2078.
201. Casartelli to Amigo, 22 March 1916, A.A.S., Amigo Papers, Correspondence with Bishops.
202. Keating to Fr Parkinson, 24 March 1916, O.C.A., Fr Parkinson Papers.
203. Casartelli to Bourne, 20 March 1916 (copy), Sal.D.A., Casartelli Papers, Box 161.
204. W. Buscot, *The History of Cotton College* (London: Burns Oates and Co., 1940), p. 263.
205. *The Oscotian: The Jubilee 1838-1888* (Birmingham: St Mary's College, Oscott, 1888), Appendix 15.
206. Keating to Cardinal Gotti, 16 January 1908, S.C.P.F., 443 (1908), rubr. 140.
207. J. Gillow, *Bibliographical Dictionary of the English Catholics*, vol. V (London: Burns and Oates; New York: Benziger Books, 1902), pp. 87-8.
208. B. Aspinwall, 'Towards an English Catholic Social Conscience, 1829-1920', *Recusant History*, 25 (May 2000), 107-8. Aspinwall mentions Fr James Nugent and Rev. Lord Archibald Douglas of London and Annan.
209. J. F. Bromfield, *Souvenir of the Centenary of St Mary's Parish, Wednesbury 1850-1950* (Wednesbury, 1950).
210. Sermon given at St Chad's on 1 January 1901, A.A.L., Keating Papers, S7 A/1.
211. Ibid.; sermon given at St Chad's on 25 August 1901, ibid.
212. Sermon given at St Chad's on the second Sunday after Easter 1901, ibid.
213. Inglis, *Churches and the Working Classes*, pp. 314-8.
214. Sermon given at St Chad's on Easter Sunday 1899, A.A.L., Keating Papers, S7 A/1.
215. A. W. W. Dale, *The Life of R. W. Dale of Birmingham* (London: Hodder and Stoughton, 1898); D. M. Thompson, 'R. W. Dale and the 'Civic Gospel', in A. P. F. Sell, *Protestant Nonconformists and the West Midlands of England* (Keele: Keele University Press, 1996), 99-118.
216. Sermon given at St Chad's on 15 September 1901, A.A.L., Keating Papers, S7 A/1; *St Chad's Magazine* (August 1906).
217. Keating to Cardinal Gotti, 16 January 1908, S.C.P.F., 443 (1908), rubr. 140.
218. Terna for Northampton bishopric, ibid.
219. Hughes, 'Bishops of the Century', p. 213.
220. M. Bence-Jones, *The Catholic Families* (London: Constable, 1992), p. 168.
221. M. J., Benkovitz, M. J., *Frederick Rolfe: Baron Corvo* (London: Hamilton, 1977).
222. The Cary-Elwes family are described in M. Beard, *Faith and Fortune* (Leominster: Gracewing, 1997), pp. 75-9.

223. Cary-Elwes to Frank Devas, 21 May 1930, E.P.S.J., Frank Devas Papers.
224. *St Chad's Magazine* (August 1906).
225. Bishop Keating's *Pastoral Letter* on the Norwich Congress, 1912, Nrt.D.A, Pastoral Letters 1908–1918, Book IV, no. 19.
226. *Ad Limina*, Northampton, 562 (1912), Rome, Vatican City State, Archivio Segreto Vaticano (A.S.V.), Consistorial Congregation (C.C.). See also M. Osborne, ' 'The Second Spring': Roman Catholicism in Victorian Northamptonshire', *Northamptonshire Past and Present*, 9 (1994–5), 71–9.
227. Bishop Keating's *Pastoral Letter* on the Norwich Congress, 1912, Nrt.D.A, Pastoral Letters 1908–1918, Book IV, no. 19.
228. Keating to Fr T. Williams, 9 March 1910, Cambridge, St Edmund's College Archives, Box E Envelope 2.
229. Quoted in Cleary, *Catholic Social Action*, p. 80.
230. Fr John H. Wright, S.J. to Fr Joseph Keating, 10 September 1917, E.P.S.J., Joseph Keating Papers, 48.9.6.2.
231. Keating to Fr Joseph Keating, 11 December 1915, ibid.
232. Speech given at Southwark, u/d, entitled, 'Is religion any good for the working man?', A.A.L., Keating Papers, Series 7 III A/111.
233. Bebbington, *Evengelicalism in Modern Britain*, p. 211.
234. Dom. A. Morey, 'Benet House, Cambridge, Some Early Correspondence, 1895–1900', *The Downside Review*, 103 (July 1985), 231.
235. G. Sweeney, *St Edmund's House, Cambridge The First Eighty Years: A History* (Cambridge: St. Edmund's College, 1980), p. 44.
236. Speech to Fisher Dinner, u/d but 1914, A.A.L., Keating Papers, Series 7 III.
237. A. Marshall, *The New Cambridge Curriculum in Economics and Appointed Branches of Political Science; its Purpose and Plan* (London: Macmillan and Co., 1903), pp. 9, 20.
238. F. Keating, 'Introduction' in Plater, *Priest and Social Action*, pp. xiv, xii.
239. Hinsley to Fr O'Hea, 21 August 1936, C.S.G.A., E9, Cardinal Hinsley 1927–41.
240. Fr. Lattey, S.J. (ed.), *The Church: Papers from the Summer School of Catholic Studies held at Cambridge, August 6–15, 1927* (Cambridge: Heffer and Sons, 1928), pp. xi–xii.
241. Address to the National Catholic Congress, 'The Church and the Worker', Cardiff 1914, A.A.L., Keating Papers, Series 7 III A/116.
242. *Western Daily Mercury*, 7 July 1913.
243. Address to the CSG at Holy Name Church, Manchester, u/d, A.A.L., Keating Papers, Series 7 IV A/191.
244. Address to the Society of St Vincent de Paul, Sheffield, on 'social justice', 24 November 1912, ibid., Series 7 III A/56. Keating had originally written 'a barrier which all her energy is unable to surmount', indicating how seriously he viewed the threat of poverty for the future of religion.

245. Bishop Keating's Advent *Pastoral Letter* of 1908, Nrt.D.A., Pastoral Letters 1908–1918, Book IV no. 6.
246. Keating to Stuart Coats, 12 January 1920 (copy); Keating to Anon., 22 December 1919 (Copy), Nrt.D.A., Keating Papers, FV. 1 (G).
247. Keating to Fr J. Keating, S.J., 28 December 1910, E.P.S.J., Joseph Keating Papers, *Month* Correspondence (48.9.6.2).
248. Address to the CSG at Holy Name Church, Manchester, u/d, A.A.L., Keating Papers, Series 7 IV A/191.
249. Bishop Keating's Advent *Pastoral Letter* of 1908, Nrt.D.A., Pastoral Letters 1908–1918, Book IV no. 6.
250. Bishop Keating's Advent *Pastoral Letter* of 1914, ibid., no. 28.
251. Bishop Keating's Lenten *Pastoral Letter* of 1917, ibid., no. 38.
252. Bishop Keating's Lenten *Pastoral Letter* of 1917, ibid., no. 38.
253. A. Fox, *A History of the National Union of Boot and Shoe Operatives 1874–1957* (Oxford: Basil Blackwell, 1958), pp. 58, 313–15.
254. Doyle, 'Origins of the Catholic Social Guild', pp. 409–10.
255. Fox, *National Union of Boot and Shoe Operatives*, pp. 308–13.
256. Forty million days were lost through strikes in 1912, the most serious dispute being in the coal industry: P. Clarke, *Hope and Glory: Britain 1900–1990* (London: Penguin, 1996), p. 70.
257. Although their annual conference held at Newcastle in August 1911 was their fourth, Bishop Keating remarked that 'he had no notion that their organisation had developed to such an extent': *Catholic Federationist* (September 1911).
258. Meeting of the Bishops, 16 April 1912, A.A.W., *Acta*.
259. Casartelli to W. O'Dea, u/d (but September 1912), Sal.D.A., Casartelli Papers, Box 159. Geremia Bonomelli (1831–1914), Bishop of Cremona between 1871 and 1914, was known for his success in persuading Pope Pius X to withdraw the *non expedit* prohibiting Catholics from participating in political activities in the Italian state, and for his attacks on landowners who mistreated their workers.
260. *Catholic Federationist* (December 1912).
261. Quoted in Oldmeadow, *Bourne*, II, p. 216.
262. *The Tablet*, 15 February 1913. There were also denunications of sympathetic strikes in the provincial Catholic press, see e.g. *Birmingham and District Catholic Magazine* (December 1913); copy in B.A.A.
263. *Catholic Federationist* (September 1911).
264. F. Valentine, *Father Vincent McNabb*, O.P. (London: Burns and Oates, 1955).
265. This article forms an appendix in Valentine's biography.
266. P. Snowden, *Socialism and Syndicalism* (London and Glasgow: Collin's Clear Type Press, 1913), p. 133.
267. Ibid., p. 197.
268. *Western Daily Mercury*, 7 July 1913. Quoted in E. Larkin, 'Socialism and Catholicism in Ireland', *Studies*, 74 (Spring 1985), 81. Thomas Burns claimed that he was told by two people (one of them was Father Parkinson) at a meeting of the CTU in Birmingham in 1914 that

Whiteside had aligned himself with the 'economic views' contained in Snowden's book: Thomas Burns to Casartelli, 6 June 1914, Sal.D.A., Catholic Federation File.

269. *Western Daily Mercury*, 7 July 1913. Keating's rebuke of the Catholic unionists was greeted with 'prolonged cheering'.
270. *Catholic Federationist* (July 1914).
271. Casartelli spoke out at the NCCTU in December 1916 against the tendency of some CSG members to speak of 'certain kinds of socialism': ibid. (January 1917).
272. *Ad Beatissimi Apostolorum*, 180, p. 148.
273. Meeting of the Bishops, 17–18 April 1917, A.A.W., *Acta*.
274. Casartelli to Bourne, 5 May 1917 (copy), Sal.D.A., Casartelli Papers, Box 161.
275. Ibid.
276. Casartelli to Bourne, 13 May 1917 (copy); Casartelli to Canon O'Kelly, 16 May 1917 (copy), ibid.

2

'Imperialists and Snobs?': The Bishops and Ireland 1918–1921

The charge that English Catholicism was unsympathetic to Ireland was not without some justification. Although Cardinal Manning in the 1880s had identified himself more openly with Irish national aspirations as part of his populist, democratic vision,[1] amongst the episcopate he could count only on Bishop Bagshawe of Nottingham, a maverick and controversial figure, for support.[2] Amongst the lay elite of the Catholic community such a commitment to social reform and home rule was greeted with hostility. This chapter examines the attitudes and responses of the English bishops to events in Ireland, and in particular during the Anglo-Irish War of 1919–21, 'two years of as appalling an Irish policy as Britain had ever tempted'.[3] Although little has been written on this subject, Boyce's authoritative study on English reactions to the policy of reprisals and the role of the Black and Tans has suggested that of all sections of the Christian community Catholics were the most reluctant to engage in criticism of British policy.[4] According to Fitzpatrick the English bishops 'greeted the revolutionary movement with loyal disgust'.[5]

How are we to explain this response? One explanation is the persistence of anxieties about identification with and commitment to Irish causes. The typical reaction of English Catholic leaders to the charge that their religion encouraged civic disloyalty – a hoary Protestant refrain – was invariably to overcompensate for these perceived deficiencies in patriotism. An anxiousness not to give a handle to their critics set a limit to how far English Catholicism felt able to identify with Ireland's cause. But after the war there surely could have been no doubt about the loyalty of Catholics. Furthermore, Randall Davidson (1848–1930), Archbishop of Canterbury, who was moved to criticize the government during the Anglo-Irish War, showed that patriotism did not mean timid subservience to whoever happened to form the government of the day. The concern of the Catholic bishops to address a broader range of social and political questions after the war, exemplified by Bourne's 1918 pastoral letter *The Nation's Crisis*, indeed suggested a growing political maturity and confidence which might have extended to the Irish question. With the influence of Catholic Tory peers in decline, had not the time arrived for a thoroughgoing commitment to the radical, populist agenda which Manning had envisaged?

There was a perception amongst Irish Catholics that their English co-religionists were no friends. When the Catholic sculptor and artist Eric Gill visited Ireland in October 1919 he recorded in his diary: 'Long talk on Ireland and English politics with reference to the attitude of English Catholics to Ireland. Irish people very bitter (this we found everywhere) about this. They much resent anti-Irish attitude and regard English Catholics as imperialists and snobs and also bad Catholics.'[6] Of course, English Catholicism was a broad church in which many views towards Ireland were heard, but it is certainly the case that the attitudes of the most prominent Catholics gave ample support to such criticisms. For some English Catholics opposition to Irish home rule was a natural consequence of class allegiance. A tradition of Catholic Unionism was kept alive by the fifteenth Duke of Norfolk (hereafter 'Norfolk'), who regarded himself as the spokesman for the pope in Great Britain. Fearful of social radicalism and home rule,[7] Norfolk defected Gladstone's party in 1886 – although the traditional allegiance of leading Catholics to the Whigs had already been strained over issues such as the papal temporal power[8] – and went on to hold minor office in Salisbury's Conservative government of 1895–1900. Irish distrust of English Catholics was fuelled by Norfolk's involvement in the efforts of Salisbury's government to re-establish diplomatic relations between Britain and the Vatican.[9] These moves were seen in Ireland as an attempt by the British government to gain 'more leverage in Irish affairs at Rome', with the aim of securing papal condemnation of the Plan of Campaign and possibly even the home rule movement.[10] Norfolk earned Irish opprobrium when, during the crisis surrounding the Third Home Rule Bill, he appeared on the same political platform as Edward Carson and made gestures of support for the Ulster Volunteer Force's campaign of armed resistance in Ulster.[11]

The main vehicle for English Catholic Unionist sentiment was the CUGB. Its membership, according to a list printed in 1916, stood at around 1,000,[12] but its active membership was far smaller[13] and drawn mainly from the higher social classes. It was imperialist in political outlook and conspicuously loyal to Crown and country: this could create tensions with ecclesiastical authority, as during the Boer War when Norfolk, the CUGB's President, protested to Rome at the anti-British tone adopted by the *Osservatore Romano*, the paper subsidized by the Holy See.[14] There was, however, no doubting Norfolk's staunch devotion to the papacy; according to David Mathew his 'position was valued by the "Black" Roman aristocracy and at the Vatican he had great authority'.[15] During the late nineteenth century the CUGB's influence within the Church had been out of all proportion to its size, which created some resentment. V. M. Durnford, President of the Catholic Association, informed Norfolk of the 'strong feeling amongst them that the Catholic Union is not sufficiently representative of the Catholic body; and that it is not fair to other Catholic societies that the Union should be selected on every occasion as embracing all parties of the Catholics of this land'.[16] The Irish community in Britain had good reasons to challenge the CUGB's claim to speak on behalf of British Catholics. Under the proprietorship and editorship of the truculent Charles Diamond *The Catholic Herald*, an organ of Irish national sentiment, contained vituperative attacks almost every week on the Catholic peers.[17]

Norfolk's death in 1917 saw the leadership of the CUGB pass to Admiral Lord Walter Kerr, who became its President, and Rudolph Fielding, ninth Earl of Denbigh. But this did not lead to any lessening of anti-Irish feeling. In 1918 the CUGB attacked the Irish Catholic hierarchy over its stance on conscription. The introduction on 9 April 1918 of the Military Service Bill, which gave the British government power to extend conscription to Ireland by Order in Council, had provoked massive demonstrations of Irish nationalist solidarity, to which the Irish bishops had added their voice. They contended, in a joint letter, that 'conscription forced in this way upon Ireland is an oppressive and inhuman law, which the Irish people have a right to resist by all means that are consonant with the law of God'.[18] Emanating from a traditionally cautious bench, it was evidence of the feelings of passionate indignation aroused. Typically, the Ulster Unionists denounced the action as a Vatican-inspired attack on the rights of the sovereign state.[19]

The conscription crisis had raised the spectre of Catholic disloyalty. Although during the war Catholics had surpassed other sections of the Christian community in bellicosity,[20] the conservative press, led by *The Times* and the ultra-Tory *Morning Post*, converged on what they saw as further confirmation of the inherent disloyalty of Catholics. *The Tablet*, ever since the 1850s the main organ of Catholic Toryism,[21] was particularly anxious that the reputation of English Catholics would be tarnished by association: 'Life for Catholics all over the Empire will be made much more difficult, and they will find themselves surrounded by a new atmosphere of prejudice and suspicion'.[22] The previous year English Catholics had been made distinctly edgy by Pope Benedict XV's 'Peace Note', which the Western Allies suspected as having been formulated at the behest of the Central Powers.[23] It was even suggested that Cardinal Bourne's reluctance to agitate on the education question during 1917–18 was due to the unpopularity of Catholicism in Britain because of the Pope's attitude.[24] Bourne, who had previously warned Benedict of the likely response in England to any initiative,[25] dissociated English Catholicism from the Peace Note when he declared: 'We do not want a peace which will be no more than a truce or armistice between two wars ... We English Catholics are fully behind our war leaders'.[26] With conspicuous displays of loyalty a marked feature of the public utterances of English Catholic leaders, a sympathetic response to the Irish conscription protest was most unlikely.

The CUGB moved with alacrity to announce its patriotism. Denbigh wrote in *The Times* on 29 April that 'it almost make me ashamed of the word Catholic to see the action now taken by the Irish hierarchy to combat and resist the law'.[27] The next day the CUGB moved four resolutions condemning the stance of the Irish hierarchy:

1. The Catholic Union has viewed with the deepest regret the action which the Catholic bishops have deemed it necessary to take for resisting compulsory service in the present war, action which appears to support the movement for organized disobedience to the law.
2. The Catholic Union is of the opinion that it is just and right that the people of every portion of the United Kingdom should take their share in the defence of the liberties of mankind from the grave peril to which they are exposed through the conflict wantonly forced upon the world by a real and unscrupulous enemy.
3. Catholics cannot but regard with serious misgivings any interference by ecclesiastical authority in questions which are purely temporal and political, and in no way connected with faith or morals.
4. The Catholic Union desires emphatically to dissociate itself from a movement which cannot but fail to hamper the full development of the military forces of the Allies, and thereby endanger the cause of humanity.[28]

The resolutions proved to be controversial even within the CUGB. Lord Braye, a member of the Executive Council, dissented;[29] Marjoribanks Egerton resigned for the reason that '"Ecclesiastical authority" including as it does the Holy Father himself, makes it quite impossible for me as a member of the Papal Household to continue to belong to the Union'.[30] It was this third resolution which also troubled James Britten of the CTS: he informed Mark Sykes, a CUGB member, 'it has been thought that it applies even to the Holy Father himself; and though I am sure such was not the intention of those who drew it up I think that, strictly interpreted, it would justify such a conclusion'.[31]

Worse still for the CUGB they succeeded in antagonizing the English bishops. Most were indignant that lay people would dare to upbraid bishops, and in some cases there was sympathy for Irish political grievances.[32] It is worth examining this response in detail for it shows the political cleavage which had opened up between the episcopate and Catholic peers since the late nineteenth century. But what is also notable is that criticism of the CUGB remained private and mute just when a hard-pressed Irish Church might have expected and welcomed a firmer repudiation.

The most vehement opponent of the political tendencies represented by the CUGB was Bishop Cotter of Portsmouth (1866–1940). One of three Irishmen on the English bench (the others being Keily of Plymouth and Lacy of Middlesbrough), Cotter was born in Cloyne, County Cork, but spent most of his childhood in Portsmouth where his father served on HMS Active. After training for the priesthood at Maynooth he returned, in 1892, to England where, apart from a short spell as a curate in Cork, he was to remain for the rest of his life.[33] He was something of a loose cannon, unafraid of offending polite English sensibilities. 'I am not skilled in the dialectics of diplomacy', he once remarked to Amigo with nice understatement.[34] 'During the war', Maisie Ward recalled, 'he had written a pastoral so violent in its attack on England that I had gone to the sacristy afterwards and told the priest I had found it hard to go to Communion after listening to his words – and if I, why not others? The Isle of Wight was, after all, English.'[35] Cotter's antipathy towards the self-styled leaders of English Catholicism was uncontained. In a letter to Amigo he excoriated the CUGB:

> I am not surprised at the English Catholics finding fault with the 'Catholicity' of the Irish – even with the Hierarchy thrown in! When ever did they agree that the Irishman could do right, except when he happened to be doing something which was a benefit to the Englishman? Isn't it marvellous that the rough heroic Irishman's Catholicity has managed to survive as genuine and undefiled – when the polished, expedient profession of the same by the English Catholics, has so often been suspect.[36]

Cotter was voicing a frequent complaint that whilst English Catholics seemed to demand the support of Irish politicians for their schools as of right, they were indifferent when faced with the political aspirations of the Irish.[37] The letter also expresses his conviction that the Catholicism of the English was of an inferior variety to the robust faith of the Irish – a prejudice which may explain why he was loath to accept English or English-trained priests in his diocese.[38] His anti-English feelings would intensify during the Anglo-Irish war, so much that he would declare, 'I only wish I could clear out from this country'.[39] He wrote this not long after his mother suffered personally during a Black and Tan arson attack which destroyed a large part of Cork on 11 December 1920. However, Cotter was to labour in the diocese of Portsmouth for another twenty-three years, an ordeal he made more tolerable by surrounding himself with manly Irish priests.

A more constructive, but no less passionate advocate of Irish causes was Bishop Amigo of Southwark. He was, like Cotter, an outsider to English Catholicism having been born in Gibraltar in 1864; he 'never entirely lost a slight Spanish accent'.[40] Possibly this predisposed him to other outsiders. Amigo was to tell Lloyd George that his 'sympathy and love for the Irish began by my working among the poor in the East End of London, and since then I have been honoured by the friendship of many Irish Bishops, Priests and lay-people'.[41] Among these friends was John Redmond, the leader of the IPP, whom he had met at the outbreak of the war: Amigo was instrumental in bringing him together with Cardinal Mercier to secure relief for Belgian refugees.[42] He numbered several Irish bishops among his correspondents including Robert Browne, Bishop of Cloyne; Denis Kelly, Bishop of Ross; Patrick Foley, Bishop of Kildare; and Michael Logue, Cardinal Archbishop of Armagh. They welcomed the vocal support Amigo gave at the time of the conscription crisis. Speaking in Southwark Cathedral, Amigo declared: 'The Bishops of Ireland are learned and holy men, and I, for one, will not presume to sit in judgement on them. As a matter of fact, knowing them as I do, I am in agreement with them ... the policy they have adopted is one that has had the effect of calming the Irish people and preventing more serious evils than people realize.'[43] He also wrote to the Prime Minister appealing for a reversal of the government's decision on conscription; he warned Lloyd George in May 1918 that the 'Irish can be won, but never driven. You would have all the soldiers you need without any conscription, if the Irish could be made to trust British politicians, but every man and woman in Ireland will resist conscription.'[44] Whilst Amigo had no influence on politicians, his public action on behalf of the Irish bishops did something to mitigate the action of the CUGB, and showed to the wider Catholic world that English Catholicism was not unanimously hostile. At a time when relations between the two national hierarchies were distant, even chilly, the trust which Amigo and Logue established at a personal level[45] was a promise of a thaw.

Casartelli of Salford was the other vocal critic of the CUGB. Whilst he may have shared the anxieties of leading CUGB members about socialism, that is where the affinities ended: he insisted to Archbishop Whiteside that 'the Catholic Union does not in any way represent and has no right to speak in the name of the Catholic body'; in a letter of solidarity to Logue he dismissed them as 'scarcely known'.[46] As an ardent defender of the rights and duties of the bishops to direct lay people in political as well as spiritual matters, Casartelli was particularly irked by the nature of the CUGB's third resolution; it was to him an extreme instance of that increasing tendency of lay organizations to disregard episcopal guidance and set themselves up as the arbiters of what constituted right action. Casartelli would disparage lay attempts to exercise initiative independently of the episcopate as 'Cisalpinism' – this from a prophet of the 'age of the laity' – and frequently alluded to the power struggles within the Church of a century earlier in his correspondence. He observed the growing influence of lay professional bodies like the Catholic Teachers' Federation (CTF) with dread, likening the situation to the 'days of the Cisalpine Club'.[47] Exasperated with assertions of lay autonomy he would invoke the name of John Milner ('O for one hour of Bishop Milner'),[48] the 'foremost defender of hierarchical claims in the community'[49] and the intransigent opponent of aristocratic lay predominance. It was with Casartelli's backing that the Salford Federation issued a statement repudiating the CUGB's action,[50] and he re-emphasized this opposition to Lord Denbigh who was disturbed enough by the controversy the CUGB's statement had provoked to visit Casartelli on 3 May in an attempt to repair the fissures.[51] Casartelli informed his Vicar-General that Denbigh 'heard of our action and seemed distressed about it and very much surprised ... I gave him a very straight talking to and did not mince matters'. (At a personal level Casartelli felt some pity for Denbigh who had lost two sons in the war.[52])

Sensitive to the charge that they 'had not found a word to say in defence of the Irish Hierarchy,'[53] some bishops wanted to see the CUGB's action denounced by the hierarchy. A special meeting of the bishops to discuss the new Code of Canon Law was held on 10 May 1918, and some wanted to use the occasion to issue a public repudiation of the CUGB. But it was Bourne who controlled the agenda, and he refused to be drawn on the issue. Cotter complained to Amigo: 'the way the meeting was rushed on Friday was a disgrace ... I can only think it was to avoid the bringing up in any form the action of the Catholic Union. From what transpired at the end of the meeting when

tackled on the subject, it was evident that His Eminence did not want
to take any combined action.'[54] Bourne also refused to put his name
to a letter of protest circulated by H. S. Dean, editor of *The
Universe*,[55] which was signed by every other bishop. Possibly Bourne
was unwilling to engage in public criticism of a Catholic society,
though this seems rather lame: he was to inform the Westminster
Federation, who were also pushing him for a statement, 'So far as I
am aware the Council of the Catholic Union has never made any claim
to speak in the name of all the Catholics of Great Britain. It represents only the members of the Union, who are fully entitled to extend
its action if they think fit to do so. But apart from that I fully depre-
cate the mutual criticism of Catholic societies.'[56] Ironically, whilst
Bourne probably took a dim view of the Irish hierarchy's action, this
statement, published in *The Tablet*, was in fact interpreted by CUGB
members as a repudiation of its position, precisely because they did
claim to possess a mandate to speak for the Catholics of Britain – they
were not merely representing themselves. One member, J. S. Franey,
referred to Bourne's comments when he asked Cardinal Gasquet to
seek verification in Rome that 'Pius IX actually appointed the Union
to represent the lay voice of Great Britain'.[57] Whatever the basis of
this claim Gasquet evidently felt that such an assertion was now
redundant. Almost fifty years since the CUGB's formation it was a
very different political world, and Gasquet, despite his reputation as
a veritable John Bull,[58] was not blind to this. He told Franey that he
thought a real Catholic Union impossible 'so long as Irish troubles
exist',[59] which does not seem to indicate great sympathy; indeed a few
years earlier he had complained to Denbigh about the association of
prominent Catholics (though not Denbigh) with Orange 'No-
Popery'.[60] Yet despite the ambiguity surrounding the exact scope of
the CUGB's authority, H. S. Dean was uncertain enough to refrain
from publishing his memorial, for 'the Union would have immediately
have confronted us with an unrevoked mandate, and all concerned
would have found themselves in an extremely difficult position'. Dean
might have hoped for some episcopal reassurance but none, so it
appears, was forthcoming; he contented himself with the thought that
'They [the bishops] had given encouragement and countenance to the
representative laymen who are interested in the matter'.[61]

Ironically it was a CUGB member, Mark Sykes, who did something
to restore the reputation of English Catholicism in the eyes of the
Irish. A further irony was that Sykes, a Unionist MP,[62] had an intense
dislike of the Irish believing that they 'pay little, take much, do
nothing, and yell and screech about their grief and sufferings of a 100
years ago as if they were going on today'. He had only contempt for

the Irish bishops, believing that they had 'denied men to the Entente in the hour of direst need'.[63] Yet Sykes could not but feel uncomfortable at the anti-Catholic and anti-papal feeling which had been whipped-up by sections of the national press, to which the CUGB, by its attack on the Irish hierarchy, had, however unwittingly, helped ferment. Members of the House of Commons, foremost among them Edward Carson,[64] had seized on a statement made in the upper House by Lord Curzon which made the claim that the Irish clergy had 'advised their flocks . . . under penalties of eternal damnation, to resist Conscription to the utmost'.[65] The effect of Sykes's intervention in a House of Commons debate on 25 June was to expose the absence of authority for such allegations. In that debate Sykes, recalling the Ulster campaign of resistance in 1914, turned on Carson himself, stating that the 'reason why there is no law in Ireland is this – that he himself challenged the law . . . he entered into a covenant which imagined resistance to law'.[66] Bishop Dunn of Nottingham (1870–1931), no friend of the CUGB, was moved to contrast Sykes's stance with the hesitancy which characterized the English bishops' response: 'I fear we are, as a body, timorous rather than prudent . . . Promptitude was vital and Mark Sykes came to the rescue of the Church. But where were the Bishops that a layman should have to speak for the Church!'[67]

The feeling amongst the English hierarchy that they had failed the Irish bishops lingered. On 9 May 1920, whilst in Rome, Bishop Keating received a visit from Cardinal O'Connell of Boston, a conspicuous Irish nationalist, and recorded in his diary that he 'spoke of the anti-British feeling in America, largely on account of the Irish trouble and complained that the English Bishops had not done more to counteract the bad effect of pronouncements by the Duke of Norfolk and the Catholic Union'.[68]

*   *   *

The attitudes of the English bishops towards Catholic Ireland were, however, changing – there was a desire for closer relations and harmony. Whilst Cotter and Amigo were prickly outsiders in English society, the same could not be said of Bernard Ward (1857–1920), a distinguished historian who became the first Bishop of Brentwood in 1917. A humorous, rotund, cricket-loving man with an enormous capacity for work,[69] Ward had spent twenty years as President of St Edmund's College, Ware, during which time he wrote his monumental histories of English Catholicism; it was these works which encouraged a more positive assessment of Irish immigration. Irish immigration, Ward insisted, 'affected the future of Catholicism in this country more even than the Oxford Movement'.[70] His father, W. G. Ward, had been one of the foremost figures in the Oxford Movement and was Tory to the marrow. Bernard's niece, Maisie Ward, said that her uncle 'found himself regarded almost a traitor in old English Catholic circles for making obvious statements about the Irish immigration – its proportionate numbers, the degree to which it had strengthened English Catholicism'.[71] This was a challenge to those 'second spring' historical accounts which, as Fielding points out, 'emphasised the conversion of intellectual Anglicans, the renewal of faith within indigenous adherents and the efforts of the papacy, at the expense of the Irish influx'.[72] An indefatigable researcher, Ward spent many hours in ecclesiastical archives in Ireland and during a period of research in 1910 stayed for a week with Archbishop Walsh of Dublin, whom he came to greatly admire. Whilst from a research point of view his labours were apparently unproductive,[73] he told Walsh that he had 'returned with more knowledge and appreciation of Catholic Ireland, and ... more friends among the clergy here ... and more acquaintance with Catholic life in Ireland'.[74] Again, in 1911, he told Walsh, 'the week I spent in your great house and the knowledge I gained of the Irish Catholics are among the pleasantest recollections connected with the writing of it [*The Eve of Catholic Emancipation*]', although he regretted 'the small part occupied with misunderstandings with the Irish Bishops'.[75] To bring out the significance of these modest gestures of friendship it should be remembered that Ward's brother, Wilfrid, was deeply antipathetical to home rule: at the same time as Bernard was attempting to forge relationships with Irish Catholics, Wilfrid was closely involved with Tory diehard opposition to the Third Home Rule Bill.[76]

Bishop Keating of Northampton came from a very different social background to Ward and had little sympathy with aristocratic influence, yet there was a similar desire to build bridges with Catholic Ireland; soon after Norfolk's death he commented that 'Politically we have suffered from association with the poor Duke ... Already the bulk of our people look to Ireland rather than to us for a lead'.[77]

A visit to the United States for Cardinal Gibbons's golden jubilee in 1918 brought home to Keating the level of Irish antipathy towards England; heightening his discomfort was the feeling expressed in ecclesiastical circles that English Catholicism had failed Ireland. Although Keating was aware that his visit had been arranged through the Foreign Office,[78] he was naively innocent of Foreign Office motives. With the Paris Peace Conference looming, there was a concern within the British government that President Wilson would

come under strong Irish-American influence to take up the Irish cause
as part of the overall peace settlement. Yet within British diplomatic
circles there was a belief that the American Catholic hierarchy was
'more inclined to be friendly than they have been for years',[79] that the
Church was possibly 'the only remaining organisation through which
American influence can be brought to bear on Ireland'.[80] It was seen
as important, therefore, to make friendly overtures to the American
hierarchy. At the British Embassy, Colville Barclay saw the opportunity provided by the presence in America of Keating and his Secretary
Mgr Barnes. Barnes was asked by Barclay to contact Gibbons and
Cardinal O'Connell of Boston and obtain the names of two prelates
who would be willing to go to England as guests of Cardinal Bourne
and the English bishops.[81] But this gesture met with a damp response.
O'Connell, who was seen as the 'dominant figure among Irish
Americans', informed Barnes that 'all the Irish Americans were in a
state of ebullition which would soon break out into hostile utterances
against England unless some definite action were taken against Home
Rule ... if England acted generously he would do his best to see that
the great body of Irish Americans met her action in a similar spirit'.[82]
No further links between the English and American hierarchies were
attempted. The same visit saw Keating excited about the thought of
collaborative ventures between social Catholics in England and
America; he took the opportunity to visit leading Catholics in several
American cities to discover whether there might be common ground.[83]
But he naively misjudged the public mood: sections of Irish opinion
excoriated him as an 'agent of the English Tory enemies of Ireland'.[84]
He was berated in the Irish nationalist press for having reputedly said
that the 'Home Rule question was not the fault of England, but of
Ireland'.[85] As the tour progressed he was made aware of the strong
anti-English feelings of many American Catholics: 'No appeal for
cooperation between English-speaking Catholics would be listened to,
we were told, unless Catholic England was prepared to express her
sympathy, plainly and unreservedly with Catholic Ireland'.[86]
Keating's original decision to eschew references to politics in his
public addresses – probably on Foreign Office advice – no longer
seemed appropriate; he had been informed by American Catholic
leaders that silence on his part would be construed as implying support
for the British government's Irish policy. At a lunch at the Catholic
University, Washington DC, which was attended by Mgr Benzano,
the Papal Delegate, and chief personnel from the British Embassy, he
declared: 'Ascendancy must end in Ireland as it must end in Prussia
and elsewhere. No British party, certainly no British Government,
will ever again be willing to play Ulster's hand or seek to perpetuate

the intolerable situation which has brought misery for so many generations.'[87] This was clearly not from the script provided by the Foreign Office, but it helped to placate O'Connell. At the same time Keating was always anxious to tread a careful line on Ireland: in October 1919 he reprimanded Shane Leslie, a cousin of Winston Churchill's who supported Sinn Fein, for his talk of rebellion, insisting that it would draw 'multitudes of good fellows into a hopeless enterprise'. He thought that Ireland's cause would be best served by the Labour Party, 'who will come into power when the Coalition crushes, and who are under no sort of pledge to the Orangemen. And then the band will play!'[88]

Ward and Keating did not go as far as Amigo and Cotter in their identification with Irish causes, yet from them we get a sense of the direction which English episcopal opinion was taking – this was clearly away from Catholic Tory assumptions.

*   *   *

The rout of the IPP in 1918 and the emergence of Sinn Fein, a party committed to physical force nationalism, marked a new stage in the Anglo-Irish conflict. Sinn Fein set up an independent Irish parliament, the Dáil, and reaffirmed the 1916 declaration of independence. Early 1919 saw the emergence of a more militant nationalism in the form of the Irish Volunteers, later known as the IRA. Without the authority of the Dáil, Volunteers launched an armed assault on the forces of the Crown: the ambush and killing of two members of the Royal Irish Constabulary (RIC) at Soloheadbeg were the first shots in the Anglo-Irish War. The British government responded by proscribing the IRA in August 1919, and the following month it declared the Dáil illegal. In March 1920 the counter offensive was accelerated when Sir Hamar Greenwood, the new Chief Secretary for Ireland, sent back-up support to the beleaguered RIC in the form of the Black and Tans and the Auxiliary Division. The Black and Tans gained a notorious reputation for violence and intimidation, behaving 'more like independent mercenaries'[89] than policemen. The violence and counter-violence reached its bloody apogee on 21 November 1920, the day known as 'Bloody Sunday', when the IRA killed eleven unarmed British officers, and the Black and Tans engaged in reprisals, firing on a football crowd at Croke Park, Dublin, causing many deaths and injuries.

Where did the sympathies of the English bishops lie during the Anglo-Irish War? Although Mews points to the support of Amigo and Cotter for the republican hunger-striker Terence MacSwiney, Lord Mayor of Cork, in the authoritative study of English reactions to the

Anglo-Irish war, Boyce contends that the Catholic hierarchy, more than any other section of religious opinion, were 'not only reluctant to criticise the government but seemed at times to lend it support, or at least approval'.[90] The two events which served to bring the Irish question most forcibly to the attention of the English bishops were the arrest of Archbishop Mannix of Melbourne and the hunger strike of Terence MacSwiney.

Mannix, former President of Maynooth College, Ireland, was a conspicuous advocate of Irish independence. In 1920, en route to his *ad limina* visit, he embarked on a tour of America to galvanise support for the Irish cause.[91] Around this time, Mannix was being mentioned as a possible successor to the seriously ill Archbishop Walsh of Dublin, and an exaggerated alarm about the possible appointment of a nationalist, and such a vehement and imprudent one, spread in the Foreign Office and filtered through to the Vatican. The Foreign Office, through its envoy Count de Salis, lobbied against the appointment – which was not in fact a realistic possibility – and urged that Mannix's political activism be curbed.[92] But whether through disinclination or inability, the Vatican made no attempt to silence Mannix. When it was discovered that Mannix intended to stop off in Ireland on his journey from America to Rome, the British government, anxious that he would stir up unrest, prevented him from landing, took him to England under arrest and banned him from visiting Ireland. Yet Mannix was allowed to move freely throughout England and Scotland; accompanied by Shane Leslie he pursued a propaganda campaign for seven months. This made some of the bishops, notably Bourne, distinctly uneasy. It did not help that Mannix's cause and reports of his public appearances were given extensive coverage by *The Catholic Herald*, whose editor, Charles Diamond, had recently emerged from prison after his article on the attempted assassination in 1919 of Lord French, Lord Lieutenant of Ireland, ('Killing no Murder') was deemed seditious.[93] Diamond was regarded by the Catholic hierarchy as a baleful influence: Bishop Burton, although a critic of British rule in Ireland,[94] referred to Diamond as a 'neurotic Scotsman' (he was actually born in Maghera, Ireland, although he spent most of his life in Glasgow), and expressed the hope that 'some of *his* enemies will break his windows, or administer to him a sound post-ternal correction'.[95] Much as they were made uncomfortable by Mannix's presence, there was still some sympathy for his plight amongst the English bishops and a feeling of indignation that a prelate of the Church should be treated so disrespectfully. A story circulated that Bourne had been consulted prior to Mannix's arrest; the Cardinal repudiated the charge in a letter to the bishops of 6 November 1920,[96] but there were those only too ready to believe the worst of Bourne: 'I couldn't help laughing over the recent disclaimer from H[is] E[minence] re Mannix', Dunn remarked.[97]

A number of bishops identified themselves directly with Mannix's cause. Bishop Cotter hosted what proved to be a controversial reception in Mannix's honour on 23 September 1920 at the Cannon Street Hotel. Bishop Amigo was present along with 300 priests, including a considerable number of the clergy of the Westminster province. Bourne, claiming ill-health, was unable to attend. In his opening speech Cotter referred to Amigo's presence as 'amply filling a gap'.[98] There was a truculence in the tone of some of the speeches which offended the sensibilities of some observers. H. S. Dean, who was otherwise sympathetic to Mannix's plight, described the reception as 'a Sinn Fein demonstration of the most insolent kind'.[99] Fr Baston protested to Mgr Jackman, Bourne's Private Secretary, that Cotter had 'let his political tongue loose about His Eminence'.[100]

The following month the Irish bishops issued a joint pastoral letter which described the exclusion of Mannix as 'one of the most unwise steps that purblind and tyrannical oppression could take'.[101] Although Bourne came under further pressure from bishops and clergy to speak out,[102] his ingrained reluctance to antagonize authority meant that this was never likely. He may also have been aware that when Cotter read the statement of the Irish bishops from the pulpit he was greeted with hostile abuse. Cotter's typically defiant attitude was that 'right must prevail, and the Catholic Protestants must be made to realise it'.[103]

During his time in England, Mannix was a frequent visitor to Terence MacSwiney, who was on hunger strike in Brixton Prison. One month before his death on 25 October 1920, Mannix administered to him the sacrament of extreme unction.[104] MacSwiney had been sentenced to two years imprisonment for possession of an RIC cypher and documents 'whose publication might cause disaffection'.[105] The thought that MacSwiney might starve himself to death in a British prison was deeply repugnant to sections of English opinion – even King George V urged Lloyd George to intervene to prevent this. It was natural that Amigo, in whose diocese MacSwiney was imprisoned, should have become involved in the case. Amigo began lobbying government ministers to secure the release of MacSwiney. A telegram to Lloyd George appealed for clemency and warned that 'Resentment will be very bitter if he be allowed to die'. A further letter stated that 'the good name of England will be much affected throughout the civilised world' and again appealed for MacSwiney's immediate release.[106]

A sensitive and hotly debated question within the Church was whether the death of a hunger striker should be deemed a suicide. The British government, through their envoy Count de Salis, pressed Rome for an authoritative condemnation of hunger strikes; this would have undermined the moral force of MacSwiney's actions.[107] But no condemnation was ever issued despite pressure from pro-British voices in the Vatican, Merry del Val and possibly also Gasquet.[108] It does not appear, however, that the English bishops were involved in pressurizing for a pronouncement.

In the debate that ensued in the English Catholic journals and press the examples and precedents adduced were on occasions put to the service of existing political prejudices. Fr Bernard Vaughan was of the opinion that the sacraments should not be given to a hunger striker;[109] but then Vaughan was a fanatical patriot, popular with royalty,[110] whose bellicose outpourings during the war had embarrassed even the government.[111] Vaughan's view was not echoed by the bishops. Amigo told one layman a few weeks before MacSwiney's death: 'My Lord Mayor of Cork has been an excellent Catholic all his life and he took advice off good theologians before he acted. Knowing the circumstances of this particular case I am convinced that Mr MacSwiney is not committing suicide and that the priest is fully justified in giving him the sacraments.'[112] H. S. Dean informed Amigo that in Westminster the view was that MacSwiney was 'a man in extremis ... he has got his conscience fixed and is in apparently invincible ignorance, he should be given the benefit and given the sacraments'. It is not known whether this was the view of Bourne. Dean also mentioned that the sacraments had been refused to a hunger striker in a Birmingham prison,[113] but it seems likely that this action was the individual decision of the chaplain rather than a rule laid down by the Archbishop, for Ilsley's illness had meant that his responsibilities had been assumed by his Auxiliary,[114] John McIntyre (1855–1934), who was known to be fervently pro-Irish.[115] McIntyre's view was probably reflected in the publication in the diocesan magazine of November 1920 of a poem dedicated to MacSwiney; the sale of photographs of the hunger striker had been announced in an earlier edition.[116] In the Clifton diocese the chaplain of Shepton Mallet prison, Fr T. O'Connell, asked Bishop Burton for 'suggestions, instructions, or restrictions on the matter'[117] as a number of Irish inmates were on hunger strike. Here the ultimate responsibility was left with the priest, although Burton's comment that 'You are the confessor of these *good people*' [Burton's italics] perhaps suggests where his sympathies lay:

As, however, you ask for my counsel, I will tell you what I should do, were I in your place. 1) I shall point out *very kindly* to them the unlaw-fulness of omitting the ordinary means of sustaining life, where, as here, no one else's life is saved by the food rejected, and where the partaking of it does not symbolize participation in sin. If they persisted in abstention, I should not absolve them. 2) But when death seemed to be near, and the faster, after every means of persuasion has been used, persisted to refuse the *food in good faith*, I should require an expression of *contrition for all sins*, and then absolve him.[118]

MacSwiney's funeral at Southwark Cathedral was a highly-charged and controversial affair with Sinn Fein banners unfurled, the Irish Volunteer uniform draped over the body, and six IRA men standing as guard of honour.[119] Amigo may have been displaying a cleric's insouciance of political realities when he claimed later to have been taken completely by surprise by the nature of the funeral,[120] but Mannix and Cotter, who also presided, were not so green. Some of Amigo's flock were outraged. A typical protest came from a convert, Major John Edgecombe, who saw the funeral as simply an 'Irish demonstration of disloyalty'.[121] Lord Walter Kerr, President of the CUGB, in a letter to Cardinal Gasquet stated: 'I do submit that it is deplorable that any bishop should have officiated at a solemn funeral in his honour', however, despite great pressure for a CUGB protest he remarked, somewhat unconvincingly given its previous record, that it would be 'unseemly in a lay body to publicly censure bishops for action taken in the discharge of purely spiritual functions'.[122] A member of the Southwark Chapter, Canon Sheehan, expressed his unease at events in the Cathedral, although his main concern appears to have been the likely effects on the Sunday collections. Cotter reassured Amigo: 'I do not know Canon Sheehan but he ought to have a longer outlook than collections. I wonder what the countervailing effect on the boxes would be if the Irish element of your diocese took umbrage at opposite action on your part.'[123] There was talk of a condemnation from Rome for the manner in which the funeral was conducted, but whilst Pope Benedict XV was concerned that 'at the funeral there was too much parade' and 'a certain element of farce with it all', Amigo was only mildly reprimanded.[124]

*   *   *

In the month of MacSwiney's death there was an attempt to heal the fissures which the Irish question had opened in the Catholic community. Fr Plater was behind one such initiative. He began to show an interest in Ireland in 1920, and, although dangerously ill (he was to die the following year), he spent a week in Galway to view the political situation, 'asking questions, offering suggestions, trying to make up his mind about land-hunger, emigration, the tragedy of politics, and all that he should have forbidden himself'.[125] Ever the initiator and organizer, what emerged from his new pre-occupation with Ireland was the Committee of British Catholics for Reconciliation between Great Britain and Ireland (CBCR). His CSG colleague Henry Somerville described its purpose as to 'promote unity and good feeling between different sections of Catholics in England';[126] Plater explained it as an attempt to address the criticism 'that Catholics of the middle-classes and upper-classes and also "English Catholics" are no friends of Ireland'.[127] Plater was clearly concerned that the reputation of the CSG might suffer if it remained aloof from events in Ireland.

A memorial was drafted and the support of leading social Catholics and representatives of all shades of political opinion was canvassed – it was a typically Plater attempt to avoid any hint of political partisanship. 'It would be useless', he told Edward Eyre of the Westminster Federation, 'to have the signatures only of so-called "moderate" men. We must reconcile Unionists and self determinists or we shall do nothing.'[128] As Plater had anticipated, the attitude of Bourne was typically non-committal: although he had the Cardinal's verbal backing he had refused to append his name to the memorial.[129] Similarly, Archbishop Whiteside 'warmly approved' but did not wish to put his name to the memorial, insisting its signatories be laymen only.[130] Bourne and Whiteside evidently saw this as a political movement from which they as bishops should remain detached. The ailing Archbishop Ilsley's name headed the memorial although it is likely that John McIntyre prompted him. Plater succeeded in bringing together a broad spectrum of political opinion, from Unionists such as Denbigh to avowed Sinn Feiners like Shane Leslie. Unsurprisingly, what finally emerged was a somewhat anodyne document which reflected the current clamour for dominion home rule as a way of reconciling the claims of nationalists for self-determination and the concerns of those who feared that self-government would portend the break-up of the British empire.[131] It stated that 'freedom and equality are compatible with the real and permanent union between the two countries', and was couched in terms acceptable to all shades of opinion avoiding reference to either nationalist violence or the Black and Tans. It made little impression on public opinion, and, significantly, was ignored altogether by the main organ of Irish nationalist opinion in England, *The Catholic Herald*. It did, however, secure the approval of Archbishop Mannix and members of the Irish hierarchy, including Cardinal Logue and Archbishop Gilmartin of Tuam, and may be seen therefore as a successful exercise in public relations.[132]

The memorial might have attracted more attention if Bourne had not issued a public statement only days after its publication which sent out a very different message to that of conciliation. What prompted Bourne to write to *The Times* (12 November 1920) on the situation in Ireland is not clear – he was not usually given to airing his views in the press – although at the foot of the letter he claimed that he had received an 'urgent request' to place 'before my fellow countrymen in both countries' his thoughts on the current situation.[133] (I have not been able to establish where this request came from.) In the letter Bourne affirmed his conviction that the widest possible self-government was 'the only possible solution of the many difficulties that confront us', whilst at the same time stressing that the union of the two countries within the British empire should be maintained. His views approximated, therefore, to the CBCR memorial. Where the statements differed was on the question of violence, an issue which the CBCR had studiously avoided. Whilst recognizing that the Black and Tans had exacerbated the situation in Ireland and were a cause of great 'shame' to 'the vast majority of those who live in England', Bourne viewed their withdrawal with apprehension, pointing to the existence of an uncontrollable 'murder gang', 'a secret oath-bound society using assassination as its weapon' which the 'real and legitimate Sinn Fein' could not control. No Catholic could be a member of a secret society, Bourne stated, recalling the papal condemnation of Fenianism in the 1860s. Bourne had shifted the main burden of the responsibility for the violence on to the IRA; to his critics he appeared an apologist for state violence. The letter invoked his 'Irish mother', but if anything this gave a disreputable flavour to the whole effort. Bourne's knowledge of Ireland and Irish politics was actually very limited, and he was upbraided by Bishop Cohalan of Cork and *The Catholic Herald* for his references to the existence of a secret oath-bound society.[134] Bourne did not enjoy close relations with the Irish episcopate, the more informed of who would have provided a more sympathetic and nuanced interpretation of the actual situation on the ground. Neither did he have first-hand knowledge of Irish questions: until he attended the Eucharistic Congress of Dublin in 1932 he had only ever visited the city of his mother's birth once in his life.[135]

Also controversial was Bourne's decision to hold a Requiem Mass in Westminster Cathedral for three Catholic British army officers who had been shot dead in their beds on the morning of 21 November by Michael Collins's Dublin Brigade Active Service Unit. Lloyd George thanked Bourne for 'the most moving and impressive service in your beautiful cathedral and the part you yourself took in it'.[136] The accusation of partisanship was directed at Bourne by Irish Catholics angered that he made no reference in the service to the shootings at Croke Park by troops in search of IRA men later that day. The suspicion was that Bourne had 'indulged himself in a reprisal for the funeral service of the Lord Mayor of Cork in Southwark Cathedral a month before'.[137] Of the event, Mews states that 'The Westminster requiem gave considerable satisfaction to English Catholics, while the premier's letter demonstrated that although the government might have lost all patience with the Irish hierarchy, it still had some confidence in the Catholic leadership of England'.[138] Of course, Bourne did not speak for all the Catholic bishops. At Southwark Cathedral Amigo sent out a very different message, declaring that 'the murderers were not only the men who used the revolver, but the people who incited them to murder. They condemned murder, and they also condemned the murder of men, women and children by the forces of the Crown.'[139] This was in line with the views expressed by Cardinal Logue and the Irish bishops in a strongly-worded pastoral letter on the events of 'Bloody Sunday'.

By December 1920 it was becoming apparent to most bishops that benevolent proclamations of good-will and vague general statements were not enough to heal divisions between Irish and English Catholics. The policy of force employed by the government to put down insurrection in Ireland had roused 'respectable' opinion. Archbishop Davidson of Canterbury was moved by reports of events in Ireland to issue a protest against the government's Irish policy. In the House of Lords he made two forthright speeches on 2 November 1920 and 22 February 1921. His intervention underlined the extent to which 'moderate' opinion had lost confidence in the government's Irish policy. 'It looks as if the British public are wakening to what is being done in Ireland', Mgr Brown wrote after Davidson's second speech, 'Canterbury's intervention followed by the Crozier revelations[140] are all doing much to move people who were incredulous before.'[141] Davidson's stance had impressed Irish sympathizers in the Catholic Church who now began to look to him, rather than their own leaders, to voice their concerns. Having given up on Bourne and recognizing his own lack of influence, Amigo began to work through Archbishop Davidson. He wrote to Davidson on 21 February 1921 with details of Black and Tan outrages in the town of Ardee, and these were incorporated into the speech in the House of Lords the next day.

Opinion in England had turned sharply against the government's Irish policy in the last two months of 1920. It was more the stigma on England than concern for the Irish which was behind this shift in the public mood. The Catholic bishops, at least the majority of them, began to join the chorus of criticism, although Bourne resisted any corporate statement against reprisals. There was even criticism from surprising quarters: Joseph Cowgill (1860–1936), Bishop of Leeds, a mild, gentle man known as the 'children's bishop, who came from an old Catholic family,[142] declared: 'When will English politicians see that Ireland is in all likelihood destined to prove the pivot upon which the Empire may turn? A running sore . . . may well bring on the death of the body in the end.' Cowgill also deplored the 'anti-Irish prejudice of some English Catholics'.[143] Such views were echoed by Bishop Dunn of Nottingham in his Advent pastoral letter:

> With the political aspect of the Irish crisis we have no concern. But we shall be well within our province and shall not, we trust, offend the sensibilities of anybody if we point out that the present condition of affairs in Ireland is a public scandal which grievously offends the Christian conscience. As the Catholic Bishop of an English diocese we should be wanting in our duty if we did not declare this openly to you, and to all whom it may concern, and exhort you all to demand that some effectual remedy be found for it without a moments delay. We speak out more readily because bred of an English stock and born of English parents we are nothing if not a plain John Bull, ardently jealous for the honour of England and the prestige of her good name. At present these things are, alas, in jeopardy and peril amongst the nations of the world.[144]

The cry of political partisanship was invariably raised when churchmen ventured to criticize government policy, which goes to explain the defensive tone of the letter. Dunn was keen to stress that his concern was entirely with the moral issues involved, and the emphasis on his Englishness was to counter the inevitable charges of disloyalty and to present himself as one performing a patriotic duty. Although similarly guarded, it was a statement more in line with episcopal feeling than Bourne's, which Bishop Burton dismissed in a letter to Amigo as 'a little milk-and-watery, despite the "Irish Mother?" Nottingham *per contra* has been telling his flock that he himself is a full-bodied John Bull of English father and English mother, and yet he declaims hotly against the iniquities of our rulers in Ireland! Good!'[145]

Going further than the studied caution of Dunn's pastoral letter, a number of bishops gave their support to a protest meeting against reprisals, held towards the end of December 1920 at the Caxton Hall, London, under the auspices of the Catholic Women's Suffrage Society, a society which had in fact encountered considerable resistance from the hierarchy.[146] Presiding at the meeting were McIntyre and Cotter. According to a *Catholic Herald* report, Cotter described

British policy as 'Hunnish' and Cork as the '"Louvain on the Lee"
. . . bringing shame and disgrace on the name of England, at home and
abroad'. Bishop Burton, although not present, sent a letter which
stated: 'The tragedy of Ireland deepens, and it is a scandal of the
British Empire. I would rather see the Empire perish, than to see it
held together by such methods.'[147]

With the absence of any corporate expression of these views, the
general impression that the bishops were unwilling to speak out
against reprisals lingered. 'They are silent, consenting as did Paul to
the murder of Stephen', wrote Charles Diamond with characteristic
lack of deference.[148] By now the bishops had become immune to
Diamond's interminable outpourings of invective; what really
prompted Bishops Dunn and Amigo's attempt to persuade Bourne to
take up a more critical stance was not the invective of a turbulent journalist, but rather their sense of shame that a Protestant leader had
spoken out against reprisals whilst they had remained silent. But
Dunn's visit to Bourne proved futile: 'I told His Eminence that it was
a great shame that Canterbury and many other Protestant Bishops
were speaking against reprisals and we should be dumb. He would not
hear any of a joint statement.'[149] Amigo met with a similar response:
'Learning . . . that Canterbury was going to make a pronouncement, I
went to His Eminence and pointed out that the Irish Bishops would be
annoyed to see that even the Anglicans spoke and that we collectively
took no trouble to show sympathy with our fellow Catholics, but he
would have none of it.'[150] 'He and Gasquet are both quite fascinated
by Lloyd George which is a terrible pity', Amigo told Dunn.[151] The
fact that it was Davidson and not Bourne who had spoken was a
source of embarrassment to many in the Catholic community. As one
'English Priest' put it: 'We naturally expect to see a Cardinal of
England denounce the red reign of terror and the scarlet regime of the
Black-and-Tans . . . It is the Protestant Archbishop of Canterbury who
has stepped into the breach and denounced the British terrorism in
Ireland. The English Hierarchy looks on complacently – aye, cyni-
cally.'[152] James Britten thought it 'rather humiliating to find the
Protestant Archbishop protesting against reprisals upon a *Catholic*
country'.[153]

The bishops' frustration intensified when the Belgian hierarchy
issued its own joint pastoral letter protesting against reprisals. It was
the protest of a nation which had recently experienced oppression to
another, and it made the English bishops deeply uncomfortable. It
stated: 'The Belgians owe you this act of charity out of gratitude, for
when we were oppressed by the foreigner, deprived of food, heat and
clothing, you generously came to our aid . . . we range ourselves

beside you to demand of that Government that an inquiry of unques-
tionable impartiality shall be set up with a view of strengthening the
public conscience'.[154] 'This makes our silence all the worse', Dunn
remarked to Amigo.[155] Matters were made worse when the CUGB,
unchastened by the conscription crisis controversy, issued a protest
against the Belgian hierarchy's action, taking the opportunity once
more to hammer the Irish hierarchy. 'No corporate effort has been
made by the spiritual leaders of Ireland to stamp out the murderous
spirit which has been a reproach to their people and their faith', wrote
Kerr in a letter to Cardinal Mercier, which was circulated to the
press.[156] On this occasion the CUGB met with a more robust challenge from the English bishops. The charge of pusillanimity that
Cardinal O'Connell levelled at the English bishops earlier that year in
Rome had weighed heavily on Bishop Keating, convincing him to take
up a more public opposition to the CUGB.

> Lest silence should be construed as consent, and the whole body of
> English Catholics should be committed to the views on the Irish tragedy
> expressed in their latest *motu proprio* by the Catholic Union ... I ask
> space to repudiate on my own behalf, (1) specifically and emphatically
> the grave censure passed upon the bishops, who are infinitely better
> informed upon the facts of the case than their self-constituted critics,
> and who deserve all our sympathy and confidence in their official
> handling of a most perilous and perplexing politico-religious problem;
> and (2) generally, the purely *ex-parte* statement of the situation, which
> is neither better nor worse than the clap-trap of the secular party press.
> My sole motive in making this protest is to obviate, as far as lies in
> one person's capacity, the serious danger to our own domestic solidar-
> ity and our cordial relations with our fellow-Catholics, in Ireland and
> elsewhere, arising from what I feel to be the officious, though doubt-
> less well-intentioned, action of the Catholic Union.[157]

Keating explained later to Burton, who needed no persuading, that the
'plain fact is that this "frightfulness" in Ireland is as great a scandal
as the Hun's performance in Belgium: *and is so recognised* in England
and America. To allow the Catholic Union to put out such a document
as theirs, without repudiation on our part, would surely compromise
us in the eyes of the civilised world.'[158] Episcopal opinion was, as in
1918, ranged overwhelmingly against the CUGB, although as before
Bourne made no protest.

Why did Bourne remain so impervious to episcopal pressure for
corporate action? Discussing his refusal to consider a joint pastoral
letter, Burton speculated that Bourne 'may have anticipated a refusal
on the part of one or two bishops to sign'.[159] Certainly the recent troubled history of his relations with the bishops had only served to

heighten his sense of isolation, and made him ill-disposed to joint action. There was also his insistence on remaining above the political fray: his self-perception was that of a mediator between the diverse traditions in English Catholicism. Acutely conscious of the divisive nature of Irish politics, Bourne wanted to avoid committing the hierarchy to any position which could have been construed as partisan, although he failed to recognise that not acting could itself be interpreted as a partisan stance. In an interview he gave to a hostile American reporter at his country residence, Hare Street, in the spring of 1921, it was apparent that Bourne saw it as no part of his duty to tie the hierarchy to the Irish cause. He viewed his episcopal role in the following terms: 'I am an Archbishop in England, and in London at that; I have the interests of my own archdiocese to think of first and the interest of the Church in England second. I cannot afford to forget that in any public statement I make.' The welfare of his co-religionists in Ireland was of lesser moment. Neither was Bourne willing to accept the government's responsibility for the situation in Ireland: 'You have to expect a slightly different point of view on the Irish question from one whose duty it is to be English as well as a Catholic and an Archbishop'.[160] There was no sense that one's duty as an Englishman may involve on occasions taking courses antagonistic to the government of the day. Bourne was very anxious not to upset authority.

With Bourne opposed to a joint statement the bishops had to content themselves with alternative expressions of solidarity. Fundraising was one way. The expulsion of an estimated 8,000 to 10,000 Belfast Catholic shipworkers from their employment by Protestant mobs in 1920 provoked a massive international relief campaign, conducted by the Irish Church. Several English bishops made appeals for the expelled workers: Dunn requested that during the penitential season of Lent, alms collected over and above what the diocese needed would be sent to Bishop MacRory of Down and Connor. Burton and Amigo made personal contributions to the fund and McIntyre, outraged by the 'outburst of orange fury against our Catholic brethren in Belfast', led an appeal in Birmingham.[161] Casartelli approached Bourne to open a national fund for the relief of the expelled Catholic workmen in January 1921, arguing 'that such a movement would go a long way to promote better feeling between Irish and English Catholics'.[162] But Bourne refused, claiming that there was 'much greater distress in England, owing to unemployment, than there is in Ireland', adding 'we must be careful to avoid anything that might appear to have a political complexion'.[163] The issue of relief had indeed become highly politicized, with the Irish White Cross organization, of which Michael

Collins was a trustee, especially suspect in the eyes of Bourne.[164] Cotter's attempt at the next Low Week meeting to arrange a collection for the White Cross was to fail for the reasons that Bourne gave to Casartelli.

Despite his apparent concern to remain outside politics, Bourne returned to the subject of Ireland in his Lenten pastoral letter, read out in the churches of the archdiocese on 13 February 1921. It appears to have been aimed at curbing the activities of the Irish Self-Determination League (ISDL) in the diocese, although this organization was not referred to by name. Started in 1919, the ISDL, Hart maintains, 'was a front for republican activities of all kinds in England and Wales', which were 'more extensive and effective than is usually assumed'.[165] The most controversial aspect of the pastoral letter was that it was actually a re-issue of Cardinal Manning's 1867 condemnation of Fenianism, with only a short foreword from Bourne himself:

> In the midst of this confusion I have grave reason to fear that some of my own flock, impelled by legitimate love of country and urgent longing for the realisation of lawful aspirations, are unwarily allowing themselves to become implicated, by active sympathy or, even, actual cooperation in societies and organisations which are in opposition to the laws of God and the Catholic Church ... A similar danger arose in 1867, and my great predecessor, the then Archbishop Manning, in words inspired by zeal for God's honour, and burning with his constant and unfailing love for Ireland and her faithful people, uttered the needful warning. I take that warning, heard fifty-four years ago, and I make it my own today. The name 'Fenianism' is now no longer in use, but the activity that it connoted is still alive, and the denunciation of the second Archbishop of Westminster applies in unchanging measure to that activity today, by whatsoever name it be called.[166]

Again he had raised the spectre of secret societies, but few believed that Manning's pastoral letter, issued the year after Cardinal Cullen, the Irish primate, and his bench of bishops had themselves condemned Fenianism, was pertinent to the current situation.[167] The current Irish hierarchy had certainly moved a long way, even if Bourne had not. The invocation of Manning, who had been hugely popular amongst Irish Catholics, offended many: Jeremiah MacVeagh, an Irish MP, accused Bourne of sheltering under 'Cardinal Manning's mantle' and pointed to his silence 'when his co-religionists were being hunted from the factories, mills, and workshops of Belfast for no other crime than that they worship God at the same altar as himself'.[168] Typically, Bourne's biographer jumped to his defence by claiming that if the condemnation had come directly from him the point would have been lost because of the passions he aroused on personal grounds.[169] But if Bourne hoped that he could deflect personal criticism by invoking Manning he was mistaken: his standing with the Irish was never lower and the sobriquet the 'Black and Tan Cardinal' was attached to him by those who assembled at the Kingsway Hall, London, on 21 March to protest.[170]

Bourne was possibly oblivious to the anger his statement had aroused because he was in Rome for most of March. In his absence the bishops continued to inveigh against government policy. In a letter to Gasquet, Amigo stated that the actions of the Black and Tans sapped 'the foundation of all Government'.[171] But English Catholicism remained linked in the mind of the wider Catholic world with the resolutions of the CUGB. Bourne's pronouncement fastened the impression that English Catholics cared nothing for Ireland.

Those bishops who had been dismayed at Bourne's handling of the Irish issue saw the Low Week meeting of 4 and 6 April 1921 as perhaps the last opportunity for English Catholicism to declare its outrage at reprisals. Keating thought it 'impossible to meet without making some sort of pronouncement on the Irish troubles'. Dunn welcomed it as an opportunity to 'decide which are to be masters, – the Hierarchy or the Catholic Union'.[172] It was also an opportunity to remedy the difficulties caused by Bourne's Lenten pastoral letter. But even among those bishops most critical of British policy towards Ireland there was a certain anxiety. Keating urged that any pronouncement should be prudent 'to avoid making ourselves the tools of politicians and journalists'.[173] The Low Week agenda contained an item from Amigo asking: 'Is it too late for a Joint Letter of sympathy with the Irish hierarchy in their troubles?'[174] Cotter thought so: he had earlier told Amigo that he thought it 'too late for the Hierarchy to butt in now. The opportunities were lost.'[175] At the meeting Cotter said that 'while they [the hierarchy] might shelve an expression now on the past, that it might be a test of their willingness, to suggest an all England collection for the Irish White Cross'.[176] No decision was made to follow Cotter's suggestion. However, Bourne, though reluctant, was persuaded to issue a protest against reprisals. The printed resolutions of the meeting show that a letter to Lloyd George expressing grave concern about the condition of Ireland was approved on 6 April.

> They feel that the good name of England in other countries has been and still is being obscured by terrible happenings which it is impossible to explain or to justify. They desire me to impress upon you most

earnestly that all ground should at once be removed for the definite charges which are constantly being made of reprisals exercised by the Crown upon perfectly innocent persons. In this connection they are convinced that much could be done towards promoting a good understanding and the restoration of law and order were the auxiliary troops withdrawn without delay from Ireland.[177]

Bourne's use of the third person throughout the letter was possibly more than a formality, and suggests that he was attempting to distance himself from the opinions expressed. Aptly illustrating the rival pulls that troubled Bourne when faced with Ireland, Lord Edmund Talbot, recently appointed Lord Lieutenant of Ireland,[178] on hearing of the proposed course of action that evening, told Bourne that he had gone too far in 'demanding the actual recall of the Black and Tans', insisting that 'a change of method in the system of their discipline would have more weight'. Talbot cautioned Bourne that 'if you adhere to the letter I am afraid many of those who really understand the present position will only say "Here's another instance of those who might be expected to know better simply showing ignorance of the situation"'.[179] But Talbot's appeal, with which Bourne probably sympathized, was too late and the letter went out unmodified. At the meeting Bourne directed that the content of the letter be made known to the clergy, and that a letter be sent to Logue making him aware of their protest. The Low Week resolution seems therefore to have been more an attempt to mollify the Irish hierarchy and Irish Catholics in England than to influence policy. If this was the case it was probably, as Cotter had suggested, 'too little, too late'.

The truce called in July 1921 brought an end to the Anglo-Irish war. It had been an uncomfortable period for the English hierarchy. From opposite ends of the political spectrum their record on Ireland was attacked: some accused the bishops of pusillanimity, others of disloyalty. Late in 1921, Mgr Brown wrote to Archbishop Davidson and thanked him for speaking 'out boldly against outrages in Ireland when few voices were raised in defence of the suffering people ... I have never hesitated to point out the value of your timely intervention – at a time when prominent persons in our own Church here were silent about the excesses ...'[180] But episcopal attitudes had undergone a shift, and the attitudes to Ireland of the late nineteenth century were not the attitudes of the early 1920s. That this was so was underlined by a memorandum sent by several leading members of the CUGB to Gasquet in July 1923.[181] It argued that the events in Ireland had compromised the Catholic religion in the eyes of English people by its 'revolutionary associations', and stated that some of the English bishops had condoned 'political crime'. It went on to argue that would-be converts were 'repelled by the atmosphere, too often clouded in politics, in which her spiritual life is distorted and obscured'. They appealed to Gasquet that

> when an English See becomes vacant it should be taken into consideration that there are priests in this country, imbibed with the ancient traditions of England, and free from the entanglements of secular controversy, who combine a loyal devotion to the Holy See with an understanding of the feelings and inspirations of their countrymen and who by their exemplary life and high abilities are capable of bearing the burden of the Episcopate. We would on no account seek to limit the selection in any narrow racial principle, but we do humbly submit that an understanding of English ways, a sympathy with English traditions and a knowledge of English institutions, together with abstinence from secular politics should be considered essential qualifications for appointment to English Sees; and we trust that Your Eminence may find it possible to convey our sentiments to the Holy Father, among the number of whose spiritual children there are none more loyal than ourselves.[182]

But the response of the English hierarchy to Ireland – *pace* the CUGB – fell far short of sprinkling holy water over the IRA. Mgr Brown was far nearer to the truth than these beleagured Catholic peers. The weakness of the bishops' response was that they could not give corporate expression to what they felt individually. The general impression that Catholic England cared little for Ireland persisted.

Notes

1. See McClelland, *Manning*, pp. 161–98; see also D. Gwynn, 'Manning and Ireland' in J. Fitzsimons (ed.), *Manning: Anglican and Catholic* (London: Burns and Oates, 1951), pp. 111–35.
2. E. G. Bagshawe, *The Monstrous Evils of English Rule in Ireland: especially since the Union* (Nottingham: Watchorn, 1886). See Norman, *English Catholic Church*, pp. 194, 355; Quinn, *Patronage and Piety*, pp. 163–4, O. Rafferty, 'Nicholas Wiseman, Ecclesiastical Politics and Anglo-Irish Reflections in the Mid-Nineteenth Century', *Recusant History*, 21 (May 1993), 381–400; R. O'Neil, *Cardinal Herbert Vaughan* (London: Burns and Oates, 1995), pp. 281–6; there is a good discussion in M. Hickman, *Religion, Class and Identity* (Aldershot: Avebury, 1995), pp. 95–120; Gilley, 'Roman Catholic Church, 1780–1940', pp. 360–1.
3. Hastings, *English Christianity*, p. 21.
4. D. G. Boyce, *Englishmen and Irish Troubles: British Public Opinion and the Making of Irish Policy 1918–22* (London: Jonathan Cape,

1972), pp. 77–9, for the response of the churches to the Irish question. See also S. Mews, 'The Hunger Strike of the Lord Mayor of Cork, 1920: Irish, English and Vatican Attitudes', in W. J. Sheils and D. Wood (eds), *The Churches, Ireland and the Irish* (Studies in Church History, 25; Oxford: Blackwell, 1989), 385–99; J. Davies, 'A Liverpool Priest and the Anglo-Irish Treaty of 1921', *North West Catholic History* 24 (1997), 22–41.

5. D. Fitzpatrick, 'A curious middle place: the Irish in Britain, 1871–1921', in R. Swift and S. Gilley (eds), *The Irish in Britain 1815–1939* (London: Pinter Publishers, 1989), p. 33.

6. Eric Gill's diary entry for 24 October 1919; quoted in E. Gill, *In a Strange Land* (London: Jonathan Cape, 1944), 44.

7. The best source for the Duke of Norfolk is Quinn, *Patronage and Piety*; see also W. M. Kuhn, *Democratic Royalism: The Transformation of the British Monarchy, 1861–1914* (Basingstoke and London: Macmillan; New York, NY: St Martin's Press, 1996), ch. 5.

8. C. T. McIntire, *England and the Papacy 1858–1861: Tories, Liberals and the Overthrow of Papal Temporal Power during the Italian Risorgimento* (Cambridge: Cambridge University Press, 1983), pp. 106–12; J. L. Altholz, 'The Political Behaviour of the English Catholics, 1850–1867', *Journal of British Studies*, 4 (November 1964), 89–103.

9. Described in E. Larkin, *The Roman Catholic Church and the Plan of Campaign 1886–1888* (Cork: Cork University Press, 1978), *passim*.

10. Ibid., p. 48.

11. J. Biggs-Davison and G. Chowdharay-Best, *The Cross of Saint Patrick: The Catholic Unionist Tradition in Ireland* (Bourne End: Kensal, 1984), pp. 283–304. Norfolk supported the Tory diehard Willoughby de Broke's British League for the Support of Ulster and the Union, although he did not sign the British Covenant of 1914: D. Cannadine, *The Decline and Fall of the British Aristocracy* (New Haven, Conn. and London: Yale University Press, 1990), p. 528.

12. *The Catholic Union Gazette* (January 1916).

13. Its meetings were usually attended by twenty to thirty: W. S. Lilly to Mark Sykes, 18 June 1918, Hull, University of Hull, Brynmor Jones Library, Mark Skyes Papers, DDSY(2)/1/38.

14. Cardinal Rampolla to Norfolk, 13 February 1900; Norfolk to Cardinal Vaughan, 6 February 1900; Vaughan to Norfolk, 14 February 1900; Vaughan to Norfolk, 25 February 1900, A.C.A., Norfolk Papers, MD 2078.

15. Mathew, *Catholicism in England*, p. 233.

16. V. M. Durnford to Norfolk, 22 May 1901, A.C.A., Norfolk Papers, MD 2078.

17. The bad feeling was reciprocated: Mr Fitzherbert-Brockholes to Norfolk, 31 February 1893, ibid.

18. Quoted in M. Harris, *The Catholic Church and the Foundation of the Northern Irish State* (Cork: Cork University Press, 1993), p. 66

19. Ibid., pp. 66–8.

20. Ceadel, 'Christian Pacifism in the Era of Two World Wars', p. 404.
21. Altholz, 'Politicial Behaviour of the English Catholics', p. 96.
22. Harris, *Catholic Church and the Foundation of the Northern Irish State*, p. 68
23. A. Rhodes, *The Power of Rome in the Twentieth Century: The Vatican in the Age of Liberal Democracies* (London: Hodder and Stoughton, 1983), p. 242.
24. Amigo to Whiteside, 4 February 1918, A.A.L., Correspondence 1874–1929 (A).
25. Pollard, *Unknown Pope*, p. 123.
26. Rhodes, *Power of Rome*, p. 242.
27. Quoted in Biggs-Davison and Chowdharay-Best, *Cross of Saint Patrick*, p. 321.
28. *Manchester Guardian*, 1 May 1918.
29. *The Catholic Herald*, 11 May 1918.
30. W. S. Lilly to Stuart Coats, 24 May 1918, D.A.A., Gasquet Papers, File 889.
31. James Britten to Mark Sykes, 16 June 1918, B.J.L., Mark Sykes Papers, DDSY(2)/1/38.
32. Amigo to Archbishop Walsh, 3 May 1918, Dublin, Archives of the Archdiocese of Dublin (A.A.D.), Walsh Papers, 379/6.
33. G. Dwyer, *Diocese of Portsmouth Past and Present* (Portsmouth, 1981), pp. 88–103.
34. Cotter to Amigo, 13 February 1920, A.A.S., Amigo Papers, Correspondence with Bishops.
35. Ward, *Unfinished Business*, p. 106. The priest in question reassured Ward that if anymore such letters came from Bishop's House 'he would read them only in the evening at Benediction and announce in the morning what we had ahead of us' (pp. 106–7). See also Sheed, *Church and I*, p. 96.
36. Cotter to Amigo, 26 April 1918, A.A.S., Amigo Papers, Correspondence with Bishops.
37. A point made in Brown, *Through Windows of Memory*, p. 181.
38. J. Furnival and A. Knowles, *Archbishop Derek Worlock: His Personal Journey* (London: Geoffrey Chapman, 1999), p. 38.
39. Cotter to Amigo, 29 December 1920, A.A.S., Amigo Papers, Correspondence with Bishops.
40. Clifton, *Amigo*, preface.
41. Amigo to Lloyd George, 28 May 1918 (copy), A.A.S., Amigo Papers, J54A.
42. Clifton, *Amigo*, p. 71.
43. *The Tablet*, 18 May 1918.
44. Quoted in Clifton, *Amigo*, p. 73.
45. Amigo to Logue, 15 June 1918, Armagh, Armagh Archdiocesan Archive (A.A.A.), Logue Papers, Correspondence with European Bishops; Logue to Amigo, 21 August 1918, A.A.S., Amigo Papers, Correspondence with Bishops.

46. Casartelli to Whiteside, 1 May 1918 (copy); Casartelli to Logue, 10 May 1918 (copy), Sal.D.A., Casartelli Papers, Box 163.
47. Casartelli to Keating, 18 November 1917 (copy), ibid., Box 162.
48. Casartelli to Whiteside, 14 March 1912 (copy), ibid., Box 159.
49. Bossy, *English Catholic Community*, p. 334.
50. Other branches of the Federation followed Salford's lead: *The Catholic Herald*, 18 May 1918.
51. Bishop Casartelli's Diary, 3 May 1918, Sal.D.A., Casartelli Papers.
52. Casartelli to Fr O'Kelly, 3 May 1918 (copy), ibid., Box 163.
53. Dunn to Gasquet, 3 May 1918, D.A.A., Gasquet Papers, File 874.
54. Cotter to Amigo, 17 May 1918, A.A.S., Amigo Papers, Correspondence with Bishops.
55. H. S. Dean was no admirer of the Catholic Union. 'I have to write next week on the 50th anniversary of the Catholic Union, and shall be as nasty as I dare': H. S. Dean to Burton, 24 January 1921, Bristol, Clifton Diocesan Archives (C.D.A.), Burton Papers.
56. *The Tablet*, 6 July 1918.
57. J. S. Franey to Gasquet, 5 January 1920, D.A.A., Gasquet Papers, File 889.
58. See D. A. Bellenger, 'Cardinal Gasquet (1846–1929): An English Roman', *Recusant History*, 24 (October 1999), 552–60. Gasquet is thought to have used his influence in the Vatican against the Irish: Keogh, *Vatican, the Bishops and Irish Politics*, pp. 16–18.
59. Gasquet to J. S. Franey , 16 January 1920, D.A.A., Gasquet Papers, File 889.
60. Gasquet to Lord Denbigh, 16 July 1914, Warwick, Warwickshire County Record Office, Feilden MSS, CR 2017/C681.
61. H. S. Dean to Burton, 14 May 1918, C.D.A., Burton Papers.
62. For Sykes's career see R. Adelson, *Mark Sykes: Portrait of an Amateur* (London: Jonathan Cape, 1975). See also Cannadine, *Decline and Fall*, pp. 382–3.
63. Mark Sykes to James Britten, 5 July 1918, B.J.L., Mark Sykes Papers, DDSY(2)/1/38.
64. H[ouse] of C[ommons] Deb[ate], 25 June 1918, 107, 923
65. Ibid., 951–54. See also Amigo to Curzon, 21 June 1918 (copy); Amigo to Mark Sykes, 25 June 1918; Mark Sykes to Amigo, 26 June 1918 (copy), B.J.L., Mark Sykes Papers, DDSY(2)/1/38. The correspondence shows that Sykes was responding to Amigo's request for information regarding the authority of Lord Curzon's statement.
66. H C Deb. 25 June 1918, 107, 951–54
67. Dunn to Amigo, 30 March 1917, Nottingham, Nottingham Diocesan Archives (Not.DA), Dunn Papers.
68. Archbishop Keating's Diary of his Visit to Rome, 9 May 1920, A.A.L., Keating Papers.
69. Ward, *Insurrection versus Resurrection*, pp. 114–6; S. Foster, 'A Bishop for Essex: Bernard Ward and the Diocese of Brentwood', *Recusant History*, 21 (October 1993), 556–71.

70. Quoted in D. Gwynn, 'The Irish Immigration' in Beck (ed.), *English Catholics*, p. 270.
71. Ward, *Unfinished Business*, p.104.
72. Fielding, *Class and Ethnicity*, p. 41.
73. 'I have found any numbers of Milner's letters: but not much else of moment': Ward to Fr Parkinson, 21 September 1910, O.C.A., Fr Parkinson Papers.
74. Ward to Walsh, September 1910, A.A.D., Walsh Papers, 382/7.
75. Ward to Walsh, 19 December 1911, ibid., 376/5.
76. Ward, *Insurrection versus Resurrection*, pp. 405–11.
77. Keating to Amigo, 31 March 1917, Amigo Papers, Correspondence with Bishops.
78. For papers relating to this see A.A.W., Bourne Papers, Bo. 5/48a.
79. Geoffrey Butler to Colville Barclay, 7 October 1918, London, Public Record Office (P.R.O.), F.O. 115, 2398, fos. 107–8. Geoffrey Butler, a Cambridge historian, occupied the position of director of the British Bureau of Information. Colville Barclay was *Chargé d'Affaires* at the British Embassy in Washington.
80. Despatch by Colville Barclay to the Foreign Office, 15 October 1918, ibid., fos. 125–6.
81. Mgr A. P. Barnes to Colville Barclay, 9 November 1918, ibid., fo. 151.
82. Despatch by Colville Barclay to the Foreign Office, 15 October 1918, ibid., fo. 153.
83. *New York World*, 20 October 1918. From Keating's cuttings file, A.A.L., Keating Papers.
84. *Gaelic American*, 28 October 1918.
85. *New York World*, 20 October 1918.
86. F. Keating, 'Impressions of Catholic America', *Dublin Review*, 164 (April – June 1919), 182.
87. *New York Times*, 25 October 1918.
88. Keating to Shane Leslie, 30 August 1919, N.L.I., Shane Leslie Papers, MS 22, 838, Acc 3669.
89. R. F. Foster, *Modern Ireland 1600–1972* (London: Allen Lane, 1988), p. 498.
90. Boyce, *Englishmen and Irish Troubles*, p. 77.
91. B. A. Santamaria, *Daniel Mannix* (Carlton. Ashford [Middx]: Melbourne University Press, 1984), p. 106; Keogh, *Vatican, the Bishops and Irish Politics*, p. 48.
92. Ibid.
93. *The Catholic Herald*, 27 December 1919.
94. The British government in its handling of Ireland had given in to the 'very Prussianism we set out to destroy': Burton to Archbishop Walsh, 31 December 1918, A.A.D., Walsh Papers, 379/6.
95. Burton to Amigo, 7 December 1920, A.A.S., Amigo Papers, Correspondence with Bishops
96. There is a copy of this letter in C.D.A., Burton Papers.

97. Dunn to Amigo, 9 November 1920, A.A.S., Amigo Papers, Correspondence with Bishops.
98. Quoted in Mews, 'Hunger Strike of the Lord Mayor of Cork', p. 396.
99. Quoted in ibid., p. 395.
100. Fr Baston to Canon Jackman, 28 April 1921, A.A.W., Bourne Papers.
101. Keogh, *Vatican, the Bishops and Irish Politics*, p. 51.
102. Dunn to Amigo, 9 November 1920, A.A.S., Amigo Papers, Correspondence with Bishops.
103. Cotter to Amigo, 26 November 1920, ibid.
104. Santamaria, *Mannix*, p. 118.
105. D. W. Miller, *Church, State and Nation in Ireland 1898–1921* (Dublin: Gill and Macmillan, 1973), p. 461.
106. Amigo to Lloyd George, 27 September 1920, A.A.S., Amigo Papers, J54A.
107. Keogh, *Vatican, the Bishops and Irish Politics*, pp. 51–6.
108. Mews, 'Hunger Strike of the Lord Mayor of Cork', pp. 397–8.
109. Ibid, pp. 391.
110. Mathew, *Catholicism in England*, p. 236.
111. One of Vaughan's war-time speeches which, his biographer notes, 'raised even in England a storm of indignation', referred to a duty 'to keep on killing Germans': C. C. Martindale, *Bernard Vaughan, S. J.* (London: Longmans and Co., 1923), pp. 195–7.
112. Amigo to Marchant, 2 October 1920 (copy), A.A.S., Amigo Papers, J54A.
113. H. S. Dean to Amigo, 9 September 1920, ibid.
114. Ilsley eventually resigned on 15 January 1921.
115. *The Venerabile* (April 1935).
116. *Birmingham and District Catholic Magazine*, August 1920 and November 1920.
117. Fr T. O'Connell to Burton, 7 December 1920, C.D.A., Burton Papers.
118. Burton to Fr T. O'Connell, 8 December 1920, ibid.
119. Clifton, *Amigo*, p. 77.
120. Amigo to Rowland Wedgewood, 28 October 1920, A.A.S., Amigo Papers, J54A
121. Major Edgecombe to Amigo, 26 October 1920, ibid.
122. Quoted in Mews, 'Hunger Strike of the Lord Mayor of Cork', p. 394.
123. Cotter to Amigo, 26 November 1921, A.A.S., Amigo Papers, Correspondence with Bishops.
124. Keogh, *Vatican, the Bishops and Irish Politics*, p. 56.
125. Martindale, *Plater*, p. 307.
126. Henry Somerville to Bourne, 20 October 1920, A.A.W., Bourne Papers, Bo.5/36a.
127. Henry Somerville to Bourne, 20 October 1920; Fr Plater to Edward Eyre, 31 August 1920, A.A.W., Bourne Papers, Bo.5/36a.
128. Ibid.
129. Bourne to Edward Eyre, 8 September 1920, ibid.
130. Henry Somerville to Bourne, 20 October 1920, ibid.

131. Boyce, *Englishmen and Irish Troubles*, esp. pp. 123–5.
132. *The Tablet*, 13 November 1920.
133. *The Times*, 12 November 1920.
134. Ibid., 15 November 1920; *The Catholic Herald*, 20 November 1920.
135. Bourne to Archbishop Byrne, 19 September 1929, A.A.D., Byrne Papers, Foreign Bishops File.
136. Oldmeadow, *Bourne*, II, p. 180.
137. Ibid., p. 181.
138. Mews, 'Hunger Strike of the Lord Mayor of Cork', p. 397.
139. *The Catholic Herald*, 4 December 1920.
140. A reference to General Crozier, the commander of the auxiliaries, who resigned after his superior, General Tudor, overturned his decision to dismiss twenty-six cadets for looting.
141. Brown to Cotter, 26 February 1921, Por.D.A., Cotter Papers, 6.05.29
142. Heenan, *Crown of Thorns*, p. 24.
143. *Universe*, 19 November 1920.
144. Bishop Dunn's Advent *Pastoral Letter* of 1920, Not.D.A.
145. Burton to Amigo, 7 December 1920, A.A.S., Amigo Papers, Correspondence with Bishops.
146. F. Mason, 'The Newer Eve: The Catholic Women's Suffrage Society in England, 1911–1923', *Catholic Historical Review*, 72 (October 1986), 620–38.
147. *The Catholic Herald*, 25 December 1920.
148. Ibid., 4 December 1920.
149. Dunn to Amigo, 2 December 1920, A.A.S., Amigo Papers, Correspondence with Bishops.
150. Amigo to Burton, 6 December 1920, C.D.A., Burton Papers. See also Amigo to Dunn, 2 December 1920, N.D.A., Dunn Papers.
151. Ibid.; See also Amigo to Gasquet, 25 February 1920, D.A.A., Gasquet Papers, File 917a.: 'He [Bourne] is very friendly with Lloyd George but I am sorry he trusts the Prime Minister who will use him without helping us'.
152. *The Catholic Herald*, 5 March 1921.
153. James Britten to Burton, 8 December 1920, C.D.A., Burton Papers.
154. *The Catholic Herald,* 27 November 1920.
155. Dunn to Amigo, 2 December 1920, A.A.S., Amigo Papers, Correspondence with Bishops.
156. *The Catholic Herald*, 18 December 1920.
157. *The Tablet*, 18 December 1920.
158. Keating to Burton, 16 January 1921, C.D.A., Burton Papers.
159. Burton to Amigo, 7 December 1920, Amigo Papers, Correspondence with Bishops.
160. From a press cutting held in A.A.W., Bourne Papers, Bo. 1/72, dated 10 April 1921.
161. Dunn to the Canons, 2 November 1920, Not.D.A., *Acta.*; Fr O'Doherty to Burton, 2 November 1920, C.D.A., Burton Papers; MacRory to Amigo, 3 March 1921, A.A.S., Amigo Papers,

Correspondence with Bishops; *Ad Clerum*, 8 October 1920, B.A.A., *Acta*.

162. Casartelli to Bourne, 10 January 1921, A.A.W., Bourne Papers, Bo. 5/36a.
163. Bourne to Casartelli, 11 January 1921, ibid.
164. Harris, *Catholic Church and the Foundation of the Northern Irish State*, p. 90.
165. P. Hart, ' 'Operations Abroad': The IRA in Britain, 1919–23', *English Historical Review*, 65 (February 2000), 75. Fitzpatrick minimises the role of the ISDL in 'A curious middle place', pp. 43–4. See also Fielding, *Class and Ethnicity*, p. 102.
166. *The Tablet*, 9 February 1921.
167. For a good treatment of the Church's response to Fenianism, with much material on Manning, see O. P. Rafferty, *The Church, the State and the Fenian Threat 1861–75* (London: MacMillan, 1999), esp. chps 4 and 5. See also E. R. Norman, *The Catholic Church and Ireland in the Age of Rebellion* (London: Longmans, Green and Co, 1965).
168. *The Times*, 15 February 1921.
169. Oldmeadow, *Bourne*, II, p. 182.
170. *Daily News*, 19 March 1921. Press cutting held in Irish File, A.A.S.
171. Amigo to Gasquet, 16 March 1921, D.A.A., Gasquet Papers, File 917a.
172. Dunn to Amigo, 29 December 1920, A.A.S., Amigo Papers, Correspondence with Bishops.
173. Keating to Amigo, 29 March 1921, ibid.
174. Meeting of the Bishops, 4–6 April 1921, A.A.W., *Acta*.
175. Cotter to Amigo, 1 April 1921, A.A.S, Correspondence with Bishops.
176. Meeting of the Bishops, 4–6 April 1921, A.A.W., *Acta*.
177. *The Catholic Herald*, 7 April 1921.
178. Talbot's appointment was badly received in Ireland. 'Logue, when asked for his comment on the appointment, said that he received it in the same manner as he would the appointment of a Catholic hangman': O. P. Rafferty, *Catholicism in Ulster 1603–1983* (London: Hurst and Co., 1994), 209. Papers relating to Lord Edmund Talbot's role in Ireland can be found in H.L.R.O., Lloyd George Papers, F/17/2/7–28.
179. Lord Edmund Talbot to Bourne, 6 April 1921, A.A.W., Bourne Papers, Bo. 1/72.
180. Quoted in Bell, *Davidson*, II, p. 1064.
181. It was signed by Lord Denbigh, Lord Edmund Talbot, James Hope, Sir Henry Jerningham, Lord Walter Kerr, Lord Lovant, Lord Stafford and Lord Crichton Stuart.
182. A Confidential Memorandum sent to Gasquet, July 1923, D.A.A., Gasquet Papers, File 889.

3

Social Reconstruction and the Labour Party Question 1918–1924

The acute sense of dislocation felt in the aftermath of the war provoked a fresh outburst of interest amongst the churches in the social question. Anxiety about the collapse of the existing social and economic order, as much as enthusiasm for social change, was the inspiration. Many feared that Bolshevism was on an unstoppable march across Europe, and everywhere the traditional landmarks of stable, hierarchical society were being uprooted. Others welcomed the possibilities of social reconstruction and the creation of a more equal, just society.

The Catholic Church in England did not remain unaffected by these currents. Bourne's 1918 pastoral letter, *The Nation's Crisis*, exemplified the greater sense of commitment to the public realm – the very choice of title betokened a broadening of the Church's responsibilities, a sense of a mission to the nation. The sorts of questions which had previously preoccupied the relatively small number of Catholics who joined the CSG were now to the front of the Church's agenda as it attempted to assert itself in national life. That there was a less defensive mood about the Church in these years is shown by the participation of Catholics, with the encouragement of Bourne, in the initial stages of the Conference of Christian Politics, Economics and Citizenship (COPEC), the great inter-church contribution to social reconstruction. There were some bishops who did not share Bourne's expansive confidence and vision of a socially progressive Church at ease with the wider society. Furthermore, there were factors which inhibited the development of the populist agenda adumbrated in *The Nation's Crisis*. The education question, as ever, dispersed energies. Irish troubles, as I have shown, introduced a divisive element into the Church. Furthermore, serious discord between Bourne and the bishops, which the historian cannot ignore, created a climate unpropitious for greater corporate effort.

Contemporaneous with Bourne's elevation to the cardinalate in November 1911, the apostolic constitution *Si Qua Est* created two new ecclesiastical provinces with archbishoprics at Liverpool and Birmingham. (Bourne had also hoped that his pre-eminence would be recognized by the title of 'primate', but this the Holy See refused although certain prerogatives were formally recognized.[1]) Bourne envisaged that a consequence of the creation of new provinces would be the corresponding increase in the number of dioceses. He was convinced that the only way the Church could expand was if more dioceses were created, and was encouraged in this view by Merry del Val, Secretary of State, who believed 'Catholic evangelization in England ... deficient or stagnant in many parts'.[2] In view of the subsequent controversy surrounding the plan to divide the dioceses, Oldmeadow takes great pains to demonstrate that this was an idea that originated in Rome and was not the personal campaign of Bourne.[3] However, the personal element clouded the issue. When it became known that the proposals included the creation of one London diocese and a new diocese of Brighton at the expense of Southwark, the suspicion grew amongst the bishops that Bourne's motive was to rid himself of a troublesome neighbour – Amigo – and to aggrandize his position over the English Church. Casartelli told Amigo as early as January 1912 that the English bishops 'are coming to feel that, in one sense, your cause is theirs'.[4] Keating was also sensitive that the the status of English bishops vis-à-vis Westminster was becoming precarious, but whilst declaring himself to be 'strongly opposed to an aggravated form being perpetuated of what seems to have been the autocratic policy of past Archbishops of Westminster', he was at least reassured that *Si Qua Est* 'expressly prescribes that, in *civil* matters, Westminster is to be our spokesman, but only our spokesman ...'[5] It was not until 1916 (the year in which Bourne became a full member of the Consistorial Congregation), when further plans were revealed which involved the division of Northampton to create a new see centred on Cambridge, the separation of Essex from Westminster (which occurred when the diocese of Brentwood was created in 1917),[6] and the separation of Kent from Southwark, that feeling against Bourne became more widespread and intense.

Bourne pursued his goal to create more dioceses with unrelenting vigour in the early part of 1917. 'Change and separation are the law and condition of all development and progress on this earth', he stated pointedly in his allocution on the occasion of the creation of the diocese of Brentwood.[7] Bourne was away in Rome for much of the early part of 1917 and this extended stay created apprehension at home – with some justification the bishops feared that questions of ecclesiastical jurisdiction would be decided over their heads. Keating confided to Bishop Ward that 'Whenever His Eminence goes to Rome for his frequent and prolonged stays, we are always on tenter-hooks, knowing from past experience that some project disturbing our peace, about which we have heard nothing except the gossip that trickles to England, will be sprung upon us as a fait accompli or so far advanced that we can scarcely expect more than a formal hearing'.[8] What comes through strongly in the episcopal papers is the bishops' sense of impotence in the face of Roman authority. 'Inarticulate' was a word some bishops used to describe their condition.[9] Although Bourne was the object of much hostile criticism, was there not also underlying this a sense of a wider grievance against the Holy See's modus operandi in matters affecting the English Church? As one would expect, such feelings, if they existed, remained latent. In a letter to Merry del Val, Casartelli referred to the bishops' 'natural shyness and diffidence at addressing the Holy See or the Sacred Congregation, based I suppose on an innate reverence for authority'.[10]

These stirrings of disaffection crystallized at a meeting, held in Bourne's absence, at Oscott College on 11 March 1917. The meeting had been called by Bourne's suffragans, but was attended by bishops from other provinces, amongst them the Archbishops of Liverpool and Birmingham. Keating had become increasingly vexed about the use of 'un-English Roman procedure'[11] in matters affecting the English bishops: what was at stake, he stressed to Ward, 'was *not* the policy of subdivision, but the policy of consulting the Hierarchy as a whole, and individual members individually so far as they may be individually affected, before such proposals are launched'.[12] The 'temper of the meeting was a most painful one', Dunn told Gasquet, 'It almost amounts to a scandal, and it is a grievous pity that the Cardinal of Westminster should *despise* all the other Bishops in the land ... just at a time when it is so important that we should all be working in harmony together! I'm not *angry* with him, but I am unutterably saddened. Can't you muzzle him!'[13] The resolution which was passed voiced the bishops' 'strong conviction that the subdivisions of the diocese of this country will be detrimental to religion in England', urging 'the Holy Father not to allow even the first steps to be taken in such an undertaking until the Hierarchy of England has been heard'.[14] The Oscott resolution, Keating explained to Ward, was a demand that 'a more English method be followed'.[15] Archbishop Whiteside explained the significance of Oscott to Ward as the occasion 'when at last the Bishops who had been so long inarticulate as a body, spoke their minds on the whole policy. After such a declaration, the Holy See will no longer push the sub-division theory.'[16]

Relations after Oscott were at their nadir. Bourne protested to Amigo that 'no one is entitled to call, or to preside at a meeting of my suffragans without my knowledge or consent',[17] and even talked of resigning,[18] though this was a threat, according to Amigo, he frequently made when he felt slighted.[19] With inhibitions released, the Low Week meeting held on 17–18 April was focused directly, as Dunn put it, on the 'whole attitude H[is] E[minence] has seen fit to take up – treating Bishops, as he treats everyone else, as so much dirt under his feet'.[20] Casartelli recorded in his diary that the meeting was 'rather painful' with some 'very strong speaking'.[21] Bourne appeared to concur with a resolution which stated that in matters affecting the English bishops there should be prior consultation by the Holy See, but the drafting of this created the impression that Bourne was committed to nothing more than transmitting the Oscott resolution to Rome, the content of which the Holy See had already been made aware of by telegram. Bishop Ward had taken the minutes of the Low Week meeting, but as he was regarded as close to Bourne the suspicion grew that 'some other hand' had censored the draft.[22] Ward reassured Keating on this point, but added that whilst he sympathized with all he said about 'un-English Roman procedure' he did not see that this would be improved by sending up resolutions and suspected that things would go on very much as before.[23] Subsequent events tended to support Ward. In November 1924 the diocese of Lancaster was created by the division of Liverpool and Hexham and Newcastle; Keating, Archbishop of Liverpool from 1921, was to claim that he had received a pledge in July 1922 from Cardinal de Lai, Merry del Val's successor as Secretary of State, that because of the financial burdens of the Cathedral project and the diocesan seminary at Upholland the proposed division would be put on hold,[24] and that his first knowledge of the new diocese was when he received the papal Bull.[25] 'I have received bad treatment, having had my diocesan and metropolitan rights absolutely ignored', he told Amigo.[26] To Cardinal de Lai he complained of 'broken faith'.[27] Although the strength of feeling in 1917 did persuade the Holy See to postpone plans to divide the dioceses, it is ironic that one of the effects of this successful assertion of episcopal pressure may have been to encourage in the Holy See an even greater stealth in its dealings with the English bishops, as the Lancaster case was to illustrate.

The frank airing of differences did not lead to an improvement in the domestic situation. Bourne stubbornly carried on with his project to divide the dioceses, even though attitudes in Rome were turning against him as surely as they were at home.[28] Bishops spoke of Bourne in the most savage terms. Keating thought him an 'autocrat of the most Prussian type, who consults noone but himself and wishes to stifle all opinion opposed to his own'.[29] Dunn thought Bourne 'an autocratic spirit much stronger than Manning's'.[30] 'Although he has many admirable qualities, we all know that openness and frankness are not amongst them. He is ... what they call in Rome a "politicone"', he remarked to Amigo, 'and a dark horse and a lover of secrecy for its own sake at that.'[31] Cotter described him as a 'bad judge of men'.[32] 'He is a strange mentality', Amigo told Ward, 'He wants something and discovers it is the will of God.'[33] The manner of Bourne's chairmanship of the Low Week meeting was a common cause of frustration. 'All deplore the attitude of His Eminence towards the Bishops', Amigo told Dunn, 'The meetings, with him in the chair, are useless as they say that he has made his mind up about matters beforehand and will not abide by the wishes of the rest.'[34] He forged only one close link amongst the bishops; that was with Richard Collins, Bishop of Hexham and Newcastle, a contemporary at Ushaw, who before the afternoon session of the hierarchy's Low Week meeting was always invited to share the Cardinal's room for a little repose: 'Sit there, Dick, and put your feet up on the chair', Bourne would tell him.[35] (Rather different was Keating's response to the offer of Bourne's hospitality: 'will you invite me instead?', he begged Amigo.[36]) The atmosphere of mutual recrimination was at its peak during the period under consideration and it was clearly a factor which inhibited common causes.

The lack of a coherent and united response to H. A. L. Fisher's Education Bill, first introduced in August 1917 then again in 1918 after a false start, added to the sense of disaffection. Bourne came under fire for his perceived indifference to the cause of denominational education. Despite Fisher's assurances that the Bill would leave the dual system of 1902 untouched,[37] there were still concerns amongst the episcopate, especially in the north, that the appointment and control of teachers in Catholic schools would be handed over entirely to the local authorities.[38] If the 'whole situation had changed since the days of Mr. Birrell's Education Bill',[39] it was news to Casartelli. As ever, it was he who led the sabre-rattling, seeing every measure of educational reform in apocalyptic terms, as bringing the 'ruin of our Catholic schools'. He urged Bourne to mobilise the clergy and laity in an opposition on the scale of 1906.[40] But the ground had shifted since 1906. Bourne was unwilling to countenance popular agitation during wartime. Furthermore, his political adviser Lord Edmund Talbot pursued a number of concessions but was on the whole satisfied with the Bill and could not understand the opposition from the north.[41] Unlike 1906 there was no united voice. Significantly, the Catholic teaching profession had its own ideas about what was best for the future of the Catholic schools, and these views did not always mesh with those of the episcopate. The CTF,[42] founded in 1907 and led by a Manchester teacher W. O'Dea, mainly welcomed the proposals; like other professional associations of teachers, it had much to gain through the Bill because of its emphasis on the supply and training of teachers.[43] In contrast with the intransigence that usually characterized the hierarchy's stance, the CTF appeared as a voice of moderation, as for instance when it expressed the hope, to Casartelli's chagrin, that 'Catholics would not unnecessarily raise the religious question'.[44] Casartelli saw it as an attempt by a lay 'clique' to determine a policy which was the sole responsibility of the hierarchy.[45]

Casartelli's sense of disenchantment grew as it became more obvious that the Catholic hierarchy was becoming a marginal voice in educational debate. They had always been able to rely upon the Church of England's equally committed championship of the denominational schools, even if it was not always as intransigent. But when, after his Bill had been given the Royal Assent on 8 August 1918, Fisher set himself to settling the religious problem once and for all, it appeared that the Catholic bishops would have to stand alone. As Bell notes, 'There was a far more cordial feeling between the representatives of the different churches'.[46] But no Catholics were present at the gathering of church leaders invited by Fisher in July 1919 to discuss the issue. A consensus emerged at this meeting: the existing dual system would be replaced by a national system; the appointment and dismissal of teachers would be placed in the hands of the local education authorities; there would be statutory provision for religious instruction from suitably trained teachers in all elementary schools. Fisher's proposals were outlined in public for the first time in March 1920, and were embodied in a Private Member's Bill in 1921. The Catholic response was negative, as Fisher had expected. The safeguards for religious instruction were regarded as inadequate. (In the event, with the end of the post-war boom in 1922 and the so-called Geddes axe, measures for educational reform were suspended and the dual system remained.) Bourne's lack of firm leadership and command of the issue during the course of the negotiations frustrated his fellow bishops. When news leaked out that he had met Fisher in private in March 1920,[47] his critics leapt on what they saw as another example of his secrecy and underhand behaviour.[48] Bourne's long bout of illness in 1920, which made him unwilling to call a meeting of the bishops, was spreading further disaffection.[49] So disheartened was Casartelli by the hierarchy's 'acquiescent silence and apparent apathy'; by the question constantly raised by clergy and laity, 'Why don't the Bishops guide us as in former times?'; by his own lack of 'ability to grapple with the situation any longer', that he began to contemplate resignation.[50] 'It is painful to be told by our clergy ... that we Bishops have abdicated our leadership and let it go by default to the schoolmasters', Casartelli lamented to Ilsley.[51] As John Coventry noted, it was in the teaching profession that lay autonomy first took hold, as its own professional standards and expertise developed;[52] the assumption that this body could simply be mobilized at the behest of the hierarchy was no longer a credible one. With the religious question of less import in the determination of and the response to post-war educational measures, the role and attitudes of the bishops were, as Casartelli dolefully acknowledged, of increasingly marginal significance.

* * *

Casartelli's feeling of impotence in the face of social change was one attitude, but not the dominant one, amongst the episcopate in the post-war years. Catholics shared in the 'high religious hopes of a better society'.[53] Anxiety and fear were not the only responses. The post-war years found Catholics willing to assert their presence more vigorously in national life and to take their part in the work of social reconstruction (albeit they were negative in the field of education). Anti-Catholic and anti-clerical prejudice was breaking down, which was in large part due to the courageous witness of Catholic military chaplains, who, unlike their higher-class Anglican counterparts, found it easier to mix socially with the ordinary soldier.[54] Amongst the episcopate there was a greater interest in social and political questions after the war. This was partly as a consequence of anxieties about the rise of socialism, but also because they were increasingly aware, as they had perhaps been slow to grasp before, that the success and progress of the Church was bound up with the poorer classes. Unlike the other churches they already had a strong presence amongst the working class: now was the time to exploit this fact.

The demand for a more effective witness to the nation prompted calls for institutional structures appropriate to the situation. The lack of internal cohesion, accentuated by personal animosities and rivalries, troubled many of the bishops. Amigo informed Cardinal Gasquet that 'we have the new Code which needs special attention and there are questions regarding both Primary and Secondary Education to be carefully considered ... there are social problems in abundance and also ways of helping poorer dioceses which should be dealt with'.[55] He believed that there needed to be greater consultation and more coordinated episcopal action, suggesting 'an Emergency Committee of the Hierarchy on the lines of the Irish one',[56] a reference to the standing committee of the Irish bishops which enabled senior members of the hierarchy to meet on a more regular basis and to discuss matters demanding urgent attention. Incoherence and lack of direction were also perceived by Casartelli: 'We are already developing separate 'provincial' policies, and in some matters, e. g. education, this process may become serious'.[57] It was a view echoed by Bishop Doubleday of Brentwood, who observed to Dunn, an astringent critic of Westminster's high-handed methods who argued persistently for a standing committee system as a counterweight: 'At present each bishop is a law unto himself, and though no doubt this tells for the good of the Church in England, much confusion and wasted energy would be avoided if there were centralised discussion and decision'.[58]

Behind these calls for institutional change lay a fair amount of personal animosity towards Bourne, who was seen as increasingly detached from the hierarchy and underhand in his dealings. There were other factors: the feeling amongst the bishops that they had allowed themselves to be sidelined over the schools question, and that they had not given the same strong lead as in the past, was extremely discomforting to those who had agitated against the Liberal bills of 1906–8. There is a sense that for bishops such as Casartelli the ability to defend the schools was their most important task, the touchstone of episcopal authority. More positively, the greater stress placed by the bishops on social questions from the late 1910s and the generally optimistic view of the future for Catholicism in England encouraged some of the less parochially-minded to consider ways in which the bishops as a corporate body could become a more visible presence in national life.

As ever, it was Keating who was encouraging his brother bishops to become more outward-looking. His range of concerns, social and political, regularly took him out of the diocese and gave him a stronger sense of the Church's mission to the nation. His name was frequently mentioned in connection with high ecclesiastical office, as in 1917 when there was talk of Archbishop Ilsley of Birmigham resigning on the grounds of ill-health. (In order to relieve the burden, John McIntyre was made Auxiliary Bishop in August 1917.) Keating dismissed such talk in a letter to Amigo in December 1917:

> I have no ambition but to be left alone. Northampton suits me down to the ground: no 'curia' to interfere between me and my clergy: no seminary to empty the till and add to my cares: no endless confirmations, ordinations and visitations: but just enough to keep me from rusticating at home and the whole of England from my surplus energy! Does

the old goose envy his domesticated relative? Therefore don't talk to me of Archbishoprics and such like vanities. Not being consciously a prodigal, why should I want to 'go back'?[59]

Yet his translation to the see of Liverpool in 1921 was evidence that the Holy See was now looking for more than mere administrative prowess in its senior appointments. It is worth noting that shortly after Keating's death in 1928, Merry del Val, who boasted of influence in the matter of episcopal appointments,[60] said that a successor to Keating was needed who would 'be acceptable and equal to that high and important office, not only for local needs but also in view of the position and prestige in England generally'.[61] This was not a note struck at the time of Bourne's appointment to Westminster when the emphasis was on diocesan rather than national needs, and suggests, perhaps, that for the most important sees candidates were identified who possessed the qualities and outlook that would speak to a democratic and increasingly secular world. Keating certainly fitted the bill.

Foreign travel played its part in broadening Keating's outlook. He was a keen observer of social conditions in the places he visited, as, for instance, when he wandered through the poorest, most overcrowded and insanitary parts of Naples in April 1920, and recorded the impression 'that Socialism was almost a natural result'.[62] His 1918 visit to America for the golden jubilee of Cardinal Gibbons's episcopate provided an opportunity to survey developments in American social Catholicism at first-hand, and gave him a fresh perspective on the English scene. (He was, for instance, confronted with the unpleasant truth that the English Catholic leadership – lay and clerical – was viewed by substantial parts of American Catholicism as the enemy of Ireland.) Keating was especially enthused by the movement in the American Church to more corporate activity on social questions. The formation, in 1917, of the National Catholic War Council (which later became the National Catholic Welfare Conference) was a response to the perceived lack of unified direction in the public activities of the Church, and was conceived as a way of bringing the Church's influence to bear more effectively on the pressing social issues of the day.[63] Despite the anxieties of those who saw the project as threatening the rights of the bishop as the supreme arbiter of affairs in his own diocese, and the grudging acceptance of this institutional innovation by Rome, the National Catholic Welfare Conference did succeed in becoming a vehicle 'for far less parochial, more general political activity on the part of the hierarchy'.[64] Clearly the idea appealed to Keating, as he made the need for more corporate episcopal activity a theme of his war-time and post-war pastoral letters and addresses. The pastoral letter he wrote shortly after his return from America asked whether some means could not be devised whereby the 'three or four hundred English-speaking bishops' would not only 'rule each his own flock, but ... formulate a common policy of social and individual reconstruction on frankly Christian lines'.[65] Developments closer to home may also have influenced Keating's thinking: the creation of the Church Assembly by the Enabling Act in 1919, for instance, facilitated greater corporate effort in the Church of England, encouraging hopes that religious influence could be brought to bear more effectively on social and political questions.[66]

But despite the calls for more unified action there were no changes made to the existing system in the post-war years. Bourne's troubled relations with the episcopate was to render him suspicious of projects which appeared to challenge his pre-eminence. In a letter to Archbishop Whiteside, Dunn remarked of Bourne: 'I know he is difficult to move. I know he is instinctively against things which are not his own 'conceits' ... he is apt to be touchy and to look on any initiative except his own as the work of an enemy bent on discrediting him.'[67] Personal differences were one factor, but the more ambitious social programme envisaged by Keating, involving cooperation across the national hierarchies, would hardly have recommended itself to Rome. Although the American Church managed to keep hold of its coordinating agency in the face of considerable opposition from within the Roman Curia, the idea of episcopal collegiality savoured too much of Gallicanism to be encouraged by a centralising and Romanising papacy. Indeed, the scope for national hierarchies to act in concert was diminished in this period by the greater stress placed by the papacy on the *ad limina* visit, and which meant, at least in theory, that individual bishops could settle the problems of their diocese together with the Roman congregations, and which tended to obviate the need for discussions at the local level.[68] During an audience with Benedict XV at the time of the diocesan division controversy, Bishop Dunn was told that 'nothing could possibly be more advantageous for due diocesan administration than that local ordinaries should be in continual communication with him. He said that in a short personal interview more could be done than by months of correspondence and he added, significantly, that there would be less possibility of misunderstanding.' The Pope told Dunn to 'let this desire of his be made known to Bishops'. Cardinal de Lai later stressed that 'the local Ordinary was the Chief Official with whom the Holy see wished to deal in all diocesan matters'.[69]

The impression of a Church leadership turned in on itself, endlessly bickering, is hard to avoid – but it was not the whole story. The post-war years did see an upswing in the Church's concern with social questions. Although its leadership may not have spoken with one voice, it is possible to discern a more conciliatory attitude towards labour and a positive view of social reform. The fear of Bolshevism after 1917 was partly the reason for the appeal to moderate labour, although it is important also to note that some bishops were hardened further against socialism and the Labour Party as a consequence. In his Lenten pastoral letter of 1919, Casartelli stressed the threats to social order posed by projects for social reform and greater state activity. Class war was his great anxiety. Drawing attention to the 'terrible spectacle of chaos and rampant bloody disorder in Russia', Casartelli saw the present wave of industrial unrest – the immediate post-war period saw the police, railwaymen and Lancashire cotton operatives on strike – as a product of the 'same anti-Christian self-ishness'.[70] He was not alone in expounding this view. Keating told Gasparri: 'In their Lenten Pastorals, many of the Bishops adverted to the general state of social unrest, and to the terrible atrocities of the Bolsheviki in several European countries; and gravely warned against association with revolutionary socialism'.[71] For instance, Bishop Collins of Hexham and Newcastle asserted the rights of private property, warned against excessive state activity and inveighed against the false optimism which underpinned all projects of social reform. The inherent sin of mankind, Collins maintained, meant that 'They ... who promise to reconstruct all human institutions, in such wise as to eliminate all evil, are promising a vain thing'.[72] Such anxieties were also a feature of Keating's social thought: in a speech given at Manchester on 24 October 1921 he described society as 'like a volcano in eruption, trembling with frequent convulsions, emitting noxious vapours from huge fissures in all directions, and momentarily threatened by the burning lava of Bolshevism, the negation of all civilisation'.[73] This was explicit and violent language from one who generally took a more positive view of social reform than either Casartelli or Collins. But perhaps none of the bishops went as far as Fr F. Askew, a priest of the Nottingham diocese, in condemnation of modern class politics. Askew became interested in social questions whilst a student of Fr Parkinson's at Oscott and joined the CSG, writing regularly for the Birmingham diocese magazine on contemporary political issues.[74] His articles demonstrate very nicely the point that under the CSG umbrella many political views could be found. His attack on the coal miners who went on strike in October 1920 is worth quoting at length:

In any typical mining district ... the 'skilled labourers' have too little to think of save food, work, sleep and beer. The unutterable ugliness of these parts – the depressing effect of living like troglodytes – and of cooling one's heel between whiles (awaiting the next shift!) The complete absence of architecture, of verdure and of the refining and aesthetic influence of women (other than those who go about in shawls over their heads or in men's caps and overalls!). The banalities of clingy rows of sordid dwellings ... The racing and betting ... the many 'sluts' at home – who go 'dead off' after the first or second kiddy (fact!). These, and other such, influences tend to make the typical miner all too often a grumbling and grabbing and growsing fellow who knows precisely what he wants ultimately – and who would but have little *real joy* in life were his wages ten times what they were at the present moment

Urging restraint and 'mutual self sacrifice' he went on: 'The miner must work out his own salvation ... Not by dint of brutal and all too-recurrent strikes and hold-ups, but more by the sane and cogent cultivation of character ... When they have learned to wash their faces before going to the pub for the evening, there will be some remote chance of their taking a cleaner view of the intricate issues involved.'[75] Not surprisingly this was one of Askew's last contributions to the diocesan magazine. Illness forced an early retirement in 1920 and he spent the great part of his life (he died in 1962) in various 'retreat' homes.

Such vivid fears did not dispel the front of upbeat optimism which English Catholicism showed in the years following the war. Many believed, with Fr William Barry, the veteran author and theologian, that 'The Catholic Restoration must come'.[76] The Catholic Church appeared to stand for what was stable, unchanging and certain in a world where political structures and institutions had been overthrown, authority and hierarchy in social relations were shaken, and religious faith was losing its strength. Far from repelling, the uncompromising and authoritarian character of the Church was the main reason for its appeal in this period. Ronald Knox, the son of an Anglican bishop who Cardinal Heenan regarded as 'perhaps the greatest figure in the Church of the twentieth century',[77] was one of an illustrious band of converts who saw the Roman Catholic Church as the last bastion against Modernism and moral and social chaos. Conversions to Rome reached a peak in 1920 with 12,621,[78] but it was the prominence of some of these which encouraged sanguine hopes. Further grounds for optimism were offered by a revivified papacy. As John Pollard has argued, Benedict XV succeeded in rescuing the prestige of the papacy from the oblivion into which it descended during the reign of Pius X. Although excluded from the Versailles Peace Conference (which would at any rate have seriously compromised the Vatican's neutrality and its ability to give a moral lead) and the League of Nations, the diplomatic standing of the papacy was transformed by Benedict and it was once again, Pollard maintains, a force in international affairs.[79]

A mood of confidence and optimism pervaded Cardinal Bourne's public statements of the later 1910s, no more so than in his pastoral letter of 1918, *The Nation's Crisis*. Even the difficulties with his brother bishops did not dent this mood – he earned the unlikely sobriquet, 'The Cheerful Cardinal'.[80] Merry del Val, who was inclined to take a more pessimistic view of the Church's situation,[81] remarked to Fr J. Broadhead of Ushaw College: 'it seems strangely incongruous to speak of joy in these days . . . the flood of evil on every side is very distressing and I am at a loss to understand what Cardinal Bourne means when he speaks as if the world were better after the war from a religious standpoint. I am afraid the evidence is all the other way at present and it is no good closing our eyes to the facts.'[82] Yet Bourne was convinced that the war had opened up great possibilities for evangelization, that many previously hostile or indifferent were turning to the Church, and that it should be alert, therefore, to the new opportunities.[83] Bourne's project to divide the dioceses is usually mentioned only to illustrate his autocratic dealings and rivalries with his fellow bishops, but a more positive way of viewing it is that he saw an expanded episcopate as giving the Church a more solid basis and enabling it to become a more effective and visible presence in national life.

Bourne's *The Nation's Crisis* was a striking statement of this more assertive, less defensive vision. It was very much the product of the CSG, which in the post-war years was at the zenith of its influence. 'The Guild really promises to come into its own at last', Plater told Keating in July 1919. He reported that membership had almost doubled in a year, and cited the example of the St Dominic's Branch, Leicester, where ninety soldiers had been recruited in just a matter of weeks. The St Dominic's branch was organized from the Holy Cross Priory at Leicester, and was led by young Dominican priests such as John-Baptist Reeves, who provided comment on social questions in the *Blackfriars* journal, and Edwin Essex, who edited that journal for a short period in the mid-1920s; also based at Holy Cross in 1919 was Fr Theodore Bull, who as a very effective military chaplain in Gallipoli and France would have played a part in recruiting soldiers to the CSG.[84] In January 1921 the CSG launched a monthly journal, *The Christian Democrat*, and in that year also (in October) the Catholic Workers' College was opened as a sort of counterpart to Ruskin College, Oxford, so fulfilling Plater's long-standing commitment to the training of an elite of Catholic working men. (Sadly, Plater did not live to see the latter development: never a healthy individual he died on 21 January 1921 in Malta at the age of forty-five.) It seemed also that the CSG was beginning to win over the episcopate. Although Plater was to express a concern to Keating that some bishops appeared afraid of the CSG,[85] Bourne, importantly, was regarded as an enthusiast.[86] In 1917 Bourne approached Plater for his assistance with the writing of a pastoral letter on the social question,[87] who in turn drew on Leslie Toke's confidential letter on 'The Social Unrest' which had been sent to him in October of that year.

Toke's letter was Bellocian in spirit. 'The English have very nearly lost the instincts of a free people', he declared in a phrase which recalled Belloc's *Servile State* (1913). Toke, like Belloc, traced the social and economic dislocations of the age back to the Reformation and the 'robbery of church property'. His characterization of the political system relied heavily on Belloc's *Party System* (1911), the bitter fruit of the former Liberal MP's despondency with the party political gene,[88] and was similarly replete with references to the corruption and manipulative role of capitalist plutocrats, 'Jewish financiers' and 'alien money lenders'. Belloc's anti-semitism has been well documented,[89] but it interesting that Toke and, in the light of his endorsement of Toke's letter, Plater, who in many respects represented the progressive element in early twentieth-century English Catholicism, accepted a view of the Jew as a symbol of 'acquisitive finance capitalism'.[90] Toke's letter closed on a more familiar CSG note, urging the Church to take up social questions:

> At any rate, to *encourage* and *reassure* timid Catholics, would it not be possible for the Bishops to issue a joint pastoral, carefully worded, but certainly *not* reactionary in tone, urging the laity of all classes both to study social problems and to enter into and assist the efforts of their non-Catholic fellows to attain some modicum of justice and enlightenment? Surely, where the Popes have shown the way the Bishops need not be shy of following![91]

The Nation's Crisis, which was published by the CSG and sold 25,000 copies,[92] did not, as Toke had hoped, appear as a joint pastoral letter but under Bourne's name alone. It was, of course, a more temperate document than its source, and was minus the overt anti-semitic references, although the attack on plutocrats remained a feature.[93] Its tone was confident and positive, and marked a shift away from the defensive concerns of the early years of his archiepiscopate; its concern was 'not with exclusively Catholic interests, but with those common problems of national importance which have recently become so acute'.[94]

Most significantly it was conciliatory in its attitude towards the labour movement, perhaps reflecting something of the more accommodating approach to trade unions and labour organizations taken by Pope Benedict XV.[95] But there was also anxiousness about social radicalism. With events in Russia reverberating Bourne took the opportunity to warn against 'suicidal projects' to overturn the existing social order, but clearly he saw an appeal to moderate labour at this juncture as a far more constructive approach than further anti-socialist invective.[96] Bourne's main focus, therefore, was on those 'points of contact' between Catholic social principles and the 'modern labour unrest'. The 'task must be, not to denounce them as impious revolutionaries, but to show them that the Catholic Church alone can purify and realise their aspirations'.[97]

> Now there are certain leading features of the modern labour unrest which, though their expression may be crude and exaggerated, we recognise as the true lineaments of the Christian spirit. Its passion for fair treatment and for liberty; its resentment at bureaucratic interferences with family life; its desire for self-realization and opportunities of education; above all, its conviction that persons are of more value than property – these surely give us points of contact and promise a sympathetic welcome to our message.

The role that Bourne envisaged for the Church was to harness those feelings and legitimate aspirations, and to show the 'sundered and embittered classes' that Catholic social teaching 'has denounced in terms as strong as they themselves are likely to use, the greed and self-seeking which have laid upon the working classes "a yoke little better than slavery itself"'.[98]

Pervading the pastoral letter was a sanguine optimism about the potential for the advance of Catholicism in England. Bourne averred that since the 'religious disruption of the sixteenth century ... gradually and almost imperceptibly a new relation of society came into being; and men of high aim and of avowedly Christian belief, came to be dominated by ideas which had no ground in, or dependence upon, any Christian principle'. The economic individualism of the nineteenth century, when 'Desire of gain at all cost' was 'a ruling principle',[99] was the culmination of this process. Yet Bourne observed that in the last thirty years there had been a change of atmosphere, a reaction against materialism and individualism, and a 'return to saner doctrines and sounder principles in the teachings of our economists and in the practice of our people'. The war had accelerated this movement away from materialism: 'Youthful ardour, self-sacrifice in face of common danger, recognition of the rights of all who do their part in the nation's struggles, no less than the compelling necessity of the moment, have led the peoples of the Empire to an abandonment of materialistic aims and to a giving up of desires based purely on the present life, which would have seemed incredible not so many years ago.'[100] It was a climate that Bourne believed would be receptive to vigorous Catholic evangelization: there were none of the self-critical references to the 'failure of the Church' which, for instance, marked the Church of England's Fifth Report.[101]

> They [English people] are impressed with a new sense of the reality of religion. They observe its effectiveness in the face of danger and death; its power to heal, tranquillise and uplift; the definiteness and uniformity of Catholic teaching. In England, too, many have adopted Catholic emblems, beliefs and practices which before the war would probably have repelled them. The message of war-shrines, crucifixes and rosaries, finds an echo in the heart of the people, a stirring, it may be, of the old Catholic tradition, never wholly obliterated. Belief in the efficacy of prayers for the dead is becoming more frequent; and it is dawning upon many that their choice must be between the religion of Catholics and no religion at all.[102]

There were other stirrings, no less 'revolutionary': a growing resentfulness and suspicion against public authorities and political leaders; a questioning of the 'whole system of society'[103] and a 'passion for social righteousness'.[104] The implication was that these parallel movements could converge under the influence of the Church and its social teaching; that the Catholic Church could become the Church of ordinary English people.

As far as practical proposals for the building of a Christian social order, *The Nation's Crisis* was somewhat vague: brotherhood, a catch phrase of Christian socialists, and 'cordial cooperation among all classes of society' were urged.[105] But no fundamental change in the existing order of society need be implied by the use of such terms – they were employed by churchmen of all political complexions.[106] The priority of individual conversion over social reform was affirmed: it was through 'earnest prayer, in the frequentation of the Sacraments, and in the example of a good Catholic life' that *The Nation's Crisis* placed its ultimate hopes for the building of a Christian social order.[107] There were also echoes of a Bellocian antipathy to state action: 'Legislation under the guise of "social reform" tended to mark off all wage earners as a definitely servile class'.[108] Belloc's *The Servile State*, a highly influential book in social Catholic circles, was partly based on a speech in protest against the National Insurance Act of 1911, which he viewed as a 'vile enslaving measure'[109] and a portent of further encroachment by the state into the liberties of individuals and families.[110] It is interesting that *The Nation's Crisis* appeared to endorse Belloc's view of social reform, especially since leading CSG members such as Mgr Parkinson had been involved in the movement for the reform of the Poor Law,[111] and, according to Sir Henry Slesser (Solicitor-General in the first Labour government of 1924), one who had worked alongside Parkinson and other Catholics on the issue, had welcomed the measures for unemployment insurance initiated by Lloyd George.[112] An aversion to state action, therefore, did not characterize mainstream social Catholic thought, although similar arguments to Belloc's would be heard late into the 1950s.

A striking indication of the broadening of perspective encouraged by *The Nation's Crisis* was its appeal to the laity to participate in the efforts of other Christian organizations to 'remedy our unchristian social conditions'.[113] This opened the way for subsequent Catholic involvement in inter-church social movements, the most significant being COPEC. Closer relations with other like-minded Christian groups had been one of the aspirations of the CSG from the outset, but this was almost certainly a non-starter during the reign of Pius X. A few English bishops remained grudging in their attitude to cooperation. Thomas Dunn, the rebarbative Bishop of Nottingham, was an ardent supporter of temperance work, yet found it hard to tolerate the interdenominational group that was promoting this cause: 'I don't like the idea of going in with the heretics but it seems to be our only chance', was his typically acerbic response.[114] Casartelli was slightly warmer: he had shown a marked hostility to cooperation in the past,[115] but was now prepared to admit that Catholics 'can co-operate with Anglicans, – (e.g. in defence of religious education) as with the Free Church or Salvation Army, – (e.g. in temperance reform)'.[116] Elsewhere a more positive view was in evidence. The most significant gesture came from Archbishop Whiteside of Liverpool, for his was a city where sectarian animosities were a pronounced feature of its public life.[117] He was in many ways an improbable advocate of inter-Church effort, having a reputation for unremitting opposition to any mixing with non-Catholics. According to a later Archbishop of Liverpool, John Heenan, Whiteside of all the bishops cleaved to the most rigid interpretation of the *Ne Temere* decree of April 1908, which underscored the Church's opposition to mixed marriages.[118] It was a reflection of the more open mood that Whiteside could issue a Lenten pastoral letter in 1919 urging his flock to take their part in the work of social reconstruction: 'Catholics may co-operate with non-Catholics in promoting the social and even moral amelioration of those whom amidst they live, as far as always without compromise of principle'.[119] Temperance, housing, sweated labour, secular education and divorce were admitted by Whiteside as appropriate areas for cooperation. Whiteside's successor in 1921, Frederick Keating, reaffirmed this commitment.

Bourne's greater prominence in national affairs both during and after the war brought him into closer contact with other church leaders. He became a joint President of the Temperance Council of the Christian Churches of England and Wales in 1915 along with Archbishop Davidson, General Booth of the Salvation Army and John Clifford, the Baptist leader.[120] With Davidson and other church leaders he attempted to mediate in the railway strike which began in September 1919.[121] Probably as a result of this closer accord, Bourne was nominated for membership of the Athenaeum Club by Davidson. Bourne regarded his election in 1920 as a great honour and expressed the hope to Davidson that it would enable him 'to do something more for the causes which we all have at heart'.[122] He would often drop in at the Athenaeum in the afternoon,[123] but whether he overcame his natural diffidence to converse with other members is not known. Bourne and Davidson never really got close; all meetings between them were on neutral ground and neither was Bourne invited to visit Lambeth Palace, nor Davidson Archbishop's House.[124] It is certainly the case, however, that amongst the episcopate the Archbishop of Westminster had the opportunity for moving in a wider orbit, and it is no coincidence that Bourne and Hinsley later were more open to forging contacts with other church leaders than those whose horizons were necessarily more narrow.

The great expression of inter-church social concern was COPEC. In 'the brief period of post-war excitement even Roman Catholics took part in the production of the reports on which the Copec meetings were based'.[125] The subsequent withdrawal of the Catholic delegation by the bishops, which will be discussed in the next chapter, should not obscure the fact of the initial involvement, which would surely have been inconceivable before the war. The originator of the idea of COPEC was William Temple (1881–1944), Anglican Bishop of Manchester (later Archbishop of York and Canterbury). It was at Temple's 'Collegium', an inter-church discussion group on social questions, that the idea for COPEC was first mooted. Preparations for the conference, which took place in Birmingham in 1924, began in 1920 with the establishment of twelve commissions to prepare reports on specialized areas of social concern. Plater approached Bourne in 1921 about the possibility of official Catholic involvement and drew a favourable response. At this stage, Bourne was demonstrating a 'lively and friendly interest' in COPEC.[126] At the Low Week meeting of 1923 it was resolved to send an official delegation to COPEC, with the responsibility of appointing delegates representative of the range of 'Catholic opinion and teaching' resting with the bishops.[127] A number of the bishops later expressed themselves as having been against COPEC from the beginning, but at this stage their opposition remained mute. The extent of episcopal involvement in the appointment of delegates is unclear, although in 1922 Bourne informed Temple that he had handed over responsibility for the matter to the CSG. Its leaders were prominent on the various commissions.

COPEC is discussed at greater length in the next chapter, however, it is interesting to consider several of the delegates at this stage for it shows that fairly liberal and progressive winds were blowing in these post-war years. Some were known for their work in the movement for Christian reunion. Fr Leslie Walker of Campion Hall, Oxford, who along with Fr Leo O'Hea, Principal of the Catholic Workers' College, coordinated Catholic involvement in COPEC, had taken a prominent role in the Malines conversations, assuming the role of 'contact person' between the Archbishop of Canterbury, Cardinal Gasparri and Cardinal Mercier, and was regarded by Lord Halifax, the initiator, as 'friendly'.[128] Fr McNabb, appointed to the commission on the *Social Function of the Church*, was also well-disposed to the Malines conversations, and throughout his life had a strong affection for the Church of England.[129] From his Leicester days, McNabb had imbibed a strong appreciation of Nonconformity;[130] at the National Catholic Congress in 1913 he delivered a sympathetic address on 'Catholics and Nonconformists' which was later published by the CTS.[131] McNabb's commitment to Christian reunion is less well known than his political activism or his abilities as a preacher, yet it was a commitment which stretched throughout the length of his priestly career, furthermore, whereas most of his Catholic contemporaries could envisage no other view of reunion save through corporate conversion to Rome, McNabb soon arrived at the view that an insistence on 'submission to the Holy See' constituted an insuperable barrier to reunion.[132] Not surprisingly he was regarded by the Church hierarchy as something of a turbulent priest. His social radicalism, always worrying to the Catholic hierarchy, troubled even the well-disposed: W. F. Brown, a fellow worker in the social and political field, commented that McNabb had 'somewhat missed the mark ... His sermons on purely religious subjects held me almost spellbound: but unfortunately it became his habit to deal with social questions, whether preaching or giving a retreat.'[133] Brown was also a COPEC delegate. He was to establish a reputation as the foremost clerical educational expert in Britain, and was appointed Auxiliary Bishop of Southwark with the titular see of Pella in 1924. Clearly to the left of the political spectrum, he had moved within the Fabian orbit, and his public support for the Labour Party was to earn him the opprobrium of Catholic conservatives. It was possibly because of his political involvement that he informed Gasquet, who had heard him described as 'undoubtedly episcopabalis' by Amigo,[134] that 'To be a Bishop would in some ways be an embarrassment to me. I should have to consider episcopal dignity and could not take part as freely as I now do in various works.'[135]

But the progressives by no means dominated the COPEC delegation. The insistence of the bishops on the representative nature of the delegation meant the inclusion of those who had little sympathy with the dominant Christian socialist outlook of COPEC. There were also those who do not fit so easily into the categories of 'progressive' or 'conservative'. This is certainly the case with the delegate to the commission for *Christianity and War*, Francis Urquhart. The son of David Urquhart, the great diplomat,[136] Francis was a Fellow of Balliol College, Oxford. Perpetually youthful, 'Sligger' (as he was known) endeared himself to Balliol's brightest and most attractive undergraduates, in whose company he revelled:[137] 'it is unlikely that any other don has ever known and earned the affection of so many undergraduates', Balliol's most recent historian has stated.[138] He did not achieve any great academic distinction, seeing his task, a Balliol contemporary commented, as 'the education of young men rather than any addition to knowledge.'[139] He had little involvement in the wider life of Oxford. But it would be unfair perhaps to suggest that Urquhart's sense of responsibility as an educator stopped at the college gates: while he did not act on a vague whim to take up adult education work amongst the labouring classes of the East End of London[140] – a path that many Balliol men of his generation took[141] – from 1921 he took on unpaid tutorial work at the Catholic Workers' College.[142] Although a liberal in political sympathies, he was 'inclined to regard politics as the politician's job', noted Bailey, taking the view that 'it was a man's duty to live as good a life as he could in his own sphere and not to busy himself with external 'causes' and 'movements''.[143] Nevertheless, the sense of national crisis did prompt an interest in the CSG,[144] and he published numerous articles on questions of international morality.[145] It was his deep knowledge of European political and diplomatic history which explains his appointment to that particular COPEC commission.

Several letters Urquhart wrote to Fr Frank Devas, S.J., son of the economist C. S. Devas and fellow Stonyhurst alumnus, shed some light on his prejudices and preoccupations. They reveal a liberal's enthusiasm for Montalambert and Lacordaire,[146] and an Englishman's disdain for the 'follies and iniquities ... of the system in which the Index is worked'.[147] But in other respects he was thoroughly ultramontane in outlook: 'After all though many foolish things are done in Rome, still during the nineteenth century as far as England is concerned Rome has been much more enterprising than our old fashioned Catholics at home.'[148] The papal assault on critical scholarship did not upset this faith: he dismissed George Tyrrell as creating a sort of 'esoteric Christianity which takes nearly all the dogmas in a different sense to the world at large'.[149] A well-travelled francophone,[150] Urquhart was scathing about the parochialism and insularity of the English Catholic community:

> We are the most intellectually indolent of races in some ways. How few English people there are who can understand a French point of view – well *mutatis mutandis* this is true I think of most Catholics who have been brought up in a narrow way – whose homes are uninteresting – who have had to depend on school for all their education ... Who are the people who have broader ideas! Well I suppose they are the people with more imagination, people who have come across intelligent non-Catholics and really tried to understand and not confute them.[151]

People like Urquhart, in other words. A key to his involvement in COPEC can be found in a letter from 1917, which in its confident assertions that England was in need of Catholic social principles anticipated *The Nation's Crisis*.

> I have got a great theory about it being our business as Catholics to mix as much as possible with the rest and to give those who still profess to be Christians the principles which they ought to have behind their religion. England simply cannot go on now on instincts and traditions alone. It must have more principles and we must try to give Protestants the principles of Christianity which they ought to have ... This should be done without any introduction of controversial questions – but with the deliberate intention of making them intelligent Christians as far as their lights allow. No doubt it is sure to lead to conversions in some cases. But we shall not aim at this directly, but rather of giving England in religion, in social questions, in international politics, the principles, the intellectual basis, she so badly wants.[152]

It is ironic that whilst Urquhart kept any proselytising tendencies under wraps at Balliol,[153] and whose self-image was that of one progressive, broad-minded and outward-looking, he shows himself here to be possessed of the triumphalism and assertiveness typical of many English Catholics of the time. It was a mood which was to jar with the self-critical and reflective nature of the COPEC meetings he attended. There was a chasm which even shared political attitudes could not bridge.

* * *

Whilst COPEC was of mostly marginal interest to the bishops until January 1924, when the concerns of some of the Catholic delegates about its political tendencies forced it onto the agenda, questions about the nature of socialism, and particularly the question of whether Catholics could support the Labour Party, were live issues after the war.

The Labour Party's adoption, in February 1918, of a new constitution in which clause four committed the party to 'secure for the producers by hand or by brain the full fruits of their industry, and the most equitable distribution thereof that may be possible, upon the basis of the common ownership of the means of production',[154] changed the nature of the party. For the first time the party had committed itself, albeit cautiously, to socialist objectives, whereas previously it had seen itself as the parliamentary vehicle for trade union aspirations, involving no official commitment to a socialist programme. The Labour Party was now converted into a national party with local branches and individual membership, laying the basis for a concerted appeal to the British electorate.

It became apparent that the reluctance of the Catholic hierarchy to issue a pronouncement on the question in 1917 was not a posture that could be easily maintained in the changed context. Now the Labour Party posed a serious electoral challenge. Many working-class Catholics were newly enfranchised in 1918 and would find the Labour Party's promise of social reform alluring. This would further erode the traditional identification of this section of the Catholic community with the Liberal Party. Furthermore, the rout of the IPP, to which the bishops had always looked for support on the education question, would denude the House of Commons of its Catholic presence. If only for pragmatic reasons the bishops could no longer afford to remain indifferent to the Labour Party, which after all was at its strongest in the very northern industrial heartlands where Catholicism too had its strength. Where the Catholic hierarchy situated itself on the Labour Party question was no longer merely 'academic'. As Bishop Ward put it to Amigo, if the Labour Party was now socialist 'does not that modify our attitude towards it?'[155]

The Labour Party question weighed the more heavily on the bishops because of the interest shown by the Holy See. There was no surprise in the fact of Rome's interest: Fr Plater told Bishop Keating that the Secretary of State, Cardinal Gasparri, had approached the CSG for material on the matter a few years previously.[156] The Holy See had long harboured concerns at the spread of socialist ideas amongst Catholics, and, as one would expect, probed diocesan bishops about the extent of the threat. One of the questions asked of a bishop at his quinquennial *ad limina* visit to Rome was whether socialism and other practices condemned by the Church, such as Freemasonry, existed in his diocese. But the English bishops had rather downplayed the threat that socialism posed to the faithful: typical was the reply given by Bishop Lacy in 1917, who admitted that socialist societies had made inroads amongst non-Catholics but that very few Catholics were attracted to them.[157] Even Casartelli, who was more anxious about socialism than most, stressed in his 1912 *ad limina* report that the faithful generally did not engage in 'evil' practices such as socialism and Freemasonry, although he added that there was a great danger that such errors would arise if a vigorous stance, such as that adopted in Salford, was not taken to combat the threat.[158] Only Bishop Collins of Hexham and Newcastle displayed any real anxiety, stating in 1912 that socialism was propagated amongst Catholics 'with some damage to souls'.[159] But with the bishops on the whole maintaining a temperate attitude, zealous anti-socialists like Stuart Coats and Thomas Burns of the Federation appeared to be fighting lonely crusades. It was only after the Labour Party's adoption of a socialist constitution that their isolated campaigns found a focus.

The involvement of the Vatican authorities began after Cardinal Gasparri received what Bishop Keating was to describe as 'Alarmist reports ... regarding the grave danger to which English Catholics are said to be exposed by the association of our working class with the Labour Party, which has been represented as a Socialist organization of a virulent type'.[160] The first group moving in the matter was the Salford Federation, supported one must assume by Casartelli. In contrast to the conciliatory note struck by Bourne in *The Nation's Crisis*, Casartelli's opposition to the 'modern labour unrest' took an increasingly shrill tone after the war. The more positive attitude to social reform adopted in *The Nation's Crisis* was emphatically not the view of all. Casartelli went further, however, in identifying the Labour Party with dangerous social radicalism. He gave encouragement to Thomas Burns, who arrived at the conclusion that the effect of clause four was that 'the Labour Party, for the first time, became the Socialist Party'.[161] When, in September 1918, Burns along with other disaffected Catholic trade unionists formed the Centre Party,[162] it enjoyed Casartelli's full support. Fielding has argued that Burns acted without episcopal approval in forming the Centre Party and that his independent action led to a breakdown of relations with Casartelli.[163] But whilst Casartelli was increasingly exasperated by Burns's tendency to harangue political opponents,[164] there was no fundamental disagreement between the two. Although the Centre Party was a dismal failure, folding after a poor showing at Gorton, Manchester, in the 1919 municipal elections,[165] Burns's stock with Casartelli remained high. In July 1919, Casartelli, in response to Gasparri's request, entrusted Burns to draft a memorandum on the relation of the Labour Party to socialism.[166] In the same year Casartelli was reported as having said that 'the Labour Party is now committed to Socialism, and as Catholics may not be Socialists, they must not be associated with it, though they retain their freedom of vote at elections'.[167]

Prominent members of the CUGB were also agitating on this issue. Stuart Coats, who had complained to Gasquet in 1917 about the hierarchy's unwillingness to curb the message of socialism and class hatred emanating from 'some of the leading Dominicans and others of the clergy',[168] now accused the bishops of failing to respond to Mgr W. F. Brown's alleged statement that it was the 'most natural thing in the world that the bulk of the Catholic electors of this country will vote for the frankly Socialist programme of the Labour Party'. Coats stated in a letter to Gasquet:

> Really, when one thinks of the repeated condemnations of Socialism in the Encyclicals of recent Popes, and the Papal directives given to the German Episcopate on the subject of men's unions, and the condemnation of the Sillon, it is more than surprising to observe the attitude of the Catholic hierarchy in this country, with not a word of warning given to those hundreds of thousands of Catholic electors at the approach of the election, just when the Labour Party has finally announced itself as a definitely Socialist Party.

He drew an analogy between the hierarchy's unwillingness to condemn the Labour party and the 'Archbishop of Canterbury's permitting Hensley Henson's utterances'. Coats was referring to the recent controversy surrounding the elevation of Henson, who apparently denied the two miracles of the creed, to the see of Hereford. Coats insisted that the 'only difference is that the Anglican failure to warn and condemn is in the sphere of faith, and the Catholic failure is in the sphere of morals ... We Catholics scoff at the helplessness of Anglicanism in the face of the denials of Bishop Hensley Henson, but is there not a more or less close parallel to be found in the face of the helplessness of the Catholic Church in England and Scotland in the face of Socialism?' Coats's intention in writing to Gasquet was to ask him to bring the matter to the attention of Rome so that 'Catholics in this country can have some authoritative warning given them that they cannot support a Party by their votes which is pledged to Socialism'.[169]

In July 1919, Gasparri wrote to several bishops (Amigo, Bourne, Casartelli and Keating) to solicit opinion on the Labour Party and its relation to socialism, and on the attitude that Catholics should adopt towards it. Clearly Casartelli and Keating were thought to represent different sides of the question. Keating's response is the most interesting and considered. Keating had touched on the question earlier in his Lenten pastoral letter of 1919, *Faith and Country*. Whilst expressing grave concern that the effective leadership of the Labour Party was being 'gradually monopolised by men of extremist and most pernicious views', Keating drew a distinction between the socialist clique who had committed the party 'on paper at least' to a 'programme which no conscientious Catholic can wholly accept', and the 'genuine trade-unionism' of the mass of its members. The duty of Catholic trade unionists was 'to purge the party rather than leave it. Let them employ their voting strength and influence manfully, to dismiss from office and power those who misrepresent the true aims of trade-unionism, and replace them by honest men who will promote the interest of their own class without declaring an unjust war on every other class.'[170] His letter to Gasparri amplified these points. One of the most interesting aspects of it was that it drew heavily on a letter which Sidney Webb wrote to Mgr W. F. Brown. Brown, who had been on close terms with Webb since their common interest in Poor Law reform had brought them together in 1910,[171] had approached him for his views on questions such as the Labour Party's attitude to private property. Webb could pass on the reassuring message that the Labour Party emphatically did not intend to abolish private property.[172] Echoing Webb's analysis, Keating informed Gasparri that the socialism of the Labour Party could be distinguished from the 'socialismo ateo, materialista e antichristiano' continental Europe. First, because the 'common ownership of the means of production involves no denial of the right of private property, and has absolutely no resemblance to that "community of goods" which is distinctive of Communism'; secondly, 'In all its schemes of nationalisation or municipalisation of industries the Labour Party insists on compensation for the expropriated shareholders'. On the question of nationalization, Keating insisted that many Catholics denied that 'the common ownership of the means of production' had been condemned by the Church, 'apart from adventitious circumstances, such as revolutionary and confiscatory methods'. 'They point to the nationalisation, without serious protest, of such public services as posts, telegraphs, telephones, railways, canals &c, and contend that the Legislature might, without any manifest violation of justice, extend State-ownership indefinitely to the greater industrial undertakings, on similar terms and for the general good'. The second half of Keating's letter informed Gasparri of the predominant attitude of the bishops towards the Labour Party. It is clear where Keating's sympathies lay in the matter. The Labour Party, Keating insisted, was 'opposed by other political parties representing the wealth and vested interests of the Country; but this opposition is based not on moral, but on purely economic or party grounds'. Therefore to 'shift the discussion to theological issues would provoke the ridicule of many and the lasting resentment of all sections of the labouring classes. For them it could only have one meaning, – i.e. that the Church was siding with the rich against the poor, and was using her spiritual influence for political objects.' The working classes, Keating went on, were 'heartily sick of the inhumanity and injustice of the industrial system' and found themselves 'defeated time after time by the superior advantages of entrenched wealth'. If the Church 'seems to forbid them every avenue of escape, the more reckless will surely abandon the Church, while even the more docile will grow cold in their loyalty'. Employing a phrase of Cardinal Newman's to describe the Church of England, Keating argued that the Labour Party formed 'a serviceable breakwater against errors more fundamental than its own'. 'At such a crisis, it seems to me that a well-organized popular party, committed to moderate views and constitutional methods, is a valuable asset, which the Church and all temperate minds ought to respect ... I venture to think that many Continental nations may envy us the possession of such an instrument of social stability, and would counsel us to keep on the best possible terms with it, as long as we can.'[173]

Keating's conciliatory views were echoed by Southwark and Westminster. 'Your reply is on thoroughly right lines', Amigo assured Keating.[174] Less confident than Keating on such matters, Amigo gathered a wide range of views before he wrote to Rome,[175] and his letter to Gasparri of 25 November 1919 reflected the dominant feeling:

> My own considered opinion after inquiry is that the Labour Party will probably be in power in a short time and that it is for us to try and work with them ... it would be a profound mistake to condemn the Labour Party. Our own people consist mainly of working class, and

mostly in favour of the Labour Party, and they look upon it simply as a political party willing and ready to help them with their difficulties, whereas the others have promised much and done little for them.[176]

There was a similar pragmatism in evidence at Westminster. Canon Moyes, Bourne's closest adviser, wrote to Canon Jackman expressing his concern that 'the Salford Federation is committing the Church in England, and leading us into a calamitous war with the Labour Party, to which seven-tenths of our own people belong'.

> If they elicit a condemnation ... it will mean that the Catholic labour-ing man will have his religion put in antagonism to his political and professional interests and sympathies, resulting either in alienation from the faith, or in ostracism from his Trade Union and the odium of disloyalty to his fellow workman. If all that were for a matter of *faith*, no-one would complain. But we have only the word and opinion of these Federationists in the North, that it is so. It seems to me to be utterly unwise and futile to condemn 'Socialism' as a whole. A great deal of what people call 'Socialism' is not forbidden by any law, natural or Divine. Neither is Socialism an inseparable whole, nor is the Labour Party committed to it as such ... The matter seems one which may deeply affect the whole future of Catholicism in England. But I hope sincerely that Rome will not be pushed by these Northerners into saying undemocratic things which will have to be explained away after-wards.[177]

Similarly, Archbishop Whiteside, like Moyes, did not wish to make an issue out of the Labour Party's formal socialist commitment, urging that a distinction should be drawn between its programme and the 'measures it seeks to pass, *de facto*'.[178] This was a position he had maintained since his reading of Snowden's *Socialism and Syndicalism* several years earlier had convinced him that the Labour Party's social-ism was not shot through with atheism and anti-clericalism.

A decision on the matter had to wait until 1924, yet the weight of episcopal opinion could not be ignored by the Holy See. A cautious stance was maintained until then with the bishops maintaining that 'Where the Church had not spoken one was at liberty to take whatever side he wished'.[179] Bourne, speaking at Leicester in October 1919, insisted that Casartelli's declaration that Catholics should not associate themselves to the Labour Party was merely 'an expression of opinion not binding on Catholics generally'.[180] In the absence of any authorita-tive pronouncement, Burns and the Federation continued their agitations. A resolution was passed at the annual conference of the Catholic confederation held in Sheffield in November 1921 stating that as Catholics could not be socialists, Catholic trade unionists should not pay the political levy.[181] Bourne, responding to a protest from Westminster branch members opposed to Burns's campaign, insisted that a note be added in the report of the conference that 'those who passed the resolution with regard to Catholics and the Labour Party do not adequately represent the Catholics of this country'.[182] But by then the bishops' patience with Burns had already worn exceedingly thin. Keating referred to that 'That dreadful man Burns' who 'is still girding at every Catholic who ventures to traverse his *ipse dixit* of what is condemned under his name of "Socialism"'.[183] Bourne remarked to Casartelli that 'Mr Burns causes a good deal of irritation' and appeared to 'think that the Bishops must make pronouncements as and when he wishes'.[184] Casartelli's position was clearly discredited by implication.

The post-war years saw a broadening of the Church's concerns. A new urgency was attached to the social question and for a brief period even inter-church initiatives were viewed by some, if not all of the bishops, in a positive light. Behind this was a confident optimism that the times were propitious for the Church to make an impact in national life. The debates over socialism and the Labour Party demonstrated that there were sections of Catholic opinion anxious about the new class politics, and who hoped to see the episcopate denounce these tendencies in unambiguous terms. A few progressive bishops, however, insisted on the distinction between continental socialism and its domestic expressions, and even those more concerned about the political tendencies exhibited in the Labour Party perceived that a condemnation would only drive a wedge between the Church and its people. Whether for pragmatic reasons, or because of a commitment to social reform, with one lone exception the episcopate urged on Rome the dangers of intemperate condemnation.

Notes

1. Oldmeadow, *Bourne*, II, pp. 85–6.
2. Merry del Val to Gasquet, 2 July 1912?, D.A.A., Gasquet Papers, File 882. See also Oldmeadow, *Bourne*, II, p. 89.
3. Ibid., pp. 123–39.
4. Casartelli to Amigo, 20 January 1912, A.A.S., Amigo Papers, Correspondence with Bishops.
5. Keating to Amigo, 10 January 1912, ibid. 'I gather that Westminster has *always* been somewhat autocratic. The outline of a better system is sketched in the "Si Qua Est"...': Keating to Mgr Brown, 8 January 1912, ibid., Brown Papers.
6. S. Mews, *Religion and Society in the First World War* (unpublished Ph.D. dissertation, University of Cambridge, 1973), 194–6; S. Foster,

'A Bishop for Essex: Bernard Ward and the Diocese of Brentwood', *Recusant History*, 21 (October 1993), 556–71.

7. *Ad Clerum*, 12 March 1917, B.D.A., Ward Papers, Establishment of Diocese 1917–18 File.

8. Keating to Ward, 24 May 1917, ibid.

9. Casartelli to Amigo, 8 December 1916, A.A.S., Amigo Papers, Correspondence with Bishops; Whiteside to Ward, 27 December 1917, B.D.A., Ward Papers, Establishment of Diocese 1917–18 File.

10. Casartelli to Merry del Val, 22 April 1917 (copy), Sal.D.A., Casartelli Papers, Box 161.

11. Ward to Keating, 28 May 1917, B.D.A., Ward Papers, Establishment of Diocese 1917–18 File.

12. Keating to Ward, 24 May 1917, ibid.

13. Dunn to Gasquet, 15 March 1917, D.A.A., Gasquet Papers, File 874.

14. *Acta* of the Meeting of the Bishops at Oscott College, 11 March 1917, copy held in B.D.A., Ward Papers, Establishment of Diocese 1917–18 File.

15. Keating to Ward, 24 May 1917, ibid.

16. Whiteside to Ward, 27 December 1917, ibid.

17. Amigo to Gasquet, 2 April 1917, D.A.A., Gasquet Papers, File 917a; copy of Bourne's letter to Amigo, 22 March 1917, A.A.L., Early Bishops' Collection, Series 2 V A/73.

18. Casartelli to Cardinal Merry del Val, 22 April 1917 (copy), Sal.D.A., Casartelli Papers, Box 161.

19. Amigo to Whiteside, 21 May 1917, A.A.L., Early Bishops' Collection, Series 2 V A/55.

20. Dunn to Amigo, 30 March 1917, A.A.S., Amigo Papers, Correspondence with Bishops.

21. Bishop Casartelli's diary, 17–18 April 1917, S.D.A.

22. Keating to Ward, 19 May 1917; Keating to Ward, 24 May 1917, B.D.A., Ward Papers, Establishment of Diocese 1917–18 File.

23. Ward to Keating, 28 May 1917, ibid.

24. Keating to Pius XI, 5 April 1925 (copy), A.A.L., Keating Papers, Series 2 I A/1.

25. R. Kollar, 'The Reluctant Prior: Bishop Wulstan Pearson of Lancaster', *Recusant History*, 20 (May 1991), 412; L. Gooch, 'An Archbishop for Darlington?', *Northern Catholic History*, 39 (1998), 60–2.

26. Keating to Amigo, 10 December 1924, A.A.S., Amigo Papers, Correspondence with Bishops.

27. Keating to Cardinal de Lai, 2 April 1925 (copy), A.A.L., Keating Papers, Series 2 I A/1.

28. Gasquet to Amigo, 13 March 1920, A.A.S., Amigo Papers, Correspondence with Bishops; Leslie, *Gasquet*, pp. 207–9.

29. Keating to Amigo, 31 March 1917, A.A.S., Amigo Papers, Correspondence with Bishops; see also Keating to Amigo, 4 April 1917, ibid.

30. Dunn to Amigo, 22 March 1921, ibid.
31. Dunn to Amigo, 14 February 1920, ibid.
32. Cotter to Mgr Brown, 21 April 1917, ibid., Brown Papers.
33. Amigo to Ward, 1 June 1918, B.D.A., Ward Papers, Establishment of Diocese 1917–18 File.
34. Amigo to Dunn, 19 August 1918, Not.D.A., Dunn Papers, G03.01.35; see also Casartelli to Gasquet, 10 November 1917 (copy), Sal.D.A., Casartelli Papers, Box 162; Keating to Amigo, 8 March 1925, A.A.S., Amigo Papers, Correspondence with Bishops.
35. *The Ushaw Magazine* (March 1953), 3. It is interesting, however, to note that Collins was present at the Oscott meeting – surely not the actions of a close friend.
36. Keating to Amigo, 24 March 1922, A.A.S., Amigo Papers, Correspondence with Bishops.
37. Whiteside to Singleton, 3 November 1917, Shr.D.A., Singleton Papers, Box 6; L. Andrews, *The Education Act 1918* (London: Routledge and Kegan Paul, 1976), pp. 29–32.
38. Casartelli to Mgr Brown, 27 July 1917 (copy), Sal.D.A., Casartelli Papers, Box 162; Whiteside to Singleton, 3 November 1917, Shr.D.A., Singleton Papers, Box 6.
39. Bell, *Davidson*, II, p. 1125.
40. Casartelli to Whiteside, 6 November 1917 (copy); Casartelli to Gasquet, 10 November 1917 (copy); Casartelli to Bourne, 19 October 1917 (copy), Sal.D.A., Casartelli Papers, Box 162.
41. Lord Edmund Talbot to Bourne, 20 July 1918, A.A.W., Bourne Papers, Bo.5/25d.
42. J. Finan, *Struggle for Justice: A Short History of the Catholic Teachers' Federation* (Nelson, 1975).
43. Andrews, *Education Act*, p. 42.
44. Casartelli to Mgr Brown, 17 November 1917 (copy), Sal.D.A., Casartelli Papers, Box 162.
45. Ibid.; also Casartelli to Mgr Tynan, 22 September 1917 (copy); Casartelli to Keating, 18 November 1917 (copy), ibid.
46. Bell, *Davidson*, II, p. 1125.
47. Dunn to Whiteside, 5 April 1920 (copy), Not.D.A., Dunn Papers, G.04.01.
48. Amigo to Whiteside (copy), 7 April 1920, B.A.A., D Series; Dunn to Whiteside, 30 March 1920 (copy), Not.D.A., Dunn Papers, G.04.01.; Dunn to Whiteside, 5 April 1920 (copy), ibid.
49. Casartelli to Whiteside, 19 April 1920 (copy), Sal.D.A., Casartelli Papers, Box 164.
50. Casartelli to Whiteside, 1 December 1920 (copy), ibid. Casartelli's health was failing rapidly around this time.
51. Casartelli to Ilsley, 29 April 1920, B.A.A., D Series.
52. J. Coventry, 'Roman Catholicism', in R. Davis (ed.), *The Testing of the Churches 1932-1982: A Symposium* (London: Epworth Press, 1982), p. 17.

53. G. I. T. Machin, *Churches and Social Issues in Twentieth-Century Britain* (Oxford: Clarendon Press, 1998), p. 14.
54. Norman, *Roman Catholicism in England*, pp. 126–7. See also T. Johnstone and J. Hagerty, *The Cross on the Sword: Catholic Chaplains in the Forces* (London: Geoffrey Chapman, 1996).
55. Amigo to Gasquet, 14 February 1918, D.A.A., Gasquet Papers, File 917a.
56. Amigo to Whiteside, 20 February 1917, A.A.L., Early Bishops' Collection, Series 2 V A/50.
57. Casartelli to Gasquet, 6 December 1916 (copy), Sal.D.A., Casartelli Papers, Box 161.
58. Doubleday to Dunn, 29 March 1920, Not.DA., Dunn Papers, G.03.02.17.
59. Keating to Amigo, 3 December 1917, A.A.S., Amigo Papers, Correspondence with Bishops.
60. Merry del Val to Fr Broadhead, 31 October 1925, Ushaw College Archives, OS/J 77. It seems unlikely that Merry del Val had such an influence in 1925, though without access to the Vatican Archives for this period it is not possible to say.
61. Merry del Val to Fr Broadhead, 12 February 1928, ibid.
62. Archbishop Keating's Diary of his 1920 Visit to Italy, 23 April 1920, A.A.L., Keating Papers, Series 6 I A/I.
63. Fogarty, *Vatican and the American Hierarchy*, ch. 9; see also J. McShane, *'Sufficiently Radical' Catholicism, Progressivism, and the Bishops' Program of 1919* (Washington: Catholic University of America Press, 1986); T. A. Byrnes, *Catholic Bishops in American Politics* (Princeton: Princeton University Press, 1991), ch. 2.
64. Ibid., p. 26.
65. Bishop Keating's Advent *Pastoral Letter* of 1918, Nrt.D.A, Pastoral Letters 1908–1918, Book IV no. 44; see also Lenten *Pastoral Letter* of 1919, entitled *Faith and Country*, ibid., Book V no. 1; Notes for a speech entitled 'New Horizons' given at Dublin, undated but c. 1917–8, A.A.L., Keating Papers, Series 7 IV A/204.
66. Norman, *Church and Society*, p. 246.
67. Dunn to Whiteside, 25 March 1920 (copy), Not.D.A., Dunn Papers, G.04.01.
68. E. Fouilloux, 'The Antepreparatory Phase: The Slow Emergence from Inertia (January, 1959 – October, 1962)', in G. Alberigo (ed.), *History of Vatican II: Vol. I Announcing and Preparing Vatican Council II Toward a new Era in Catholicism* (Maryknoll: Orbis; Leuven: Peeters, 1995), p. 67.
69. Dunn to Whiteside, 4 July 1917, A.A.L., Early Bishops' Collection 1873–1921, Series II Box V.
70. Bishop Casartelli's Lenten *Pastoral Letter* of 1919, Sal.D.A.
71. Keating to Cardinal Gasparri, u/d but 1919, Nrt.D.A., Keating Papers, FV. 1 (G).
72. Bishop Collins's Lenten *Pastoral Letter* of 1919, H.N.D.A

73. Address entitled 'Christ or Chaos', 24 October 1921, A.A.L., Keating Papers, Series 7 IV A/8.
74. For Askew see the obituary in *The Oscotian* (1963).
75. *Birmingham and District Catholic Magazine* (October 1920); see also the March 1921 edition.
76. Fr William Barry to Sir James Marchant, 9 December 1917, Oxford, Bodleian Library, MS Eng lett d. 314.
77. Quoted in Norman, *Roman Catholicism in England*, p. 125.
78. Gilley, 'Age of Equipoise', p. 40.
79. See Pollard, *Unknown Pope*, esp. ch. 6.
80. 'H[is].E[minence] has lately been saluted as a "cheerful Cardinal" in contrast with "a gloomy dean"': Address entitled 'Christ or Chaos', 24 October 1921, A.A.L., Keating Papers, Series 7 IV A/8.The 'gloomy dean' referred to was Dean Inge of St Paul's.
81. Pollard, *Unknown Pope*, p. 158.
82. Merry del Val to Fr Broadhead, 5 April 1920, Ushaw College Archives, OS/J 54.
83. Oldmeadow, *Bourne*, II, p. 124.
84. Fr Plater to Keating, 18 July 1919, Keating Papers, Nrt.D.A., FV. 1 (G). I am grateful to Fr David Lannon for his assistance on these points. Biographical information on these Dominicans is taken from S. F. Gaine, *Obituary Notices of the English Dominicans from 1952 to 1966* (Oxford: Blackfriars Publications, 2000).
85. Fr Plater to Keating, 25 September 1919, Nrt.D.A., Keating Papers FV. 1 (G).
86. Fr Plater to Leslie Toke, 9 February 1918, C.S.G.A., Miscellaneous Letters 1909–20, E 6.
87. Fr Plater to Leslie Toke, 20 December 1917, ibid.
88. H. Belloc and C. Chesterton, *The Party System* (London: Stephen Swift, 1911). J. P. McCarthy, *Hilaire Belloc: Edwardian Radical* (Indianapolis: Liberty Press, 1978), pp. 137–99; J. P. Corrin, 'Labour Unrest and the Development of Anti-Statist Thinking in Britain 1900–1914', *The Chesterton Review*, 8 (August 1982), 225–43; W. H. Greenleaf, *The British Political Tradition: Volume Two The Ideological Heritage* (London and New York: Methuen, 1983), p. 89; G. R. Searle, *Corruption in British Politics 1895–1930* (Oxford: Clarendon Press, 1987), pp. 158–9.
89. See the references to Belloc in ibid.; R. Barker, *Political Ideas in Modern Britain: In and after the twentieth century* (London and New York: Routledge, 1997 edn), p. 131.
90. Searle, *Corruption in British Politics*, p. 120.
91. Leslie Toke's letter on 'The Social Unrest' , C.S.G.A., E 11.
92. Keating, 'Roman Catholics, Christian Democracy', p. 70.
93. Francis Cardinal Bourne, *The Nation's Crisis* (London: CSG, 1918), p. 10.
94. Ibid., p. 8.
95. Duffy, *Saints and Sinners*, p. 254; Pollard, *Unknown Pope*, p. 178.

96. Bourne, *Nation's Crisis*, pp. 6, 13.
97. Ibid., p. 12.
98. Ibid., p. 13.
99. Ibid., pp. 2–3.
100. Ibid., p. 4.
101. Norman, *Church and Society*, p. 241.
102. Bourne, *Nation's Crisis*, p. 7.
103. Ibid., p. 11.
104. Ibid., p. 12.
105. Ibid., p. 14.
106. Kent, *William Temple*, p. 119.
107. Bourne, *Nation's Crisis*, p. 16.
108. Ibid., p. 10.
109. Quoted in Barker, *Political Ideas in Modern Britain*, p. 94.
110. H. Belloc, *The Servile State* (London and Edinburgh: T. N. Foulis, 1913)
111. Wraith, 'English Catholic Church and the "Social Question"', p. 536.
112. Sir Henry Slesser to Archbishop Grimshaw, 5 January 1959, B.A.A., Archbishops' Papers 1929–65, AP/S8/5.
113. Bourne, *Nation's Crisis*, p. 17.
114. Dunn to Amigo, 23 November 1918, A.A.S., Amigo Papers, Correspondence with Bishops.
115. Casartelli to Bishop Knox, 9 February 1917 (copy), Sal.D.A., Casartelli Papers, Box 161.
116. Casartelli to Thomas Burns, 30 November 1918 (copy), ibid., Box 163.
117. See P. J. Waller, *Democracy and Sectarianism: a Political and Social History of Liverpool 1868–1939* (Liverpool: Liverpool University Press, 1981).
118. Heenan, *Crown of Thorns*, p. 230.
119. *The Tablet*, 5 April 1919.
120. Oldmeadow, *Bourne*, II, p. 192.
121. Bell, *Davidson*, II, p. 951.
122. Bourne to Davidson, 4 February 1920, L.P.L., Randall Davidson Papers 520, fo. 327.
123. Oldmeadow, *Bourne*, II, p. 345.
124. Bourne to Bede Jarrett, 11 March 1931 (copy), A.A.W., Bourne Papers, Hi 2/66.
125. Kent, *William Temple*, pp. 115–6.
126. Bourne to an anonymous Manchester COPEC supporter, 5 December 1922 (copy), A.A.W., Bourne Papers, Bo. 5/76a.
127. Meeting of the Bishops, 10 April 1923, A.A.W., *Acta*.
128. R. J. Lahey, 'Cardinal Bourne and the Malines Conversations', in Hastings (ed.), *Bishops and Writers*, p. 89; J. A. Dick, *The Malines Conversations Revisited* (Leuven: Leuven University Press, 1989), pp. 76–7, 81–8; For Walker's involvement see B. Barlow, *'A Brother Knocking at the Door': The Malines Conversations 1921–1925* (Norwich: The Canterbury Press, 1996), pp. 76–91.

129. Ibid., pp. 112, 137–8; A. White, 'A History of *Blackfriars* and *New Blackfriars*', *New Blackfriars* (July/August 1996), pp. 324–5.

130. Valentine, *McNabb*, p. 115.

131. This was published again in 1942 with an introduction by Nathaniel Micklem, Principal of Mansfield College, Oxford. Micklem stated that McNabb had written about Nonconformity with 'restraint and sympathy and charity': V. McNabb, *Catholics and Nonconformists* (London: CTS, 1942 edn), p. 3.

132. Fr McNabb to Bishop Bell, 14 December 1938, L.P.L., Bell Papers 210, fo. 330.

133. Valentine, *McNabb*, p. 191.

134. Amigo to Gasquet, 5 March 1918, D.A.A., Gasquet Papers, File 917a.

135. Mgr Brown to Gasquet, 10 March 1918, ibid.

136. G. Robinson, *David Urquhart: Some Chapters in the Life of a Victorian Knight Errant of Justice and Liberty* (New York: Augustus M. Kelley, 1970 edn). This has an introduction by Francis Urquhart.

137. Waugh, *Ronald Knox*, p. 86; C. Bailey, *Francis Fortescue Urquhart: A Memoir* (London: Macmillan and Co., 1936), pp. 32–3, 45–50, 60–84; M. Secrest, *Kenneth Clark: A Biography* (London: Wiedenfeld and Nicholson, 1984), p. 54; Dom Bernard Green, 'David Knowles's First Book', *Downside Review*, 107 (April 1989), 79–80; N. Annan, *Our Age: The Generation that Made Postwar Britain* (London: Fontana, 1991 edn), p. 4.

138. J. Jones, *Balliol College: A History* (Oxford: Oxford University Press, 1997 edn), p. 235.

139. Bailey, *Francis Fortescue Urquhart*, pp. 41.

140. Ibid., p. 105.

141. L. Goldman, *Dons and Workers: Oxford and Adult Education* (Oxford: Clarendon Press, 1995), pp. 54, 246–7.

142. MacEntee, *Catholic Social Movement in Great Britain*, p. 235.

143. Bailey, *Urquhart*, p. 103.

144. Ibid., pp. 133–4; Fr Plater to Henry Somerville, 31 January 1916, C.S.G.A.

145. MacEntee, *Catholic Social Movement in Great Britain*, pp. 276–7.

146. Francis Urquhart to Francis Devas, Feast of St Stephen 1897, E.P.S.J., Francis Devas Papers, MS/3; Francis Urquhart to Francis Devas, 15 January 1899, ibid.

147. Francis Urquhart to Francis Devas, 19 December 1901, ibid.

148. Ibid.

149. Francis Urquhart to Francis Devas, 14 July 1906, ibid.

150. Bailey, *Urquhart*, pp. 37, 39, 85–96, 99–100.

151. Francis Urquhart to Francis Devas, 19 December 1901, Francis Devas Papers, MS/3

152. Francis Urquhart to Francis Devas, 2 January 1917, ibid.

153. Bailey, *Urquhart*, pp. 134–5.

154. Quoted in R. T. McKenzie, *British Political Parties: The Distribution of Power Within the Conservative and Labour Parties* (London:

Heinemann, 1963 edn), p. 479. For the background to the adoption of the 1918 constitution see D. Coates, *The Labour Party and the Struggle for Socialism* (London: Cambridge University Press, 1975).

155. Ward to Amigo, 3 October 1919, A.A.S., Amigo Papers, Correspondence with Bishops.

156. Fr Plater to Keating, 29 July 1919, Nrt.D.A., Keating Papers, FV. 1 (G).

157. *Ad Limina*, Middlesbrough, 497 (1917), A.S.V., C.C.

158. *Ad Limina*, Salford, 705 (1912), ibid.

159. Ad Limina, Hexham and Newcastle, 377 (1912), ibid.

160. Keating to Cardinal Gasparri, u/d but 1919, ibid. This is an English copy of the letter which was then translated into Italian and sent to Rome. The Italian translation can also be found in the Keating Papers. The original letter, along with other correspondence on the subject, is held at A.S.V., Segretaria di Stato, fasc. 7, rubr. 2. These papers could not be located for me at the time.

161. *Catholic Federationist* (October 1918).

162. The idea of a specifically Catholic political party appears to have held some appeal after the war: at a meeting of the Westminster Federation in May 1918 a majority of the 100 present voted in favour of a Catholic party, *The Tablet*, 18 May 1918.

163. S. J. Fielding, 'The Irish Catholics of Manchester and Salford' (unpublished Ph.D dissertation, Warwick, 1988).

164. Casartelli to Canon Sharrock, 1 September 1916 (copy), Sal.D.A., Casartelli Papers, Box 161; Casartelli to Mgr O'Kelly, 26 November 1918 (copy), ibid., Box 163; Casartelli to T. F. Burns, 14 July 1919 (copy), ibid.; 'Our friend T.F.B. is always hitting out at friend and foe alike and antagonising almost every other Catholic organisation or publication': Casartelli to Canon O'Kelly, 15 December 1920 (copy), ibid., Box 164.

165. Fielding, 'Irish Catholics of Manchester and Salford', p. 287.

166. Casartelli to Mgr O'Kelly, 25 July 1919 (copy), Sal.D.A., Box 163.

167. *Leicester Daily Post*, 24 October 1919. Press cutting held in A.A.W., Bourne Papers, Hi. 2/128.

168. Stuart Coats to Gasquet, Easter Day 1917, D.A.A., Gasquet Papers, File 889. Fr McNabb was almost certainly the target of Coats's invective.

169. Stuart Coats to Gasquet, 27 October 1918, ibid.

170. Bishop Keating's Lenten *Pastoral Letter* of 1919, Nrt.D.A., Pastoral Letters 1919–1933, Book V no. 1.

171. Brown, *Through Windows of Memory*, p. 52.

172. Sidney Webb to Mgr W. F. Brown, 1 August 1919, Nrt.D.A., Keating Papers, FV. 1 (G).

173. Keating to Cardinal Gasparri, u/d but 1919, Nrt.D.A., Keating Papers, FV. 1 (G).

174. Amigo to Keating, 28 August 1919, ibid.

175. There are letters in 'Political 1919' file in the Amigo Papers from

George Milligan, a Liverpool trade unionist, Archbishop Whiteside of Liverpool, Hilaire Belloc, Bishop Keating of Northampton, Joseph Devlin of the UIL and James Hope.

176. Quoted in Clifton, *Amigo*, p. 110. A copy of a draft letter which argues in a similar vein can also be found at Nrt.D.A., Keating Papers, FV. 1 (G).

177. Canon Moyes to Canon Jackman, u/d but probably October or November 1919, A.A.W., Bourne Papers, Hi. 2/128.

178. Whiteside to Amigo, 24 September 1919, A.A.S., Amigo Papers, 'Political 1919'.

179. *Catholic Federationist* (November 1919).

180. *Leicester Daily Post*, 24 October 1919.

181. *The Tablet*, 8 October 1921. See *Catholic Federationist* (November 1921), for a full account of the proceedings.

182. Canon Jackman to Edward Eyre, 17 December 1921, A.A.W., Bourne Papers, Bo. 5/43d.

183. Keating to Amigo, 9 January 1920, A.A.S., Amigo Papers, 'Political 1919'.

184. Bourne to Casartelli, 20 May 1919, Sal.D.A., Catholic Federation File.

4

The Eclipse of Social Catholicism 1924–1935

The involvement of Catholics in preparations for COPEC was an example of the interest attached to social questions in the period following the war. As an inter-church venture, Catholic participation carried with it the high expectations of those Catholics, Bourne among them, that the Church would begin to assert its presence more vigorously in national life. However, the resignation of the Catholic delegation at the beginning of 1924 was a turning point in the fortunes of the social Catholic movement. Social Catholics parted ways with progressive elements in other churches and the potential for Catholic influence on public life was correspondingly reduced. The policy of accommodation which most bishops adopted towards labour in the aftermath of the war also came under severe strain. Bourne was very publicly to take the side of the government during the General Strike of May 1926 – a dramatic shift from his positive endorsement of the claims of labour in *The Nation's Crisis*. This chapter also examines the Church-labour strains which appeared in Liverpool in the mid–1920s. Paradoxically given his earlier support for the Labour Party, Archbishop Keating, reflecting shifts in papal social thought, urged a distinctively Catholic presence in the public life of the city. This narrowing of vision typified the direction English Catholicism took once the high hopes of the immediate post-war years had withered.

There were, of course, elements in the Church implacably hostile to the tendencies which COPEC appeared to embody. Bourne did not carry the episcopate with him: some were averse to anything that smacked of social radicalism; others viewed any dealings with Protestants as anathema; not a few were hostile on both counts. The inclusion of Fr McNabb amongst the delegates raised particular concern. Bishop Casartelli traced the CSG's tendency to 'coquette with socialism' back to McNabb's *Tablet* article of a decade earlier. In his attitudes to McNabb were distilled all the anxieties about

socialism which had been such a prominent feature of his episcopate.[1]
Bishop Cary-Elwes of Northampton (1868–1932), Keating's very
conservative successor, was possessed of a similar animus towards
McNabb, disliking intensely his 'socialist proclivities'.[2] Yet from the
acta of the hierarchy's Low Week meeting of 1923 it is not possible
to ascertain whether dissenting voices were raised to sending a delegation to COPEC. It was only with the resignations in January 1924
that the full extent of episcopal opposition became known.

Historians have commented on the part English Catholic anxieties
about the Malines conversations may have played in the withdrawal of
episcopal support from COPEC.[3] Started in December 1921, they
were intended as an unofficial discussion between three Anglicans, led
by Lord Halifax, and three Catholics from continental Europe, led by
Cardinal Mercier of Belgium, on the prospects of reunion. Papal
approval was given for these discussions.[4] As Lahey has demonstrated, whilst Bourne was not opposed to the idea of discussions, he
was piqued by the apparent disregard shown for his position as the
foremost representative of the 'Latin Church in England'.[5] Almost
from the beginning he was kept in the dark about proceedings, possibly because of a perception on the Anglican (and perhaps the Catholic)
side that English Catholics were more antagonistic to the idea of
reunion, more ultramontane than the papacy itself. English Catholic
opposition was led by editor of *The Tablet*, Ernest Oldmeadow, a
former Nonconformist minister who brought with him a virulent
animosity towards the Established Church. *The Tablet* in the
Oldmeadow years (1923–36) was thought to reflect closely Bourne's
views; typically the two met once a week to discuss matters that
should be covered, and while a fairly free hand was granted to the
editor, Bourne's guidance, Oldmeadow pointed out to Fr S. J. Gosling
(editor of *The Sower*), enabled the 'ordinary Catholic reader to feel
that in matters of supreme importance he was getting a policy that *at
least* did not run counter to the wishes of the hierarchy as represented
by the Cardinal'.[6] It was a typically Bourne way of operating.
Although Lahey contends that Bourne had no connection with some of
Oldmeadow's more hostile articles,[7] it is hard to believe they ran
completely counter to his views – it was a question of tone and
degree. Evelyn Waugh, though not an impartial witness,[8] thought
Oldmeadow a 'man of meagre attainments and deplorable manners,
under whom the paper became petty in its interests and low in tone'.[9]
Waugh was hardly equipped to pronounce on manners, but clearly
Oldmeadow was not the man to represent the more 'open' Catholicism
Bourne had appeared to endorse in the immediate post-war years.
Oldmeadow's *Tablet* was 'a journal of such un-ecumenical slant that

Anglican Bishops were referred to by the title of 'Mr' in its columns',[10] and in the view of a later editor it became 'sectarian and puritanical, pompous and parochial'.[11]

The reasons for the COPEC withdrawal were not, however, directly related to the Malines conversations, although the resignations did spark off a wave of episcopal invective against inter-church initiatives which was probably as much a release of pent-up resentment at the drift of these discussions as it was a reaction against social radicalism. Ironically given the progressive attitudes of many of the Catholic representatives on the COPEC commissions, it was concerns expressed by the delegation itself about the social views represented at COPEC which prompted the resignations.

Ada Streeter, a member of the CWL and CSG, emerged as COPEC's most astringent critic. She was the delegate to the *Industry and Property* commission whose report represented *par excellence* the dominant concerns and ideals of the Christian socialist tradition.[12] Streeter was clearly the wrong choice. She was contemptuous of her colleagues, who included Christian socialists of such distinction as R. H. Tawney and Sir Henry Slesser (soon to become Solicitor-General in the first ever Labour government): 'The majority of the members are avowed Socialists of a more or less pronounced type and include representatives of the 'intelligentsia', of the Labour Party, several Nonconformist Ministers, and some rather fanatic idealists who are looking for the realisation of the "Kingdom of God" in the reconstruction of society on the basis of egalitarianism'. The 'only articulate minority', Streeter told Bourne, 'was an employer in the North and myself.'[13] The northern businessman was Sir Max Muspratt, Vice-President of the Federation of British Industry, whose 'industrialist's realism', Edward Norman observed, 'was quite at variance with the academic tone of the other leading speakers'.[14] Muspratt had maintained that wealth was perfectly justifiable: 'It is the successful and wealthy industrialist who normally sets the example to the less wealthy in wages and conditions and wide philanthropy, and it is the nations with the largest number of wealthy people which have in practice the highest standards of living all round'.[15] Streeter was to commend the work of Christian employers like Muspratt in establishing 'understanding with their Employees, through Work's committees, Welfare, and other agencies ...' Urging resignation, Streeter commented that 'it is my conviction that the motive is not an unbiased enquiry into the social applications of Christian Doctrine, but a deliberate endeavour to clothe the whole programme of the Labour Party in the garb of the "Teaching of Jesus"'.[16]

A weightier opposition came from Francis Urquhart, who sat on the

Christianity and War commission. A couple of meetings were enough to disabuse Urquhart of his earlier hope that Catholic social ideas would capture COPEC. Urquhart told Bourne in December 1923 that he was close to resigning as he found 'the whole thing ... to be of very little use'. His principal objection was that the commission 'were nearly all pacifists at heart and instead of having a fruitful attempt to insist on sound principles in international relations, there will simply be a barren discussion on the wickedness of *all* war'.[17] (Few Catholics of this period are known to have held pacifist views.)[18] Urquhart also took exception to idealistic attempts to model international relations on early Christianity:

> The whole thing is deplorably impractical – I am tempted to call it "amateur". "Christianity" for them means the conditions which existed in Palestine in Our Lord's time, and the words He used to individuals are applied by their loose talk directly to the conduct of nations. They seem to have no conception of the Moral Law which is something older even than Christianity and which Our Lord came to fulfil.[19]

Such criticisms were to prove decisive. On 4 January at Archbishop's House, Westminster, a meeting was convened to address the mounting disquiet. Bourne was too ill to attend and in his absence the chair was taken by his Auxiliary, Bishop Bidwell (1872–1930). The delegates were divided over whether they should withdraw from COPEC. Most expressed the view that they could not put their names to their commission's report, but others sought a way of remaining within COPEC whilst at the same time having the opportunity to make known their objections to the views contained in the final reports.[20] Only Mgr Brown, shortly to become Auxiliary Bishop of Southwark, Miss Fortey of the CWL, and Canon James Hughes of the Liverpool archdiocese expressed their unqualified support. Hughes was a veteran of the Catholic social movement: according to MacEntee his involvement with social questions began whilst ministering to a Wigan parish during the coal strike of 1893–4; his labour sympathies also led him to collaborate with trade union leaders to find a settlement to the Liverpool dockers' strike of 1911.[21] Reflecting his Liverpool experience, Hughes saw the cooperation of churches in social questions as an important factor in helping to allay religious prejudice and bigotry.

With a substantial body of opinion opposed to COPEC and with other delegates uncertain as to the collective position they should adopt at Birmingham, it was left open for others to make up their mind for them. Bidwell recommended withdrawal to Bourne, who agreed. On 7 January, Bourne informed Fr O'Hea that 'I have come to the conclusion that Catholics, while being ready to give advice and information on the subjects considered by the Conference on Christian Politics, Economics and Citizenship, might not cooperate formally with it or in future participate in any of its activities'.[22] On 21 January, O'Hea was told by Bourne that the 'occasional presence of Catholics, as benevolent outside well-wishers, on a COPEC platform does not present much difficulty; the danger consisted in service on committees being regarded as a close identification with the principles, or non-principles, of the organisation'.[23] The frantic efforts of several leading CSG and COPEC representatives to find some way of maintaining an official Catholic delegation came to nothing.[24]

It was only after the resignations that the true extent of episcopal hostility was revealed. COPEC found only one defender: Archbishop Keating.

> Your Eminence's letter re 'Copec' has put us into a quandary in these parts. Some years ago, religious antagonism was so acute that nothing similar to the 'Copec' movement would have been possible, or would have received a moments consideration. Recently there has been a marked and growing disposition to get on a more friendly footing ... Would it not be well before withdrawing formally *en bloc* from 'Copec', and especially before publishing the reasons of our retirement, to give the Council of 'Copec' a chance of considering and replying to our strictures.[25]

But elsewhere irenic feelings were in short supply. A day before the resignations Casartelli wrote to Amigo castigating both the Malines conversations and COPEC, which he believed to be 'dangerous, or at least misleading'.[26] Amigo made his feelings known to his flock in an editorial in the *Southwark Record*:

> Copec suggests to us astronomical observations, but we prefer to look upon it as a ship of very modern construction starting on a voyage of discovery, that commands the sympathy of all good-hearted men. But to take a passage in it – never! It is commanded by as many captains as there are men, having hazy and contradictory ideas as to the course they should take, and it is manned by a crew that seems to threaten mutiny every day. The Catholic who has taken his passage in the barque of Peter, a vessel of more enduring material, and commanded by a pilot who knows where he wants to go, and is never surprised by currents and winds, is well content to trust to a good ship and to a united crew. Copec does not understand but we do![27]

A year later, in response to reports that Fr McNabb was again involving himself in COPEC activities, Bishop Dunn informed Bourne that my 'impression has always been that Copec was an organisation which Catholics ought to shun and ignore altogether'.[28]

But the most emphatic broadside was delivered in an *ad clerum* of 12 February by Archbishop McIntyre of Birmingham; as the conference was being held in this city his strictures were guaranteed much publicity. It was also signed by his suffragans: the Bishops of Clifton, Plymouth and Shrewsbury. In McIntyre's view, COPEC was but a local instance of that dangerous tendency towards religious indifferentism which he believed was being given encouragement by the Malines conversations. There is a clear sense that McIntyre was venting pent-up resentments against the wider movement for Christian reunion. The whole COPEC project was underpinned by certain objectionable doctrinal assumptions which he believed no Catholic bishop could subscribe to. The Church with its 'clear, definite, dogmatic teaching, coming down through the ages' was now being told 'that "organized Christianity" has failed; that conferences, now being prepared, should voice "a confession of guilt from the Christian Church"'. Another objectionable feature was talk of the 'nebulous something, called "our common Christianity"', a negation of the 'historic, visible Church; nothing but Modernism in action, on a large scale'. Playing directly on the sensitivities surrounding the schools question, McIntyre twisted the knife further into COPEC by insisting that an admission of 'this so-called "common Christianity" as a practical basis for a common Christian teaching in the schools ... would tempt, and indeed has tempted, educational authorities to try their hand at evolving a standardized Christianity which, in their judgement, ought to satisfy all denominations. The prospect of thus forging a fresh argument against dual control, would make the temptation irresistible.'[29] The letter closed by warning the faithful against COPEC. Casartelli was delighted by Birmingham's uncompromising stance, as shown in his letter to the Bishop of Clifton:

> Many thanks for the fine Pastoral and 'provincial letter'. Roma locuta est. Deo Gratias! This 'Copec' tomfoolery was an emetic business from the first and your lordship may remember my sentiments when Fr Lucas (or was it Lester?) S.J. first 'sounded' the see of Clifton about it.
>
> There is a great need for more such pastorals from other Bishops too. Clear thinking, clear teaching, clear preaching, clear action are the needs nowadays and it will do a world of good to hear these fluffy phrases and mouldy mottoes pilloried. 'Our Common Christianity' is an excellent example of such eye-wash.[30]

McIntyre's pronouncement had the effect of frustrating the attempts of Catholic delegates to negotiate new terms on which they might participate at the conference. Fr O'Hea, who harboured hopes that Bourne would reconsider his decision, described the Birmingham letter as 'objectionable', but Bourne defended the pronouncement,[31] and it is clear that he had intended his letter of 7 January to be the last word on the matter. However, in the absence of a public resignation, and despite Bourne's letter, McIntyre was concerned that a Catholic delegation, albeit with certain safeguards, would find a way of attending the conference.[32] McIntyre's intervention can be seen as an attempt to forestall attempts in that direction, although his avowed motive, expressed in a letter to Bishop Burton, was to take 'on our shoulders the odium of their withdrawal, and enable them to get free without seeming unfriendly'.[33]

Understandably, there was some recrimination at the Birmingham conference, although William Temple was restrained, expressing his 'profound regret' that the Catholic delegation had withdrawn, thanking them for 'the valuable aid which they brought and for the cordiality of their cooperation', and welcoming those 'who are attending the Conference not as representatives but as individuals'.[34] Fr O'Hea was one of those individuals; it was he who bore the brunt of the recrimination. On 12 April, O'Hea told Bourne that 'non-Catholics not connected with the inner circles of the movement are already asking why we withdrew and some are being led to think that the cause is sheer high-mindedness on our part and that we are against all cooperation'.[35] He heard one leading Anglican, Charles Gore, declare that it was 'almost unbelievable that any leader of the Christian Church could hold that the Church had not failed to make men understand the meaning of Christianity and brotherhood.'[36] Gore had highlighted an important point: English Catholicism, confident and assertive after the war, could not indulge in the mood of guilty self-criticism which invariably accompanied Christian social witness at the time. This kind of complacency was the dominant note of Casartelli's editorial on COPEC in 1923: if, as COPEC leaders maintained, the 'social ethics of Christianity have been greatly neglected', then 'Catholics decline to accept responsibility for this neglect ... the existing social chaos is the product of Protestantism'.[37]

There was to be no further Catholic participation in inter-church efforts during Bourne's archiepiscopate, although there were minor initiatives at the local level. After the promising developments of the immediate post-war years relations between Church leaders became decidedly chilly. Bourne's attitude towards the Malines conversations hardened, and at a meeting in September 1924 he offended Anglicans by 'using the word 'impertinence' of their claim to continuity with the prae-Reformation Church'.[38] The mid-1920s saw his relations with

Archbishop Davidson deteriorate; this may have been due to Bourne's role during the General Strike. The cooling between them is very evident by 1927. On hearing from Sir James Marchant that Bourne, usually so phlegmatic, was moved to tears 'when he spoke to me of his longing desire to see more friendly relations established and his constant prayer for reunion', a distinctly unmoved Archbishop Davidson remarked that Bourne had 'throughout maintained that the conversion of individuals and the bringing of them into the fold is the only policy he could further in England, and his addresses and references to Anglicans have never indicated ... any desire for corporate conversions or approaches or for ultimate corporate reunion save by absorption'.[39] By this time the Malines conversations had ended and with them any hope of further discussions on reunion. A papal encyclical issued in January 1928 soon after this meeting between Davidson and Marchant, *Mortalium Animos*, revealed a hardening of Roman attitudes to reunion: 'Such attempts can nowise be approved by Catholics, founded as they are on that false opinion which considers all religions to be more or less good and praiseworthy ...'[40] Bourne's contribution to Marchant's *The Reunion of Christendom*, published the following year, had all the coldness of that encyclical (which Bourne incorporated into his chapter): the Church, he insisted, 'must ever be, as she has been from the beginning, an *exclusive* Church both in her teaching and in her worship'.[41]

* * *

The period which followed the COPEC resignations in 1924 through to 1935 was largely one of decline for English social Catholicism. The mood of post-war idealism had passed. Fr Parkinson feared that the CSG was 'declining towards extinction' and noted that intellectuals had 'disappeared from our meetings'.[42] A disappointed man, Parkinson died in 1924; the same year saw the death of another stalwart of the Catholic social movement, Canon James Hughes. In many ways 1924 was proving a gloomy year.

Strong episcopal leadership might have helped in these testing times. But commitment from the top was markedly absent. Even Archbishop Keating, now extremely ill[43] and immersed in diocesan cares, could no longer give it the necessary push. High office imposed demands which he had not experienced at Northampton. There was not only a cathedral to be built, a task to which Keating promised in 1922 to 'devote the rest of my days, every ounce of my strength and every penny I save ...',[44] there was also considerable work to complete the seminary at Upholland. Keating refused an appeal for financial support from a local branch of the CSG because the proposed cathedral for Liverpool was draining diocesan resources.[45]

The lay apostolate had lost much of its drive and purpose. In Salford the Catholic Federation was in disarray. Its unremitting campaign against the Labour Party had won them few friends: Bourne's declaration in August 1924 that membership of the Labour Party was compatible with Catholicism[46] seemed like a repudiation of all it had stood for. Between 1921 and 1926 membership of the Salford and Manchester branches fell from 7,000 to 4,000, and the number of branches from twenty-five to thirteen.[47] The Westminster branch was in similar decline.[48] Contemporary explanations of the organization's declining appeal suggested that its role had been primarily negative, consisting of agitations against threats to the schools, but that it had contributed little of constructive or positive value. In his unpublished history of the organization, Ford suggested that its 'negative performance during the steadily growing depression failed to have any attraction for the industrial workers'.[49] Federationists on the other hand began to express some disenchantment at the negative, defensive role assigned to them. An editorial in the *Catholic Federationist*, for instance, warned: 'Let those who would discourage initiative by the Catholic body face the dread alternative. The alternative to Federation is a shoulder-shrugging laity.'[50] It was an outburst of frustration that its opposition to socialism and the Labour Party had not received support from above. The Cardinal's declaration of 1924 was, however, the final word on the matter and Casartelli warned Burns to desist from further comment: 'we cannot allow a controversy with H[is] E[minence], the scandal and consequent trouble would be too great'.[51] With the death of Casartelli in January 1925 the demise of the Salford Federation was brought closer. It seemed as if a distinctive kind of political Catholicism, uncompromising in its stance towards progressive social and political movements, had finally ran its course.

Strangely something of the spirit of Casartelli and the Federation continued under Keating at Liverpool. In the dormant mid–1920s the appeal of Catholic Action in England had been decidedly limited. The odd social Catholic like Mgr Parkinson, who had never been enthusiastic about movements like COPEC,[52] began to urge a distinctively Catholic presence in public life;[53] but this was not at the time part of mainstream thinking. Yet a shift to distinctively Catholic social and political action was now encouraged by Keating; this was surprising since he more than any other bishop of the period had encouraged Catholics to channel their political energies into the main political parties, rejecting the idea of a specifically Catholic presence.[54] How are we to explain this shift?

It can be partly explained by reference to tendencies in contemporary papal social thought. Achille Ratti, a former Vatican librarian, was elected Pope in February 1922, taking the name Pius. The main themes of Piux XI's early encyclicals, *Ubi Arcano Dei Consilio* (1922) and *Quas Primas* (1925), were assimilated faithfully into Keating's pastoral letters and sermons of the period. Denunciations of personal immorality became a marked feature of Keating's social thought in the 1920s. The immodesty and frivolity of current feminine attire, a bugbear of Pius XI's,[55] was a development Keating alluded to frequently;[56] although his commitment to social reform remained it was far less pronounced. The printed resolutions of a special meeting of the hierarchy in 1922 reveal that Keating was wanting to put a question on socialism to electoral candidates; evidently this was causing him greater anxiety than previously, and has much to do with the Liverpool context. (Typically, the bishops decided 'to let the question rest until Low Week, as the Education matter alone seemed pressing'.[57]) His adoption of military metaphors pointed also to the influence of contemporary papal social thought: a militant, confrontational vision of the Church was encouraged which brooked no compromise with a sinful society. As Pius put it in *Quas Primas*, 'if the faithful were generally to understand that it behoves them ever to fight courageously under the banner of Christ their King, then, fired with apostolic zeal, they would strive to win over to their Lord those whose hearts that are bitter and estranged from him, and would valiantly defend his rights'.[58] At St Charles's, Liverpool, on 1 March 1925, Keating's Manichean view of society was revealed in a homily on the theme 'Soldiers of Jesus Christ', when he urged his congregation to do battle against satanic forces manifested in the world through money, dress and the 'pleasures' of eating, drinking and comfort.[59] The corollary of this disdain of the world was the attempt to create a distinctive Catholic movement which would engage in a militant crusade for the reChristianisation of society. Central to this vision was the cult of 'Christ the King', which was inaugurated as a feast day by Pius XI in the encyclical, *Quas Primas*.[60] Keating took the theme of 'Christ the King' for his Lenten pastoral letter of 1923 when he urged his flock to 'sink all ... differences, racial, political, social, industrial, or personal', and to combine 'with the zeal, self-sacrifice, and the pertinacity of monarchists for the restoration of our Heavenly King'. Party politics, echoing *Ubi Arcano*,[61] were deprecated as simply carrying on 'the futile and discredited tradition of secularism ...'

> Something more heroic than that, one would think, is demanded by the stress of the times, and by the summons of 'Catholic Action'. If we

cannot command a majority; we can at least command a hearing on any public bodies to which we may be elected; and outside those bodies, we can promote the cause of Christianity by speech, by pen, and by discussion, if we have the courage of our convictions, untrammelled by human respect and worldly considerations.[62]

The denigration of party politics and the call for Catholic Action sound strange coming from Keating – they are themes which featured more prominently in continental Catholic social thought where the call for the reChristianization of society and the establishment of Christ's reign evoked an enthusiastic response. Young Catholics in France and Belgium, especially students, increasingly rejected mainstream Catholic parties in place of movements which offered a more direct involvement in the life of the Church:[63] pilgrimages, parades, demonstrations and rallies were core activities of the Catholic Action groups which sprang up on the continent in the 1920s; party politics were eschewed and energies directed instead into 'campaigns against pornography, proselytisation among the deChristianised working classes and glorification of the virtues of motherhood, youth and the family'.[64]

Catholic Action, it has been argued recently, was of marginal significance in English Catholicism: first, because there was not that sense of crisis in the Church to provoke such a combative counter-movement; secondly, because its leaders, following in the tradition of Cardinal Manning, have rather encouraged lay people to take their full part in a democratic, plural society, working through existing political parties and with other religious groups where possible.[65] It is my contention that whilst the ultimate failure of Keating's efforts to promote a distinctively Catholic political party in 1920s can be cited in support of these arguments, the very fact that such an initiative was attempted, and not by a marginal figure but by one who had more than any other bishop of the period continued Manning's tradition of social and political concern, suggests a declining commitment in mid–1920s England to these ideals and a preparedness to consider other, more exclusivist traditions of political Catholicism.

In the febrile, sectarian political culture of Liverpool,[66] with its numerically significant Catholic presence, the idea of a separate political party to defend Catholic interests at municipal level was regarded as a realistic alternative. The Irish Nationalist Party had, after all, constituted a major force in Liverpool politics and had the support of the majority of the city's Catholics. Keating's Catholic Representation Association (CRA), started in 1925, was an attempt to maintain a united Catholic presence in local politics after the Irish political settlement of 1922 deprived the Nationalist Party in Liverpool of its *raison d'être*. 'The Catholic Representation Association', Keating told W. Friel of the South Scotland Labour club, 'was set up under my auspices to secure the Catholic representation in the six wards of the Scotland Road area where the organisation of the old Irish party fell to pieces.'[67] Yet out of the remnants of the Nationalist Party the Labour Party also hoped to profit. Although the Nationalists continued to contest elections after the Irish Treaty, and had found themselves at the 1922 municipal elections in a strong position in Liverpool,[68] Labour's improved performance in bastions of Nationalist strength did suggest realignment.[69] Whilst Labour attempted to draw the beleaguered Nationalists to its side, Nationalists threatened that a specifically Catholic, anti-socialist party would emerge to take its place. Brushing aside these threats, Labour continued to make gains from the Nationalists, taking two seats from them in the 1924 municipal elections. At this point, Nationalist fears of political demise dove-tailed with Keating's vision of a reinvigorated, assertive Catholicism: with his active encouragement the Nationalist Party transformed itself into the CRA.

It was therefore a combination of political opportunism and militant Catholicism which inspired the most significant attempt to create a specifically Catholic political party during the period discussed in this study. Of course, in the mid-1920s 'party politics' had no place in Keating's lexicon; so the CRA claimed that it was not a political party but rather, as the constitution adopted in September 1927 stated,[70] an organization for the furtherance of the 'moral' and 'social' interests of the Church. Its avowed aims were to ensure that Catholic education received financial equality with all other forms of education recognized by the state; to secure the right of all Catholics to practice their religion in all public institutions and hospitals; to see that the religion of Catholic children was safeguarded by law in the administration of the Adoption Act. The inclusion in the constitution of a section devoted to the 'social' objects of the CRA was probably intended to counter the charge that it was an anti-Labour front: the CRA pledged itself to 'work for the social betterment of the working classes as regards a living wage and to secure better conditions of labour' and 'to provide decent sanitary and sufficiently large dwellings for the working classes and for the poor'. The main focus of CRA activity was, however, the defence of the Church's educational interests, and this is reflected in the fact that Mgr Thomas George of St Joseph's, the CRA's Chairman and Keating's right-hand man, went on to sit on the City Council's Education Committee.

The constitution of 1927 also gave emphasis to the two key principles of Christian democracy, as defined in the papal encyclical *Graves de Communi*. First, it should not 'mix itself up with politics' or 'serve political parties and political ends'; secondly, it should 'be subordinate to Ecclesiastical Authority, giving loyal obedience to the Bishop and their representatives'. It went on: 'It is neither meritorious zeal nor genuine piety to undertake any work, excellent though it may be in itself, when the Bishop does not approve'.[71] The purpose of the constitution was, of course, to define CRA activity; yet it also appears to have grown out of Keating's feelings of dissatisfaction and anxiety at the course of political developments amongst Catholics in the city. In Keating's opinion, too many Catholics were taking the authority of bishops lightly: it was an opportune moment to remind lay people of the virtues of submission, obedience and docility.

The CRA was to prove highly damaging to Keating's reputation. The attempt to mobilize his flock into a non-political movement for specifically Catholic causes in itself involved the very political methods he purported to disdain and sought to transcend. Political divisions within the community were in fact accentuated in the process. Moreover, the introduction of a Catholic party into the volatile political climate of Liverpool only served to incite further bigotry. Protestant opinion viewed the CRA – and particularly the prominent role of clerics in the party – as confirmation, if any was needed, of Rome's political pretensions and its complete subjection of the laity. The *Liverpool Daily Post* believed that it would herald 'a greater interference of the Priest in Politics'.[72] It was a view shared by leading Catholic Labour men. Soon after the formation of the CRA was announced, a group of these men (Alderman W. A. Robinson, Luke Hogan, David Logan, Richard McCann and J. O'Donoghue) drew up a letter of protest against the intrusion of the clergy into politics. It stated that the 'Catholic Church can boast that it has retained its adherents when apathy and indifference characterized most other churches. In a great measure this is due to the fact that the Catholic people have been taught to reverence their clergy and to regard them as widely removed from the cockpit of politics with its inevitable wire-pulling.' The letter went on to cite statements by the popes, Bourne, and Keating himself against the creation of a Catholic party, and concluded that they would be advising Catholics 'not to be misled on this issue, but to exercise the franchise on matters affecting the material well-being of the people as ordinary citizens', expressing the hope that 'the Catholic clergy of this city will, in the interests of the Catholic Church and of their own personal dignity, refrain from interfering with the judgement of the people in deciding what form of political representation is best for the toiling masses'.[73] Keating's initiative had threatened that 'unspoken' understanding of the scope and limits of clerical authority.[74]

Obdurate, Keating ignored this protest and attempted to bring the Labour men to heel through the ballot box. Against all intentions and rhetoric, his fine ideal of Catholic unity was vitiated in the quagmire of party politics. There was some initial success: arguably the greatest blow they inflicted on Labour was when Mgr George stood for the Scotland North ward in the 1925 municipal elections, the first time clerics could stand, and routed the ex-Nationalist Labour candidate, Richard McAnn, by 3,465–617 votes.[75] The CRA had seven seats as opposed to the three elected as Nationalists in 1924, and in four of the five wards where they opposed Labour candidates in 1925 they triumphed.[76] But this was as good as it got. In 1926 the Labour Party halted the CRA's advance: the most significant defeat was in the Scotland North Ward when Fr T. Rigby fell to W. A. Robinson, the Catholic former leader of the Labour group.[77] If there was ever proof that lay people were becoming hostile to clerical incursions in the matter of their political preferences, then this was it. Earlier that year Keating had intensified efforts to bring Catholic Labourites to heel after they rejected his demand that where a Catholic was seeking re-election he should be left unopposed by Catholics in other parties. He told George that 'you have no choice but to teach them the stern lesson they are asking for. You can give no quarter. You must enlist the zealous and undivided support of all Catholic voters in your area, priests and people alike, to ensure the return of your full list of eight candidates by decisive majorities. We have no use for political dictators. The Catholic voter must be master in his own house: – especially when he lives in Scotland Road!'[78] In a further letter of the same day, Keating urged George 'to work up a strenuous and I hope victorious campaign, with the help of all the clergy' and to 'provide every voter with a voting card, and to bring them up at the poll'. Significantly he also remarked, 'I am not sure that I have not gone beyond the bounds of prudence in the enclosed letter',[79] a reflection of his unease at the unhappy direction his campaign for Catholic unity was taking.

In 1927 Keating tried again, once more unsuccessfully, to persuade Labour to withdraw and leave the field clear for CRA candidates. Controversially, a CRA candidate threatened to set himself up in opposition to James Sexton, the veteran Catholic trade unionist and Labour M.P for St Helens (1918–31), who was standing for the St Anne's ward, despite Keating's admonitions that no CRA member should challenge a sitting Catholic candidate.[80] Somewhat unconvincingly given his active role in promoting the CRA, Keating insisted to

Sexton, an indefatigable fighter for Catholic causes,[81] that he had 'no idea that you were due for re-election and that you were being opposed by the C.R.A.' But after admitting that it was 'deplorable that such opposition should have been set up against you with all your years of faithful service behind you', Keating again attempted to secure a deal:

> I cannot coerce the C.R.A. who are responsible for their own line of action. But I have privately intimated my strong desire that the opposition in your case should be withdrawn. If this is the case, I hope you will use your influence with the Labour Party in the Scotland Division to come to a friendly understanding ... with the C.R.A. If your Party persists in trying to oust our 'sitting members', the C.R.A. cannot be blamed for retaliation. Catholic fighting Catholic is a sorry spectacle and it ought to cease.[82]

But another acrimonious contest between two Catholic candidates ensued, and Sexton's eventual victory over C. Devlin, who stood despite Keating's guarded assurances, combined with other CRA defeats to Labour in the Scotland North and Sandhills wards, hastened its political demise.

The clergy of the Scotland Rd area had been divided as to the efficacy of a Catholic political party from its inception, but the embarrassments of 1927 brought dissentient voices out into the open. A meeting of the clergy of central Liverpool was held on 24 January 1928 to address the mounting disquiet. In his absence through illness, Keating's Auxiliary, Robert Dobson, presided. Several priests testified to the bitterness the CRA-Labour clashes had caused in their parishes, with stories of fights during election campaigns and a general falling away from mass attendance and the sacraments due to the politically-charged atmosphere. Far from being an organisation promoted to serve Catholic interests, the CRA was seen by many as simply an anti-Labour movement. This was the opinion of Fr Kavanagh of St Alexander's:

> Its action during the last few years have lowered the prestige of the clergy and if our people lose respect for the clergy they would cease to respect religion. Our poor people regard opposition to the Labour Party as opposition to the working man: it would be difficult to educate them out of this confusion. Spiritual harm was being done to our poor people – better lose our representatives than our poor people. They would always be loyal to the voice from the pulpit if any crisis arose.

There were some prepared to stand by the CRA; some felt with the bishop that the very existence of the CRA at least prevented the

Labour Party from putting up non-Catholic candidates in 'Catholic wards'. But there few unqualified supporters of the CRA. Probably out of a sense of deference and respect to Keating (who was on his death-bed), the meeting stopped short of calling for the disbandment of the CRA, satisfying itself with an expression of dissatisfaction at the current functioning of the CRA.[83]

Keating's death less than a fortnight later changed the situation. The new Archbishop, Richard Downey, was keen to improve relations with the Labour Party and to avoid any repeat of the 'turmoil which obtained in the last municipal elections in November with regard to the Catholic vote'.[84] After meeting with Labour leaders on 10 October 1928 Downey decided that:

1a) no priest should stand as candidates in wards b) take active part in elections c) allow schools to be used (or ecclesiastical property) for political purposes

2) sitting members who are Catholics should not be opposed by fellow-Catholics this year

3) Catholic party was a misleading term. 'I would not recognise the claims of any political party to the exclusive use of the term "Catholic"'.[85]

Although the CRA was disbanded, some of its members continued under the name 'Centre Party'. This party eventually folded in the 1930s.

Not only was Downey's action inspired by the desire for *rapprochement* with the Labour Party, he also held very pronounced ideas about the duty of Catholics to participate fully in civic life. It became clear to him that an exclusively Catholic party was an obstacle rather than an aid to this – it was the introduction of a divisive element into the body politic. The changed attitude to Catholic political parties also reflected current papal policy, which came to see them as a distraction from or a danger to the avowedly religious and spiritual message of Catholic Action. The Pope's desire, as Odo Russell, British Legate to the Holy See, described in a letter to Archbishop Davidson in 1927, was to 'withdraw the Church as far as possible from the political arena, so that Catholics will unite on a moral and religious basis and cast their voting strength in favour of whichever of the existing political parties seems most likely to advance the aims of the Church ... any tendencies on the part of the clergy to mingle politics and religion beyond the prudent limits laid down by the Holy See will be severely repressed'.[86] In Italy, for instance, Pius XI withdrew support for Don Luigo Sturzo's Partito Populare, although this had the effect of leaving the field clear for Mussolini's Fascist Party.[87]

*   *   *

Church-labour tensions also surfaced at the national level. Bourne's denunciation of the General Strike of May 1926 imposed severe strains on the loyalty of many working-class Catholics. It was in many respects a curious episode in church history: Archbishop Davidson of Canterbury, the cautious primate who had previously refused to become involved in COPEC, attempted to mediate in the dispute and unwittingly found himself cast in the role of champion of the people; Bourne, on the other hand, presiding over the church with the largest proportion of working people, became a spokesman for middle England and a defender of lawfully constituted authority. Here, as over the Irish question, Davidson was closer to the instincts of the Catholic community than their Cardinal.

Since the war the miners and coal-owners had been locked in an ongoing dispute about wages and hours, played out against a backdrop of uncertainty about the future of the coal industry. In 1919 the Sankey Commission had reported in favour of nationalization, but the owners stubbornly rejected any change; with the industry in decline after the occupation of the Ruhr in 1923 they were more intent on keeping down wages and increasing hours. The miners' leaders were equally intransigent. The dispute came to a head in 1926 when the owners ignored the recommendations of the Samuel Commission. Reporting in March, this had rejected the idea of any further government subsidy to help the ailing industry and proposed an immediate reduction of wages, whilst dismissing the idea of a longer day; proposals for the reorganization of the industry and improvements in working conditions were for the future. The miners' leaders were unwilling to make concessions and deadlock ensued. When, on 1 May, the miners rejected the owners' demands for district agreements and lower wages, they were locked out. On 3 May the General Council of the Trades Union Congress (TUC), which had committed itself to supporting the miners, called for a national strike.

Central to the strategy of Conservative government hardliners like Winston Churchill, Chancellor of the Exchequer, and Sir William Joynson-Hicks, Home Secretary, was to portray the General Strike as an attack on the constitution. They hoped this would alienate the sympathies of middle England, thereby making it easier to hammer the miners into submission. But a political attack on constituted authority was emphatically not the intention of the General Council of the TUC. Political extremists were not to the fore: TUC leaders were rather motivated by feelings of loyalty and sympathy to the miners, and concerns about the lowering of wages; overthrowing the government was not on the agenda. The government's interpretation was tendentious and widely seen as such. Although the government ensured wide publicity for the views of Sir John Simon, a Liberal MP and notable lawyer who, in the House of Commons on 6 May, declared the strike to be an illegal proceeding, there were many dissenting legal voices. Sir Henry Slesser argued that the strike was a trade dispute and not an attack on the constitution. He claimed there was nothing illegal about a sympathetic strike as long as it was not accompanied by criminal acts.[88] It was this view, not Simon's, which gained support in the main legal journals.[89]

The churches were equally divided over the General Strike. The constitutional question inevitably polarized opinion, making the attempts of some church leaders to conciliate a hazardous task. The expectation of the government was that the respected elements of society should denounce the General Strike in emphatic terms and uphold the constitution. However, it was not only Christian socialists who saw this as an unhelpful and divisive position: churchmen of a conservative hue sensed also that it was their duty to stand above the fray and promote peace. Whatever his view on the rights and wrongs of the tactics employed by the strikers, this was clearly the view of Archbishop Davidson. His attempt to conciliate in the General Strike originated in a meeting on 5 May between Henry Carter, a Wesleyan temperance and social welfare worker, Dr Scott Lidgett, and P. T. R. Kirk of the Industrial Christian Fellowship. The idea of an intervention by church leaders was mooted. On 6 May, Luke Thompson, a coal-owner and Conservative MP for Sunderland, sensing an opportunity for the church leadership to break the impasse, suggested three points on which to base a joint church appeal: the cancellation of the strike, the continuance of the subsidy and the withdrawal of the mine-owners' notices. Davidson had previously spoken of the iniquity of the strike in the House of Lords, but following a conversation with Lord Londonderry, a mine-owner, who pointed out the futility of asking the TUC to call off the strike in advance of negotiations, Davidson was persuaded that his intervention might help the situation. He gave his approval to Londonderry's proposal that the three points should be acted upon 'simultaneously and concurrently'. Londonderry urged Davidson to inform the government and the TUC 'that it was "up to them" to support the honest effort made by the churches to secure a resumption of negotiations'.[90]

Bourne's role during the General Strike is surrounded by ambiguity. On the afternoon of 7 May a representative of Davidson called at Archbishop's House to ask him to put his name to the appeal. He was out, but on his return apparently informed Lambeth Palace that he broadly supported the appeal, although he insisted that ending the strike should be the first proposal.[91] But this was a significant divergence from the point of Davidson's appeal, which had used the words 'simultaneously and concurrently'.[92] Somehow Davidson was under the impression that Bourne was thinking along the same lines: one Conservative MP, Joseph Nall, who later remarked on the contrast in the church leaders' attitudes, was told by Davidson that Bourne had suggested some of the words inserted in the appeal.[93]

Precedents for conciliation would certainly have been in Bourne's mind. In 1919, along with Davidson and Free Church leaders, he had attempted to mediate in the railway strike. Looming in his mind no doubt was the example of Cardinal Manning. At the age of eighty-two, Manning had thrown himself with great energy into the task of conciliation in the dock strike of 1889:[94] there were not a few quick to remind Bourne of Manning's great success, who suggested that he also could 'save the country'.[95] However, Bourne had neither the desire to adopt Manning's mantle, nor did he have the public standing to bring the sides together even if he wanted to. Furthermore, Manning's success was achieved against a background of huge public support for the dockers,[96] whereas, as an apparent war between capital and labour, the General Strike divided the country. Bourne ignored the precedent.

There were other considerations in Bourne's mind at the time. There was a Roman Catholic Relief Bill before the House of Commons, so it was prudent to avoid taking action which may have upset the government.[97] Although hostility to Catholicism was in decline, the removal of the remaining Catholic disabilities from the statute-book was a cause close to the hearts of many Catholic conservatives. It had been the great campaigning issue of CUGB members since the organisation began, but despite its success in having the offensive references to the Catholic religion removed from the monarch's accession oath in 1910, there were still some formal disabilities to be swept away. Their removal would symbolise the public acceptability of Catholicism. It was, therefore, a cause in which Bourne was closely interested and which he brought before the Prime Minister, Stanley Baldwin.[98] Francis Blundell, Conservative MP for Ormskirk, was moving in the matter, along with Dennis Herbert, who, though not a Catholic, had since his time as a history student at Oxford been 'deeply impressed by the injustices done to Catholics'.[99]

Although the Bill was concerned with the 'repeal of obsolete and unworkable laws' which could not be objected to by 'even the most intolerant Protestants',[100] its parliamentary passage was far from assured. As a private member's bill it was vulnerable to sabotage from backbenchers, and as late as 1926 there were one or two in parliament implacably hostile to popery. The most controversial provision of the Bill was the repeal of section twelve of the Catholic Emancipation Act 1829, which had excluded Catholics from the office of lord chancellor. This was an issue upon which Bourne insisted with a passion.[101] Dennis Herbert was attempting to persuade the government to ease the passage of the Bill by giving facilities at the second reading stage: Baldwin was sympathetic to his case although the Home Secretary, Joynson-Hicks, was a vehement anti-Catholic opposed to any government support.[102] It was made clear to Baldwin that the repeal of section twelve was a measure likely to anger grass-roots 'ultra Protestant' opinion, and that this would be further aggravated if the government were seen to be assisting the Bill's passage.[103] It was with these sensitive negotiations not far from his thoughts that Bourne considered his response to the General Strike.

Dramatically, at Westminster Cathedral on 9 May, just two days after Davidson had apparently elicited support for a conciliatory policy, Bourne denounced the General Strike in the most emphatic terms.

1. There is no moral justification for a General Strike of this character. It is a direct challenge to a lawfully constituted authority and inflicts without adequate reason immense discomfort and injury on millions of our fellow countrymen. It is therefore a sin against the obedience which we owe to God, Who is the source of that authority, and against the charity and brotherly love which are due to our brethren.
2. All are bound to uphold and assist the Government, which is the lawfully constituted authority of the country and represents therefore in its own appointed sphere the authority of God Himself.
3. As God alone can guide both rulers and ruled to a wise and successful understanding, it is the duty of all to pray earnestly and constantly for His guidance, that the day may be hastened when these unhappy conflicts shall terminate in a just and lasting peace.[104]

A rumour circulated at the time that Churchill himself had visited Bourne to ask him to say something;[105] but there is nothing in the archives to substantiate this, although it was certainly the kind of message Churchill wanted to hear from Church leaders. Indeed, Bourne's pronouncement was broadcast that night and given prominence by the *British Gazette*, Churchill's anti-strike sheet. By contrast, Davidson's appeal was not heard after J. C. W. Reith, Managing Director of the BBC, came under pressure from J. C. C. Davidson, Deputy Civil Commissioner, not to do anything that might antagonize government hardliners.[106]

Bourne's pronouncement pleased the Establishment immensely. At the beginning of the strike Baldwin had written to Bourne thanking him for his prayers 'during these difficult times through which our country is passing',[107] now he had even greater reason to be thankful: 'Your clear and strong pronouncement will be of the greatest value to the Government in the present crisis, and I am most grateful to you for your support', Baldwin told the Cardinal.[108] Lord Northcliffe informed Bourne that 'Your endeavour to support our cause and your support of the government do not go unrecorded', an allusion perhaps to the legislation with which Bourne was currently preoccupied.[109] Dorothy Gordon, a convert and stepdaughter of a Privy Counsellor told Bourne, 'My Stepfather was here yesterday and he was dining with all the Judges at Lincoln's Inn a few days ago and they talked of almost nothing else – saying that they were all going to become R.C.'s in consequence!!! And even that arch-protestant "Jix" the Home Secretary told Mother it was one of the best speeches in the strike!'[110] Significantly the weight of support for Bourne came from Anglicans dismayed by the conciliatory stance of Davidson. The chaplain of Benet House, Cambridge, Dom Bede Camm, O.S.B., a convert of conservative political leanings, told Bourne, 'Canon Adams, the Vicar of the Round Church here and the Rural Dean, stopped me in the streets to express his great admiration of your Eminence's statement. He said that, in contrast with the remarks of the Archbishop of Canterbury and other Protestant leaders, your Eminence shone out as a real leader.'[111] Hensley Henson, disliking Bourne but sharing his view of the strike, was deeply troubled by such talk and wrote a sharp letter of protest to Davidson:

> Your Grace knows how strongly I feel on the national character and responsibility of the Church of England. Surely that character and that responsibility did require at such a crisis as the General Strike created, a clear and imperative call to fundamental civic duty. What could be more unfortunate – I might also say grotesque – than a procedure which made it possible for Cardinal Bourne to become the mouthpiece of national sentiment and civic duty – a role which belongs pre-eminently to the National Church, and therein conspicuously to the Primate.[112]

Henson was privately convinced that Bourne's pronouncement was an opportunistic grasp for public acclaim. 'The wily Cardinal', his diary entry for 14 June recorded, 'was quick to seize the opportunity of presenting himself to the public in the character of the good citizen in vivid contrast with the fumbling and untimely peacemaking of the Primate. If he knew, and had assented to, the Archbishop's proposals, his conduct can hardly be purged from the charge of disingenuousness.'[113]

Bourne certainly did not let the government forget the role he had played. With some members of the government, notably Joynson-Hicks, reluctant to give the Roman Catholic Relief Bill parliamentary time despite Bourne's stance on the General Strike,[114] Blundell relayed a warning to the Home Secretary on Bourne's behalf that the omission of section twelve of the 1829 Act, 'could be exploited in mining areas where there was any considerable Catholic element (and there are many of these) as a further instance of the intolerance and oppressiveness of the Government'.[115] It was unlikely that Bourne would have attempted to exert such pressure if he had not demonstrated himself to be on the government's side during the General Strike. But Bourne was eventually persuaded by Blundell that to save the rest of the Bill the repeal of section twelve should be jettisoned.[116] Yet most of the demands were met and clearly Baldwin, though he was not personally sympathetic to Catholicism,[117] sensed that he had a duty to ensure that the Bill was given every chance.[118]

Whilst critics within the Church believed that Bourne had simply presented the opinion of government hardliners in the garb of Catholic social teaching, Bourne himself would have been confident that he was speaking from within a well-established body of teaching on labour questions. As noted in chapter one, Bourne had argued as early as 1913 'that the sympathetic lock-out or strike ... appears contrary to every principle of justice and charity'.[119] In a contemporary English treatment of the issue, the Jesuit Fr Bampton declared that a general strike was 'a direct attack upon the rights of the community; it is holding a pistol at its head, with the demand to stand and deliver; it is a criminal conspiracy against society at large, and any Government – if it had the courage – would have a perfect right to deal with it as such'.[120] Whilst it was clearly difficult to mount a direct challenge to Bourne on the grounds of his interpretation of Catholic social teaching on strikes, critics focused instead on the lack of sympathy and balance in his statement. All the blame, so it seemed, lay with the workers.

Within the Catholic community Bourne's pronouncement caused great disquiet. Reactions recorded in his own papers and published references are naturally weighted against him: those who approve are less inclined to submit their thoughts to paper than those who disapprove. There must also have been those who submitted to the pronouncement after much pain and heart-searching. It provoked a great deal of anger – one Catholic working man wrote to Bourne calling him a 'miserable sycophant of the owning classes'.[121] There were more temperate but equally strong criticisms from representatives of labour. But it was amongst the ranks of social Catholicism that the pronouncement caused most perturbation. Maisie Ward recalled that one Catholic Evidence Guild member had been so shattered by the pronouncement that 'she had felt unable to go to the sacraments until after a long conversation with Fr Vincent McNabb'.[122] Fr Winsborough of St David's Cathedral, Cardiff, who as a former railwayman understood working people and who himself took an active interest in social questions,[123] had to reassure several hundred upset trade unionists at a meeting of the CSG that Bourne had not condemned the right to strike, rather 'he has condemned the abuse of this right, that all workers in the country should withhold their labour and so make community life impossible, and thus in effect subvert lawful constituted authority'.[124] Evidently there were complaints that the Cardinal had no right to pronounce on politics. Fr Hind, Rector of St Mary's, Warrington, addressed Bourne's critics in a sermon which stated that

> it was one of the chief duties of the Church to teach on matters of faith and morals; and it was the duty of the priest in the parish, the Bishop in his diocese, and even more so the Cardinal, the chief representative of the Church in England, to teach not infallibly, but at any rate with the special guidance of God, therefore, such a pronouncement as that made by the Cardinal carried enormous weight from the Catholic point of view, and, at any rate, by Catholics, should be received with the greatest support and reverence.[125]

Another Warrington priest, addressing the same criticism, stated that 'if the Church had no right to pronounce on such a vitally important moral question, then it was futile to speak out at all of her right to direct men in matters concerning morals'.[126]

One of the consequences of the pronouncement was a cooling in relations between Bourne and the CSG, an organization he had previously held in high esteem. This distancing was partly the product of Bourne's increasingly conservative stand on social questions since the early 1920s. But it was also because he detected a critical tone in some of the comments relating to the General Strike in *The Christian Democrat*. According to Cleary, one analysis of the strike 'made Cardinal Bourne, usually the Guild's warm but undemonstrative supporter, distinctly cool towards it for some time'.[127] The Oxford-based Dominican Fr John-Baptist Reeves, writing in that journal, said that the pronouncement came to CSG members 'As a shock and an embarrassment ... It found us in a state of excited tension which made calm reflection difficult, and obedience as painful as obedience can be, and must be if it's Christ-like. Some of us were assailed by a horrible fear that his Eminence had been misinformed on a question of fact, and so won over as an ally by a party which we felt it a sacred duty to oppose.'[128] Reeves did not carry these comments forward into an analysis of the moral issues involved in this kind of strike action, but it was probably this frank admission which upset Bourne. The following month a Benedictine priest, Fr James Mclaughlin, contributed an article on the subject of resistance to authority ('He that Resisteth the Authority').[129] 'Wherever there exists, or there is reason to fear, an unjust oppression of the people, etc., it is lawful to seek for such a change of government as will bring about due liberty of action', McLaughlin, quoting the papal encyclical *Libertas Praestantissimum* (1888), reminded the reader. Although McLaughlin did not specifically apply the Church's teaching to the General Strike, with events still reverberating and with the stress heavily on obedience to authority, Bourne would not, one suspects, have appreciated this disquisition on resistance.

Bourne's views were by no means shared by the rest of the bishops, but so emphatic was his pronouncement that more conciliatory voices struggled to make themselves heard. Fr McNabb, who not surprisingly took a very different view to Bourne,[130] was told by Archbishop Keating that 'It would never do for me or any other Bishop to publicly disown the Cardinal's lead, whatever we may think about it, among ourselves'.[131] Private disquiet was not converted into public dissent. Prompted by the publication of J. Symon's *The General Strike* (1957) into recalling the events of May 1926, Fr O'Hea maintained that Bourne did not consult the other bishops, and whilst some agreed with him, others did not; some were annoyed that he had been taken as speaking on behalf of the Catholic hierarchy.[132]

One bishop who certainly agreed with Bourne was Dudley Cary-Elwes of Northampton. Cary-Elwes was from one of Northamptonshire's leading Catholic families; his father, Valentine, who was received into the Church in 1874, was a prominent figure in local Conservative politics.[133] At the age of thirteen Dudley was certain he too would always be a Conservative.[134] Quiet and retiring, as a young priest in Peterborough Dudley did not follow Bishop Keating's lead in public affairs, preferring 'to be in the background, and look on rather than be looked at'.[135] As a bishop, Cary-Elwes disliked priests meddling in politics and had a frequently troubled relationship with Fr John Lopes, an eccentric and unpredictable Cambridge University chaplain who held strong socialist beliefs.[136] During the General Strike, Lopes was disgusted that many so undergraduates enlisted enthusiastically as strike-breakers; he declared that

'If there is ever a class war in this country the universities of Oxford and Cambridge began it in 1926'.[137] Neither did Lopes take kindly to Cary-Elwes's instructions to have a handbill of Bourne's pronouncement pinned to the Chaplaincy door.[138] For his outspoken stance Lopes earned a severe reprimand from Cary-Elwes.

Other bishops were less convinced that Bourne had got it right, but to a great extent their sense of duty to the Cardinal set limits on what they could say. Some felt a sympathy for the miners, whilst sharing Bourne's view that the General Strike constituted an attack on the whole community. It was not surprising that episcopal statements reflected this tension. Archbishop Keating, who felt the tension more than most, tried to steer a middle course. In his sermon of 9 May he insisted on the 'clear duty ... to stand by lawfully constituted authority' and on the duty of obedience. This seems to suggest that Keating saw the General Strike as an unlawful attack on the community.[139] Indeed, in a private letter to a Catholic trade unionist he stated that the General Strike was an 'unlawful weapon' adopted by the trade unions at the behest of 'extremist politicians'. He drew an analogy with the Labour Party's adoption of a 'socialistic ... formula' in 1918, and urged the trade unionist to 'fight hard to keep Trade Unionism as an industrial movement'.[140] Clearly his was not the ringing endorsement of the claims of the strikers that some historians have suggested.[141] But neither did Keating go as far as Bourne in condemnation: he stressed to Fr McNabb that 'we are not in a position to apportion blame for the beginning or the continuance of the deadlock', and left out any reference to sin. Bourne's pronouncement had clearly put Keating in an awkward position: the civil authorities in Liverpool had asked him to distribute notice of it throughout the parishes, but fortunately, Keating told McNabb, the 'calling off of the Strike saved me from the dilemma'.[142] Keating's letter to McNabb, who had probably been trying to elicit episcopal criticism of the Cardinal's position, also suggested that Catholic social teaching could point in other directions than the one set out by Bourne: 'it is open to anyone to say that he spoke on the theological aspect of the question, as Sir John Simon spoke on the legal aspect, *in his individual capacity*: and that, whatever respect the speaker's public position entitles him to, he cannot, in either case, commit his Church or his party to the opinion expressed. Could a confessor e.g. refuse absolution to a striker on the strength of His Eminence's utterances?'[143] But this was a view he was understandably unwilling to state in public. On 16 May at Seaforth, he spoke again on the theme of obedience to the higher powers, contending that though there were bad or imperfect governments 'where so much human passion and selfishness issues in oppression of the poor

... neither our Lord nor his Apostles nor his Saints ever organized a rebellion – they suffered painfully'. He was not entirely one-sided: he also emphasized that as civil authority held its power from God it must 'respect the Law and the spirit of Christianity'.[144]

It was only when it appeared that the government and the mine-owners were intent on crushing into submission the miners who remained on strike after May 1926 that Keating cast off his earlier caution. His editorial in the June edition of the *Liverpool Catholic Parishioner*, which historians have quoted from to show Keating's social radicalism, was an emphatic condemnation of political economy and the treatment of the miners:

> In those mining villages, however unprepossessing they may appear to a stranger's eye, the native population, at all events, have found elements of that earthly and supernatural happiness. Is all this human tackle to be lightly 'scrapped', together with all the rest of the machinery, because the mines no longer 'pay'? Or must the miners submit to ruthless inroads upon their living wage, in order that private enterprise may be able to make it 'pay' to employ them? The mere formulation of such questions is enough to show that economic considerations are not the sole, nor even the primary factors in the solution of these difficult problems. No doubt there will always arise desperate cases where a 'deserted village' is inevitable. But no decent country will tolerate the wholesale devastation of our mining areas, and the deportations of the inhabitants, until science and management have exhausted every resource to let the poor live where they have made their home.[145]

In the fraught months following the General Strike, Keating's exasperated statement in the diocesan newsletter that 'if private enterprise cannot provide the worker a living, it must clear out for a system that can', moved Lord Stourton, a prominent local Catholic Tory, to accuse him of fermenting social radicalism. It was a charge Keating stiffly repudiated in a letter of 21 July:

> I am sure you will recognize that I have no time for controversial letter-writing on social questions ... The alternative to unrestricted exploitation of the coal-fields by capitalists, if they fail to provide a living family wage for miners who have no other means of subsistence, is not socialism, but, as I expressly said in my notes, some such re-organization of the industry as is outlined in the Report of the Coal Commission. In my opinion, the intransigence of the Coal Owners is mainly responsible for the hold established on the miners by Cook and his associates.[146]

Keating was referring in this letter to the Sankey Commission set up in 1919 to consider the issues of wages and hours and the question of nationalization; although deferring the question of nationalization, the Commission had condemned the current system of ownership and working in the coal industry, and stated that some other system must be substituted for it. Again, speaking to CSG members on 9 September at the Picton Hall, Keating declared that the cause of the coal trouble was the obsession with the 'axioms of economists' to the neglect of the 'human element'.[147]

Bourne's interpretation of the General Strike as an attack on the constitution was clearly not the view of all the bishops. A conciliatory note was sounded by John Keily (1854–1928), Bishop of Plymouth, in a letter read out at High Mass:

> It has been a grievous thing ... for the country to struggle against two bodies of men who stood particularly high in its esteem; the miners whose work is repeatedly heroic and always dangerous, and the fine railwayman, who if hurried into breaking through their contract, seemed to mean (one is convinced) more a chivalrous standing by an industry in trouble than any profit of their own. In such a quarrel it is hard to take sides and villainous to maintain them.[148]

Amigo, as ever, found himself in disagreement with Bourne. Always looking for points of disagreement with the Cardinal, Amigo wrote to a number of bishops expressing his conviction that though the General Strike was a 'big blunder' it 'was no attack on the constitution'.[149] He did not, however, express this view in public. There are two replies to his letter in his papers. Joseph Thorman (1871–1936), Bishop of Hexham and Newcastle, Keating's successor as President of the CSG, hoped 'he was not blind to the situation here' but thought that Bourne's pronouncement 'caused no real perturbation'; that the clergy had 'heard no question or complaint but rather acknowledge that his Eminence had power aright to speak'.[150] It is entirely possible given the disruption to communications during the General Strike that many did not hear Bourne's pronouncement; this would explain why there was no 'real perturbation'. Discussing the response to it amongst Catholics in the north east, Mews stated that many Catholics had not heard of it, and that others refused to believe anything which appeared in the 'capitalist press'.[151] Thomas Henshaw (1873–1938), Bishop of Salford,[152] proved more willing than Thorman to grapple with the question. He insisted that the trade union movement had been hijacked by political extremists, and that the General Strike was 'bound to injure the country at large and workmen most of all'. He also stated that the General Strike 'was a sin'. But this is where his agreement with Bourne ended. He believed the Cardinal's pronouncement 'failed to convey a true impression of where the blame for the General Strike was to be attributed. It seemed to exempt the Government from all blame ... it singled out for condemnation the "hewers of wood and the drawers of water".' Furthermore, the worker was now subject to the commands of his trade union, so it was unfortunate that Bourne appeared 'to apportion the sin and responsibility of this evident false step ... to the individual workman'. Significantly, Henshaw also pointed to the failure of the Church to prevent the growth of social radicalism: 'The ultimate blame devolves on those who have allowed him [the workman] to "coquette with socialism" in the past and in this connection it may not be amiss to remark that neither the Bishops nor the clergy of England are exempt from censure'.[153] He was of course citing the expression used by his predecessor Casartelli to deride the CSG's conciliatory attitude towards the Labour Party. Evidently Henshaw thought the time had arrived for a reversal.

The General Strike heightened anxieties amongst the episcopate about social and political involvement. Indeed, enthusiasm for social reform declined in all the churches as a result. Amongst Nonconformists there had been a marked decline in social concern since the war,[154] and the effect of the General Strike was only to intensify the feeling that 'tampering with the social order was inopportune'.[155] Archbishop Davidson, once bitten, declined to throw his weight behind William Temple's well-intentioned but ultimately futile effort to conciliate between the union leaders and mine-owners in the months following the General Strike.[156] As Edward Norman put it, 'In 1926 the door had been opened and a very cold blast had withered the hot-house growths. The Church's passion for social criticism survived the experience, but its growth was stunted.'[157]

*   *   *

Not surprisingly the sectional meeting of the CSG at the Manchester National Catholic Congress of September 1926 proved to be a low-key affair.[158] June 1926 had seen a revision of the statutes of the CSG which resulted in increased hierarchical control: from then on the four archbishops of Great Britain would nominate the president whereas previously the decision had rested with members.[159] CSG leaders had good reason to feel on the defensive. At other sectional meetings the mood was buoyant. The Tory convert Algernon Cecil declared that Bourne's clear lead 'had given many people quite a new feeling towards Catholicism. They were completely in sympathy with His Eminence, and they made no bones about saying so.'[160] Leo Ward of the Converts' Aid Society stated: 'If men of the older England like

Dr. Johnson came to life to-day they would understand a pronouncement of Cardinal Bourne far more easily than one by the Archbishop
of Canterbury'.[161] Speaking at the Congress, Bourne, wisely given the
divided opinion, took as his main theme the well-tried rallying cry of
unity in defence of the schools; only at the end of his address did he
advert to recent events, observing that Catholics had recognized 'the
claims of lawful authority' and had thereby performed a 'real service
to their country in those difficult economic crises'; he trusted that his
fellow-countrymen would now treat Catholics 'as other Englishmen'
and release them from 'the remaining disabilities whereby the law still
unjustly discriminates against us'.[162]

Bourne was never again to display the sort of commitment to the
CSG and social questions he had shown earlier in his archiepiscopate. Renewed obsession with the education question also served to
keep social questions off the hierarchy's agenda, with the Labour
Party determined on settling the denominational question after its
victory at the 1929 election. Bourne's address at the National
Catholic Congress of 1929 (which turned out to be the last such
gathering), coinciding with the triumphalist celebrations surrounding
the centenary of Catholic emancipation, exhorted the faithful to turn
all their thoughts to the schools and to the crisis in morality, and
not dwell complacently on the momentous achievements of the
preceding century.

Bourne was seriously ill for much of the early 1930s; in March
1934 *The Catholic Herald* commented that the Cardinal 'seems to be
forgotten by the masses of his flock'.[163] Richard Downey, appointed
Archbishop of Liverpool after the death of Keating in 1928, was probably the most prominent Catholic ecclesiastic of the late 1920s and
early 1930s. Unusually for such a senior appointment he had no experience of running a parish, had held no intermediate ecclesiastical
office, and at the age of forty-seven he was the youngest archbishop
in the Catholic Church. His family had settled in Liverpool when
Richard was in his early teens and he often described himself as the
'Lancashire lad from Kilkenny': his appointment was a sign that the
Irish element in the English Church was finally being taken seriously.
Up until his appointment he had spent most of his life in the classroom, first as Professor of Philosophy at Sacred Heart College,
Hammersmith, latterly as a Professor of Dogmatic Theology at
Upholland College, where he was also Vice-Rector. Anthony Kenny,
as a junior seminarian at Upholland, remembered Downey as someone
'small, round, and pompous' who 'looked as if he lived rather
well'.[164] Five feet four inches in height, there was some alarm in 1932
when he ballooned to eighteen stone (when asked by a little girl what

the difference was between a bishop and an archbishop Downey pointed to his stomach and said 'the arch'[165]), but a regime of exercise and dieting saw this reduced by nearly half.[166] However, the lengthy period he presided over the see did nothing to diminish his sense of self-importance: 'Do not forget, Your Eminence, that I rule the north', he once told Cardinal Griffin.[167] A monarch requires a palace, and on 6 June 1933, accompanied by a great fanfare, the foundation stone was laid for what was to be the cathedral for the northern province. In the book published that year to launch the Metropolitan Cathedral Building Fund, Downey recalled how on 'the occasion of my own episcopal consecration, thousands were unable to gain admission to the Pro-Cathedral. We need a cathedral, we need it urgently, and it must be a vast one.'[168] Indeed Lutyen's design was far greater in size than Westminster Cathedral, second only to St Peter's in Rome itself. Downey's view of what a cathedral stood for was bound up with an exalted conception of the episcopal office and in particular his emphasis on the primacy of the teaching function: in 'the ages of faith a cathedral was built so that on occasion the whole far-flung diocese should draw nigh and listen to the authoritative words of the Church speaking in the person of the bishop'. Dismissing those critics who urged him to build on financially modest lines, Downey stated: 'A Cathedral is at least a counterblast to such materialism. It serves to arrest the attention of the thoughtless throng, to remind them that man liveth not by bread alone, to recall them to the things of the spirit, the eternal values; to set before them the pledge of their immortality.'[169] But the cathedral project was to prove one of the less successful aspects of Downey's archiepiscopate: Lutyen's design was far beyond the pockets of the faithful and never rose above the crypt (but as Nikolaus Pevsner remarked, 'what a crypt!'[170]). The sheer size of the undertaking was underestimated. Financial mismanagement may have been another factor: among the donations Downey received towards the cathedral was a silver christening mug from C. C. Martindale, but allegedly this remained in a glass case with other sumptuous objects.[171] Downey left £63,000 in his will to the consternation of many of his flock.[172]

Like his predecessor, Downey was eloquent and assured on the public stage, though perhaps too pat. John Heenan recalled that his occasional sermons, whether for the opening of a new church or the jubilee of an old nun, would begin: 'This is a red letter day. The joy bells ring in the belfry of our hearts.'[173] Nevertheless, Downey had the knack of finding the right words for the occasion. In contrast to the increasingly negative strictures on politics which had flowed from the later Keating, Downey's early pastoral letters and addresses struck a positive note extolling the virtues of civic participation. Ever the Aristotelian, 'Civic Virtue' was the theme Downey took for his consecration ceremony sermon at St Nicholas's Pro-Cathedral on 23 September 1928, in which he laid special stress on the duty incumbent on Catholics to play their part in the public life of the city, a duty which cut across religious or political differences:

> Why should we be tied to ancient hates that have long since paled their fires? Let the dead bury their dead, and let us who are numbered amongst the living, whatever be our religious beliefs or political opinions, salute with the kiss of peace those who are opposed to us, waiving nothing of our essential principles because we respect those of others, standing fast by the known truth whilst holding out the right hand of fellowship to all within the city gates.[174]

In a sermon delivered on 6 December 1931 he once more venerated civic life. 'Good citizenship', he argued, '. . . is not an anaemic negative virtue consisting simply of not breaking laws or in not falling into the hands of the police . . . it is something active, dynamic, energetic.' He lamented the fact that the idea of duty had been squeezed out by the current emphasis on rights; this had the effect of promoting 'insubordination, a selfishness and a self-seeking, which glorifies license into liberty'.[175] Downey's emphasis on civic participation was part of his broader aim to ameliorate sectarian tensions in the city, and this desire to inaugurate a new era of religious peace also explains his decision to disband Keating's CRA.

There was indeed a lessening of sectarian feeling in Liverpool in the 1930s although the extent to which Downey's interventions played a part is difficult to assess. There were still violent incidents: one of the most notorious took place in 1932 when Canon Dawber's jubilee celebrations provoked local Protestants who turned on the parishioners, drove them into the Church and laid siege to it for three days.[176] Neither can it be said that Downey was always an emollient influence. His grandiose cathedral project antagonized local Protestant opinion: Revd H. D. Longbottom, a prominent anti-papist and local councillor stated that he would rather see 'a poison germ factory' on the Brownlow Hill site.[177] (After the battle to acquire the cathedral site was won in 1930, Downey quipped: 'Well it's all over, the site is ours. Not that it was a resounding victory, far from it. In fact we only won by a short head. But I suppose it is better to win by a short head than be beaten by a Longbottom!').[178] It was also the period of *Mortalium Animos* and any mixing with non-Catholics was discouraged, although the English bishops needed no prompting from Rome: after COPEC the line that separated Catholics from Protestants was drawn more firmly by the hierarchy; the very month of the Birmingham conference they expressed their concern at the attendance of 'Catholic Mayors and like officials at non-Catholic religious services' and 'earnestly appealed to all to whom it may apply to adhere faithfully to the well-established tradition of the past'.[179] Downey, despite all his noble sentiments, was very much a man of his time. After he declined an invitation to a joint Remembrance service, the Anglican Bishop of Liverpool launched a scathing attack on Downey in which he stated that there could be no community spirit when Catholics could not even join with other Christians to sing hymns at the cenotaph. Downey's riposte to Bishop David, that 'an Archbishop of the Catholic Church can hardly be expected to accept the spiritual leadership of an Anglican Bishop',[180] provoked a fresh outburst of sectarian violence, vitiating his high-minded civic ethic.

Neither was the education issue, burning again in 1929, ever a dissolvent of religious antagonism. Liverpool witnessed some of the most aggressive campaigning, which had the effect of exacerbating religious divisions within the community. Despite Downey's admonitions against clerical involvement in politics this did not prevent individual priests throwing the weight of their influence behind particular, usually Conservative Party, candidates at the general election of that year. Fr O'Ryan, a former CRA activist, was quite explicit in guiding his flock to vote Conservative; it was clearly a factor which contributed towards Sir James Reynolds's narrow victory of 209 votes over the Labour candidate, W. A. Robinson, this despite similar assurances on the religious question.[181] Reynolds, a prominent Catholic, had always been afforded a certain amount of deference by the Liverpool clergy: Archbishop Keating once described him as a 'rabid Conservative', but because of his 'generous support of causes in which he has confidence' thought it advisable 'not to make him an enemy'.[182] Claiming intimidation of voters,[183] the local Labour Party considered petitioning. The affair undid much of the progress Downey had made in improving relations between the Church and the local Labour Party.

The bishops for the most part did little to restrain this sort of pressure. Downey tried to retain a neutral stance at the general election of May 1929,[184] conscious of the fact that 'our . . . people here are nearly all Labour',[185] but elsewhere partisanship was very much in evidence. 'H[is] E[minence] praises Lord Eustace Percy[186] on every occasion', Amigo remarked to Downey, 'and even at the Albert Hall just before the General Election, it was taken for granted by the audience that he wanted them to vote for the Conservatives. He believed that they would be returned to power and therefore thought that our case was never as hopeful as then.'[187] The Auxiliary Bishop of Southwark, W. F. Brown, writing to Sir John Gilbert, Chairman of the London County Council (LCC) Education Committee and Secretary of the CEC, bemoaned the extent to which episcopal influence had been thrown behind the Conservative Party:

> The Labour Party quite realised that the weight of official Catholics and the Catholic press was thrown against them, and that extreme pressure was put upon Catholics by Bishops and priests to vote Conservative ... The attempt to coerce the working-class Catholic to vote Conservative utterly failed in most constituencies, and Labour members assure me that while they know that the Hierarchy, many priests, and the Catholic papers were their enemies, the rank and file disregarded their leaders and voted Labour. Whether it is wise to advertise the fact that the Church can no longer hold the mass of its working-class people or not I leave those responsible for the action taken at the election to decide. One thing, however, it has taught politicians that when in public questions the Hierarchy threatens, for practical purposes it is only *brutum fulmen*.[188]

Catholics were clearly in bad odour with the government. The new Labour Prime Minister, Ramsay MacDonald, was according to Brown indignant at the attitude of the bishops.[189] That their interventions could have prejudiced the new government against Catholic claims was also privately admitted by Amigo in a letter to Downey of 19 September 1929: 'We need the financial support of the Government, but we shall find it difficult with the Labour Government owing to our attitude at the time of the election'.[190] Again: 'I fear that H[is] E[minence] will have little or no influence with the present Government as they don't trust him. He was too much for Eustace Percy.'[191] At the 1931 general election similar pressure was brought to bear: Andrew Thorpe's study found that at 'almost every by-election from 1930 onwards, in a seat with a fair proportion of Catholics, the issue damaged Labour'.[192]

There was little movement away from entrenched positions on the schools question in these years, although Bourne did indicate a willingness to consider modifications in the method of appointing teachers in return for greater financial assistance. The northern bishops were more intransigent: monster demonstrations were held in protest against the Education (School Attendance) Bill of 1929 and the revised version of 1930, which proposed that local authorities would be entitled to spend money on the repair of existing schools in return for the right to appoint all teachers. Despite certain safeguards for denominational interests there were concerns that in areas where local authorities were unsympathetic (e.g. Liverpool) Catholic claims might be ignored.[193] Downey's bellicose opposition only served to harden Nonconformist opinion against any further compromise with the denominationalists.[194] The second Education Bill was lost because of the difficulties of parliamentary time; Sir Charles Trevelyan, President of the Board of Education, attributed the lack of progress to the 'intrigues of Catholics'.[195] Trevelyan pushed ahead with a third Bill in October 1930; this permitted local authorities to contribute a proportion of the cost of reorganising non-provided schools, fixed at 50 per cent as a minimum and 75 per cent as a maximum. At the same time, Trevelyan was preparing the ground for a further Bill (the Non-Provided Elementary Schools Bill) which would have given the denominational schools financial assistance in return for greater local authority control. Trevelyan was optimistic that a settlement acceptable to the denominationalists was near, although Nonconformist hostility was aroused by concessions relating to denominational teaching in the newly reorganized schools, in particular the proposal to extend the number of so-called 'reserved' teachers (those responsible for giving denominational instruction). Progress was again frustrated when the denominationalists insisted that any future reorganization of the schools should be dependent on a settlement satisfactory to the non-provided schools. An amendment was secured by John Scurr, a Catholic Labour MP, which had the effect of delaying the operation of the Bill until the claims of the non-provided schools had been secured.[196] However, the Lords rejected the Bill completely and Trevelyan resigned.

*   *   *

The absorption with the education question was a significant factor in explaining the mute response of the bishops to the social and economic distress of the early 1930s. Contemporaries lamented the apparent absence of social concern. Bishop Brown remarked to the Archbishop of Birmingham in March 1934:

> People are asking how is it that Anglican archbishops, bishops, monks, rectors are vocal in prominent places – e.g. St Paul's cathedral, on unemployment cuts, means test, housing, while our High Ecclesiastics preserve silence. It is pointed out that the Hierarchy vigorously denounce the sins of the people but say nothing about their sufferings. Yet we boast that we are *the* Church of the poor. Our people are hard pressed to find an answer when challenged as to the Church's teaching.[197]

What prompted these observations was Bourne's cancellation of a conference on the housing question planned for March 1934. Despite John Wheatley's Housing Act of 1924, the Slum Clearance Act of 1930 which provided subsidies for this purpose, and the National government's Housing Act of 1933, there remained a lamentable shortage of habitable houses for working people. The slow rate of progress in this area was of great concern to many church leaders.[198] Cyril Garbett, as Anglican Bishop of Southwark and later York, made himself an expert on the housing question; his *The Challenge of the Slums* (1933), with its call for the abolition of the slums and for 'decent housing of the people', did much to rouse the public conscience and keep the issue before the government. The Housing Act of 1935, which legally obliged local authorities to end overcrowding, was in no small part due to Garbett's informed agitations. But as Bishop Brown noted, housing was rarely mentioned by the Catholic bishops; if it was it was usually considered solely as a pastoral problem. After the 1935 Act accelerated the pace of slum clearance, Bishop Henshaw became concerned at the 'altering of the conditions of the parishes' near the city centre of Manchester, and issued questions to the candidates in forthcoming municipal elections seeking assurances that before clearance orders were made due regard was taken of the religious needs of the tenants.[199] In other words, the Church was mainly concerned about the break-up of existing parish life. In October 1933 the CSG planned a conference on the housing question to take place in March of the following year. According to Brown, this was cancelled because it coincided with the LCC elections, and Sir John Gilbert, a leading lay Catholic whose Municipal Reform Party held the majority of seats, was sensitive to anything that could be construed as a criticism of the council's housing policy.[200] Gilbert and the Municipal Reform Party were right to be sensitive: as *The Times* noted a few days after the Labour Party had overturned Gilbert's party to win its first ever majority on the LCC, sustained criticism of the housing organization of the LCC was probably the main reason for the defeat of the Municipal Reform Party.[201] Bourne's calculation, encouraged by Gilbert,[202] was that denominational schools would get a better deal under the Municipal Reform Party than Labour. It is a telling example of how the hierarchy's obsession with the schools question overrode all other concerns. Despite assurances to Bourne from the CSG that there was 'no idea of criticising the L.C.C.', that they were simply adding their 'contribution to the removal of what as Your Eminence so justly points out threatens the "moral well-being of the nation"',[203] the concern that nothing should be said that might prejudice the LCC against the Church acted as a negative pressure. Neither did the CSG receive any support from Thomas Williams (1877–1946), Archbishop of Birmingham, to whom they turned to host and address the meeting. He commended the record of the Birmingham authorities in building 'more houses than any other public authority outside London ... Consequently it does not seem to be opportune to choose Birmingham as the place for holding this conference'. He added that he did 'not believe Catholic men and women will make any valuable contribution to public opinion or action on the question of improved housing'.[204] The absence of any sustained Catholic contribution in this most crucial of areas of social policy was highlighted by Fr Martindale at the 1935 Summer School of Catholic Studies:

> You are all going home, I hope, to pleasant homes. But millions have no proper house. Here certainly the national conscience is turning in its sleep: but has the Catholic Conscience woken up wide, and taken the initiative in arousing the rest? I see no signs of it. If pity does not move us nor a sense of human justice, at least we believe in sin, and the fact that bad housing directly promotes sin should concern us. We speak loudly of contraception; but many a man can exhibit his house to you, and say, incontrovertibly: 'If I have another child, where am I to put it?' I do not dwell upon the quite common and often humanwise inevitable sin of incest.[205]

There is a sense, therefore, that the episcopate had lost its belief in the possibility of any distinctive Catholic contribution to social questions, a fact that appears all the more remarkable when one considers the confidence and assertiveness with which successive popes, most recently Pius XI in *Quadragesimo Anno* (1931), held forth on such issues. It was as if the bishops thought an abstract knowledge of the broad Catholic social principles sufficient; they tended to look askance at anybody who actually suggested that they might be applied to social realities. It is important to note that Williams, who was so opposed to the idea of a housing conference, was possibly the one member of the hierarchy who might have taken on Frederick Keating's mantle as an advocate of social and political involvement. A Cambridge History graduate, Williams struck up a good relationship with Keating, a fellow alumnus of Cotton College, whose Northampton episcopacy roughly coincided with his term of office as Master of St Edmund's House, Cambridge (1909–18). Williams's vision for St Edmund's, which Keating undoubtedly shared, was that of a centre of 'picked men' who would go on to become opinion formers on the important subjects of the day, including socio-economic questions.[206] His reluctance to enter public debate in the early 1930s illustrates the extent to which social Catholicism was in recession.

Bourne also discouraged attempts by Catholics to lend their support to the chorus of Christian criticism against the plight of the unemployed for similar reasons to those given by Williams. In a speech at east London in October 1932, George Lansbury, a government minister, declared: 'What do the leaders of the Church intend to do regarding the unemployment problem? It is now a question of life or death for your religion.' The appeal prompted Fr Worsley of Notting Hill to write to clergymen of various denominations in his area suggesting a conference on the issue; in seeking Bourne's approval he remarked on the possibility of the Labour Party 'introducing some adverse Education Bill if they are persuaded the Church is indifferent to the distress caused by unemployment'.[207] Worsley was attempting to prick Bourne's conscience by referring to the area of greatest sensitivity for the Church – education. But Bourne was not moved.

> I know Mr Lansbury and, while I admire his earnestness, I have no confidence in his judgement. What can the 'leaders of the Church' reasonably advise of a useful character concerning unemployment? They are not experts either in politics or economics, and the wisest heads are perplexed how to act. We have no reason for thinking that the Government is not doing its best. As far as the Catholic Church is concerned, all our organisations are, I believe, doing their best to relieve the existing distress. I am very reluctant to venture into questions in which I feel no competence.[208]

In September 1933, Fr C. C. Martindale led a pilgrimage of 400 unemployed Catholic men to Rome, the purpose of which was to pray for 'the temporal welfare of the millions of their fellow countrymen and women now suffering in the economic blight . . .'[209] But again this received no episcopal backing. At a meeting of the bishops on 4 July 1933 it was decided that 'as the Hierarchy were not approached before this pilgrimage was announced, the Bishops were not prepared to take common action in promoting it'.[210] In the face of the surrounding social tumult Bishop Barrett of Plymouth's resolutely apolitical attitude was typical: his Lenten pastoral of 1933 declared: 'Compared with this fact [the Passion and the Death of Our Lord Jesus Christ] all the other happenings in this world fade into significance. They may have had some effect on our mortal life for a few swiftly passing years, but our true concern is with eternity . . . what a fool he is who allows worldly concerns to distract him from that all important affair of his salvation.'[211]

Yet it would be misleading to suggest that social Catholicism was an entirely negligible factor in Church life in the later 1920s and early 1930s, even though its influence upon the episcopate had clearly diminished. An interest in back-to-the-land ideas was encouraged by the Distributist League, founded in September 1926, which converged around Hilaire Belloc, G. K. Chesterton and A. J. Penty. Although this was not in any formal sense a Catholic organization, the Catholic element came to dominate. Yet the anti-urban, mediaevalist orientation of Distributist thought alienated many more mainstream social Catholics: 'Belloc and his friends became classed as political eccentrics worshipping strange gods in Sussex', the Catholic journalist Douglas Jerrold remarked.[212] Fr O'Hea of the CSG dismissed them as inconsequential utopians, 'merrie Englanders' detached from the social and economic realities facing the great mass of urban Catholics.[213] One historian has stated that the appeal of Distributism was limited in England and that its main impact was amongst Scottish Catholics.[214] Yet some Distributist ideas, such as the idea of land resettlement or back-to-the-land, did find episcopal support. Back-to-the-Land was not necessarily a ruralist fantasy: such prominent politicians as George Lansbury could be heard espousing the idea of land resettlement as a solution to unemployment,[215] and one Catholic MP, Francis Blundell, was a vocal proponent. Archbishop Downey was the most serious advocate of back-to-the-land amongst the episcopate; his interest in land resettlement can be traced to a visit to Italy in 1933, where Mussolini's achievements in this area impressed on him that 'ultimately a country derives its strength from the soil'.[216] It is slightly comical to hear Downey extolling the virtues of peasant proprietorship and simple living, but the number of lectures he devoted to the subject suggests that he was sincere. The main appeal for Downey was that it appeared to offer a solution to unemployment which avoided both excessive state interference in the lives of individuals and the 'opiates' and 'palliatives' offered by much current voluntary effort.[217] A typescript amongst the Downey papers, dated February 1933 and entitled 'Back to the Land', argued: 'Cultivation of the land to the full extent of its capacities is the only remedy for unemployment which really touches the root of the problem. Technocracy, the nationalization of banks, insurance companies and railways, nationalization of industries and other similar schemes are all at the best mere temporary expedients and at the worst dangerous experiments of doubtful utility to the community as a whole.'[218] In June 1933, Downey presided at a back-to-the-land conference held at Manchester Town Hall, and his address bore traces of the Distributist critique of industrialism and the existing financial system. He argued that 'Land alone affords new opportunities of work and creative wealth. This does not commend itself to financiers who are bent on making money out of money, a vicious circle which is largely responsible for our present awful predicament. It is time that we got back to the real values of Mother Earth to which all monetary values are necessarily subsidiary.'[219]

Downey was not a lone figure in his interest in land resettlement. The Catholic Land Association (CLA) was formed in 1929 to establish training farms for the unemployed, and by 1933 there were five such diocesan groups in existence.[220] At a meeting of the CLA in 1934, John McNulty (1879–1943), Bishop of Nottingham, commended it as a 'national, Catholic, traditional and English movement. They were out to restore peasant proprietorship. The movement was dead against Communism and the Socialisation of the means of production and for that reason it should have the support of all Catholics.' He believed it offered the only solution to unemployment.[221] At his consecration as Bishop of Northampton in July 1933, Laurence Youens (1872–1939), who subsequently became Vice-President of the South of England CLA, referred to 'back to the land', stating optimistically that when Catholics followed this precept Northampton would 'blossom out into a province'.[222] Yet few practical initiatives flowed from this interest, and those that did could not be counted as successes. Maisie Ward's conclusion based on her dismal experiences with the Scottish CLA is not without application elsewhere: 'a farm could not be run on Christian principles if no one knew anything about the techniques of farming'.[223] In Birmingham, Sir Martin Melvin, proprietor of *The Universe*, sought funds from the diocese to buy Billesley Manor, near Stafford, but the plan came to nothing, with one priest suspecting that Melvin's principal motive in promoting the scheme was profit and that he would do little to encourage the 'development of simple thrift and the spirit of peasant contentment'.[224] In Salford the CLA did not start any practical work on the land until 1935 when it merged with the Liverpool group, who had a farm at Prior's Wood Hall near Wigan. Financial constraints and the poor quality of many recruits meant that the experiment failed to meet up to the sanguine expectations of its founders.[225] Despite the evident commitment of a number of bishops to the ideas of the CLA, the decision of the hierarchy in 1935 that it 'would not at present be justified in giving any official sanction to the Catholic Land Movement',[226] was effectively the death-blow. It was felt that all available funds should be devoted to the building of schools and churches in new housing areas.[227]

To varying degrees all the churches had turned in on themselves in the late 1920s and early 1930s,[228] but it was arguably the Catholic Church which became the most introverted. Even the enthusiasm of back-to-the-land that some bishops exhibited can be interpreted as part of this recoil from social and political engagement – certainly Fr O'Hea thought so. This chapter has catalogued a dismal period in the history of English social Catholicism during which the high-hopes of the post-war years withered and a myopic conservatism took hold. During the latter part of his episcopate Bourne was a sick man simply holding on; the direction and impetus he had given to Catholic political engagement in the immediate post-war years had given away to indifference and reaction. After hearing of Bourne's death on 1 January 1935, Arthur Hinsley, the sick and elderly former Rector of the Venerabile, wrote to his friend Bishop Amigo: 'May we all meet in heaven, where there will be no question of divisions but unending peace and unbroken friendship'.[229]

Notes

1. Casartelli to F. W. Aspinall, 15 September 1912 (copy), Sal.D.A., Casartelli Papers, Box 159; Casartelli to Thomas Burns, 20 August 1916 (copy), ibid., Box 161; Casartelli to Bishop Knox of Manchester, 9 February 1917 (copy), ibid., Box 162.
2. Cary-Elwes to Dom Bede Camm, 29 December 1924, D.A.A., Bede Camm Papers, Vol. II (C).
3. Oliver, *Church and Social Order*, p. 66; Kent, *William Temple*, p. 116.
4. R. J. Lahey, 'Cardinal Bourne and the Malines Conversations', in Hastings (ed.), *Bishops and Writers*, p. 87. See also the more recent treatment by B. Barlow, *'A Brother Knocking at the Door': The Malines Conversations 1921–1925* (Norwich: The Canterbury Press, 1996).
5. Lahey, 'Cardinal Bourne and the Malines Conversations', pp. 88–9.
6. Fr S. J. Gosling to Williams, 31 December 1936, B.A.A., Archbishops' Papers 1929–65, AP/P21.
7. Lahey, 'Cardinal Bourne and the Malines Conversations', pp. 90–1.
8. Gilley, 'Age of Equipoise', p. 43.
9. Quoted in Waugh, *Ronald Knox*, p. 243.
10. Scott, *Historian and his World*, p. 96.
11. T. Burns, *The Use of Memory* (London: Sheed and Ward, 1993), p. 45. See also, J. J. Dwyer, 'The Catholic Press', in Beck (ed.), *English Catholics*, pp. 487–88.
12. Which Kent describes as the 'radical margin' of COPEC: *William Temple*, p. 130.
13. Ada Streeter to Bourne, 16 December 1923, A.A.W., Bourne Papers, Bo. 5/76a. On Streeter's role at COPEC see Kent, *William Temple*, p. 122.
14. Norman, *Church and Society*, p. 300.
15. Ibid.
16. Ada Streeter to Bourne, 16 December 1923, Bourne Papers, Bo. 5/76a.

17. Francis Urquhart to Bourne, 20 December 1923, ibid.
18. Ceadel, 'Christian Pacifism in the Era of the Two World Wars', p. 404. Fr J. Keating, S.J, found the pacifism of many delegates the most objectionable feature of COPEC: *The Month* (May 1924), pp. 457–8.
19. Francis Urquhart to Bourne, 20 December 1923, A.A.W., Bourne Papers, Bo. 5/76a.
20. Memorandum to Bourne on the outcome of the meeting held on 4 January 1924, A.A.W., Bourne Papers, Bo. 5/76a.
21. MacEntee, *Social Catholic Movement in Great Britain*, pp. 220–1.
22. Bourne to Fr O'Hea, 7 January 1924 (copy), A.A.W., Bourne Papers, Bo. 5/76a.
23. Bourne to Fr O'Hea, 21 January 1924 (copy), ibid.
24. Fr O'Hea to Fr Parkinson, 31 January 1924 (copy); Fr O'Hea to Fr Parkinson, 4 February 1924 (copy), C.S.G.A., CSG Correspondence 1922–4, E 3.
25. Keating to Bourne, 19 January 1924, A.A.W., Bourne Papers, Bo. 5/76a.
26. Casartelli to Amigo, 6 January 1924, A.A.S., Amigo Papers, Correspondence with Bishops.
27. *Southwark Record* (May 1924).
28. Dunn to Bourne, 21 February 1925, A.A.W., Bourne Papers, Bo. 5/76a.
29. *Ad Clerum*, 12 February 1924, B.A.A., *Acta*.
30. Casartelli to Burton, 28 February 1924, C.D.A., Burton Papers.
31. Fr O'Hea to Bourne, 12 April 1924; Bourne to Fr O'Hea, 14 April 1924 (copy), A.A.W., Bourne Papers, Bo. 5/76a.
32. McIntrye to Burton, 26 February 1924, C.D.A., Burton Papers.
33. Ibid.
34. *Proceedings of C.O.P.E.C.: A Report of the Meetings of the Conference on Christian Politics, Economics and Citizenship* (London, 1924), p. 20.
35. Fr O'Hea to Bourne, 12 April 1924, A.A.W., Bourne Papers, Bo. 5/76a.
36. *Proceedings of C.O.P.E.C.*, p. 212.
37. *Catholic Federationist* (March 1923).
38. H. Henson, *Retrospect of an Unimportant Life* (3 vols., London: Oxford University Press, 1942–50), II, 132.
39. Memorandum of meeting between Archbishop Davidson and Sir James Marchant, 22 November 1927, L.P.L., Davidson Papers 36, fo. 309.
40. *Mortalium Animos*, 201, p. 313.
41. F. Bourne, 'The Catholic Apostolic Roman Church', in J. Marchant (ed.), *The Reunion of Christendom: A Survey of the Present Position* (London: Cassell and Company, 1929), p. 21.
42. Fr Parkinson to an Oscott Priest, 21 April 1924, C.S.G.A., CSG Correspondence 1922–4, E 3.
43. 'When he was transferred to Liverpool disease had already impaired his frame': *Cathedral Record* (July 1931).
44. Quoted in ibid. (June 1933).

45. Keating to Mr Leyland, 13 January 1924 (copy), A.A.L., Keating Papers, Series 4 I A/1.
46. Buchanan, 'Great Britain', p. 264.
47. Doyle, 'Catholic Federation', p. 475.
48. Executive of the W.C.F. to Bourne, 19 April 1923, A.A.W., Bourne Papers, Bo. 5/43d.
49. J. Ford, *Notes for the C.S.G. History: Manchester and Salford Area* [typescript], copy in C.S.G.A. See also an article on the 'failure of the Federation' in *Catholic Social Year Book 1921*.
50. *Catholic Federationist* (April 1922).
51. Casartelli to Fr Sharrock, 22 August 1924 (copy), Sal.D.A., Casartelli Papers.
52. Fr Parkinson to Henry Somerville, 14 July 1921, C.S.G.A., Executive and Council Letters, E 2.
53. Fr Parkinson to Fr O'Hea, 16 January 1924, ibid., CSG Correspondence 1922–4, E 3.
54. Fr J. S. Mayne [Keating's Secretary] to Dr Bradley, 14 May 1911 (copy), Nrt.D.A., Keating Papers, FV.6.
55. *Ubi Arcano Dei Consilio*, 192, p. 228.
56. See e.g., sermon given at Colne, 11 August 1925, A.A.L., Keating Papers, Series 7 IV A/84; see also, address to the CWL, 14 February 1923, ibid., Series 7 IV A/46; sermon given at Adoration Réparatrice Convent, Liverpool, 13 February 1926, ibid, Series 7 IV A/95.
57. Meeting of the Bishops, 26 October 1922, A.A.W, *Acta*. The matter was not taken up at the Low Week meeting of 1923.
58. *Quas Primas*, 197, p. 276.
59. Sermon given at St Charles', 1 March 1925, A.A.L., Keating Papers, Series 7 IV A/77; see also, sermon given at SS Peter and Paul's, Bolton, 11 October 1925, ibid., Series 7 IV A/88.
60. Conway, *Catholic Politics in Europe*, p. 42.
61. *Ubi Arcano Dei Consilio*, p. 228.
62. Archbishop Keating's Lenten *Pastoral Letter* of 1923, A.A.L., Keating Papers, Series 2 I D/1.
63. See M. Conway, 'Buiding the Christian City: Catholics and Politics in Inter-War Francophone Belgium', *Past and Present*, 128 (August 1990), 117–51.
64. Conway, *Catholic Politics in Europe*, pp. 41–2.
65. J. Pereiro, 'Who are the Laity', in McClelland and Hodgetts (eds), *From Without the Flaminian Gate*, p. 174; Von Arx, 'Catholics and Politics', pp. 245–71.
66. Described in P. J. Waller, *Democracy and Sectarianism: A Political and Social History of Liverpool 1868–1939* (Liverpool: Liverpool University Press, 1981).
67. Keating to W. Friel, 14 October 1927 (copy), A.A.L., Keating Papers, Series 4 I A/9.
68. R. Baxter, 'The Liverpool Labour Party, 1911–1963' (unpublished D.Phil. dissertation, University of Oxford, 1969), 21.

69. S. Davies, *Liverpool Labour: Social and Political Influences on the Development of the Labour Party in Liverpool, 1900–39* (Keele: Keele University Press, 1996), pp. 69–75.
70. To the best of my knowledge there was no constitution previous to September 1927.
71. *Constitution of the Catholic Representation Association*, signed by Archbishop Keating on 22 September 1927, A.A.L., Keating Papers, Series 5 I B/3.
72. Quoted in Baxter, 'The Liverpool Labour Party', p. 24.
73. Copy of statement to the press by representatives of the Liverpool Labour Party to Keating, 12 October 1925, A.A.L., Keating Papers, Series 5 I B/3.
74. Hastings, *English Christianity*, p. 143.
75. Waller, *Democracy and Sectarianism*, p. 228. The results of municipal elections in this period form Appendix IV of Davies, *Liverpool Labour*.
76. Ibid., pp. 113–4; Baxter, 'The Liverpool Labour Party', p. 25.
77. Davies, *Liverpool Labour*, app. IV.
78. Keating to Mgr George, 18 March 1926 (copy), A.A.L., Keating Papers, Series 4 I A/6.
79. Ibid.
80. See e.g. Keating to Canon Pinnington, 26 February 1926 (copy), ibid.
81. At the Labour Party conference of 1927, Sexton led Catholic opposition to the adoption of a resolution in support of artificial birth control: Machin, *Churches and Social Issues*, p. 91. Sexton was knighted in 1931.
82. Keating to James Sexton, 5 October 1927 (copy), A.A.L., Keating Papers, Series 4 I A/9.
83. Minutes of a meeting of the clergy of central Liverpool held in St Mary's Hall on 24 January 1928, ibid., Series 5 I B/3.
84. *Liverpool Post*, 20 October 1928.
85. Ibid.
86. Odo Russell to Archbishop Davidson, 19 April 1927, L.P.L., Davidson Papers 215, fo. 324.
87. J. N. Molony, *The Emergence of Political Catholicism in Italy: Partito Popolare 1919–1926* (London: Croom Helm, 1977).
88. M. Morris (ed.), *The General Strike* (Harmondsworth: Penguin, 1976), pp. 254–5.
89. Ibid.; J. Symons, *The General Strike* (London: Cresset Press, 1959 edn), p. 123.
90. Quoted in Mews, 'The Churches', in Morris (ed.), *General Strike*, p. 326.
91. B. S. Bennett, 'The Archbishop of Canterbury in Politics, 1919–1939: selected case studies' (unpublished Ph.D. dissertation, University of Cambridge, 1992), pp. 84–5.
92. Oldmeadow, *Bourne*, II, pp. 220–30. Mews is similarly of the opinion that Bourne's connection with the appeal was 'fairly vestigial': Mews, 'The Churches', p. 330.

93. Bell, *Randall Davidson*, II, pp. 1312–13.
94. McClelland, *Manning*, pp. 140–8.
95. Joseph Curran to Bourne, 5 May 1926, A.A.W., Bourne Papers, Bo. 5/77.
96. A. W. Hutton, *Cardinal Manning* (London: Methuen, 1892), p. 210; McClelland, *Manning*, p. 142.
97. See also Mews, 'The Churches', p. 333.
98. Bourne to Stanley Baldwin, 1 May 1926 (copy), A.A.W., Bourne Papers, Bo. 1/108.
99. Francis Blundell to Bourne, 24 December 1926, ibid.
100. Memorandum from Sidney Herbert to Bourne, 15 December 1925, Cambridge, Cambridge University Library (C.U.L.), Baldwin Papers 52, Political 3. Sidney Herbert, Baldwin's Permanent Private Secretary, was known to support the Bill.
101. Francis Blundell to Sir William Joynson-Hicks, 1 July 1926, L.C.R.O., Francis Blundell Papers, DDB1 (Acc. 7725) Box 7; Bourne to Stanley Baldwin, 30 June 1926, C.U.L., Baldwin Papers 52, Political 3.
102. Francis Blundell to Bourne, 18 July 1926, A.A.W., Bourne Papers, Bo. 1/108.
103. Mr Topping [representative of the Lancashire and Cheshire Conservative Association] to Mr Maclachlan [Chief Organising Agent for the Conservative party], 22 January 1926; memorandum from Mr Maclachlan to Mr Wicks [Baldwin's Permanent Private Secretary], 28 January 1926, C.U.L., Baldwin Papers 52, Political 3
104. Oldmeadow, *Bourne*, II, p. 218.
105. Fr O'Hea to Joe Kirwan, 31 October 1957 (copy), E.P.S.J., 28/2/5/4.
106. Mews, 'The Churches', p. 327.
107. Stanley Baldwin to Bourne, 3 May 1926, A.A.W., Bourne Papers, Bo. 1/108.
108. Stanley Baldwin to Bourne, 10 May 1926, ibid., Bo. 5/77.
109. Lord Northcliffe to Bourne, 10 May 1926, ibid.
110. Dorothy Gordon to Bourne, 14 May 1926, ibid.
111. Dom Bede Camm to Bourne, 15 May 1926, ibid.
112. Quoted in Bell, *Davidson*, II, p. 1316.
113. Quoted in Bennett, 'Archbishop of Canterbury', p.108
114. Sir William Joynson-Hicks to Stanley Baldwin, 1 July 1926, P.R.O., HO 045/19390, 173661/39a; Home Secretary's memorandum to the cabinet, ibid., 173661/20.
115. Francis Blundell to Sir William Joynson-Hicks, 1 July 1926, L.C.R.O., Blundell Papers, DDB1 (Acc.7725) Box 7.
116. Francis Blundell to Bourne, 18 July 1926, A.A.W., Bourne Papers, Bo. 1/108.
117. P. Williamson, *Stanley Baldwin: Conservative leadership and national values* (Cambridge: Cambridge University Press, 1999), pp. 278, 282, 290.
118. P.R.O., CAB 23/53, Cabinet minutes, 23 June 1926.
119. See below, p. 59.

120. Fr Bampton, S. J., *Christianity and Reconstruction: The Labour Question* (London and Edinburgh: Sands and Co.), p. 103.
121. Quoted in Mews, 'The Churches', p. 332.
122. Ward, *Unfinished Business*, pp. 89–90.
123. Hughes, *Winds of Change*, p. 166.
124. *Catholic Times*, 18 May 1926.
125. Ibid., 28 May 1926.
126. Ibid.
127. Cleary, *Catholic Social Action*, p. 116.
128. *The Christian Democrat* (June 1926).
129. Ibid. (July 1926).
130. Ward, *Unfinished Business*, pp. 189–90.
131. Keating to Fr McNabb, 14 May 1926, A.A.L., Keating Papers, Series 4 I A/6.
132. Fr O'Hea to Joe Kirwan, 31 October 1957 (copy), E.P.S.J., 28/2/5/4.
133. Beard, *Faith and Fortune*, pp. 75–9.
134. Dudley Cary-Elwes to Valentine Cary-Elwes, 8 November 1881, Northampton, Northamptonshire County Record Office, Elwes Family Papers, E (GB) 1036.
135. Dudley Cary-Elwes to Valentine Cary-Elwes, 25 November 1907, ibid., E (GB) 480.
136. For references to Lopes see P. Gregory-Jones, *A History of the Cambridge Catholic Chaplaincy 1895–1965* (Cagliari, 1986).
137. Quoted in M. N. L. Couve de Murville and P. Jenkins, *Catholic Cambridge* (London: CTS, 1983), p. 132.
138. R. Ombres, 'Strikes: Reformulating Catholic Thinking in Britain', *New Blackfriars*, 65 (March 1984), 120.
139. *Catholic Times*, 18 May 1926.
140. Keating to Rob Georgeson, 13 May 1926, A.A.L., Keating Papers, S4 I A/6.
141. Hastings, *English Christianity*, p. 189; R. McKibbin, *Classes and Cultures: England 1918–1951* (Oxford: Oxford University Press, 2000 edn), p. 288.
142. Keating to Fr McNabb, 14 May 1926, A.A.L., Keating Papers, Series 4 I A/6.
143. Ibid.
144. Notes for a sermon on the 'Reign of Christ', 16 May 1926, ibid., Series 7 IV A/102.
145. *Liverpool Catholic Parishioner* (June 1926).
146. Keating to Lord Stourton, 21 July 1926, A.A.L., Keating Papers, Series 4 I A/6.
147. Address to CSG, 20 September 1926, ibid., Series 7 IV A/108.
148. *Plymouth Diocesan Record* (June 1926).
149. Quoted in Clifton, *Amigo*, pp. 110–11.
150. Thorman to Amigo, 9 June 1926, A.A.S., Amigo Papers, Correspondence with Bishops.
151. Mews, 'The Churches', p. 333.

152. For the life and career of Henshaw see M. Broadley, 'The Episcopate of Thomas Henshaw, Bishop of Salford 1925–1938' (unpublished M.Phil dissertation, University of Manchester, 1998).
153. Henshaw to Amigo, 11 June 1926, A.A.S., Amigo Papers, Correspondence with Bishops.
154. D. Bebbington, 'The Decline and Resurgence of Evangelical Social Concern 1918–1980', in J. Wolffe (ed.), *Evangelical Faith and Public Zeal: Evangelicals and Society 1780–1980* (London: SPCK, 1995), pp. 175–97. See also P. Catterall, 'Morality and Politics: The Free Churches and the Labour Party Between the Wars', *Historical Journal*, 36 (September 1993), 667–85.
155. Bebbington, *Evengelicalism in Modern Britain*, p. 215; see idem., 'Decline and Resurgence', p. 181.
156. Kent, *William Temple*, p. 137.
157. Norman, *Church and Society*, p. 340. See also Kent, *William Temple*, p. 134.
158. See Fr Keating's report of the proceedings in *The Month* (November 1926).
159. Keating, 'Roman Catholics, Christian Democracy', p. 78.
160. *Eighth National Catholic Congress: Official Report* (Manchester: CTS, 1926), p. 162.
161. Ibid., p. 158.
162. F. Bourne, 'A Scholarship for Every Child', in *Congress Addresses* (London: Burns, Oates, 1929), pp. 179–80.
163. *The Catholic Herald*, 24 March 1934.
164. A. Kenny, *A Path From Rome* (Oxford: Oxford University Press, 1988 edn), p. 34
165. B. Plumb, 'Remembering Dr Downey', *Catholic Pictorial*, 3 May 1981.
166. Biographical details taken from Cyril Taylor's *DNB* entry.
167. Quoted in Hastings, *English Christianity*, p. 275.
168. R. Downey and others, *Rebuilding the Church in England* (London: Burns Oates and Co., 1933), p. 3.
169. Ibid., p. 8.
170. N. Pevsner, *The Buildings of England: Lancashire I The Industrial and Commercial South* (Harmondsworth: Penguin Books, 1979 edn), p. 192.
171. P. Caraman, *C. C. Martindale: A Biography* (London: Longmans, Green and Co, 1967), p. 8n.
172. Timothy Potts to Fr Vincent Wilkin, 11 October 1953, E.P.S.J., X17/4; Kenny, *Path From Rome*, p. 34.
173. Heenan, *Crown of Thorns*, p. 19.
174. R. Downey, 'Civic Virtue', in *Pulpit and Platform Addresses* (London: Burns Oates, 1933), pp. 39–40.
175. *Cathedral Record* (January 1932).
176. D. Sheppard and D. Worlock, *Better Together: Christian Partnership in a Hurt City* (London: Hodder and Stoughton, 1988), p. 55.

177. Waller, *Democracy and Sectarianism*, p. 324.
178. B. Plumb, 'Remembering Dr Downey', *Catholic Pictorial*, 3 May 1981.
179. Meeting of the Bishops, 30 April 1924, A.A.W., *Acta*.
180. Quoted in Waller, *Democracy and Sectarianism*, p. 326.
181. Supreme Knight of St Columba to Downey, 26 September 1929, A.A.L., Downey Papers, Series 5 II Correspondence.
182. Keating to Fr O'Hea, 7 January 1927 (copy), ibid., Keating Papers, Series 4 I A/7.
183. *Liverpool Daily Post*, 30 May 1929; Supreme Knight of St Columba to Downey, 26 September 1929, ibid., Downey Papers, Series 5 II Correspondence; Waller, *Democracy and Sectarianism*, p. 318.
184. Reply to a Circular Letter from Conservative Central Office, 22 July 1929, L.C.R.O., Blundell Papers, DDBL acc 7725, Box 4 Bundle 5.
185. Downey to Amigo, 22 May 1929, A.A.S., Amigo Papers, Correspondence with Bishops; cf. Waller, *Democracy and Sectarianism*, p. 318.
186. Eustace Percy was the Conservative President of the Board of Education (1924-9). Bourne held Percy in high regard: at the National Catholic Congress of September 1929 he said that his 'untiring endeavour to promote understanding deserves universal gratitude': F. Bourne, 'Education and Morality' in *Congress Addresses*, p. 183.
187. Amigo to Downey, 15 November 1929 (copy), A.A.S., Amigo Papers, Correspondence with Bishops.
188. Brown to Sir J. W. Gilbert, 2 June 1929, ibid., Brown Papers.
189. Ibid.; Shane Leslie's diary entry for 30 March 1930 recorded that 'The PM much dislikes Catholics and their Church ...': N.L.I., Shane Leslie Papers, MS 22, 859, acc 3669.
190. Amigo to Downey, 19 September 1929, A.A.L., Downey Papers, Series 5 II Correspondence.
191. Amigo to Downey, 30 October 1929 (copy), A.A.S., Amigo Papers, Correspondence with Bishops.
192. A. Thorpe, *The British General Election of 1931* (Oxford: Clarendon Press, 1991), pp. 23-4, 49.
193. J. Davies, '"Rome on the Rates": Archbishop Richard Downey and the Catholic School Question, 1929-1939', *North West Catholic History*, 23 (1991), 18.
194. Cruickshank, *Church and State in English Education*, p. 129.
195. R. Barker, *Education and Politics 1900-1951: A Study of the Labour Party* (Oxford: Clarendon Press, 1972), p. 62.
196. A. J. P. Taylor commented that 'Labour had acquired its own sectarian lobby': A. J. P. Taylor, *English History 1914-1945* (Oxford: Clarendon Press, 1965), p. 280
197. Brown to Williams, 13 March 1934, B.A.A., Archbishops' Papers 1929-65, AP/C28/12.
198. Machin, *Churches and Social Issues*, p. 50.
199. H. V. Marshall, Vicar-General of Salford to Henshaw, 21 February

1938; Henshaw to Mr Dean, 3 October 1937 (copy), Sal.D.A., Henshaw Papers, Folder 3; see also the sermon preached by Henshaw on rescue work which touches on slum conditions, *Harvest* (November 1936). For a discussion of the housing problem as it impacted on Catholics in Manchester, see A. Davies and S. Fielding (eds), *Worker's Worlds: Cultures and Communities in Manchester and Salford, 1880–1939* (Manchester: Manchester University Press), p. 42.

200. Brown to Williams, 13 March 1934, B.A.A., Archbishops' Papers 1929–65, AP/C28/12.

201. *The Times*, 10 March 1934.

202. Ibid., 7 March 1934.

203. Fr O'Hea to Williams, 2 October 1933, B.A.A., Archbishops' Papers 1929–65, AP/S8/1.

204. Williams to Fr O'Hea, 5 October 1933 (copy), ibid.

205. C. C. Martindale, 'A Catholic Programme', in Fr C. Lattey, S.J. (ed.), *Church and State: Papers Read at the Summer School of Catholic Studies, Held at Cambridge, July 27th to August 6th* (London: Burns Oates and Co., 1936), p. 331.

206. Sweeney, *St Edmund's House,* pp. 45–6.

207. Fr Worsley to Bourne, 11 November 1932, A.A.W., Bourne papers, Hi. 2/223.

208. Bourne to Fr Worsley, 12 November 1932 (copy), ibid.

209. *The Tablet*, 30 September 1933.

210. Meeting of the Bishops, 4 July 1933, A.A.W, *Acta.*

211. Bishop Barrett's Lenten *Pastoral Letter* of 1933, Ply.D.A.

212. D. Jerrold, *Georgian Adventure* (London: Collins, 1937), p. 97.

213. Keating, 'Roman Catholics, Christian Democracy', pp. 70–1; idem., Discrediting the 'Catholic State' in Tallett and Atkin (eds), *Catholicism in Britain and France*, p. 41; Buchanan, 'Great Britain', p. 260.

214. B. Aspinwall, 'Broadfield Revisited: Some Scottish Catholic Responses to Wealth, 1918–40', in W. J. Sheils and D. Wood (eds), *The Church and Wealth* (Studies in Church History, 24; Oxford: Basil Blackwell, 1987), pp. 393–406.

215. See R. Skidelsky, *Politicians and the Slump: The Labour Government of 1929–1931* (London: Macmillan, 1967), pp. 400–3.

216. Quoted in J. Davies, 'The Liverpool Catholic Land Association', *North West Catholic History*, 19 (1992), 16–32.

217. *Liverpool Post*, 5 July 1932. Downey was referring to occupational clubs and centres.

218. Typescript, 'Back to the Land', 22 February 1933, A.A.L., Downey Papers, Series 3 I–IV.

219. Notes for a conference address at Manchester Town Hall, 28 June 1933, ibid.

220. *Flee to the Fields: The Faith and Works of the Catholic Land Movement; A Symposium* (London: Heath Cranton, 1934).

221. *The Catholic Herald*, 26 May 1934; *Catholic Times*, 6 July 1933.

222. Ibid., 27 July 1933.

223. D. Green, *The Living of Maisie Ward* (Notre Dame and London: University of Notre Dame Press, 1997), p. 80.
224. Fr G. Hudson to Williams, 19 May 1993, B.A.A., Archbishops' Papers 1929–65, AP/C28/43. Financial objections were also raised: Mgr C. J. Cronin to Williams, 19 May 1933, ibid. Further correspondence relating to the Midland C.L.A. can be found at ibid., AP/M18.
225. Davies, 'Liverpool Catholic Land Association', esp. pp. 36–8.
226. Meeting of the Bishops, 22 October 1935, A.A.W., *Acta*.
227. Buchanan, 'Great Britain', p. 260.
228. Kent, *William Temple*, p. 149.
229. Hinsley to Amigo, 1 January 1935, A.A.S., Amigo Papers, Correspondence with Hinsley, C4.

Peter Amigo, Bishop of Southwark (1904–49) was an outspoken critic of British policy towards Ireland.

William Brown, Auxiliary Bishop of Southwark (1924–51). Brown was one of the more progressive voices on social and political questions.

Cardinal Francis Bourne (centre) in procession.

Cardinal Francis Bourne celebrating the jubilee of his ordination in 1934.

Cardinal Arthur Hinsley.

Cardinal Arthur Hinsley in 1937. Hinsley was to become a great wartime leader of England's Catholics.

Left: Archbishop Richard Downey
of Liverpool, 'Ruler of the
North'.

Below: Richard Downey,
Archbishop of Liverpool
(1928–53), in July 1940.

John Heenan, Bishop of Leeds (1951–57); Archbishop of Liverpool (1957–63); Archbishop of Westminster (1963–75). This photograph belongs to the Leeds period.

Cardinal William Godfrey. Before he was appointed Archbishop of Westminster in 1956, Godfrey had been Apostolic Delegate to Great Britain (1938–53) and Archbishop of Liverpool (1953–56).

5

Spain, Fascism and Communism

On the day of Bourne's death, 1 January 1935, Arthur Hinsley complained in a letter to his friend Amigo of a feeling of listlessness and uselessness. 'I have very little in the way of work so far, practically nothing. Perhaps in time I shall find something to do, which will make me forget myself.'[1] From early 1934 Hinsley had been convalescing in Rome after a bout of typhoid struck him down and forced his recall from Mombasa, which had been his base since his appointment as Apostolic Delegate to Africa in 1927. In the autumn of his life at the age of sixty-seven, his recovery was setback when he contracted a severe case of eczema in the summer of 1934: 'I have been bandaged up, arms and hands, legs and feet', he complained to Amigo.[2] In late 1934, with his condition slightly improved, he settled in the Vatican City taking up the canonry of St Peter's, a position which, Moloney comments, 'was considered tantamount . . . to being shunted gently into the curial sidings'.[3] This was highly frustrating for a man of Hinsley's matchless energy, but the release that was soon to arrive was not something he could ever have envisaged. In March 1935 he heard that he had been appointed as Bourne's successor. 'It must have come upon you as a terrible shock', Amigo wrote. He was not wrong.[4] Hinsley told Amigo how he had refused and resisted and how the Pope had urged obedience.[5] On 25 March his appointment was announced. So it was that this elderly man who disclaimed any ambition – 'I dislike the ceremonial part and the fuss and bother . . . I had much rather retire at once into a monastery, and try to prepare myself for my end', he told Amigo when the prospect of a bishopric was raised in 1926[6] – returned to the country he had barely seen in eighteen years to take up the most senior appointment.

What was the thinking behind this surprise appointment? As Norman points out, he had been effective in bringing some sort of Catholic education to the African mission, and had established very good relations with the British Colonial Office.[7] According to Sir

Charles Wingfield, British Minister to the Holy See, the Pope wanted someone both as 'English and as "Roman" as possible', preferring to appoint 'a prelate advanced in years, but of tried merit, to nominating a younger man who might or might not "make good"'.[8] Evidently the feeling in Rome was that Bourne had been kicking round for far too long. As former Rector of the Venerabile (1917–28), Hinsley was well-known to the Vatican authorities and was held in high regard by Pius XI.[9] To his students Hinsley seemed to be the incarnation of Romanità – the Roman spirit.[10] Hinsley never let his students forget how privileged they were to be selected for the Venerabile.[11] Clearly it was expected of Hinsley that he would reverse the undesirable situation whereby so few priests from the Westminster diocese were currently trained in Rome. Hinsley did not disappoint expectations in this area; his appointment of a former Venerabile student, Father Valentine Elwes, as his Private Secretary, signalled his determination to bring a more Roman atmosphere to the diocese.[12] (Hinsley showed correspondingly less interest in the regional seminary, St Edmund's.) Wingfield also observed that Hinsley's appointment showed that the Vatican 'still pays attention to the influence and sentiments of the old English Roman Catholics'.[13] Whilst Wingfield exaggerated the strength of Old Catholic influence, Hinsley's appointment would certainly have been congenial to that section of the community: the Archbishop of Westminster was a national figure in the way that no other Catholic bishop was, so the reasoning went, and although it was tolerable to have an Irishman in Liverpool it would not do for an Irishman to occupy the principal see. Thus Downey, in many ways the most impressive figure on the episcopal bench, was passed over, although his relative youth (he was fifty-three) was possibly another factor.[14]

Unlike Bourne, Hinsley has been generously and sympathetically portrayed by historians. He was, in Hastings's estimation, 'a priest who had outgrown ecclesiastical fears and had somehow come to see that Church windows needed to be opened, that lay people could be trusted and Christians of other traditions welcomed as brothers'.[15] Warm-hearted and avuncular with a genius for friendship, Hinsley had a very different personal style to his frigid predecessor. William Orchard, recent converted from Nonconformity, told Sir James Marchant that when he tried to kiss Hinsley's ring at a reception during the Brighton CTS conference of 1938, he 'pulled away his hand and kissed mine'.[16] During the Second World War Hinsley was to establish a reputation as a doughty English patriot, a hammer of dictators. Winston Churchill, who held the current Anglican bench of bishops in very low esteem,[17] would identify Hinsley as one of only two men he could trust to 'speak to the nation on the aims of this country at war' – the other being, of course, himself.[18] According to Hastings, 'No archiepiscopate was effectively less ultramontane or clericalist'.[19]

It might have been very different. Hinsley's biographer and acolyte John Heenan commented: 'It will long be a matter of debate whether or not Cardinal Hinsley would have enjoyed national renown if he had ruled the see of Westminster only in peace'.[20] Contemporary expectations were modest. Indeed, it would have been too much to expect of one elderly man, appointed in all probability because he offered the safest pair of hands, to offer a radical departure from what had gone on before.

The first half of Hinsley's archiepiscopate saw bold initiatives which clearly should not be underestimated. Hastings cites his giving away of control of *The Tablet* to a group of laity as an early example of his encouragement of lay freedom and enterprise, although Walsh maintains that it was given away simply because it had become too much of a financial burden for the Archbishop of Westminster to bear.[21] Nevertheless, *The Tablet* had sunk in reputation during Oldmeadow's editorship, and with the arrival of a fresh broom in Douglas Woodruff it regained its credibility and formed a significant element in that 'little renaissance' in English Catholic cultural life in the later 1930s.[22] Another bold move on Hinsley's part was the appointment of David Mathew, then Catholic chaplain to the University of London, as Auxiliary Bishop of Westminster in December 1938. What was interesting about Mathew's appointment was not just his young age, but his educational background. Unlike other bishops with university degrees, he was not training for the priesthood at the time of going up to university,[23] and was not, therefore, subject to the clerical supervision experienced by Williams and Flynn who had to reside at St Edmund's House during their time at Cambridge. Mathew's range of social contacts was much more broad as a result, and this made him aware, and on occasions impatient, of the social limitations and inadequacies of his senior colleagues. It was Cardinal Bourne – no scholar but keen all the same to raise the presence of Catholicism in the universities – who had first recognized Mathew's talents, persuading Archbishop Mostyn to release him from his position as chaplain at the University of Cardiff in order to become the first full-time chaplain for the Catholics of London University.[24] (No doubt the fact that Mathew had private wealth also weighed with Bourne.) Being at London was a congenial position for Mathew, who was now close to key historical sources. Having recently had published two historical works of some distinction, *The Celtic People and Renaissance Europe* (1933) and *The Reformation and the Contempative Life: A Study of the Conflict between the Carthusians and the State* (1934), co-authored with his beloved brother, Gervase,[25] he set himself to writing the history of the English Catholic community, a major undertaking which was published in 1936 as *Catholicism in England 1535–1935: Portrait of a Minority: Its Culture and Traditions*. 1936 was also the year in which Mathew's talents were recognized by Hinsley: he was appointed as Hinsley's adviser and representative in political and public matters. Hinsley gave this role the title 'liaison representative of the hierarchy',[26] but really Mathew's responsibility did not extend beyond Westminster. The appointment of this precocious talent as Auxiliary Bishop in December 1938, at the age of just thirty-six and only nine years after ordination, was a remarkable act of faith on Hinsley's part.

In other ways the signs were less liberal. First, Hinsley believed that during Bourne's archiepiscopate clerical censorship of Catholic publications was not as rigorous as it should have been. The furore surrounding Sheed and Ward's publication in 1938 of the convert Alfred Noyes' *Voltaire* underlined this problem for Hinsley. The book was critically acclaimed and came to the notice of a wider Catholic public through its serialization in *The Tablet*, however, it was secretly delated to the Holy Office and Hinsley was informed that it would be condemned if it were not withdrawn from publication although its errors were never officially revealed to the author.[27] Privately Hinsley had some sympathy with Noyes' position: in a letter to Amigo he stated that the matter had been 'clumsily and inopportunely dealt with' by the Holy Office, and believed that although Noyes had made Voltaire 'too grand a character' there was nothing in the book 'against faith or morals'.[28] Through representations to Rome he managed to dampen the acrimony. But the lesson he drew was that clerical control should be tightened. The publishers of *Voltaire*, who he noted 'never submit their publications to a censor', were to be reined in. 'They have been warned about this free handed way of dealing', Hinsley told Amigo, 'I have given Sheed an ultimatum. It is neither fair to us or publishers (Catholic) to act in such an independent way. Sheed answers me that my predecessor told him not to trouble about the matter.'[29] Such incidents must have brought home to Hinsley the difficult balancing act he had to perform as a Roman bishop in an English context.

Secondly, the emphasis which Hinsley placed on Catholic Action on his arrival at Westminster emphatically did not suggest a relaxation of clerical discipline and greater lay freedom. Threats to the Church from the left and the right meant that Catholic Action had become a common clarion call in bishops' pastoral letters and speeches in the early 1930s, however, Bourne, weak in body and spirit, was disinclined to energize the laity, and all the talk of a national scheme of Catholic Action came to nothing. Hinsley's appointment saw a greater priority attached to Catholic Action. 1935 saw the first publication in English of Mgr Luigi Civardi's *A Manual of Catholic Action*, which laid down a model for the organized apostolate of the laity. But for all Hinsley's evident commitment to Catholic Action he was to find himself absorbed with more prosaic concerns in the first year of his archiepiscopate; in May 1936 Hinsley admitted to Fr Joseph Keating, whom he had begun to consult regularly on social and political questions, that 'beyond my appointment as President of the National council, all actual arrangements are not advanced beyond the paper state. The Bishops have been too much excited about the Education Bill.'[30] As late as September 1937 Hinsley was apologizing to the bishops for the delay in establishing a national scheme, the aims of which had been set out in a joint pastoral letter of the hierarchy in Advent 1936. 'I have found the extent of the field so great that I have been completely overwhelmed. My time and energies have been employed also in my proper work within the Diocese of Westminster.'[31] The appointment of Mathew eased the burden. He knew something about Catholic Action from his time in Cardiff, where, according to Hughes, Archbishop Mostyn had established the first ever Board of Catholic Action.[32]

The architect of Catholic Action, Cardinal Pizzardo, a papal envoy, had stated that Catholic Action would take different forms in different countries. For its English advocates, Catholic Action had to become domiciled in an environment in which lay people did not respond well to the clerical lash. An advisory committee on Catholic Action established by Mathew in the Westminster diocese had many prominent and distinguished lay members as well as clerics, attempting to balance lay initiative and responsibility with Catholic Action's demand for unity of purpose under strong episcopal leadership. Their July 1937 report, which was the outcome of nineteen two-hour meetings, has this sense of struggling to initiate an innovative and bold scheme of organization and activity whilst remaining cognisant of local traditions. There was a concern for how Catholic Action would be perceived by non-Catholics; the committee feared that the 'term "Catholic Action" has an aggressive and military ring' which would be liable to be misunderstood, and suggested that a new title should be adopted which would still convey the ideas of 'unity, co-ordination and activity'. There was a concern that Catholic Action should not appear to negate or disturb existing parish societies; David Mathew made the point that student bodies, a potentially fertile ground for

Catholic Action activity as continental examples testified, should be allowed to continue without outside interference in their affairs. Yet despite these caveats the report remained true to the spirit of Pizzardo's model. Defined by the committee as the 'mobilization of the laity under the direction of the hierarchy', the report cautioned against any interpretation of Catholic Action which would cast it in a democratic light. Although the committee felt that it was important that the laity were not made to feel 'that their only function is to pay a subscription' and that they should be allowed to vote for members of their parochial council of Catholic Action – for the 'method of cooperation, voting, election, is one familiar and agreeable to the English mind' – they emphasized also

> in unequivocal terms our view that the introduction of the elective principle in certain parts of the organisation by no means connotes that we envisage Catholic Action as a democratic movement dependent for its authority on the suffrage of the parish electors. In most, if not all, Catholic societies, the elective principle plays its part, but the society itself depends for its very existence on ecclesiastical approval. So too with Catholic Action.

Evidently there was a concern amongst the bishops that the introduction of a parochial council might serve as encouragement to disaffected elements to vent resentments against the clergy, but the committee thought the danger of anti-clericalism to be 'almost negligible', for the 'influence' of the parish priest 'would do much to prevent the election of unsuitable persons' – a third of the council would be co-opted by the members after consultation with the priest, who would also nominate the chairman. The report also placed heavy emphasis on the spiritual nature of the whole enterprise: members of the parochial council were required to be habitual worshippers and join the Guild of the Blessed Sacrament and the Arch-Confraternity of the Blessed Sacrament; prayers were to be said before and after the meeting; there were to be organized retreats.[33] It would appear then that there was some anxiety that Catholic Action might, against its avowed intentions, generate political action.

Like his predecessors, Hinsley soon found himself absorbed with the mundane practicalities of the schools question. In this area he was perhaps less adept than others before him. Having been away from England he found it a struggle to grasp the complexities involved. But by the spring of 1935 the education question was at the top of his agenda. The Catholic bargaining position in education questions was weakened by the fact that the National government could not be subjected to the same kind of parliamentary pressure as the previous

minority Labour government.[34] There were only eighteen Catholic
MPs at the time and such was the mood for a settlement they could
not ride on the back of Anglican opposition. Henshaw admitted
ruefully that the 'Bishops' protests carry no weight with the politicians. They attend to protests from voters only.'[35] The Education Bill,
introduced on 19 December 1935, proposed to raise the school-leaving
age to fifteen and made subsidies of between 50 and 75 per cent available for the building of new schools. These grants were to be made
at the discretion of the local authorities, and in return the denominations would, with certain safeguards, surrender their rights over
teaching appointments. At the Low Week meeting of 1936 the bishops
resolved not to reject the Bill summarily but to press for amendments,[36] and Hinsley offered further hope for a settlement when he
welcomed the Bill as a step in the right direction in a speech delivered at Birmingham.[37] (Hinsley was actually 'nauseated' by the
subject and wished it could be resolved speedily.[38]) Downey recognized that rejection was not an option yet hoped to secure episcopal
approval for the proposition that 'it shall not be lawful to force non-
Catholic teachers into Catholic schools'.[39] Elsewhere there was the
usual clamour that accompanied educational legislation.[40] McNulty of
Nottingham urged total rejection,[41] an attitude Hinsley deprecated;[42]
Amigo declared that 'We shall have to agitate if we are to get our
rights', adding 'I wish we had a Whiteside in Liverpool'.[43] Amigo
doubted that a concerted assault on the Bill would materialize and
suspected that Downey, perhaps the only bishop who could have
mobilized a major opposition, lacked the stomach for the fight.[44]
Downey in fact secured separate treatment for the Catholic schools in
Liverpool. The 1936 Act left much to the discretion of local authorities and in Liverpool, a city plagued by sectarianism, the awarding of
the building subsidy was inevitably a source of controversy. In 1938
the Liverpool education authorities' refusal to provide a grant for the
building of Catholic schools resulted in the intervention of central
government and a significant proportion of the Board of Education's
grant to the local authority was withheld. The Liverpool Act of 1939
– a version of the 1936 Act – offered a way out: the local authority
was empowered to build the schools, which would then be leased out
to the Church at a percentage of the loan charges. The local authority was given the right to appoint teachers but the Catholic authorities
could veto appointments in the case of religious instruction.[45]

The lack of accord on the schools question was nothing new, yet
Hinsley's archiepiscopate at least saw an end to the animosities and
serious divisions which had opened up during Bourne's period of
office. Hinsley was sensitive to the need to carry his episcopal

colleagues with him and on the date of his appointment wrote to each bishop to insist on cooperation so that 'the Church ... may be seen to be a single front in the bitter campaign being waged against God and His Christ'.[46] He was to adopt a more collegial approach to decision-making than his predecessor and seemed more open to institutional change. Whereas Bourne was no committee-man, Hinsley consulted regularly and widely; 'every aspect of diocesan activity ... provided a sufficient reason for forming a committee usually composed both of priests and laymen'.[47] At the first meeting of the bishops he presided over, it was resolved that the bishops would now meet three times a year instead of one and that a standing committee consisting of the four archbishops should be instituted 'to deal with matters of emergency'.[48] For Hinsley it was a matter of gaining the trust of his colleagues, although it seems that the issue of standing committees was pressed on him by those who from bitter experience had reasons for wishing to keep a tight rein on Westminster.

Another attempt to repair the divisions of the past was the creation in 1938 of a standing committee of the English and Irish hierarchies. This was probably the idea of Amigo: on hearing of Hinsley's appointment to Westminster Amigo urged him to 'Keep the Bishops united here and let us make a good advance to the Irish Hierarchy'.[49] Hinsley, who was half-Irish,[50] needed no prompting, knowing full well how strained relations had been during the Bourne years, particularly during the Anglo-Irish war. On 14 February 1922 he had presided at a potentially awkward dinner held at the Venerabile to celebrate the coronation of Pius XI, attended by three cardinals: Bourne, Gasquet and Logue. In a letter to Amigo, Hinsley described how 'Gasquet proposed the Pope, and Bourne in a very judicious speech proposed Cardinal Logue ... (Logue) spoke for peace and union among Catholics ... Count de Salis was delighted and most effusive in his congratulations on this minor "Peace Congress"'.[51] Hinsley sensed that the Irish question had damaged the standing of English Catholicism in the Vatican. A key figure in Hinsley's moves to heal the breach between the English and Irish hierarchies was David Mathew. Mathew was from Anglo-Irish Catholic stock; his father was the great-nephew of the great Irish temperance activist, Fr Theobold Mathew. His background gave him a sensitivity to the Irish question: in the short section on the 1910–18 period in his history of English Catholicism, Mathew commented that 'One of the most painful phases of all this period was the acute lack of sympathy between the English conservatives of the old faith and their coreligionists in Ireland'.[52] In the same book he wrote sympathetically of Bishop Milner, insisting that his 'good relations with the priests and people of Ireland foreshadowed what was to be one of the most fortunate aspects of Cardinal Manning's policy'.[53] Like an earlier historian of the Catholic community, Bernard Ward, Mathew's research encouraged an acute sense of English Catholicism's debt to Ireland.

In 1938 an invitation was made to the Irish bishops for closer relations between the two hierarchies, an idea to which Cardinal MacRory of Armagh gave his 'cordial agreement' in October of that year.[54] It was clearly a popular move that had broad episcopal support, for there was a general recognition that relations had deteriorated under Bourne. The question of spiritual provision for Irish emigrants was the main area of concern, and during the Second World War there was a particular anxiety for the moral welfare of Irish girls who came over for war-work.[55] Archbishop Williams of Birmingham, another pushing for closer relations, assured Archbishop McQuaid of Dublin that 'If your Grace hears of any more hardships which you think we can tackle at this end, please let me know and I will do my best. My object ... is to try to get better relations between Irish and English Catholics – no easy problem when the Irish remember their history and the English forget it! – but one can only go on trying.'[56] Political questions were more rarely discussed although at the Low Week meeting of 1941 a pastoral letter from the Bishop of Waterford condemning the IRA was read and it was 'agreed that uniformity was desirable regarding the admission of its members to the Sacraments'.[57] In general there was a keener awareness of Irish sensibilities, as when David Mathew refused an honorary doctorate from Trinity College, Dublin, an institution which Archbishop Mostyn – who had what Mathew referred to as 'something of Cardinal Bourne's approach to Irish matters' – had hoped the young scholar would attend, despite the fact it fell under a prohibition of the Irish bishops. Mathew reassured Archbishop McQuaid that '(quite apart from my strong desire for close relations with the Irish Bishops) I have a new responsibility and that I must not take any action which could be regarded as contrary to that of my Irish brethren'.[58] The emphasis on cooperation in this period also led to the formation, in 1942, of a joint committee of the northern bishops and representatives of the Scottish hierarchy. Mathew informed McQuaid that relations with the Scottish bishops were 'gradually improving' as a result.[59]

* * *

Whilst the first years of Hinsley's archiepiscopate saw him concerned mainly with the narrower sorts of questions that absorbed his predecessor, it was soon to become apparent that Hinsley's task was not to be that of steering the ship through steady waters. That Hinsley recognized this was apparent in the letter he wrote to the bishops on his appointment: he talked of the campaign 'being waged against God' by communists, and emphasized the importance of Catholic Action. All of this pointed to a more confrontational stance towards perceived anti-Christian movements.[60]

Whether or not Hinsley was ever aware of it, there was clearly scope for tension between the more aggressive, defensive politics encouraged by the papacy in the mid–1930s, and the more open strands in social Catholicism with which he had himself identified since his younger days. When Hinsley contemplated the models of church leadership provided by his predecessors at Westminster, it was to Manning, with his broad social commitment, rather than to Vaughan or Bourne, who were more at home with purely Church affairs, that he looked.[61] Indeed, Hinsley was the son of a workingman, a village carpenter, and stated once that this background imbued him with a natural sympathy for the cause of labour.[62] He was a student at the Gregorian University, Rome, at the time of *Rerum Novarum*, and recalled his friend Merry del Val arriving with a copy early on the morning of its publication (15 May 1891) and the two of them reading it avidly.[63] Whilst studying for an external degree at London University, he came under the influence of the social thought of John Ruskin, reacting violently against the 'heresy' inculcated by classical political economy that 'it was possible to study economic science without reference to ethical science'.[64] This clearly placed Hinsley within the Christian socialist tradition.

Social Catholicism in England had been in poor shape since the mid-1920s, but saw a revival in fortunes with the arrival of Hinsley. The most notable development of the later 1930s was the formation of the Young Christian Workers (YCW) organisation. This grew out of *The Catholic Worker* newspaper, started in 1935 by Bernard Wall, and was strongest in Lancashire and overwhelmingly working class in its membership. One historian has pointed out that the appeal of the YCW was due to its populism, the simplicity and directness of the message, its genuine achievements in alleviating social hardship and refusal to engage in the communist-bashing so typical of the Catholic press. By May 1937 the circulation of *The Catholic Worker* stood at an impressive 40,000.[65] Whereas the middle-class, clerical, study-circle social Catholicism represented by the CSG was now slightly unfashionable, the YCW's directness and youth seemed more relevant to the more heated political climate of the mid-1930s. R. P. Walsh, the editor of *The Catholic Worker*, was an over-zealous advocate of Catholic Action in the Liverpool archdiocese, impatient with the seeming apathy of other lay groups, namely the CSG, to embrace the new commitment the times demanded.[66] One CSG member described Walsh's political attitudes thus: 'He is convinced that to first achieve the objects of Catholic Action, Catholics must first revolutionize themselves. All Catholic Action must be based on prayer, on living to the utmost, a full Catholic life. He believes that if this is done everything will be added . . .'[67] The Catholic hierarchy had been following the development of the nascent organisation closely,[68] and would no doubt have been re-assured by this emphasis on the priority of the spiritual over the political. But occasionally the YCW were prepared to display an independence of mind in its political judgements, showing itself to be more than simply the docile agency of ecclesiastical authority. During the Spanish Civil War, for instance, Walsh resisted pressures to transform his newspaper into an anti-communist organ and the attempts of 'pro-Franco propagandists' to run a special edition on the atrocities.[69] Years later Godfrey recalled that the line the YCW took on Spain 'would certainly not have been smiled upon by the Holy See'.[70]

Such pressure to make anti-communism the central focus of social Catholicism inevitably harmed progressive causes. Hinsley may have harboured ambitions to see the Archbishop of Westminster a prominent figure in British public life once more, but events were rendering unlikely that aspiration. A considerable part of the appeal of Hinsley lay in his robust plain-speaking and earthiness, but these qualities, which would endear him to the British public during the Second World War, were stifled in the first years of his archiepiscopate. It was promising for the public image of English Catholicism that it should have had a leader with a natural distaste for authoritarian politics. Whilst some English bishops, particularly after the signing of the Lateran Treaty of 1929, held Mussolini in the highest regard,[71] Hinsley, who had been in Rome at the time of the Duce's rise to power, was under no illusions. In a notorious sermon given at Golders Green on 13 October 1935, Hinsley inveighed against Italian fascism as the 'present-day deification of Caesarism and of the tyranny which makes the individual a pawn on the chessboard of absolutism'.[72] Neither was he afraid to challenge the Vatican authorities. He was critical of the Holy See's policy towards Abyssinia, and voiced the concern to Cardinal Pacelli, Secretary of State, that it was becoming too closely associated in the public mind with the Italian fascist government.[73] Although his sermon at Golders Green attempted to explain the Pope's action regarding the war in Abyssinia, he only served to confound his position. He described the Pope as 'a helpless old man with a small police force to guard himself, to guard the priceless treasures of the Vatican, and to protect his diminutive State which ensures his due independence in the exercise of his universal right and duty to teach and to guide his followers of all races'.[74] It was said that these unflattering comments cost him the cardinal's hat.[75] (He was eventually made Cardinal in December 1937.) As a result of this unwelcome publicity, Hinsley learned to weigh his words.

This formed part of the context to the appointment in November 1938 of the first Apostolic Delegate to Great Britain, William Godfrey (1889–1963). There was a concern in the Vatican, heightened in the anxious climate of the 1930s, that Rome's interests were not being adequately represented by the English hierarchy. Hastings states it thus: it was 'the moment at which the Vatican decided that Britain was too important to be left in the hands of the Archbishop of Westminster – too frigid in the case of Bourne, too impulsive in the case of Hinsley'.[76] Although not strictly a diplomatic office like a nunciature, the apostolic delegate mediated between the Holy See and the British government; the negotiations and subsequent appointment took place in consultation with the Foreign Office without reference to Hinsley and the episcopate.[77] There was, not surprisingly, some initial resistance to the move amongst the bishops, although it appears that Amigo had been aware from the beginning of Rome's intentions and had given his encouragement to the idea, perhaps because his experience of Bourne had led him to seek ways of checking Westminster's authority. Hinsley thought the better of sending a letter he drafted to Pacelli which had insisted that an apostolic delegate would be seen as 'an agent of Mussolini in the interests of the Rome-Berlin axis',[78] and would have a deleterious effect on relations between the English Church and wider society. Hinsley evidently feared the appointment of an Italian: he was known to deplore the Italianization of the Roman Curia and diplomatic service;[79] even vigorous ultramontanes like Amigo were relieved that the apostolic delegate was to be an Englishman.[80] Hinsley eventually came to terms with the appointment and a decent working relationship was established, although it clearly helped that Godfrey was no stranger to him, indeed Hinsley thought well of Godfrey and had previously urged his appointment as Rector of the English College.[81]

More than any other factor, it was the Spanish Civil War which inhibited the development amongst English Catholics of a more progressive and constructive political engagement. The English bishops, like all Catholic hierarchies, were encouraged by the Holy See to see the civil war, which began with Franco's military uprising of 18 July 1936 against the Second Republic, as a struggle to the death between Christianity and 'godless communism'. Events in Spain provided the context for the English hierarchy's joint pastoral letter of 1936 which inveighed against those 'Anti-God forces' which 'were sapping and mining the foundations of society', and which urged the laity to unite behind the banner of Catholic Action 'in one solid compact line against the battalions of evil.[82] Progressive elements in the Church found themselves increasingly on the defensive in the later 1930s. English Catholicism hardened itself against movements which seemed to be bound up with communism, but this meant also that many a progressive baby was thrown out with the bath-water.

One target of this hardening of attitudes was the League of Nations Union (LNU), which had received Catholic support ever since its formation by Lord Robert Cecil in 1920. By the mid-1930s, however, there was a concern on the part of the Catholic bishops that the LNU was getting involved with false friends. LNU leaders were pushing for closer association with the International Peace Campaign (IPC), but this organization was seen by its critics to be a communist front. Downey was one such critic: in April 1937 he resigned his position as Vice-President of the Liverpool branch citing the 'sinister connection between alleged peace movements and Communism'.[83] The breach with the LNU was more painful in the Westminster archdiocese, for here the link was strong owing to the involvement of John Eppstein, a member of the LNU Executive and formerly Cecil's Private Secretary. Eppstein had tried to interest his fellow Catholics in international politics since the early 1920s,[84] writing much on the subject including one weighty book, *The Catholic Tradition of the Law of Nations* (1935). According to Fr O'Hea, Eppstein had been instrumental in fighting against 'Fascist tendencies among Catholics and . . . combating the tendency of our people to retreat into their own rabbit burrows, out of public life and such things as LNU'.[85] The problems for Eppstein began after he lampooned IPC enthusiasts at the LNU Christmas party of December 1937;[86] some senior figures did not share Eppstein's sense of fun and even thought it a disciplinary matter. Unless Eppstein signed a pledge 'to forward the complete cooperation between the L.N.U. and the I.P.C.' and to 'seek to remove the prejudices against the latter which still exist in certain quarters', he would find himself sacked.[87] Hinsley thought it a 'detestable formula',[88] however, Eppstein, who faced the loss of his livelihood, reluctantly signed a revised and marginally more acceptable formula which had been extracted from Lord Cecil by Mathew (who along with Fr O'Hea represented Hinsley on the Christian Organisations Committee of the LNU). This committed Eppstein to 'loyally carry out such forms of cooperation between the L.N.U. and I.P.C. as are determined by the Executive Committee' and to 'seek to remove unfounded prejudices against the latter'.[89] It was an unhappy compromise for Eppstein who told Mathew he would be looking for other work, but at this stage avoidance of public controversy was everyone's wish. Privately, O'Hea and Mathew were coming round to the view that the attempt by the LNU Executive to force the IPC connection would probably result in the Catholic withdrawal.[90] The thought pained O'Hea: he viewed with alarm the growing isolation of Catholics from currents of progressive thought. On 3 April 1938, O'Hea told Hinsley that if the hierarchy insisted on withdrawal it would confirm the prejudice of non-Catholics 'that we act through blind obedience to instructions from higher authority without using our own judgement'.[91] But events were moving against O'Hea. The identification of the LNU with Republican Spain was upsetting the Catholic authorities. On 7 April, Hinsley communicated his growing concerns about the LNU's apparent breach of its policy of non-intervention on Spain,[92] informing Cecil that he was considering resignation because 'It is essential for the Archbishop of Westminster to remain remote from that political sphere in which the League under our direction now feels that it must pursue its peace activities'.[93] At the hierarchy's Low Week meeting a resolution was passed stating: 'The Bishops wish it to be understood that they cannot be held responsible for, nor associate themselves with, any political resolutions passed by the Executive Council of the League of Nations Union'.[94] By the end of 1938 the LNU and the IPC were further committed in support of Republican Spain.[95] The final straw for Hinsley came after a questionnaire was issued by the IPC (and distributed by some LNU branches) which urged its members to 'take the side of Barcelona'. The resignation of Hinsley in December 1938[96] prompted a robust response from Cecil: 'your Eminence's action will be received with great pleasure by the Governments of Berlin and Rome'.[97]

The Holy See need not have worried that English Catholics would not take the 'right side' during the civil war. The persecution of priests and religious in Republican Spain made it almost inevitable that the Church would look on the Nationalist leader Franco as the only defence for religion. As most historians have argued, English Catholics, and certainly those at the top end of the Church, threw their support overwhelmingly behind Franco.[98] Tom Buchanan, who has written the authoritative history of English responses to events in Spain, has stated that progressive Catholics who were critical of Franco's 'crusade' were made to feel like a 'beleaguered minority in the face of the 'corporate' outlook ... of the hierarchy and priesthood'.[99]

As a leading authority on Spanish Catholicism has stated, the persecution of Catholic priests and religious only partly explains the 'emotional and nearly unanimous commitment to the Nationalist cause', for the Spanish hierarchy 'knew what it wanted, namely, a government ready and willing to act aggressively on behalf of a Church anxious to seize the moment to realize old dreams of religious reconquest'.[100] These fantasies were reflected in English Catholic opinion. Hastings has suggested that, reared on a diet of Belloc and little enamoured of parliamentary democracy, it was more or less inevitable that the Catholic intelligentsia should hail Franco.[101] Buchanan has suggested that social Catholics inclined to Franco for, like Dollfus of Austria and Salazar of Portugal, he seemed to hold out the promise of a new political order based on the corporatist social principles set out in *Quadragesimo Anno*. Many intellectual converts were 'sympathetic to the idea of an authoritarian state based on Catholic social principles'.[102] Possibly even Hinsley, who was clear-minded about other European dictators, fell into this way of thinking. In a letter of March 1939, Hinsley wrote to Franco in the following terms: 'I look upon you as the great defender of true Spain, the country of Catholic principles where social justice and charity will be applied for the common good under a firm peace-loving Government'.[103] This may, of course, have been no more than an expression of future hope, written after the victory of the man who seemed to hold out the only hope for the Spanish Church. Yet this is not to say that there was not an ideological dimension to the episcopate's support for Franco: they readily propagated the interpretation of the civil war as a fight between Christianity and 'godless communism'.

The most partisan exponent of this interpretation was Amigo. With his Gibraltarian origins it was hardly surprising that he felt events in Spain more acutely. He had observed the fate of the Church under the Second Republic (1931–3) with despair,[104] and now embraced whole-heartedly the cause of the insurgents. His papers contain a considerable amount of pro-Franco propaganda in both Spanish and English. On 16 August 1936 at St George's Cathedral, Amigo declared: 'The people who are fighting the Spanish Government are described as rebels. If they are rebels, then thank God, I am one . . . they are fighting for the Church of God.'[105] Later, pro-Franco organizations like the United Christian Front and the Friends of National Spain, founded in July 1937 to promote the Nationalist cause,[106] tried to enlist Amigo's support.[107] After a local Labour MP expressed his alarm that a dignitary of the Church appeared to be supporting a revolutionary war against a constitutionally-elected government, Amigo issued a statement claiming that 'any nation may rise against a government that is guilty of grave injustice and unable to maintain public order'.[108] The line of argument recalled Amigo's stand during the Anglo-Irish War, but was not invoked by other pro-Franco voices on the bench of bishops who would have baulked at the radical implications of this sort of thinking. They justified their support for Franco on the far safer ground that he offered the only means of defence for a persecuted Church.

Despite their protestations of neutrality, the bishops became increasingly partisan as the civil war progressed and Amigo did not appear such a lone voice. The anti-communist crusade reached its height in 1937 and the civil war was viewed increasingly in monochromatic terms. This was perhaps to be expected given the stories of anti-clerical atrocities. Positions hardened further when the Vatican heard that a deputation of Anglicans and Free Churchmen led by the Marxist Revd Iredell had gone to Spain early in 1937 to investigate alleged anti-clerical outrages, concluding that the Spanish Church had brought the attacks on itself for its neglect of social justice. This was not an official church deputation, and its members, who included Hewlett Johnson, the 'red dean' of Canterbury, were to the left of the political spectrum and therefore far from representative figures; nevertheless, the group's findings created an impression that English church leaders were indifferent to the plight of the Spanish Church.[109] Francis D'Arcy Godolphin Osborne, British Minister to the Holy See, stated in his annual report to the government that the delegation appeared to belittle 'the extent and savagery of the attacks to which the Church in Spain had been exposed'.

Osborne further claimed that it was due to the prompting of the Vatican that the English hierarchy became pronouncedly anti-Republican during 1937.[110] Maximum publicity was afforded to the Spanish hierarchy's collective letter to the Catholic bishops of the world issued in July 1937, which interpreted the civil war as a struggle between Christianity and atheism, justified the military uprising and urged foreign Catholics to support their cause.[111] A vigorously anti-communist line was encouraged by the papal encyclical of 1937 *Divini Redemptoris*, published in England by the CTS as *Atheistic Communism*. This portrayed events in Spain as the natural fruit of communism. Following this papal lead, the hierarchy's Low Week meeting the following month resolved that 9 May should be set aside as a day of prayer against the 'menace of Communism', and ordered the encyclical to be read out at the principal mass of the day.[112] This undoubtedly reinforced the impression that what was happening in Spain was a war between religion and irreligion.

It was Liverpool, not Westminster, which saw the most intense Catholic Action campaign against communism. Archbishop Downey was the most zealous advocate of Catholic Action on the bench of bishops; he was also the most vigorous anti-communist. It was Downey who provided the introduction for Mgr Luigi Civardi's *A Manual of Catholic Action*. He was even commended by the Pope for 'the zeal with which Your Grace has undertaken the expansion of Catholic Action in ... accordance with the directions and recommendations of the Sovereign Pontiff'.[113] It was in Liverpool, in December 1937, that the first major gathering in England of the forces of Catholic Action was orchestrated. More than in any other diocese the programme of Catholic Action introduced in Liverpool conformed to the model laid down by Pizzardo: the concerns raised in Westminster that Catholic Action should not disturb existing patterns of parochial activity, and the anxieties that the name was too aggressive, were either not raised or were simply ignored in Liverpool. Had not Liverpool Catholicism always had to fight its corner?

The Catholic Action programme in Liverpool was designed to co-ordinate and direct all lay activity in the diocese, whether it be dedicated to needlework, nursing or rambling. In August 1937 the Pro-Deo Commission (PDC) was formed to advise the Liverpool Archdiocesan Board of Catholic Action 'on matters concerning the Communist menace'.[114] Previously, in January 1937, Downey had ordered anti-communist leaflets to be distributed throughout the parishes,[115] but the aim of the PDC was to give a 'more permanent status' to these propaganda exercises.[116] One of its first tasks was advising parish priests to bring *Divini Redemptoris* to the notice of the people.[117] The PDC were not the only organization engaged in propaganda work: in September 1937 the CTS printed 20,000 leaflets on communism.[118] But in March 1938 the CTS delegated responsibility for all anti-communist propaganda to the PDC.[119] It is worth, therefore, examining in closer detail the activities of this organization for they reveal a far more rancorous and confrontational tone to this campaign than a bare assertion of numbers of leaflets distributed can ever hint at.

The main tasks of the PDC were the publication of pamphlets and leaflets, organizing conferences and lectures on the communist threat, ensuring that public libraries were stocked with 'sound' literature on the subject through the participation of its members on relevant public bodies, and monitoring the political activities of 'suspect' Catholics. Orchestrating the anti-communist agitation and Catholic Action activity in Liverpool was Downey's Secretary, Mgr Thomas Adamson, who was assisted in his campaign by an enthusiastic young priest of

St Matthew's, Liverpool, Fr James Ellison. Ellison was entrusted with coaching lecturers who might speak on Spain throughout the parishes of the diocese,[120] and encouraged to draft pamphlets on the communist threat. He had some understanding of modern propaganda methods – he had clearly learned from the communists and the fascists:

> I would personally be inclined to go in for more 'bite' and 'kick', startling the reader either by sensational facts or the sensational manner in which commonplace or elementary truths are presented to him. To my mind the 'wayside pulpit' must arrest and grip; it must jog and jerk the wayfarer out of his rut. To succeed in provoking mild agreement is to fail in its purpose: he may or may not read it, he will certainly, like the priest and the levite, 'pass by'. Slogans these days win wars and 'sensationalism' will more easily capture the mind of the modern man than all the cold penetrating logic of the schools. Moreover, I think an anti-Communist leaflet should always be obviously and directly so, and at least a parallel drawn. The student might deduce and compare, but the man in the street has no bump of 'comparativeness': the comparison must be drawn for him in as sensational a manner as possible and slung at his head to form required excrescence. Wildly mixing metaphor it might be put this way: you have got to hit him hard on the head, preferably with a bit of his own bread and butter, for the only bit of logic that appeals to him is his 'undisturbed middle' ... All this is course is more easily said than done: don't ask me to do it.[121]

A lurid leaflet entitled 'Save the Family' bore the traces of Ellison's influence. It screamed: 'Do you realise that the family – most important of all human institutions is *in grave danger*? It is being *undermined* by divorce-laws, birth prevention, State interference and the abuses of industrial Capitalism. *Communism would completely destroy it.*' At the bottom, bold type and in upper case, it declared: 'Beware of Communists, pagans and cranks, who would destroy, enslave or corrupt the family'. Although papal encyclicals had frequently criticized capitalism, the scathing reference to 'industrial Capitalism' is surely also a pointer to Ellison. A rabid anti-semite, although this does not appear to have repulsed Mgr Adamson, Ellison, in a letter to Adamson dated 10 March 1938, endorsed a 1933 pastoral letter of the Bishop of Upper Austria which had stated: 'Depraved Jewry in alliance with international freemasonry is ... the main support of the mammonistic capitalism'.[122] On 11 March the PDC assigned Ellison the task of producing a pamphlet on 'Jewry, Masonry and Communism'; this was intended for private circulation among the elite corps of Catholic Action.[123] Ellison's ideas were influenced by two clerical Catholic social theorists from Ireland, the Jesuit Edward

Cahill, author of *Freemasonry and the Anti-Christian State* (1929) and *The Framework of a Christian State* (1932), and the Holy Ghost priest, Denis Fahey.[124] Fahey was convinced of a Jewish World Conspiracy, and spilled much ink in exposing links between Bolshevism and Jewry, as in an article carried by the *Irish Catholic* (10 February 1938) which Ellison brought to the notice of Adamson. The invitation to Ellison to compose a pamphlet on the Jewish-Masonic conspiracy came several days after Adamson had received from him an eight page diatribe on international politics and Jewish influence. Although freely admitting that his knowledge of Spain was scant, Ellison interpreted events in Spain as part of an 'ideal which Judeomasonry has relentlessly pursued for two centuries', namely a 'new de-Christianized civilisation in which reason should be supreme, the rights of man receiving consideration to the exclusion of those of God, free and independent morality, absolute laicisation of society etc. In other words a return to paganism.'[125]

The PDC's anti-communist agitations attracted the attention of sympathetic organisations. One of its pamphlets, 'The Truth about Spain: facts for Catholics', was ordered by the Friends of National Spain, the main pro-Franco pressure group in England;[126] another, 'Spain's Red Government Exposed' (previously entitled 'Spain's "Popular Front Government"' before Ellison gave it a more emotive thrust), was ordered by Nellie Driver, founder of the Nelson branch of the British Union of Fascists,[127] who expressed her gratitude that there was 'another movement besides the British Union of Fascists and National Socialists who are not afraid of telling the truth about Red Spain'.[128] (Driver came from a Nonconformist background but during a period of internment in the early 1940s she began to attend Catholic mass, eventually converting after the War; although her unpublished memoir[129] recorded that from then on her fascist beliefs receded into the background, it seems that the appeal of Catholicism was more than just spiritual, but that its political stance against atheistic communism had struck a chord long before she had witnessed a Catholic religious service.[130])

It does not appear that Ellison's pamphlet on Jewish-Masonic conspiracy was ever issued. This was not because the PDC were unsympathetic to Ellison's political sympathies: far from it, for at its meeting of 8 July 1938 it was decided that Fr William Sheppard of St Anne's would approach the Italian Council and the Italian Information Bureau of London to 'secure the wider distribution of literature explaining the true nature of Fascism'.[131] Rather, there were factors restraining the flow of literature of a more extreme nature. The archdiocesan censor, Joseph Cartmell of Upholland College, was worried

about 'involving the Archbishop and through him the Church officially in what Catholic working men might regard as pro-Fascism',
but suggested that the PDC confine its more explicitly 'political' material to the pages of the Catholic press. (Fr Sheppard dismissed the idea
that PDC material should be reduced to the level of the ephemera
which appeared in 'the little-read Catholic press', complaining to
Mgr Adamson that 'if we are to be deterred by fear of epithets "political" and "pro-fascist" ... I think we shall have to close down
altogether.'[132])

Despite the closeness of Ellison and Sheppard to Adamson, in
political terms they were fringe figures who did not quite succeed
in pushing Catholic political action in the more right-wing direction
they wanted. The most important restraining factor was the
Archbishop of Liverpool himself. Downey would simply not have
supported the anti-Jewish agitation proposed by Ellison and some
PDC officials. He was certainly acquainted with anti-semitic literature – there was an abundance of it in the social thought sections
of seminary libraries. He was familiar with the work of Fr Cahill:
in 1932 Cahill had presented Downey with a copy of his *Framework
of a Christian State*, although from the marginalia it appears that
Downey was rather more interested in its exposé of masonic influence than Jewish conspiracies.[133] Throughout his career Downey
displayed no signs of anti-semitism, and he did much to build relations with Jewish leaders. Since 1933 Downey had appeared on
public platforms to protest against the persecution of German
Jews,[134] as indeed had several other bishops. (But it was typical of
Downey to have claimed to have been the first in England to speak
out.[135]) On 19 March 1933, speaking to the Liverpool University
Jewish Society, he inveighed against the 'exaggerated and pseudo-
nationalism' let loose in Hitler's Germany.[136] A few weeks later he
spoke at a protest meeting at the Central Hall presided over by
Liverpool Church leaders: 'on broad religious principles which transcend all differences, we must protest against this persecution; this
persecution of an ancient race which, through all its many vicissi-
tudes, amidst the welter of polytheism, kept intact the worship of
one true God, and preserved monotheism upon the earth ...'[137]
During his archiepiscopate Downey also spoke at meetings of the
Liverpool Zionist Society and the Jewish Medical Society and
enjoyed close relations with several Jewish leaders. Chief Rabbi
Herz met Downey in 1933 and recalled how at an instance he could
locate a cutting relating to his friendship towards the Jewish
Community.[138] By contrast, Downey's relations with other Christian
leaders was far less cordial.[139] In 1942 Downey contributed a

preface to the first English edition of the sermons and correspondence of Count Clemens August von Galen, Bishop of Münster, the most outspoken episcopal opponent of Nazism, in which he referred to the 'perverted' and 'sadistic cruelties of the Gestapo'.[140] His foreword to Irene Marinoff's *The Heresy of National Socialism* (1941) pointed out 'the hopeless failure of this modern colossal attempt to build up a self-sufficient State without regard to Christian principles'.[141]

Downey was not the only critic of anti-Jewish feeling on the English bench.[142] In Manchester where there was a significant Jewish presence, Bishop Henshaw of Salford was another outspoken episcopal opponent of Nazism. His public commitment to the plight of the Jews was notable: at the Free Trade Hall in April 1933 he 'wholeheartedly associated himself and the Salford diocese with the other bodies present in protest against the persecution of the Jews'.[143] Nathan Laski, President of the Council of Manchester and Salford Jews, remembered Henshaw as a 'most broadminded man, and one who stood very high as a champion of the oppressed and of those who are made to suffer for their faith and religious convictions'.[144] Henshaw's attitude was in contrast with that of Bourne and Amigo who gave their reason for refusing to attend protest meetings against the treatment of Jews in 1933 as the absence of any comparative gesture from Jews when Catholics were being persecuted in Mexico, Russia and Spain.[145] Furthermore, although few were as obsessed by the wilder versions of a Jewish-Bolshevik plot as Ellison, the idea that there was a link was a commonplace. When Archbishop Williams of Birmingham took part in an inter-church meeting in May 1933 to protest that 'the discrimination exercized against the Jewish race, in Germany and elsewhere, is contrary to the spirit and principles of the Christian faith', and which called on 'Christian men and women to use their influence to overcome national and religious prejudice', in the very next breath, and surprisingly given the occasion, he went on to say that if it was true that the Jews were communists, as the Nazis were to allege in justification for their discriminatory policies, then 'my sympathy is with the Nazis, though their methods may not be wise'.[146] In fairness to Williams the sympathy did not run deep; the statement testifies more to his virulent anti-communism than any positive evaluation of Nazism.

Clearly communism, at least in the last years of Pius XI's reign and the first few years of Pius XII's, was regarded in the Vatican as a far graver threat than anything from the right. Pius XI's encyclical of March 1937, *Mit brennender Sorge* ('With deep anxiety'), warned against the Reich's deification of nation, race and state, – although avoiding explicit reference to the Nazi's anti-semitism – but its message was certainly overshadowed by the publication of *Divini Redemptoris*, with its even more vehement denunciation of communism, only five days later.

In English Catholicism there would also be a relative neglect of fascism. The Jesuit Fr Lattey, Professor of Fundamental Theology at Heythrop College, writing in the volume which emerged from the 1936 Summer School of Catholic Studies at Cambridge, held that fascism was the less dangerous of political extremes. Lattey also went on to state that 'History ... may yet come to recognize the Spanish nationalist leaders as the saviours of Europe'.[147] Whilst publishing houses churned out many volumes on the communist threat, there was very little published against fascism. The CTS archives reveal that in 1938 the Executive Committee refused a request to issue a pamphlet on fascism on the grounds that it would be viewed as an attack on the British Union of Fascists, and 'we cannot publish a pamphlet on any political party in England'.[148] Catholics were in fact well represented in the main British fascist party. According to Rawnsley, the percentage of Catholics in the British Union of Fascists was much higher than in the population as a whole. Possibly because of his outspoken stance against reprisals in 1920–1, Oswald Mosley was regarded with respect by many Irish Catholics – he was even dubbed 'the Pope' in Leeds because of his significant Catholic following.[149] Adrian Hastings has cited the publication of J. K. Heydon's *Fascism and Providence* in October 1937, six months after *Mit Brennender Sorge*, by a major Catholic publishing house, Sheed and Ward, to illustrate the point that English Catholicism was tending to the right. Heydon, a businessman and like Sheed an Australian, had a long-standing interest in Catholic social teaching and shared Belloc's hatred of 'plutocracy' and liberal democracy;[150] in *Fascism and Providence* he argued that 'Fascism, in fact, is of Catholic origin and no English Catholic has a scintilla of right to condemn the Nazis. Catholics who do, and there are some few who are busying themselves considerably, may be found to be fighting against God.'[151] Reviews of *Fascism and Providence* were mixed: the Jesuit Fr E. J. Coyne thought it 'had been better left unwritten and certainly published', deploring its 'identification of the traditional Catholic corporative-organization with Fascism',[152] whilst the scholarly Benedictine Dom Christopher Butler, later Auxiliary Bishop to Cardinal Heenan, welcomed Heydon's 'breadth and balance and appreciation of hierarchical value' and saw his contribution as a corrective to those who had overlooked the 'profounder qualities' of fascism.[153] (Whatever sympathies *Fascism and Providence* evoked it is important to note that this book did not have the *imprimatur* of ecclesiastical authority: it was precisely Hinsley's complaint against Sheed and Ward that it did not subject its output to the scrutiny of ecclesiatical censors despite styling itself a Catholic publishing house.)

Against a background of hysterical outpouring against communism even the more progressive elements on the episcopal bench found it difficult to retain a sense of balance. Archbishop Williams, then CSG President, told E. W. Record, editor of the *Birmingham Post*, that he feared the paper had swung to the left since the Spanish civil war began, declaring: 'if you believe as I do that the only real basis for European civilisation is Christianity you may be able to appreciate my feeling that all Christians ought to unite against the threat to destroy Christianity and establish Atheism for that is what is happening in Spain'.[154] Williams identified himself with the views of Douglas Jerrold, a right-wing Catholic who had organized the aeroplane which had picked up General Franco to transport him to Morocco to lead the rebellion, and Arnold Lunn, a regular correspondent on the civil war in the Catholic press with a line in lurid 'Red Terror' stories,[155] who along with Jerrold was a leading member of the Friends of National Spain.

Partisanship was further evident in the area of aid. Buchanan has found that 'Humanitarian assistance for the Nationalists was dominated, almost exclusively, by the Catholic Church'. Started in September 1936, the Bishops' Committee for the Relief of Spanish Distress 'made no pretence of impartiality'. Whilst its avowed aims were 'the relief of the sick, wounded, refugees, and destitute children of Spain', the underlying agenda was to provide moral support to those fighting 'atheistic Communism' and to dispel the belief prevalent in Nationalist Spain that the 'reds' had the monopoly on public sentiment in Britain.[156] There is support for this claim in a memorandum written by its chairman dated 22 October 1937. Although it made mention of the dining rooms established to feed 'necessitous children, both "red" and "white"', it is clear that most of the £8800 raised by this date had gone towards mobile hospitals for Franco's forces: the memorandum noted that 'General Franco's representative recently visited the Committee's hospital and expressed the greatest satisfaction with its work'.[157] By contrast, the Basque refugee children who came to Britain for safekeeping during the siege of Bilbao in April 1937 met with a lukewarm response – their plight was seen by many Catholics as a 'red' cause. Bishop Brown, who amongst the episcopate was the only one who refused to throw his support behind the Nationalists, worked alongside the Conservative MP and pro-Republican Duchess of Atholl to bring the children to England, but commented to Canon

Drinkwater: 'Many of our Extremists are furious at the Basque children being allowed to come'.[158] Archbishop Williams was one reluctant host: 'The little Red Basque children . . . hiss at the priests and spit on them, and have to be separated from the Catholic children and forcibly prevented from interfering with mass or Corpus Christi procession. They have been taught quite early to hate: and that is what the Church is up against in Spain and elsewhere.'[159]

Those Catholics who took a different line in public from the Church hierarchy were in a minority, though perhaps a less negligible one than is usually thought. Paranoid figures like Ellison tended to see reds under every bed and exaggerated the extent of opposition; the poor attendance at one of Douglas Jerrold's lecture at the Picton Hall, Liverpool, in February 1938 ('there was neither a canon to the right of him nor a dean to the left') provoked a typical outburst: 'I suggest a solemn strangling . . . of pink clericals, and a most rigid and merciless control over left Catholic authors and press . . . O for the days of the Holy Inquisition.'[160]

The 'left Catholic press' was more a figment of Ellison's overheated imagination than a reality. As one historian has stated, 'Most of the English Catholic press . . . fervently backed Franco and filled their columns with lurid accounts of Republican atrocities'.[161] Opposition to the united front of *The Tablet*, *The Month*, *The Catholic Herald*, *The Universe* and *Catholic Times*, was provided by two journals. The first was the Dominican *Blackfriars*. Although this was mainly urging restraint and non-partisanship rather than support for the Republicans,[162] to Catholics like Ellison it amounted to very much the same thing. The editor at the time was the Prior of the Dominican house at Oxford, Fr Hilary Carpenter. Carpenter resisted reducing events in Spain to the stark polarities favoured by other editors. He explained his position in a lecture on 'Catholics and European Political Development' at the Annual Conference of Catholic Colleges held at Downside on 13–14 April 1937:

> truth is ill-served and right reason impeded by dividing the sheep from the goats in too simple a manner . . . we might notice the general attitude of a great number of Catholics in this country to the Spanish question. For them, it is simply a matter of a fight for or against the Catholic religion; there are the Reds, who are militant atheists, and the anti-Reds, who are Catholics fighting for their religious lives. And all those outside Spain who are not pro-Franco are classed together as pro-Communist.[163]

One who Ellison would have certainly wished to see 'solemnly strangled' was F. H. Drinkwater (1886–1982), a priest of Small

Heath, Birmingham, who edited *The Sower* journal.[164] His career spans the period covered in this book: he commenced his studies for the priesthood at Oscott in 1903; he retired as a parish priest in 1964. Although principally know for his pioneering catechetical work, an interest in social and political questions was aroused at an early age: he was impressed by Mgr Parkinson's lectures on social science at Oscott, and on taking up a curacy at St Peter's, Leamington, in 1910, under the formidable wing of Canon William Barry, sought to transform the parish magazine into an organ for the discussion of the social question. He attended several political rallies early in 1910 and was mesmerized by the figure of Lloyd George: 'sees visions while he talks', he noted in his diary.[165] It is also significant that Drinkwater was born in Wednesbury, a Staffordshire village with a history of political priests,[166] and that Frederick Keating was a great friend of his parents. Drinkwater's father was President of the local SVP for thirty years. There were, therefore, many links into social concern. A formative experience for Drinkwater was the period he spent as an army chaplain on the Western Front during the First World War. It was a traumatic experience: he had to retire from service after suffering a mustard gas attack in which a colleague died; whilst recuperating he learned that his brother had been killed in action. During these years he began to reflect on the quality and character of Catholic education, and a desire to rectify the perceived deficiencies led him to establish *The Sower* in 1919, a journal which became influential in the movement for catechetical reform. There were early signs of Drinkwater's famous stubborn independence: he attempted to resign his army commission in December 1918 when he learned that British soldiers might be employed for 'military coercion in Ireland' and 'repression of industrial troubles at home'. The War Office refused, arguing that his duty was to minister to the religious needs of troops without any comment on political or civil administration. Drinkwater made known his objection to the notion that a chaplain's ministrations had nothing to do whatever with the justice or otherwise of the cause for which men were called on to risk their lives.[167]

The ethics of warfare were throughout Drinkwater's life a consuming interest. Although he flirted with the idea of pacifism in the late 1920s, he was concerned to distinguish his own critique of some of the methods of modern warfare – his main targets being the indiscriminate bombing of civilians and, from the mid-1940s, nuclear missiles – from outright pacifism. Besides, he always entertained high, even romantic, notions about great military exploits.[168] Characteristically, Drinkwater did not shy from airing his views on warfare in *The Sower*. During the Spanish Civil War, under the editorship of Fr S. J.

Gosling, the journal challenged those who saw Franco as engaged in a holy war against godless communism.[169] It soon came to the attention of the PDC who expressed concern at its 'unusual views' on the war.[170] Drinkwater's main themes were a rejection of the militarism of the Catholic press,[171] an insistence that coercion, even for ostensibly religious purposes, was futile and wrong; a belief that 'in an ultimate show-down a triumphant "right" would be as destructive of true religion as a triumphant "left"'.[172] On the first point he was moved to contrast the vigour with which the Catholic press pursued atrocity stories – most of which he believed were exaggerated[173] – with their silence at the bombing of Guernica in April 1937.[174] Drinkwater's strongest letter on the subject, which was published in *The Catholic Herald* in June 1937, expressed his grave concern at 'the moral disaster that has happened to us – a surrender to war-time mentality, untruth and hatred ... I see the Catholic newspapers at present as wolves ravaging my flock'.[175] On coercion for religious purposes he insisted that 'even if Franco was fighting an entirely just war' this should not be the Church's stance.[176] His position was articulated most emphatically in a letter to a Fr Burns of 12 February 1937:

> I would say the Church is sent to *teach*. You can't teach while you are making war on them. Even after victory, you can't successfully teach even the children, because they will know it was you who killed their father and perhaps their mother! ... This dilemma (between military force on the one hand or teaching-at-risk-of-martyrdom on the other) keeps recurring in the history of the Church, doesn't it? It seems to me the right answer is always the same, and that Our Blessed Lord took the trouble to dramatize it for us – Luke 22.38, and Matt. 26.51. When religion answers violence with just *teaching*, its teaching has most effect.[177]

Drinkwater's views elicited a scathing reply from Hinsley who, soon after the publication of the letter in *The Catholic Herald*, protested that 'your utterances were beyond explanation. I regret your imprudence, your own inaccuracy – and ill timed, ill placed outburst.'[178] Indeed, Hinsley's view of the civil war was not so far removed from Amigo's: he believed the Republicans were intent on destroying Christianity and civilisation,[179] stressed the need to support the Spanish hierarchy,[180] and even kept a photograph of Franco on his desk. (The Catholic actor-writer Robert Speaight was working for the BBC during the war producing features and recalled that on one visit to Archbishop's House to interview Hinsley this photograph had to be 'hastily removed' before it was spotted by a colleague.[181])

Between Drinkwater and Archbishop Williams on the other hand there was a genuine fondness which remained unbroken despite their very different views on Spain. Williams shared Drinkwater's interest in social and political opinions, and was indeed active in his role as President of the CSG in encouraging employers to heed Catholic social teaching on the 'just wage'.[182] There was a similar awareness of the 'evils in the present capitalist industrial system',[183] although Drinkwater thought Williams inclined to 'stick up for whatever system in place'.[184] Williams was certainly hostile to collectivist solutions to social and economic problems.[185] But although Williams wished that Drinkwater would concentrate more of his energy on educational work,[186] he had no desire to stifle independent characters. When a series of sermons Drinkwater gave on the social question provoked controversy in Birmingham,[187] there were some who wished to see Williams muzzle the troublesome priest. However, Williams was genuinely reluctant to suppress views which took their inspiration from the papal encyclicals, even if the particular application was contentious, and said as much in his foreword to the published sermons.[188] Although the two were far apart on Spain, Drinkwater's refusal to stock the more bellicose pro-Franco Catholic papers was greeted by Williams with only mild amusement: 'It sounds as though you were starting a new movement. Do please tell me about it?'[189]

Drinkwater had only one sympathizer amongst the episcopate, Bishop Brown. Although as Amigo's Auxiliary, Brown was in a sensitive position and had to keep his thoughts on Spain private, there are two letters in the Drinkwater papers which show clearly where his political sympathies lay. In May 1937, picking up on the issue which Drinkwater raised in the Catholic press, he expressed his disbelief at 'what has come over our clergy, press and *some* of our people. Surely Christianity teaches that even to fight Satan we must not use Satan's weapons. As you say there is no attempt to find out and tell the truth – it is all one long hymn of hate.'[190] Brown was also clear-sighted about some of the forces behind Franco. A letter of June 1937 stated: 'Our Franco supporters are in a difficulty about Hitler. They don't want to admit that he is a German Fascist and has intervened in Spain with Mussolini on Fascist grounds. Yet the treatment meted out to the Church in Germany is systematic poisoning of the wells of truth and must be much worse for Religion than outbursts of fury and burning of churches in Spain.'[191]

Although he presented a maverick figure, Drinkwater was not a lone voice. The responses to his contributions in the press reveal sympathizers amongst the clergy and laity. A memorial dated 9 February 1938 was signed by a number of priests and prominent laymen protesting against the bombing of civilians by Franco's forces.

It stated: 'The Catholic Church in this country has made the cause of the Insurgents its own, and authorities of the Church have identified the cause of the Insurgents with the cause of Christ. We respectfully submit that a grave responsibility rests on the authority of the Church to ensure that the methods employed by the Insurgents do not outrage the teaching of Christ.' Among the thirty memorialists were Fr Gosling of *The Sower*; Joseph Clayton, a convert, Fabian and historian; Monica Whateley, a Labour councillor for Wandsworth, feminist and temperance worker, who had participated in Revd Iredell's mission to Spain; Virginia Mary Crawford, the veteran social activist; and David Adams, a Labour MP.[192] Hinsley was not moved: he said it showed 'both lack of discrimination and judgement and lack of loyalty and credulity given to Red propaganda'.[193] It came also to the attention of the PDC who resolved on 20 May 1938: 'this Commission views with increasing anxiety the association of Catholic public men with the cause of Red Spain, and the consequent scandal and confusion'.[194] Other Catholics 'under review' by the PDC were Donald Attwater, a former editor of *The Catholic Herald* and the first chairman of the Pax organization, who protested against the Condor Legion's indiscriminate bombing of Basque civilian targets,[195] and Luke Hogan, leader of the Liverpool Labour Party, who chaired an 'Aid Spain' meeting.[196]

Drinkwater's main support came from the Pax organization, which was formed in May 1936 by a group of lay people who sought to encourage amongst English Catholics an awareness of the more pacific strains in the Church's recent social teaching.[197] Whilst its membership – which reached almost 100 by September 1937[198] – were drawn overwhelmingly from the Catholic community, it disavowed any claim to be a Catholic organization, which enabled it to avoid the requirement to submit its publications to ecclesiastical censorship. Partly to avoid being seen as extreme, Pax did not base itself on absolutist pacifist principles,[199] although it included several avowed pacifists amongst its membership; it sought rather to strengthen Catholic commitment to the League of Nations and international arbitration. Yet there was enough about Pax to create unease amongst the episcopate. Links with the broader peace movement, vitiated in the eyes of the Catholic hierarchy by alleged associations with communists, rendered it suspect from the beginning, and its posture of critical detachment during the civil war did nothing to allay these fears. William Orchard, who was on the absolute pacifist wing of Pax, echoed Fr Drinkwater's concerns in a letter to Sir James Marchant: 'Our Catholic papers are tying their hopes far too much to Franco and the Sword generally'.[200] Further, there were those with far more conventional political sympathies than Orchard who felt moved to express their gratitude to Drinkwater for articulating views on Spain which they felt had been suppressed by the Catholic press – this raises questions about the extent to which the newspapers actually reflected the opinions of the ordinary Catholic.[201]

* * *

The weariness of many lay Catholics with the anti-communist campaign can perhaps be gauged by the enrolment figures for the Catholic College of Social Studies founded in the Salford diocese in 1937: moral philosophy was the most popular option with 237 students enrolling; apologetics next with 227; social science with 111; social history with 95; the course on communism, however, had only 38 takers.[202] Criticisms were raised that the hierarchy's social message consisted solely of excoriations of communism. Was there nothing positive to add? Probably, even in the midst of the Spanish Civil War, Hinsley recognized the force of this point. His advent pastoral letter of 1937, for instance, stressed social justice, high-lighted the 'unjust working of the industrial machine', but unlike the joint pastoral letter of the previous year made little explicit reference to communism.[203] It also asserted, somewhat unconvincingly, that the encyclical *Divini Redemptoris* was 'less concerned with resisting Communism than with rebuilding the social order'. This point had been introduced into Hinsley's first draft by his adviser on social questions, Fr Joseph Keating.[204] Keating was aware that there were many in the English Catholic social movement growing weary of negative, vituperative anti-communist campaigning.

Historians have portrayed Hinsley as a great patriot and a robust democrat. The pre-war Hinsley was not without these characteristics: even though he got Franco wrong, the loathing of fascism and author-itarian politics were in place well before the war. The abhorrence of the all-powerful state was shared by his brother bishops – they were no different from the great majority of other English church leaders in this respect. However, it was only with the war that this commit-ment to democracy and anti-totalitarianism became explicit. This chapter has shown how Hinsley, as much as anyone else with respon-sibility for determining the course which the Church took, helped create the defensive, partisan outlook which characterized mainstream English Catholicism in the late 1930s. The emphasis on Catholic Action encouraged a sense of the Church in opposition to a hostile world, an outlook which appeared to be confirmed by events in Spain. But the Second World War was to bring a very different response from Hinsley. There was a readiness on the part of this elderly man to rethink entrenched attitudes and consider fresh approaches. We have already seen how Hinsley was prepared to give lay people greater responsibility in the Church, and was not afraid of those trained in the universities; now he was to launch himself into an ambitious programme for inter-church cooperation. But how far was it within the ability of any one man, even a Cardinal, to bring English Catholicism out from the fortress?

Notes

1. Hinsley to Amigo, 1 January 1935, A.A.S., Amigo Papers, Cardinal Hinsley 1935–43, File II.
2. Hinsley to Amigo, 18 September 1934, ibid.
3. Moloney, *Westminster, Whitehall*, p. 22
4. Amigo to Hinsley, 24 March 1935 (copy), A.A.S., Amigo Papers, Cardinal Hinsley 1935–43, File II.
5. Hinsley to Amigo, 25 March 1935, ibid.
6. Hinsley to Amigo, u/d but received August 1926, ibid.
7. Norman, *Roman Catholicism in England*, p. 112.
8. Quoted in Moloney, *Westminster, Whitehall*, pp. 23–4.
9. Brown, *Through Windows of Memory*, p. 98.
10. J. C. Heenan, *Cardinal Hinsley* (London: Burns Oates and Washbourne, 1944), p. 25.
11. Ibid., pp. 46–8.
12. Ibid., p. 23.
13. Ibid., p. 25.
14. Moloney, *Westminster, Whitehall*, p. 25.
15. Hastings, *English Christianity*, p. 273.
16. W. E. Orchard to Sir James Marchant, 3 October 1938, Oxford, Bodleian Library, MS Eng lett.d.301, fo. 135.
17. Chadwick, *Hensley Henson*, p. 310; K. Robbins, 'Britain, 1940 and 'Christian Civilization' ', in D. Beales and G. Best (eds), *History Society and the Churches: Essays in Honour of Owen Chadwick* (Cambridge, 1985), p. 281. Hinsley thought Churchill a 'man of the world, with some religion': Notes of an Interview with Cardinal Hinsley, 14–15 October 1941, L.P.L., Bell Papers 223, fo. 253.
18. Coventry, 'Roman Catholicism', p. 18. On hearing of his death, Francis D'Arcy Godolphin Osborne, British Minister to the Holy See, noted: 'He was a great patriot, though perhaps more courageously outspoken regarding the Nazi persecution of the church and other offences against the laws of God and man than would please the hypersensitive neutrals of the Vatican': O. Chadwick: *Britain and the Vatican during the Second World War* (Cambridge: Cambridge University Press, 1986), p. 220.
19. Hastings, *English Christianity*, p. 274.

20. Heenan, *Hinsley*, p. 85. A point also made by Brown, *Through Windows of Memory*, p. 99.
21. Hastings, *English Christianity*, p. 274. Following Hastings's interpretation see Burns, *Use of Memory*, p. 144. cf. M. Walsh, 'Catholics, Society and Popular Culture', in McClelland and Hodgetts (eds), *From Without the Flaminian Gate*, p. 369. For the history of the *Tablet* see M. Walsh, *The Tablet: A Commemorative History 1840–1990* (London: The Tablet Publishing Co., 1990).
22. See Hastings, 'English Catholicism of the late 1930s', in Hastings (ed.), *Bishops and Writers*, pp. 107–125.
23. Mathew was ordained in 1929.
24. Biographical details are mostly drawn from Fergus Kerr's *DNB* entry.
25. For the life and career of Gervase Mathew, including his relationship with David, see A. Nichols, *Dominican Gallery*: Portrait of a Culture (Leominster: Gracewing, 1997), ch. 7. See also the entry in Gaine (ed.), *Obituary Notices of the English Dominicans*, p. 69.
26. Hinsley to Mathew, 10 December 1936, A.A.W., Mathew Papers, Misc. 1934–43, File 1.
27. The affair is discussed in Hastings, 'English Catholicism of the late 1930s', pp. 116–7.
28. Hinsley to Amigo, 19 August 1938, A.A.S., Amigo Papers, Cardinal Hinsley 1935–43, C4.I.
29. Hinsley to Amigo, 19 August 1938, ibid.
30. Hinsley to Fr Keating, 4 May 1936, E.P.S.J., Keating Papers, 3.3.1.6.
31. Hinsley to the bishops, 18 September 1937, copy in H.N.D.A., Catholic Action File.
32. Hughes, *Winds of Change*, p. 173.
33. Report of the Advisory Committee on Catholic Action in the Archdiocese of Westminster (1937), A.A.W., Mathew Papers, Catholic Action 1937–39, File 8; copy also in B.A.A., Archbishops' Papers 1929–65, AP/A1.
34. 'With their huge majority the Govt does not care what we ... demand': Brown to Henshaw, 6 December 1935, Sal.D.A., Education 1935–6, Box 066.
35. Henshaw to Hinsley, 6 March 1936, ibid, Henshaw Papers, File '1936'.
36. Meeting of the Bishops, 18 March 1936, A.A.W., *Acta*.
37. *The Birmingham Post*, 13 March 1936; Cruickshank, *Church and State in English Education*, p. 132.
38. Hinsley to Amigo, 24 April 1936, A.A.S., Amigo Papers, Cardinal Hinsley 1935–43, C4.I
39. Downey to Amigo, 27 April 1936, ibid., Correspondence with Bishops.
40. For instance see Henshaw to Hinsley, 6 March 1936, Sal.D.A., Henshaw Papers, File '1936'.
41. McNulty to Hinsley, 12 December 1935, Not.D.A., McNulty Papers, H.32; see also a copy of McNulty to Hinsley, 12 October 1935, Sal.D.A., Education 1935–6, File 066; McNulty to Henshaw, 6 December 1935, ibid.

42. Hinsley to Amigo, 14 March 1936, A.A.S., Amigo Papers, Cardinal Hinsley 1935–43, C4.I; Moloney, *Westminster, Whitehall*, p. 158.
43. Ibid.
44. Amigo to Henshaw, 9 March 1936, Sal.D.A., Henshaw Papers, File '1936'.
45. There are accounts of the background to the Liverpool Act in Baxter, 'Liverpool Labour Party'; Waller, *Democracy and Sectarianism*, pp. 340–4; Davies, 'Rome on the Rates', pp. 28–31.
46. Hinsley to the bishops, 25 March 1935, A.A.L., Downey Papers, Series 5 I.
47. Heenan, *Hinsley*, p. 79.
48. Meeting of the Bishops, 1 May 1935, A.A.W., *Acta*.
49. Amigo to Hinsley, 24 March 1935 (copy), A.A.S., Amigo Papers, Cardinal Hinsley 1935–43, C4.I.
50. His mother was Bridget Ryan; his father, Thomas, was the village carpenter in Carlton, near Selby.
51. Hinsley to Amigo, 15 February 1922, A.A.S., Amigo Papers, Cardinal Hinsley 1935–43, C4.
52. Mathew, *Catholicism in England*, p. 250.
53. Ibid., p. 171.
54. Meeting of the Bishops, 25 October 1938, A.A.W., *Acta*. The first meeting between the hierarchies took place in Dublin on 9 March 1939, which along with the Irish representation was attended by Bishops McNulty of Nottingham, Michael McGrath of Menevia (1882–1961) and William Lee of Clifton (1875–1948).
55. E. Delaney, 'The churches and Irish emigration to Britain, 1921–60', *Archivium Hibernicum*, 52 (1998), 100–2.
56. Williams to McQuaid, 6 September 1942, A.A.D., McQuaid Papers, 523/2 (1).
57. Meeting of the Bishops, 22–3 April 1941, A.A.W., *Acta*.
58. Mathew to McQuaid, 25 July 1941; see also Mathew to McQuaid, 23 July 1942, A.A.D., McQuaid Papers, 523/2 (1).
59. Mathew to McQuaid, 23 July 1942, ibid., 523/2 (2).
60. Hinsley to the bishops, 25 March 1935, copy in A.A.L., Downey Papers, Series 5 I.
61. Heenan, *Hinsley*, pp. 158–61.
62. Ibid., p. 158.
63. Ibid., p. 153; *Catholic Social Guild Report of the 28th Annual Meeting held in Ruskin College, Oxford, on August 1, 1937, and Sixteenth Annual Report of the Catholic Workers' College* (Oxford: CSG, 1937), p. 17.
64. Ibid. Bernard Aspinwall, however, detects more conservative tendencies in the young Hinsley, 'Rerum Novarum in the Transatlantic World', in *Rerum Novarum: Écriture, Contenu et Réception d'une Encyclique: Actes du Colloque International Organisé par L'École Française de Rome et le Greco Nº 2 du CNRS, Rome, 18–20 Avril 1991* (École Française de Rome: Palais Farnèse, 1997), p. 473.

65. M. Brooke, 'Catholic Social Thought and Action in England' (unpublished undergraduate dissertation, University of Cambridge, 1994), 25–32.
66. R. P. Walsh to Mgr Adamson, 7 October u/d but probably 1937 and 4 February 1938, A.A.L., Downey Papers, Series 2 IV, CSG File.
67. Madelenie Bramble Green to Fr O'Hea, 8 August 1937, E.P.S.J., 28/2/1/1
68. Hinsley to Fr O'Hea, 15 July 1938, ibid.
69. Madelenie Bramble Green to Fr O'Hea, 8 August 1937, ibid.; Buchanan, *Britain and the Spanish Civil War*, p. 181.
70. Godfrey to O'Hara, 17 August 1955, A.A.L., Godfrey Papers, Series 1 I Documents. A Miscellany.
71. Clifton, *Amigo*, pp. 140–1. Bishop Keily of Plymouth wrote in his diocesan newsletter of the 'wonderful work of Signor Mussolini' and described Italy as 'the only land that may be said to be without "hooligans", and the sense of order, self respect and general moral well-being are very evident': *Plymouth Diocesan Newsletter* (June 1928), p. 313.
72. Quoted in Moloney, *Westminster, Whitehall*, p. 50.
73. Ibid., p. 49.
74. Ibid., p. 50.
75. A. Rhodes, *The Vatican in the age of the Dictators 1922–1945* (London: Hodder and Stoughton, 1973), p. 73.
76. A. Hastings, *Church and State: The English Experience* (Exeter: University of Exeter, 1991), p. 44.
77. Moloney, *Westminster, Whitehall*, pp. 94–5.
78. Ibid., pp. 96–7.
79. Heenan, *Hinsley*, pp. 227–32.
80. Moloney, *Westminster, Whitehall*, p. 102.
81. Hinsley to Amigo, 1 January 1929, A.A.S., Amigo Papers, Cardinal Hinsley 1935–43, File II.
82. Reprinted in *Plymouth Diocesan Record* (December 1936).
83. *Liverpool Daily Post*, 29 March 1938; see also ibid., 5 April 1938.
84. See the papers on international relations in A.A.W., Bourne Papers, B. 5/64.
85. Fr O'Hea to John Eppstein, 6 January 1938, E.P.S.J., 28/2/4/1.
86. The episode is mentioned in M. Cowling, *The Impact of Hitler: British Politics and British Policy 1933–1940* (Cambridge: Cambridge University Press, 1975), p. 228, although the author is wrong in his dating of it.
87. John Eppstein to Hinsley, u/d but January or February 1938 (copy), A.A.W., Mathew Papers, League of Nations and IPC file.
88. Hinlsey to Mathew, 2 February 1938, ibid.
89. John Eppstein to Hinsley, u/d but January or February 1938 (copy), ibid.
90. Fr O'Hea to Mathew, 2 February 1938, ibid.
91. Fr O'Hea to Hinsley, 3 April 1938 (copy), E.P.S.J., Fr O'Hea Papers, 28/2/4/1.
92. Moloney, *Westminster, Whitehall*, pp. 79–80. The LNU's stance on

Spain is discussed in D. S. Birn, *The League of Nations Union 1918-1945* (Oxford: Clarendon Press, 1981), ch. 11.

93. Hinsley to Lord Robert Cecil, 13 April 1938 (copy), Oxford, Bodleian Library, MSS Gilbert Murray 232, fo. 124.; correspondence on Catholics and the LNU can also be found at C.S.G.A., E 11.

94. Meeting of the Bishops, 26-27 April 1938, A.A.W., *Acta*.

95. Birn, *League of Nations*, p. 188; Cowling, *Impact of Hitler*, p. 228.

96. Hinsley to Lord Robert Cecil, 13 December 1938 (copy), Oxford, Bodleian Library, MSS Gilbert Murray 234, fo. 37.

97. Lord Robert Cecil to Hinsley, 16 December 1938 (copy), ibid., fos. 41-2.

98. Hastings, 'English Catholicism of the late 1930s', p. 118. The most authoritative treatments of English Catholic responses are Moloney, *Westminster, Whitehall*, pp. 63-73; J. Flint, '"Must God go Fascist?": English Catholic Opinion and the Spanish Civil War', *Church History*, 56 (1987); T. Buchanan, *Britain and the Spanish Civil War* (Cambridge: Cambridge University Press, 1997), see esp. pp. 177-88; see idem., *The Spanish Civil War and the British Labour Movement* (Cambridge, Cambridge University Press, 1991) which demonstrates the rival pulls on Catholics in the labour movement; K. L. Morris, 'Fascism and British Catholic Writers 1924-1939: Part Two', *New Blackfriars*, 80 (February 1999), 82-95, also emphasizes English Catholic support for Franco.

99. Buchanan, 'Great Britain', p. 269

100. W. J. Callahan, *The Catholic Church in Spain* (Washington, D.C.: Catholic University of America Press, 2000), p. 344.

101. Hastings, 'English Catholicism of the late 1930s', pp. 118-9.

102. Buchanan, *Britain and the Spanish Civil War*, pp. 177, 185-7. Ireland was another model of a Christian social order which attracted many educated English Catholics in the mid-1930s, T. A. Greene, 'English Roman Catholics and the Irish Free State', *Éire-Ireland*, 19 (Spring 1984), 48-73.

103. Quoted in Buchanan, *Britain and the Spanish Civil War*, p. 187.

104. Meeting of the Bishops, 4 July 1933, A.A.W., *Acta*.

105. Quoted in Clifton, *Amigo*, pp. 142-3.

106. For references to the Friends of National Spain see Buchanan, *Britain and the Spanish Civil War*, pp. 89-90, 161.

107. Arnold Lunn to Amigo, 26 July 1937, A.A.S., Amigo Papers, Spanish Civil War File.

108. *South London Press*, 28 August 1936.

109. Buchanan, *Britain and the Spanish Civil War*, pp. 172-3.

110. T. E. Hachey (ed.), *Anglo-Vatican Relations, 1914-1939: Confidential Annual Reports of the British Minsters to the Holy See* (Boston, Mass.: G. K. Hall and Co., 1972), p. 380.

111. Buchanan, *Britain and the Spanish Civil War*, p. 178.

112. Meeting of the Bishops, 6 April 1937, A.A.W., *Acta*.

113. Pizzardo to Downey, 2 January 1937, A.A.L., Downey Papers, Series 1 XI.

114. *Ad Clerum*, 16 August 1937, A.A.L., Downey Papers, Series 1 VI B.
115. *Ad Clerum*, 27 January 1937, ibid.
116. *Ad Clerum*, 16 August 1937, ibid.
117. Minutes of the Pro-Deo Commission, 10 September 1937, ibid., Series 2 IV.
118. Minutes of the CTS Executive Meeting, 15 September 1937, A.C.T.S.
119. Ibid., 16 March 1938.
120. Minutes of the Pro-Deo Commission, 25 February 1938, A.A.L., Downey Papers, Series 2 IV.
121. Fr Ellison to Mgr Adamson, 4 January 1938, ibid.
122. Fr Ellison to Mgr Adamson, 10 March 1938, ibid., Series 1 VI.
123. Minutes of the Pro-Deo Commission, 11 March and 18 March 1938, ibid., Series 2 IV.
124. Fr Ellison to Mgr Adamson, 4 March 1938, ibid., Series 1VI. See D. Keogh and F. O'Driscoll, 'Ireland' in Buchanan and Conway, *Political Catholicism in Europe*, pp. 281–83; F. O'Driscoll, 'In Search of a Christian Social Order: The Impact of Social Catholicism in Ireland', in T. M. Devine and J. F. McMillan, *Celebrating Columba: Irish-Scottish Connections 597–1997* (Edinburgh: John Donald Publishers Ltd, 1999), pp. 113–5.
125. Fr Ellison to Mgr Adamson, 4 March 1938, A.A.L., Downey Papers, Series 1VI I.
126. Minutes of the Pro-Deo Commission, 11 June 1938, ibid., Series 2 IV.
127. Driver has been described as one of the 'driving forces of fascism in Lancashire', R. Thurlow, *Fascism in Britain: A History, 1918–1985* (Oxford: Blackwell, 1987), p. 121.
128. Nellie Driver to the Pro-Deo Commission, 20 February 1938, A.A.L., Downey Papers, Series 2 IV.
129. This is entitled 'From the Shadows of Exile. An unpublished autobiography by Nellie Driver, Women District Leader of the Nelson branch of the BUF, 1935–1940', and is held at Bradford University Library.
130. D. Mayall, 'Rescued from the Shadows of Exile: Nellie Driver, Autobiography and the British Union of Fascists', in T. Kushner and K. Lunn (eds) *The Politics of Marginality: Race, the Radical Right and the Minorities in Twentieth Century Britain* (London: Frank Cass, 1990), pp. 19–39; J. Gottlieb, *Feminine Fascism: Women in Britain's Fascist Movement 1923–1945* (London and New York: I. B. Tauris, 2000), pp. 297–8. I would like to thank Dr Julie Gottlieb of Manchester University for pointing me to references to Driver.
131. Minutes of the Pro-Deo Commission, 8 July 1938, A.A.L., Downey Papers, Series 2 IV. The 'Italian Council' referred to was the British-Italian Council for Friendship and Peace, founded in 1935 to disseminate pro-Italian propaganda at the time of Mussolini's Abyssinian campaign: See D. Waley, *British Public Opinion and the Abyssinian War 1935–6* (London: Maurice Temple Smith, 1975).
132. Joseph Cartmell to Mgr Adamson, 18 December 1938; Fr Sheppard to

Mgr Adamson, 28 December 1938, A.A.L., Downey Papers, Series 2 IV.

133. This edition is in the possession of the author.

134. *Jewish Chronicle*, 12 August 1938.

135. *Liverpool Jewish Gazette*, 10 July 1953.

136. *Liverpool Post*, 20 March 1933.

137. *Liverpool Jewish Gazette*, 10 July 1953.

138. Ibid.

139. There was a similar situation in Manchester. J. Davies, 'Bishop Henry Vincent Marshall: Relations with the Manchester Jewish Community and the Other Christian Churches', *North West Catholic History*, 26 (1999), 96–109.

140. P. Smith (ed.), *The Bishop of Münster and the Nazis* (London: Burns Oates and Co., 1942), p. vi.

141. I. Marinoff, *The Heresy of National Socialism* (London: Burns Oates and Washbourne, 1941), p. 8.

142. Ulrike Ehret's doctoral work on English (and German) Catholic attitudes to the Jews promises to be a very interesting study of a previously neglected area.

143. *Harvest* (June 1938).

144. Ibid. (November 1938).

145. Quoted in Moloney, *Westminster, Whitehall*, p. 205; quoted in Clifton, *Amigo*, p. 139.

146. *The Universe*, 20 May 1933.

147. Fr C. Lattey, S.J. (ed.), *Man and Eternity: Papers Read at the Summer School of Catholic Studies, Held at Cambridge, July 25th to August 3rd, 1936* (London: Burns Oates, 1937), pp. vii–viii; see also his comments in Lattey, *Church and State*, p. xi.

148. Minutes of the CTS Executive Meeting, 16 February 1938, A.C.T.S.

149. S. Rawnsley, 'The Membership of the British Union of Fascists', in K. Lunn and R. Thurlow (eds), *British Fascism: Essays on the Radical Right in Inter-War Britain* (London: Croom Helm, 1980), pp. 161–2. Mosley took the Catholic vote seriously and this was particularly seen in his attempts to avoid offending Catholic sensibilities on questions of eugenics and birth control: Gottlieb, *Feminine Fascism*, p. 115.

150. J. K. Heydon, *Wage-Slavery* (London: John Lane the Bodley Head, 1924), pp. 7–8, 50–1, 69–76; J. K. Heydon, *Fascism and Providence* (London: Sheed and Ward, 1937), pp. 102–5.

151. Hastings, *English Christianity*, p. 326; Heydon, *Fascism and Providence*, p. 142.

152. *The Clergy Review* (April 1938), pp. 355–9.

153. *The Downside Review* (January 1938), pp. 104–5.

154. Williams to E. W. Record, 7 April 1937; Williams to E. W. Record, 10 April 1937, B.A.A., Archbishops' Papers 1929–65.

155. A. Lunn, *Spain: The Unpopular Front* (London: CTS, 1937), p. 5.

156. Buchanan, *Britain and the Spanish Civil War*, pp. 118–9.

157. Memorandum of 22 October 1937 of Major General Sir Cecil Pereira

Chairman of the Executive Committee of The Bishops' Committee for the Relief of Spanish Distress, A.A.L., Downey Papers, Series 5 I.

158. Brown to Canon Drinkwater, 26 May 1937, B.A.A., Drinkwater Papers, FHD/Q2.

159. Williams to Canon Drinkwater, 5 June 1937, ibid.

160. Fr Ellison to Mgr Adamson, 4 March 1938, A.A.L., Downey Papers, Series 1 VI.

161. Flint, '"Must God go Fascist?"', p. 368.

162. Ibid., p. 370; White, 'History of *Blackfriars*', pp. 325–8.

163. Fr Hilary Carpenter, 'Catholics and European Political Development', in *Report of the 40th Annual Conference of Catholic Colleges and of the Annual Conference of the Convent Schools' Association* (London: Cole and Co., 1937), pp. 81–98.

164. For a survey of Drinkwater's career see J. D. Crichton, *The Secret Name: Selected Writings of Francis Harold Drinkwater* (Leominster: Fowler Wright, 1986), pp. 11–45. I would like to thank Mgr Crichton for his helpful correspondence on Drinkwater.

165. Diary, 12 January 1910, B.A.A., Drinkwater Papers, FHD/A2.

166. See below, p. 50.

167. Most of the details of Drinkwater's early life are taken from Crichton, *Secret Name*, and the autobiography Drinkwater contributed to an American magazine, the typescript of which is held at B.A.A., Drinkwater Papers, FHD/A11. See also FHD/A3 for Drinkwater's war-time correspondence.

168. Crichton, *Secret Name*, p. 13.

169. See e.g. *The Sower* (January 1938); Flint, '"Must God go Fascist"', p. 371.

170. Minutes of the Pro-Deo Commission, 6 May 1938, A.A.L., Downey Papers, Series 2 IV.

171. Canon Drinkwater to Gregory Macdonald [editor of *The Catholic Times*], 23 August 1937 (copy); Canon Drinkwater to H. S. Dean, 22 October 1937 (copy), B.A.A., Drinkwater Papers, FHD/Q2.

172. Drinkwater reviewing D. Attwater's *Why Communism Gets Away With It* in the *Dublin Review* (October–December 1937), p. 391.

173. Canon Drinkwater to Sir Martin Melvin, 24 September 1936 (copy), B.A.A., Drinkwater Papers, FHD/Q2.

174. Typescript, 'Some reasons for regretting the attitude of our Catholic newspapers in regard to the Spanish War', dated 23 May 1937, ibid. For a typical pro-Nationalist response to Guernica, see Lunn, *Unpopular Front*, p. 25.

175. Canon Drinkwater to Michael de la Bedoyère, 7 June 1937 (copy), B.A.A., Drinkwater Papers, FHD/Q2.

176. Ibid.

177. Canon Drinkwater to Fr Burns, 12 February 1937 (copy), ibid.

178. Hinsley to Canon Drinkwater, 16 June 1937, ibid.

179. Hinsley to Mr O'Hanlan, 22 February 1938 (copy), A.A.S., Amigo Papers, Spanish Civil War File.

180. Hinsley to Amigo, 16 August 1937, ibid., Cardinal Hinsley 1935–43. C4.I.
181. R. Speaight, *The Property Basket: Recollections of a Divided Life* (London: Collins and Harvill Press, 1970), p. 220.
182. Williams to Fr O'Hea, 23 March 1937 (copy); Williams to Pat Taggart, 22 January 1938, B.A.A., Archbishops' Papers 1929–65, AP/S8/1.
183. William to Lord Rankeillour, 11 January 1937 (copy), ibid., AP/C28/52.
184. Canon Drinkwater to Revd Drolet, 14 February 1936 (copy), ibid., Drinkwater Papers, FHD/P4.
185. Williams to Fr O'Hea, 23 March 1937 (copy); Williams to Pat Taggart, 22 January 1938, B.A.A., Archbishops' Papers 1929–65, AP/S8/1.
186. Canon Drinkwater to Revd Drolet, 14 February 1936 (copy), ibid., Drinkwater Papers, FHD/P4.
187. These were published as *Seven Addresses on Social Justice* (London: Burns Oates and Co., 1937).
188. Crichton, *Secret Name*, p. 29.
189. Williams to Canon Drinkwater, 11 November 1936, B.A.A., Drinkwater Papers, FHD/C502.
190. Brown to Canon Drinkwater, 26 May 1937, ibid.
191. Brown to Canon Drinkwater, 6 June 1937, ibid.
192. Memorial to Hinsley and the Bishops of England and Wales, 9 February 1938, A.A.L., Downey Papers, Series 1 VI.
193. Quoted in V. Flessati, 'Pax: The history of a Catholic peace society 1936–1971' (unpublished Ph.D. dissertation, University of Bradford, 1991), p. 36.
194. Minutes of the Pro-Deo Commission, 20 May 1938, A.A.L., Downey Papers, Series 2 IV.
195. M. Vincent, 'Spain' in Buchanan and Conway, *Political Catholicism in Europe*, p. 119.
196. Minutes of the Pro-Deo Commission, 28 January and 4 February 1938, A.A.L., Downey Papers, Series 2 IV.
197. For a valuable account of the organization's history see Flessati, 'Pax: The history of a Catholic peace society'.
198. Ibid., p. 5.
199. Ibid., pp. 17, 27.
200. W. Orchard to Sir James Marchant, 26 January 1938, Oxford, Bodleian Library, MS Eng lett. d. 301, fo. 127.
201. Christian Lucas to Canon Drinkwater, 31 January 1937; T. Fish to Canon Drinkwater, 2 February 1937; Helen Parry Eden to Canon Drinkwater, 7 February 1937, B.A.A., Drinkwater Papers, FHD/Q2. There are other letters from sympathizers, including Enrique Moreno [Lecturer in Spanish at the University of Oxford].
202. Sal.D.A., Catholic Social Guild Papers, Folder 9, 181/47.
203. The pastoral letter was published in *The Tablet*, 4 December 1937, and in pamphlet form.

204. Ibid. Hinsley's original draft, with Fr Keating's notes, can be seen at E.P.S.J., Keating Papers. Hinsley remarked, apologetically, in the letter which accompanied the draft, 'I find it very hard to get time to think or to read, much less to compose a sermon or an address': Hinsley to Fr Keating, 7 September 1937, E.P.S.J., Fr Keating Papers.

6

The Sword and the Spirit

There had been no episcopal encouragement to Catholic involvement in inter-church social or political organizations since the COPEC resignations. Bourne's reluctance to engage with social questions, coupled with the hardening of papal attitudes after *Mortalium Animos* created an unfavourable climate. There were no Catholic representatives at the most important inter-church expression of social concern of the 1930s, the Universal Christian Council for Life and Work conference held at Oxford in July 1937. But just as the experiences of the First World War broke down barriers to cooperation, so the Second World War was to have a similar effect.

Even before the war Hinsley's archiepiscopate promised a thaw in inter-church relations. He shared a platform with Temple in the protests against the persecution of Jews; Temple's biographer notes that between the two men 'there was a notable sympathy ... and each had a warm regard for the other'.[1] Archbishop Lang of Canterbury's relations with Hinsley were 'mostly unofficial, but of a cordiality without precedent'.[2] Hinsley appeared as 'the very antithesis of a wily Roman prelate';[3] his openness and warmth would disarm even those ill-disposed towards Roman Catholicism. Unpretentious and seemingly devoid of guile, more worldly men mistook this for a lack of intelligence[4] – yet it would be an injustice to assume that Hinsley was no more than merely a nice man. There was certainly a reassuring and solid quality about him; his habit of employing metaphors drawn from cricket was part of his popular appeal, and what Englishman (or Australian in this instance) could fail to be stirred by a radio broadcast which contrasted those 'upright' men who were upholding by 'straight bat and vigorous driving' the 'team spirit of humanity', with those 'fellows who do not play the game, who have no decent cricket in their upbringing'.[5] Such speeches, according to William Godfrey, pleased the government very much.[6] With Anglican leaders reticent in response to calls for another crusade for Christian Civilization, this sure spokesman would assume a prominence in national life which no other English Catholic prelate since Manning had attained. When the see of Canterbury fell vacant after the retirement of Cosmo Lang in 1942, Churchill was reported to have said, 'A pity we can't have the old man at Westminster'.[7] But Hinsley was more than a mere drum-banging apologist for British war aims: underpinning this commitment was a passionate belief that core religious and moral values were at stake; that ultimately it would be a religious and spiritual movement of all Christians that would ensure the final and complete victory over tyranny. This was the thinking behind the Sword of the Spirit organisation (hereafter referred to as the 'Sword').

Encouraging and invigorating Hinsley in the area of inter-church relations was his Auxiliary, David Mathew. Mathew struck up warm relations with several leading Anglican churchmen, including Lang[8] and Temple. But it was Mathew's close relationship with G. K. A. Bell (1883–1958), Anglican Bishop of Chichester, described lately as 'amongst the first to recognise the need for international, inter-church solidarity which should be irrespective of national or confessional differences',[9] that provided much of the impetus for the Sword. Both Oxford educated with liberal, socially-concerned and ecumenical outlooks, Mathew and Bell gravitated towards one another as if old friends.[10] It may have been that Mathew, feeling constrained within Catholic ecclesiastical circles, saw the promise of a re-connection with values he associated with Anglican Oxford – moderation, liberality of expression and broad and charitable sympathies.[11] 'It is the coming together as friends which is above all desirable', Mathew maintained to Bell, 'Platform appearances are nothing without personal friendship and the easy interchange of views and above all a mutual trust and confidence.'[12] The two first came into contact towards the end of 1938 when Bell, encouraged by Pius XI's recent pronouncements, approached Mathew, who had just been appointed Auxiliary Bishop of Westminster, about the possibility of a joint Christian statement on the just international order. On 22 December, following on from a meeting at the Athenaeum, Bell stressed to Mathew that in these 'grave and troubled times' it was vital that 'responsible people ... should make more opportunities for meeting one another, though their ecclesiastical allegiances differ'.[13] Bell would establish 'most friendly relations' with Mathew during the course of 1939 and could also inform one overseas contact that the 'present Cardinal Archbishop of Westminster is very much more friendly to other Churches than his predecessor'.[14]

Whilst Bell and Mathew were growing in mutual regard over regular teas at the Athenaeum, the broader context changed with the death of Pius XI on 10 February 1939. If anything the election of Eugenio Pacelli as Pius XII just under a month later probably encouraged Bell to hasten his plans. Pius XI had made his hostility to religious cooperation known in *Mortalium Animos*, and although it was too early to tell whether Pacelli, who had spent his entire adult life in the service of the Roman bureaucracy, would emerge from the shadow of his predecessor, there were reasons to hope for a revision of attitudes. With the storm clouds gathering over Europe, Douglas Woodruff, editor of *The Tablet*, welcomed Pacelli as one who would amplify the Christian message throughout the world for and on behalf of all people of good will.[15] Indeed, Pacelli's peace efforts during the first months of his reign showed his deep commitment to the papacy's role as spiritual leader of all nations and seemed to confirm Woodruff in his optimism.[16]

Bell's approach to the Holy See was made through the Apostolic Delegate, with the full support of Hinsley, in June 1939. Bell asked Godfrey to ascertain Rome's view on the possibility of private discussions between theologians and experts from the Catholic Church and 'certain other historic churches' on the 'fundamental Christian principles involved in a true international order, and in the establishment of social justice'.[17] Despite Bell's assurances that 'it is intended to exclude dogmatic or political questions', Godfrey, who according to one contemporary observer 'had mentally lost his nationality, and ... viewed matters just as much from the Vatican point of view as any Italian',[18] doubted that such an initiative would be welcomed and suggested instead that a document issued simultaneously by the different parties would possibly be more favourably received by the Secretary of State.[19] Godfrey's suggestion appealed neither to Bell nor Mathew, who thought that the 'whole value of the meeting would evaporate',[20] but his doubts were confirmed when the Cardinal Secretary of State informed him that 'Since the various pontifical documents and the repeated utterances of the Holy Father make known his unfailing effort and clearly put forward the teaching of the Church on the questions referred to above, it is not easy to see the practical utility of eventual discussions by theologians and experts'.[21]

After this cold douche, Bell wrote an emotive letter to Mathew stating that 'there was an unprecedented opportunity for contact between some of the historic Churches and the Church of Rome, for a treatment of subjects which did not raise the dogmatic issues; and yet the only response one receives, however courteously framed, is complete rejection, and ... a failure to grasp the essential nature of the project'.[22] Bell informed one ecumenical contact that this was also the view of Mathew.[23] Hopes rose a little when, only a few days after the rebuff (21 July 1939), Bell received a letter from Godfrey which informed him of the Secretary of State's suggestion that he could approach, in confidence, the bishops or the Archbishop Delegate, or exchange information with Catholic theologians on the subject of the international order.[24] It was not what Bell had envisaged but it at least kept the lines of communication open. Bell was given further encouragement by the Pope's address of Christmas Eve 1939 which set out Five Peace Points which should form the basis of any post-war settlement.[25] In this false start lay the origins of the Sword.

Considerable academic attention has been given to the Sword.[26] Its features were social concern, commitment to democracy and disavowal of fascism, lay direction and cooperation with other Christians. As such, it has appeared as the 'authentic expression of English political Catholicism', in contrast to the exclusivist, clerically-led nature of Catholic Action.[27] But whilst the Sword so described neatly conforms to von Arx's model of Catholic political engagement in England, the ascription of 'authenticity' to this movement obscures the fact that it was an unprecedented and bold departure from what had gone before.

The fall of France in May 1940 was the immediate spur to action. The pro-Vichy sympathies of sections of Catholic opinion, led by Michael de la Bedoyère's *Catholic Herald*, and the enthusiasm of some for the idea of a 'Latin Bloc' (an alliance of the authoritarian, 'pro-Catholic' regimes of Spain, Italy and Vichy France), heightened concerns that Catholicism in England was identified with the political right.[28] Hinsley shared such concerns: in a letter to the historian Christopher Dawson (1889–1970), editor of the *Dublin Review*, he stated: 'Because we are Catholics we must be loyal and reasonable patriots. If the Latin Catholic Bloc is against our country we are against that Bloc, because it is setting up a false principle – i.e. exaggerated nationalism – against true loyalty to Fatherland.'[29] One aspect of the Sword, which was launched on 1 August 1940, was a straightforward assertion of English Catholicism's patriotism, to show, as Hinsley put it to the bishops on 7 August, 'that we in this country were loyal'.[30] There was indeed nobody more patriotic and nobody more robust in support of the allied cause: 'I see him in the car', wrote the actor and writer Robert Speaight recalling Hinsley on one of their missions on behalf of the Ministry of Information, 'as I was accompanying him from a visit to a Free French Naval establishment, shaking his fist at the sky and exclaiming: "Think of these people who are trying to disturb our peace"'.[31]

But there was much more to the Sword than drum-beating patriotism. By March 1941, with the 'anti-Catholic campaign ... robbed of its sting in good time', Hinsley began to envisage a wider purpose for the Sword than simply an 'anti-Fascist movement' – he believed it should be a movement dedicated 'to a fuller, more positive, more Catholic existence . . .'[32] This comment showed the influence of Christopher Dawson whose recent works on the relationship of religion and contemporary politics, which included *Religion and the Modern State* (1936) and *Beyond Politics* (1939), had impressed Hinsley so much that he appointed him almost simultaneously editor of the *Dublin Review* and Vice-President of the Sword. In a *Dublin Review* editorial of January 1941, Dawson urged a 'dynamic and prophetic element' within the Church committed to furthering the implications of the 'general realization that social and political issues have become spiritual issues – that the Church cannot abstain from intervention without betraying its mission'.[33] Under Dawson the *Dublin Review* carried articles by the French philosopher Jacques Maritain, who was arguing for a broad Christian democratic response to the threat of Nazism and fascism. Dawson's only wartime book, *Judgement of the Nations* (1942), which urged Catholics in the face of the threat of totalitarianism to cooperate with other Christians and make their peace with democratic society, bore strong traces of Maritain's influence. The editorial shift at the *Dublin Review* troubled the manager Douglas Jerrold, who disapproved of Dawson publishing articles by Maritain because of the anti-Franco stance he had taken in the Spanish Civil War,[34] as well as finding objectionable the contributions from non-Catholics.[35] David Mathew, who was in 'deep sympathy' with Dawson, welcomed the broadening of scope and saw the journal as a useful vehicle for ecumenical ideas, contributing an article in January 1942 'on the debt that we owe to the Caroline Anglicans'.[36] It was to Hinsley's credit that he kept faith with Dawson, threatening to move the *Dublin Review* to another publisher if Jerrold continued to destabilize the editor's position.[37] Dawson, along with A. C. F. Beales (1905–1974), a convert and Lecturer in Education at King's College, London, and Barbara Ward (1914–1981), the vivacious assistant editor of *The Economist*, would become the moving spirits of the Sword.

It was soon apparent that the liberalizing influences permeating Westminster would meet with resistance elsewhere. On 7 August, Hinsley wrote to the bishops explaining the nature of the Sword and canvassing their support. Perhaps sensing the suspicion that would greet a movement directed by progressive lay people, he suggested that 'to be spared circulars' they allow him to represent the hierarchy on the matter, and that 'notices in the Press under 'on Behalf of the Hierarchy' might be considered *official* if you consent'.[38] One of the concerns voiced at this stage was that the Sword appeared too political; it savoured too much of an anti-fascist crusade. Worryingly, the CSG President Archbishop Williams questioned the balance of political sympathies on the Sword's lay Executive, arguing that the omission of those 'who stood up for Franco', namely Douglas Jerrold, would give the impression that English Catholics regarded Nazism and fascism as greater threats than 'World Revolution'.[39] McNulty of Nottingham was also anxious. In a letter to Henry Marshall (1884–1955), who succeeded Henshaw as Bishop of Salford in 1939, McNulty said it was inevitable that the Sword would bear a 'political' complexion but insisted that it was no business of the bishops to become involved in passing judgements on political systems which had not been condemned explicitly by the papacy:

> If this is only another name for Catholic Action as explained by the Holy Father I am all for it. But if it is any sense political I shall oppose it as regards my own diocese. I do not think it is our business *as Bishops* to condemn this or that form of government unless it has already been condemned by Ecclesiastical Authority, i.e. by the Pope. For example, have Fascism or Nazism, as such, been condemned in Rome? Certain grave injustices by the Germans and others must, of course, be condemned, but we should hesitate to condemn political systems from the Episcopal Bench.[40]

This might seem a strange comment given that the papal encyclical, *Mit brennender Sorge* (1937), was regarded as a subversive act in Nazi Germany;[41] but McNulty in fact had grasped the precise point that whilst the encyclical had attacked abuses against the Church in Germany, it had indeed stopped short of outright condemnation of the political system. Furthermore, whilst the subtext may have been clear, the desire amongst key figures in the Vatican Curia, including Pacelli the future Pope Pius XII, to prevent a complete break with the Nazi regime, and the even stronger antipathy to communism, had the effect of dampening the message.[42] Nevertheless, in the very different situation of 1940 one might have expected McNulty to cast off these hesitations. Like McNulty, Bishop Marshall was also hostile to clerical politicking: 'Personally, I have kept aloof from politics of any kind all my life, and prefer to avoid even a suspicion of advertising any political view or theory', he told Hinsley in December 1940.[43] Earlier, in August 1940, he had expressed agreement with the declaration of aims, though he remained concerned that 'the methods proposed may easily pass from the Christian ideal to political propaganda'.[44] It is interesting to contrast this reticence to oppose fascism with the vigour with which the bishops conducted anti-communist campaigns, though this was of course the same across Catholic Europe.

The attitudes of a majority of bishops to the Sword were lukewarm from the outset. Downey of Liverpool would be a key figure if the Sword was ever to develop in the north of England, but he showed himself to be hostile to the idea of lay direction: in a letter to Mathew of 13 October 1940 he stated that the Sword needed 'control and guidance', suggested the appointment of a 'sound man' such as Canon Mahoney as censor (who did eventually take up this post), and hinted that local branches should come under the direct control of the diocesan bishops.[45] Only Thomas Flynn (1880–1961), appointed Bishop of Lancaster in 1939, expressed himself to be in support of the Sword at this stage (Archbishop Williams eventually came round to the idea), although he had some reservations about the quality of the Executive and thought that for it to have any influence Williams or Hinsley should take control: in other words he thought that it should be more closely tied to ecclesiastical authority.[46]

Flynn's caution was never taken to an extreme and Mathew came to see him as an ally who was both imaginative enough to grasp the opportunities for renewal in Church life yet trusted enough by more conservative colleagues. Of all the bishops, Mathew came to regard Flynn as 'perhaps the closest to my point of view in many matters'.[47] Flynn was also a link to Downey. He was a product of Upholland, and, like Downey, became Vice-Rector there. In 1932, it was Downey who appointed Flynn as co-editor (along with Edward Myers) of *The Clergy Review*. Flynn, like Downey, had an academic orientation, though his background was scientific rather than philosophical; they regularly gave papers to the Summer School of Catholic Studies and shared a similar ambition to raise the academic standing of the secular clergy. Unlike Downey, Flynn had an English university training which undoubtedly gave him a wider range of contacts in the scholarly world. This was also part of Flynn's appeal to Mathew. Flynn's social background was far more humble than Mathew's: he was born in Portsmouth, the son of a soldier; yet he distinguished himself academically and won a scholarship to study Natural Sciences at Downing College, Cambridge, which was followed by a further year of study at Fribourg.

Flynn was in fact one of a number of recent episcopal appointments who had been university, rather than exclusively seminary, educated. Whereas in 1918 not one of the bishops had been educated in the national universities, by the early 1940s the effect of the removal of the prohibition was being felt. There was Henry Poskitt (1888–1950), appointed Bishop of Leeds in 1936; a convert educated at Corpus Christi College, Cambridge, he was a countryman, quiet and retiring, never happier than when with his bees and goats.[48] Several members of St Edmund's College, Cambridge, were nominated to sees within a few years of one another: Williams to Birmingham in 1929, McNulty to Nottingham in 1932, and in that year also Edward Myers became Auxiliary Bishop of Westminster. Thomas Leo Parker (1887–1975), appointed Bishop of Northampton in 1941, was a Durham graduate. The broader perspective that a university education undoubtedly gave did not predispose all to inter-church cooperation, but what support the Sword did obtain tended to come from those with this background. Mathew dwelt on the impact of educational experience when assessing reasons for the negative attitudes to the Sword taken up by the majority of the episcopate. He told an increasingly frustrated Bishop Bell 'to remember that those who have been brought up since thirteen in a way that really shuts them out of the world, and as seminarists without a University training and so on, found it extremely difficult to understand the full force of the present situation and new proposals. They had mixed with Romans all their lives, and they did not understand the world outside.'[49]

Even though the Catholic bishops were not united behind the Sword, there were still encouraging signs of closer relations with other churches. The greater stress on social questions during the war gave the Sword momentum. Hinsley put his name to a letter signed also by William Temple and George Armstrong, Moderator of the Free Church Federal Council, supporting the Pope's Five Peace Points. This appeared in *The Times* on 21 December 1940. In addition to the Pope's Peace Points it insisted on five more: the abolition of extreme inequality in wealth and possession; equal opportunity of education regardless of race and class; the safeguarding of the family as a social unit; the restoration of the sense of divine vocation to man's daily work; and that 'The resources of the earth should be used as God's gift to the whole human race, and used with due consideration for the needs of the present and future generation'.[50] The ten points were adopted as the Sword's manifesto. Significantly there was no reference to religious liberty – a future sticking-point.

Arguably the two meetings at the Stoll Theatre on 10 and 11 May 1941, the first of which was presided over by Archbishop Lang of Canterbury, the second by Hinsley, represented a high-point for the Sword. Bishop Bell, whose *Christianity and World Order* (1940) had achieved a massive readership, was amongst those invited to speak on 'A Christian Social Order'. At the end of the first meeting, Hinsley called for 'a regular system of consultation and collaboration' between the churches. It signalled his support for the Sword Executive's 1 April resolution, which had directed Dawson, Beales and Fr John

Murray, a scholarly Jesuit who worked on *The Month*, 'to establish contact with non-Catholics'.[51] In a seminal moment at the close of the meeting, Bell asked the Cardinal discreetly whether he might lead the 'Our Father': without hesitation Hinsley led the assembly in prayer. But whilst Bell found this impulsiveness so refreshing and unusual in a Catholic prelate, it was a trait that began to worry his brother bishops. After this remarkable and unprecedented move, latent hostility or apathy towards the Sword turned into more open suspicion and antipathy. The furore that greeted the joint 'Our Father' may even have caused Hinsley to waver: several years after the event Bishop Parker of Northampton told Archbishop Griffin of Westminster that 'I hold a letter from the late H[is].E[minence]. who regretted he said the Our Father at the Stoll Theatre, and said it was done on the spur of the moment'.[52] The reason for this regret may, of course, have been due to the ferocity of the criticism rather than the action itself.

The following month Mathew wrote to Bell on behalf of Hinsley to arrange a meeting to explore the 'possibilities of joint action' and to thank him for his 'generous and continued sympathy towards us'.[53] But the mood of heady optimism created at the Stoll Theatre meeting was soon dampened. Structural issues inhibited corporate effort. The Sword's constitution instructed that any action for joint cooperation 'can be taken only in Dioceses where full approval of the Ordinary has been given for cooperation in general and for particular meetings or activities';[54] this meant in effect that the Sword could only flourish where the diocesan bishop was in support.

It soon became clear that some bishops were resistant to the Cardinal's prompting. Bishop Bell, unfamiliar with the Catholic ecclesiastical structure, had wrongly assumed that if Westminster pushed a particular scheme then that would ensure its adoption:

> I was struck once again by the fact that the Roman Catholic Bishops have a great measure of independence. *The Times* letter was circulated by the Cardinal, before publication, to all the Bishops (there are eighteen of them). He told them that he proposed to sign the letter personally, and not in the name of the Hierarchy. They agreed to this course. But it was news to me that he should have regarded it as necessary to tell all the Bishops about the letter before he signed it. Bishop Mathew also told me, some little while ago, the Bishops complained that there had been too much rule by the Metropolitans. So the Bishops claim a pretty active role in all those questions of policy.[55]

The major stumbling block was the issue of cooperation with other churches, and in particular the question of how far, if at all, it was permissible for Catholics to associate with other Christians in joint prayer. Hinsley, as we have seen, had led the prayer at the Stoll Theatre, but this went very much against the grain of current Church discipline as not a few were quick to point out. Not long after the Stoll meeting, Bishop Amigo gave a hint of the difficulties the Sword would face when he decided against any joint meetings in his diocese.[56] At a meeting with Bell on 26 June, Mathew reassured him that whilst Amigo's attitude was extremely difficult it was also 'very individual'. But flushed with the enthusiasm engendered by the Stoll meeting, Mathew had misjudged the mood of the episcopate. Bishop Flynn, by no means the most intransigent character on the episcopal bench, insisted that to avoid any scandal no prayers should be said at joint meetings: 'Is not the prescribing of the Our Father and a few other "undenominational" prayers a form of fundamentalism?', he asked Archbishop Williams on 3 August. Several days later Flynn wrote again to Williams and asked him to 'read again *Mortalium Animos* and think too of the language of the Fathers engaged with heretics in a situation very similar to our own':

> The very idea of praying with heretics would be anathema to them. I want to hang on to all we have in common; but that does not include revealed religion. Let us stick to what the Pope says, and unite for social reform with all those who, loving God and man, want to maintain the traditional Christian decencies and values. We can stand for loyalty to the pledged word, for truth and unselfishness; for decent housing, respect for the family, a living wage, freedom of conscience and speech, human equality, everything we mean by human dignity, without any common profession of faith. It is not for me to criticise the action of the Cardinal or to say that a common Our Father is a profession of common faith; but until I get further light I won't have common prayer here, because, at the best, I think it inexpedient and liable to further developments which would be certainly abuses . . .[57]

But one bishop, Godfrey informed Mathew, objected even to the more modest understanding of the Sword adumbrated by Flynn, contesting the notion that there was an area of cooperation in which questions of dogma could be excluded. The bishop instanced the housing issue, insisting, for reasons not made clear, that this raised 'not only the question of divorce, but the question of birth control'.[58]

Bell's scheme for collaboration, the Chichester memorandum, proposed that there should be two separate wings of the Sword, one containing Catholics, the other members of the Church of England and the Free Churches, linked by a joint standing committee which would have responsibility for matters of common policy and administration. Hinsley gave it his approval as did Williams who, Barbara Ward informed Bell, was 'ready for an even more drastic scheme of complete cooperation'.[59] Ward, it should be added, was disappointed with the move to a separate wing approach. In a letter to a leading Blackpool member, Barbara Ward regretted the move away from its original purpose: 'thousands have joined the Movement because it stood for Christian cooperation and they have done so on the understanding, apparently implicit in the appeal to all men of good will, that, on an agreed basis of Christian teaching such as is summarized in the "Times" letter, the different Christian Communions would cooperate on a footing of equality – a basis which cannot be reconciled with the present Constitution'.[60] But some bishops were opposed even to the more limited scheme of cooperation on offer. Mathew told Bell at their meeting of 30 July that Downey objected to the formation of a formal organ of opinion, that 'He was really afraid ... of committing himself and preferred that questions dealing with the social field and the field of natural law should be considered by experts whose results could be submitted to the Archbishops.'[61] Part of Downey's distrust of the whole enterprise was undoubtedly its lay, intellectual and London flavour: he saw the Sword as an infringement on episcopal prerogatives.

A further blow to religious cooperation was delivered by Canons George Smith, editor of *The Clergy Review*, and E. J. Mahoney, the theologians appointed by Hinsley to consider the Chichester memorandum. Their report of September 1941 stressed the 'paramount importance' of giving no impression of religious compromise, stating that 'there is only one way in which non-Catholics can be admitted to full membership of the Sword of the Spirit and that is to exclude all public religious activity, Catholic as well as non-Catholic, from the Movement'.[62] Bell's wing proposal was unacceptable as it would not 'adequately dissociate the Cardinal in public from heretical religious worship'.[63]

In October 1941 Hinsley wrote to the bishops to ascertain attitudes to the Sword, but found scant encouragement. The northern bishops met to discuss the issue; Flynn informed Mathew that Downey was 'very much against'; Thomas Shine (1872–1955), Bishop of Middlesborough, felt that the Sword would undermine his Catholic Action groups; Poskitt of Leeds and Marshall of Salford were 'eager for some cooperation', but Marshall in particular 'rather took Liverpool's line: that his priests and people would never understand his appearing on the same platform with non-Catholics'.[64] Poskitt's attitude to the Sword had actually hardened: in August 1941 Leeds was reported to have the most 'flourishing diocesan branch',[65] but now he told the Cardinal that 'If the SOS is going to be made an interdenominational affair, then our people will be scandalised and the Bishops, especially in the North, will no longer be able to support it'.[66] Ambrose Moriarty (1870–1949), Bishop of Shrewsbury, was at best lukewarm.[67] Joseph McCormack (1887–1958), Bishop of Hexham and Newcastle, who was very little disturbed by the world outside his diocese,[68] insisted that his flock would be thrown into confusion if Catholic and Church of England/Free Church wings of the same organization operated alongside one another. Archbishop McGrath of Cardiff banned the Sword from his diocese believing it to be pervaded by the 'imprudence of layfolk'; Lee of Clifton opposed the idea that non-Catholics could be admitted to an essentially Catholic organization;[69] Bishop Hannon of Menevia 'was very violent against it'; Doubleday of Brentwood and Barrett of Plymouth were also opposed.[70] Mathew could report to Flynn that only Hinsley, Williams and Parker were 'strongly pro-Sword' and that McNulty and Bishop King of Portsmouth were 'pro-Sword less definitely'.[71]

Such attitudes presented a formidable barrier to the Sword's progress, exasperating Hinsley. The frustration was all the greater since there were signs of meaningful cooperation between the Cardinal and church leaders in other areas. The British Council of Christians and Jews, founded in March 1942, brought together Temple, Hinsley and the Chief Rabbi amongst others, and although fighting anti-semitism was part of its purpose, its ultimate aims were to combat all forms of religious and racial prejudice and increase mutual understanding between Christians and Jews.[72] In a letter to William Temple of 1 November 1941, who had invited him to a lunch to discuss the initiative, David Mathew wrote, 'I have always felt that the Galilean background of our own faith should give to us Christians a particular solicitude, full of respect and charity, for all that can concern the Jewish people'.[73]

Concerns began to be expressed that under the weight of dogmatic imperatives the Sword was being squeezed of its sense of spiritual purpose. It was said that the stress on religious separation had reduced the Sword to a mere vehicle for social and political work. Dawson warned Hinsley in a letter of 4 November 1941 that there was a danger the Sword would degenerate 'into a sort of Better Britain movement which could be done better under purely secular auspices', and insisted that 'a secular Sword of the Spirit is a contradiction in terms'.[74] It was a sentiment with which Bell, who had been entangled in constitutional questions for the best part of six months, could sympathize.[75] It was clear that Hinsley felt the same way as Dawson: he informed Amigo of his dissatisfaction with aspects of the Smith-Mahoney report, stating that 'if we followed these recommendations the Sword of the Spirit movement would become a purely secular organisation', yet at the same time he felt constrained by the ban on *communicatio in sacris*.[76] He told Bell, who stayed with him over a weekend at Hare Street shortly after the Smith-Mahoney report appeared, that he found the exclusion of all public religious activity 'unfortunate', but 'could not see how it could be avoided'.[77] Silent prayer offered a way round the problem, and was recommended by those bishops who felt the same way as Dawson: Hinsley,[78] Parker and Williams.[79] But generally the position, as Mathew noted, was 'obscure'.[80]

Hinsley's repeated stress on the need for a religious dimension was by now worrying even some of the Sword's leading supporters. Bishop Flynn, for instance, cited two enthusiastic meetings in his diocese at which no prayers were said and he 'saw no reason to regret the omission'. He emphasized the 'danger of a softening of our rigid attitude towards heresy as a result of our fraternising with heretics – a danger, I mean, for those many Catholics who carry their faith too lightly already'.[81] More surprisingly, Mathew too became irritated by the constant harping about joint prayer. As a new arrival on the scene, young and with ambitions for high ecclesiastical office, Mathew was sensitive of the need not to move too far in advance of common assumptions and prejudices. He recognized that his influence amongst the bishops as a body was slight,[82] and sought opportunities to allay the suspicions of senior colleagues. He sensed that Downey had to be brought round for the Sword to stand any chance, but he was never at ease with him, finding him peculiarly prickly and unpredictable.[83] Yet he attached great weight to Downey's opinion, and was reassured to learn from him that if the Sword followed the lines of the Smith-Mahoney report then it might have a chance.[84] He believed that if Mahoney 'would guarantee the theological position much apathy would change into support'.[85] Sensing a glint of light, he came to regard Hinsley's insistence on the religious dimension as putting an unnecessary obstacle in the way of progress. With Flynn, he believed that prayer should be cut out altogether.[86] He commented to Flynn that Hinsley had failed to fully appreciate 'how much Canons Smith and Mahoney stand for when it is a question of approaching the Hierarchy';[87] he also pointed out that the Cardinal was becoming increasingly muddle-headed.[88] It is certainly the case that Hinsley's health was deteriorating badly, but it is not fanciful to suggest that this focused his mind on what seemed to him essential: common Christian witness and prayer. Sensing that he was near the end of his life had the effect of releasing him from the inhibitions that others around him were labouring under.

There was a sense that the moment for the Sword had passed even as the joint meeting of the representatives of the churches and the Sword came to an agreement on cooperation which came close to Bell's proposals. On 24 January 1942 it was decided that there would be two parallel movements, the Sword for Catholics, and 'Religion and Life' for the Commission of the Churches (the body containing prominent Church of England and Free Church representatives). (Bishop Flynn was later nominated to represent the episcopate at any joint discussions: 'no one else would be so sympathetic and yet so careful to keep "the faith" by directing the members in the right paths', Hinsley told him.[89]) A statement on cooperation was also adopted. It emphasized the obligation resting on all Christian people to 'act together to the utmost possible extent to secure the effective influence of Christian teaching in the handling of social, economic and civic problems, now and in the critical post-war period' (par. 1), and to 'unite informed and convinced Christians all over the country in common action on broad lines of social and international policy' (par. 4). It also contained a commitment to liberty of worship (par. 3): 'Full freedom must mean freedom to worship according to conscience, freedom to preach, teach, educate and persuade (all in the spirit of Christian charity), and freedom to bring up children in the faith of their parents'.[90] Hinsley gave his warm approval to the substance of this statement on 31 January, indicating that although he disagreed with some of the wording it was better to 'pass over the minutiae of phraseology and concentrate on the spirit of good will'.[91] In the same spirit he wrote to Amigo insisting that 'the danger of isolation in *practical* questions of the social order are greater than those of definite well-defined cooperation'.[92] Others were less satisfied with the direction of the Sword. Dawson repeated his concerns to Bell that the 'spiritual side has been subordinated to organisation', and bemoaned the fact that the fundamental issue of 'how to develop spiritual cooperation ... as distinct from political action' appeared to have been dropped.[93] At the opposite pole, Downey's theologians at Upholland (Hanrahan, Patten and Halsall) were unhappy with the sections in the statement on liberty of worship; Mathew told Flynn that attitudes in Liverpool to the Sword had hardened further as a result.[94]

Further difficulties arose concerning the protocol to be observed at joint meetings: Hinsley was left feeling piqued by the pre-eminence accorded to the Archbishop of Canterbury. Dawson even indicated to Bell that Hinsley was considering resigning the presidency of the Sword over this issue.[95] In March 1942 Hinsley stepped aside, his role as President was now purely titular with the burden of responsibility passing to Williams. But his faith in the project had not diminished:

'the radical solution is to make our Catholics strong enough spiritually and mentally (by sound doctrine) to meet their fellow non-Catholic citizens: rigid isolation is neither wise nor possible these days. The Kingdom of God is a *leaven*, and to leaven the lump *penetration* ... Only by frank contact shall we influence our separated brethren.'[96]

In the following months even erstwhile supporters appeared more concerned with delineating the areas in which collaboration could take place than with establishing meaningful joint action. In July 1942 Bishop Marshall issued an *ad clerum*[97] stating that 'under no pretext should Catholics take part in non-Catholic worship': 'There are a number of ways in which we, as Catholics, can associate with those who differ from us in religion, and in such case the Bishop of the diocese will decide'.[98] Bishop Amigo, never enamoured of the Sword, responded negatively to a request from Bell to allow Catholic participation at a Religion and Life weekend at Brighton in October 1942.[99] Whilst commending Bell's contribution towards Christian regeneration and reconstruction,[100] he affirmed that 'the Catholic Church alone has divine authority to define what Christian principles are, and I fear that in a joint gathering opinions would be expressed with which we could not agree, but which by our presence we should appear to countenance. Moreover the Catholic Church cannot consent to be grouped with other bodies as "one of the Churches".'[101] Williams's *ad clerum* of March 1943, which was intended to establish a clear and unified policy throughout the diocese and the province, was replete with negation: Catholics were forbidden to attend any meeting where religious matters were raised; they were forbidden to hold services or meetings in connection with Religion and Life weeks; no Catholic study club was to be addressed by a non-Catholic; and there was to be no prayer in common.[102] Hinsley's death in the same month, and the uncertainties about his successor led Flynn to remark to Mathew: 'It looks as if the Sword of the Spirit will be considerably blunted, or go back into the scabbard, if Westminster is long vacant and if no one (like Birmingham) intervenes'.[103] But the Sword had been blunted even before Hinsley's death; any hopes that it might yet be sharpened were dispelled when it became apparent that his successor, Bernard Griffin, was closer to Downey and Amigo in mindset.

An issue which historians have not really touched on concerns the attitudes of the laity and the lower clergy to the Sword. David Mathew maintained that the Sword found no support among northern Catholics and made little appeal to the lower clergy.[104] In 1941 he told Flynn that 'as far as I can make out, there is no member of the Westminster Chapter who is favourable to the Sword except possibly Jackman. As for the parish priests only about half a dozen have been associated with the Sword.' He found that members of the Executive were not in personal touch with members of the Chapter, and amongst the clergy 'a good deal of undeserved resentment against Barbara Ward'.[105] Why might this have been? Ward clearly impressed the secular mind with her intelligence – the historian A. J. P. Taylor was even prepared to admit that she was 'for a woman, very clever'[106] – but cleverness, particularly when it was displayed by a young and articulate female university graduate, rather repelled the average cleric.

Although the question of the Sword's reception requires a more thorough treatment, there is evidence which points to a more positive response. Perhaps sensing that episcopal intransigence was threatening to derail the Sword, and not wishing to identify himself with the opposition, Bishop Flynn's letter to Mathew of 24 October 1941 was an attempt to distance himself from the views of the other northern bishops. Flynn's letter is significant for he admits that despite his initial feeling that there was no great eagerness in the Lancaster diocese for the Sword, there was on the contrary a high degree of enthusiasm amongst northern clergy and laity, and he pointed to the large meetings addressed by the charismatic Barbara Ward in Blackpool, at which around 1,020 attended,[107] and at the Victoria Cinema, Preston, attended by 2,000.[108] Flynn was convinced that 'many of the Liverpool clergy, or at least some of the more far-seeing, would welcome a lead from the Sword'. Episcopal opponents of the Sword often sought to legitimize their stance by arguing that they were protecting an unsophisticated laity – and indeed clergy – from the confusion that would result from religious cooperation, however, if Flynn had gauged the mood aright, then it may have been that the bishops, sure in their paternalism, had restrained a genuine upsurge of religious feeling. Flynn warned Mathew that 'if for an *unreal* apprehension and a merely blind traditionalism, we are going to dampen down all this lay enthusiasm and miss the opportunity for effective cooperation under our own leadership, we shall *rue*, as they say in the Fylde'.[109] Neither is it certain that the lower clergy were as unanimously hostile as Mathew suggests. Amigo's refusal to allow a Catholic presence at the Brighton Religion and Life weekend brought a critical reply from Fr Flanagan, who was speaking for several parish priests of Brighton. Flanagan reminded Amigo that

> You ask us, in our own pulpits, to preach on those fundamental social principles. Then we must have the capacity. If we are bound to exercise that teaching authority in the case of an individual coming to us –

even Chichester himself – surely we ought to be prepared to carry that teaching to the hungry multitudes outside the Church ... Are we quite sure that our hesitation does not arise from mental laziness or from pure 'funk'?[110]

Flanagan was writing soon after the publication, in July 1942, of *Catholics and the New World Order*, a joint pastoral of the English Catholic hierarchy. Despite the emphasis on cooperation on social issues it is significant that even in this area developments occurred more often than not in parallel. The Malvern conference of 1941, Temple's attempt to produce a Christian contribution to social reconstruction, was a wholly Anglican affair. Nevertheless, ideas propounded in other Christian circles, and the emphasis on rebuilding a Christian social order, clearly influenced Catholic efforts. The idea of a joint statement on social questions was mooted at the Low Week meeting of 1940; a sub-committee was established, in Flynn's words, 'to clear up a lot of the social stuff cluttering the agenda'.[111] They hardly seemed fired by a vision of the 'New Jerusalem' at this stage.[112] Assisting Williams in its preparation were Bishops Lee, McNulty, Flynn and McGrath.[113] Two years later, at the bishops' meeting held at St Edmund's, Ware, 'it was decided that a pronouncement on the Social Question be issued by the Bishops, the matter to be left in the hands of the Cardinal who would be helped by the Archbishop of Birmingham'.[114] Fr T. S. Copsey, a social studies student at Campion Hall, Oxford, and Fr Vincent Turner helped with the final draft, though, Copsey recalled, its practical details 'were very much the actual mind of Archbishop Williams'.[115]

The most arresting feature of *Catholics and the New World Order* was, as *Blackfriars* noted and commended, that it descended from the level of generality which characterized much Catholic social comment: 'We have long heard the complaint that the official pronouncements of the Church are ineffective because they are too general to move the wills of individuals'.[116] With its prosaic style and practical concerns it became known as the 'Plumber's Pastoral'. Ironically, only a month before the sub-committee had been appointed, Williams had remarked to McNulty that 'it is very difficult to bring Catholic principles down to the solution of practical cases ... It is easy enough to keep to principles and to quote Papal Encyclicals but it is a very different thing to solve the problems of our country at the present day on those principles and Catholics are much more likely to differ from one another in the application of principles than they are on almost any subject.'[117] McNulty shared these sentiments. The shift in contemporary Christian social thought away from the general to more specific application of social principles – what Kent describes as the 'campaign for less abstract ideas'[118] – may have influenced Williams to cast off these earlier reservations. Arguably the most influential contribution to reconstruction was William Temple's *Christianity and the Social Order*, published in February 1942 (the month that he became Archbishop of Canterbury). This had a section entitled 'A Suggested Programme',[119] based on the six objectives which emerged from the Malvern conference which were to form the basis for a more Christian social order.[120] It is difficult to believe that Williams was not influenced by Temple, and indeed *Catholics and the New World Order* followed a similar pattern to *Christianity and the Social Order*: ten points were listed which were deemed as 'the minimum conditions for a Christian life': they included a living wage which would be sufficient to support an agreed minimum average family (three or four children); decent living accommodation (which would mean that no-one would have to sleep in the living room, and that there would be a bathroom for every family); religious education.[121] There were also concerns which did not feature in Temple's book. The spread of birth control was an issue which had troubled the Catholic hierarchy since the early 1920s, and the pastoral letter called for a ban on 'the manufacture and sale of birth-prevention appliances'.[122] But in this Catholics were not unusual: birth control was a concern of all the churches during the war, amid anxieties over increased sexual activity and promiscuity encouraged by the pressures of wartime.[123] Even tampons were a source of concern to the bishops, who viewed them as a possible means of contraception.[124] The pastoral also reflected current concern about the standard of popular entertainment, in particular the prevailing laxity with regard to obscene and irreverent material,[125] and urged that a board be set up to regulate the sale and manufacture of obscene books.[126] The final point was that the 'enormous inequality in the distribution of wealth in this country, and the control of the lives of the masses by a comparatively few rich people, is against social justice'. It further insisted that just as profits and prices were in war subject to controls in the national interest, so state authority should intervene after the war in the same national interest.[127] It was no surprise that Williams should acclaim the Beveridge Report;[128] published in December 1942 this laid the ground for a massive increase in state welfare provision. This emphasis on the distribution of wealth was the most controversial aspect of *Catholics and the New World Order*, upsetting Conservative Catholics like Arnold Lunn.[129] It prompted a Dr Walshe of Wimpole Street, London, who had attended an impassioned discussion on the pastoral letter, to suggest that by its assertions of workers' rights the

Church was seeming 'to hold less than a fair balance between the competing sectional claims in the community', contrasting the Church's reticence on international questions with its urgency 'to rush boldly into the fray' on social questions.[130] Elsewhere in the Catholic community, however, Mathew could report that the pastoral 'has had a tremendous welcome from priests everywhere. It is certainly the most popular pronouncement made for a very long time.'[131] These divergent views on social questions and state intervention were to be thrown into sharper relief when the Beveridge Report was announced.

A crucial omission from the pastoral letter was any reference to religious liberty. Indeed, Catholic social thinking in this period made only the most perfunctory gestures to this principle. The debate over whether religious liberty should be a major plank of Christian reconstruction caused serious difficulties within the Sword. David Mathew probed Bell as to how serious Nonconformists were in their insistence on this principle,[132] showing how impervious even the most liberally-minded Catholics of the period could be to the claims of religious pluralism. Hinsley had been pressed repeatedly by Bell on the question but could not commit himself to an endorsement of religious freedom: 'in principle individuals and groups and states must favour the *truth* if and when they know it and should give practical tolerance to those who profess *falsehood* which they hold as *truth*'.[133] Toleration, therefore, but not liberty. Members of the Sword's Executive were drawn begrudgingly into the debate. For the Free Church members of Religion and Life especially it was an issue of fundamental importance, with the plight of Protestants in Franco's Spain very much in their minds; unsatisfied with the text of an earlier statement, they succeeded in getting the matter before the Joint Committee for a more extended treatment. By contrast, Catholics saw the religious liberty issue as an unwelcome and potentially divisive distraction. Bishop Flynn was against the notion of an agreed statement from the beginning; Fr John Murray stated that it was 'the Free Church people that always harped on it . . . yet, it would have looked bad, and a confirmation of their worst suspicions, had we refused to make the attempt'; Douglas Woodruff, representing the Catholic side at the discussions with Murray, thought that 'good will have been done in their minds even if no statement is ever published'.[134] It was clear that no resounding commitment to religious liberty would ever emerge from the Catholic side.

The first joint meeting was held on 3 December 1942, at which prepared statements were submitted outlining the positions of the participating religious groups (William Paton represented the Free Church view and Geoffrey Fisher the Anglican.) Although Catholic members hoped privately that the idea of a pamphlet would be dropped,[135] by March 1943 a drafting committee had been established, and on 20 July 1943 the statement on religious freedom was presented to and accepted by the Joint Committee. A year later, after successive Catholic theologians had chipped away at the statement, the idea of a joint pamphlet was quietly dropped.

Deeply troubling to the Catholic theologians had been the statements' affirmation of a 'natural and civic right of every citizen to act in accordance with his conscience'. Canon Smith, the theologian charged with examining the statement, maintained that so far as it is a natural right it 'can only apply to the principles of the true religion. There can be no natural right to profess false religious principles.' Smith went further: if there can 'be no right to practise a false religion, the State cannot confer the right to practise it. Hence there cannot exist, properly speaking, even a *civic* right to practise any but the true religion.' The other objection concerned the role of the state in protecting religious freedom. The view of the joint statement was that it was 'the duty of the State to safeguard this freedom for all its members'. Recognizing that the first duty of the state is to maintain public order, the statement asserted that this 'limiting condition is capable of misuse by the State', that there was a danger that 'the argument of public order will be unjustly invoked to defend measures of discrimination and oppression'. 'Against such a misuse of the power of the State, in which limitation of religious freedom is represented as a political necessity, Christian opinion must always be vigilant.' But Canon Smith found this problematic. Considering a scenario where Catholics formed the dominant religious body in the state, he argued that considerations of public order 'would include the preservation of citizens from error – a consideration which would greatly limit freedom for the practice and propagation of non-Catholic religions'.[136] For Paton however, with his deep involvement in missionary work,[137] the propagation of religion was a key issue. He had secured those parts of the joint statement which recognized the rights of religious groups to witness to and to convert those of other beliefs, whilst also recognizing the potentially disturbing effects this may have on settled social patterns and ways of life, and the necessity therefore that missionary work be 'conducted with respect and courtesy towards existing forms of belief'. But these qualifications were not enough to satisfy Canon Smith. In his report to Archbishop Griffin of 5 June 1944 he stated that the Catholic view of religious freedom 'is a matter of policy, not a matter of principle. And it is a policy to be adopted only so far as the interests of the true religion require it, and so far as the essential freedom of the act of faith must exclude anything in the nature of constraint for the purpose of conversion.' He urged that there be no further comment or statement on the question – advice which Griffin followed.[138]

The most that Catholics could admit, therefore, was a grudging toleration. This was the position of Bishop Flynn. Although, he commented to Fr Murray, 'it is usually wise in these days to behave as if there were', there was actually no such natural right to religious freedom, for 'can there be any natural right to teach error?' Flynn decided that it was impossible for a Catholic bishop to endorse the statement: 'in practice it would be well to agree to this thing (though I regret it), but in theory it is open to criticism'. His resignation from the Joint Committee followed, although it was handled, he told Murray, so as not to give the impression that the statement on religious liberty was 'the occasion of my resignation'. He added: 'You need not be afraid that I am going to abandon the Sword altogether. I am a firm believer in it.'[139]

There was, however, decreasing conviction in such declarations of support. Although the Sword limped on through the 1940s, the experiment in cooperation had effectively ran its course. By 1944 many of the key liberalizing influences had departed the scene. Hinsley died on 17 March 1943; nine months later Bernard Griffin, a very different kind of church leader, was appointed his successor. Some thought that Hinsley had viewed Mathew as his heir apparent – a story even spread that the Cardinal's last words had been 'Poor David'[140] – but his relative youth amongst other factors rendered this unlikely. Mathew was thought to lack the common touch; some found his 'elliptical humour baffling' and his conversation 'cryptic'; his appearance was eccentric;[141] he was possibly rather too enamoured of country-house Catholicism for these democratic and austere times. He was, in short, not what a mid-twentieth-century Catholic prelate should look like. With Griffin's arrival Mathew was gradually sidelined: he was eventually appointed Apostolic Visitor to Ethiopia in 1945, so ending his close involvement in English ecclesiastical life. Another key figure off the scene was Christopher Dawson, one of the animating spirits of the Sword. Ousted in unpleasant circumstances from the *Dublin Review* and disenchanted with the contemporary absorption with 'mere' social and political work, his meaningful involvement with the Sword ended at the same time as Hinsley's, and though the second half of the 1940s was an enormously creative and successful period for him academically, he was out of sympathy and out of touch with the 'closed' variety of official Catholicism which had re-established itself.

The *Church Times* remarked on the occasion of Hinsley's funeral: 'The representation of the Archbishop of Canterbury and the presence of high dignitaries of the English Church at Cardinal Hinsley's obsequies seemed so right and proper that few people probably realised how great a departure from precedent it was. Such a thing has never happened before but then there has never been such an Archbishop of Westminster as Cardinal Hinsley.'[142] Amongst those present at the funeral was his friend Bishop Bell, who contributed one of the warmest tributes in *Blackfriars*. Bell had been encouraged to write by the editor Fr Conrad Pepler; the son of a convert, the Dominican Pepler told Bell that he had through his journal 'for long been trying to make a wide and deeper cooperation possible between the Church of England and Roman Catholics'.[143] In the obituary, Bell wrote of Hinsley's profound desire for cooperation and 'the building up of a new social, economic and political system on just and moral foundations'. Bell had been deeply moved by his conversation with the ailing Cardinal during his stay at Hare Street in October 1941: 'It was clear . . . that the Cardinal had a strong belief in personal relationships, and in the coming together, as friends, of like-minded men and women who, whatever their differences, were animated by the same Spirit'.[144]

Hinsley indeed excelled in the sphere of personal relations. During his archiepiscopate relations were established with other church leaders which were largely owing to his personal warmth, transparency and positive spirit. Yet Bishop Brown, Amigo's Auxiliary, was to offer an explanation for the failure of the Sword which pinned it to a deficiency in Hinsley himself. A man of 'strong impulses and emotional temperament', he was unable 'to maintain sustained effort to keep things going when the first months of enthusiasm were over'. Pertinacity and sheer obstinacy were required: Hinsley, aged and in very poor health, was not able to summon those resources – which Brown described as 'the Yorkshire side of him' – to bring the reluctant round to his view.[145] Good intentions, in other words, were not enough by themselves. But Brown surely exaggerates the possibility of any one man, and a elderly one at that, to change the Church. Furthermore, driving an agenda through was not Hinsley's style. Hinsley strained against dogmatic imperatives; he recognized that the times required risk-taking and a leap of faith; he was not satisfied that social and political cooperation were by themselves enough; but ultimately he was limited in what he could achieve. Despite the signs of greater openness and flexibility in Church life, currents of obscurantism and reaction were still more powerful than those for change and renewal. The casual way in which one Catholic bishop, and by no means the most reactionary, could refer to other Christians as 'heretics' gives some sense of what Hinsley and the Sword were up against.

Notes

1. F. A. Iremonger, *William Temple, Archbishop of Canterbury, his life and letters* (London: Oxford University Press, 1949 edn), p. 424.
2. J. G. Lockhart, *Cosmo Gordon Lang* (London: Hodder and Stoughton, 1949 edn), p. 366.
3. C. Scott, *A Historian and his World: A Life of Christopher Dawson 1889–1970* (London: Sheed and Ward, 1984), p. 139.
4. Chadwick, *Britain and the Vatican during the Second World War*, p. 99.
5. A. Cardinal Hinsley, *The Bond of Peace and other War-Time Addresses* (London: Burns and Oates, 1941 edn), pp. 139–41.
6. Godfrey to Williams, 8 March 1941, B.A.A., Archbishops' Papers 1929–65, AP/A6.
7. Quoted in Scott, *Historian and his World*, p. 139.
8. Lockhart, *Cosmo Gordon Lang*, p. 366.
9. D. Carter, 'The Ecumenical Movement in its Early Years', *Journal of Ecclesiastical History*, 49 (July 1998), 472. See also R. C. D. Jasper, *George Bell; Bishop of Chichester* (London: Oxford University Press, 1968 edn).
10. Mathew to Bell, 16 September 1939, L.P.L., Bell Papers 211, fo. 106; Bell to Mathew, 31 December 1941, ibid. 71, fo. 310.
11. Mathew to Bell, 3 September 1941, ibid., fos. 200–1.
12. Mathew to Bell, 13 November 1941, ibid., fo. 287.
13. Bell to Mathew, 22 December 1938, A.A.W., Mathew Papers, File 5a.
14. Bell to A Sa Grace Eveque de Novisad, 30 May 1939, L.P.L., Bell Papers 20, fos. 561–3.
15. Cornwell, *Hitler's Pope*, p. 211.
16. Duffy, *Saints and Sinners*, p. 263.
17. Bell to Godfrey, 10 June 1939, L.P.L., Bell Papers 21, fos. 29–31.
18. Quoted in Chadwick, *Britain and the Vatican during the Second World War*, p. 99.
19. Godfrey to Bell, 13 June 1939, L.P.L., Bell Papers 21, fos. 48–9.
20. Mathew to Bell, 12 June 1939, ibid., fos. 45–6.
21. Godfrey to Bell, 12 July 1939, ibid., fos. 67–8.
22. Bell to Mathew, 15 July 1939, ibid., fos. 70–1.
23. Bell to Pastor Boegner, 18 July 1939, ibid., fo. 73.
24. Godfrey to Bell, 21 July 1939, ibid., fo. 76.
25. *The Pope's Five Peace-Points: Allocution to the College of Cardinals by his Holiness Pope Pius XII on December 24th 1939* (London: C.T.S.; Oxford: C.S.G.; 1940).
26. See e.g. S. Mews, 'The Sword of the Spirit: A Catholic Cultural Crusade of 1940', in W. J. Sheils (ed.), *The Church and War* (Studies in Church History, 20; Oxford: Blackwell, 1983).
27. J. von Arx, 'Catholics and Politics', p. 266.
28. T. R. Greene, 'Vichy France and the Catholic Press in England: Contrasting Attitudes to a Moral Problem', *Recusant History*, 21 (May

1992), 111–33. See also G. White, 'The Fall of France', in W. J. Sheils (ed.), *The Church and War* (Studies in Church History, 20; Oxford: Blackwell, 1983), pp. 431–41; Keating, 'Discrediting the "Catholic State"', pp. 27–42.

29. Quoted in Scott, *Historian and his World*, p. 138.
30. Quoted in Mews, 'The Sword of the Spirit', p. 420. M. J. Walsh, 'Ecumenism in War-Time Britain. The Sword of the Spirit and Religion and Life, 1940–1945 (1)', *Heythrop Journal*, 23 (July 1982); idem., 'Ecumenism in War-Time Britain. The Sword of the Spirit and Religion and Life, 1940–1945 (2)', *Heythrop Journal*, 23 (October 1982); idem., *From Sword to Ploughshare* (London: CIIR, 1980).
31. Speaight, *Property Basket*, p. 220.
32. Hinsley to Amigo, 25 March 1941, A.A.S., 'Sword of the Spirit' File.
33. Quoted in Hastings, *English Christianity*, p. 394.
34. Scott, *Historian and his World*, p. 137.
35. Douglas Jerrold to Mathew, 15 June 1942, D.A.A., Mathew Papers, Personal and Official 1939–42.
36. Mathew to Bell, 13 November 1941, L.P.L., Bell Papers 71, fo. 287.
37. Scott, *Historian and his World*, p. 137.
38. Hinsley to the bishops, 7 August 1940, copy held in Sal.D.A., Catholic Societies, Folder 183.
39. Quoted in Mews, 'The Sword of the Spirit', p. 421.
40. McNulty to Marshall, 2 August 1940, Sal.D.A., Catholic Societies, Folder 183.
41. Cornwell, *Hitler's Pope*, p. 183; Coppa, *Modern Papacy*, p. 182.
42. See ibid.; Cornwell, *Hitler's Pope*, pp. 181–4.
43. Marshall to Hinsley, 20 December 1940 (copy), Sal.D.A., Catholic Societies, Folder 181.
44. Marshall to Hinsley, 13 August 1940, ibid., Folder 183.
45. Downey to Mathew, A.A.W., 13 October 1940., A.A.W., Mathew Papers, Misc. 1934–43, File 1.
46. Flynn to Williams, 20 August 1940, B.A.A., Archbishops' Papers 1929–65, AP/C28/20.
47. Mathew to Bell, 13 November 1941, L.P.L., Bell Papers 71, fo. 287.
48. Heenan, *Crown of Thorns*, pp. 22, 25.
49. Notes for an Interview with Bishop Mathew, 30 July 1941, L.P.L., Bell Papers 71, fos. 137–9
50. *The Times*, 21 December 1940.
51. Walsh, 'Ecumenism in War-Time Britain', I, p. 244.
52. Parker to Griffin, 17 June 1944, A.A.W., Griffin Papers, Gr.2/136a.
53. Mathew to Bell, 15 June 1941, L.P.L., Bell Papers 71, fo. 95.
54. Walsh, 'Ecumenism in War-Time Britain', I, p. 244.
55. Notes of an Interview with Bishop Mathew, 30 July 1941, L.P.L., Bell Papers 71, fos. 137–9.
56. Bell to Revd Esdaile, 17 June 1941, ibid., fo. 97; Scott, *Historian and his World*, pp. 143–4.
57. Flynn to Williams, 3 August 1941, 28 July 1941, 7 August 1941,

B.A.A., Archbishops' Papers 1929–65, AP/C28/20.

58. Notes of an Interview with Bishop Mathew, 30 July 1941, L.P.L., Bell Papers 71, fos. 137–9.
59. Barbara Ward to Bell, 26 July 1941, ibid., fo. 127.
60. Barbara Ward to Marie Patry, 15 August 1941, Lnc.D.A., Flynn Papers.
61. Notes for an Interview with Bishop Mathew, 30 July 1941, L.P.L., Bell Papers 71, fos. 137–9.
62. Quoted in Moloney, *Westminster, Whitehall*, p. 200.
63. Quoted in Walsh, 'Ecumenism in War-Time Britain', I, p. 249.
64. Flynn to Mathew, 24 October 1941, D.A.A., Mathew Papers, Personal and Official 1939–42.
65. *Report of the Honorary Secretary of the First Annual General Meeting of the Sword of the Spirit held on 9 August 1941: Branch and Group Reports (Fylde)*, L.P.L., Bell Papers 71, fos. 170–4.
66. Quoted in Moloney, *Westminster, Whitehall*, p. 202.
67. J. Davies, 'Bishop Ambrose Moriarty, Shrewsbury and World War Two', *Recusant History*, 25 (May 2000), 151–2.
68. *Ushaw Magazine* (July 1958), 58.
69. Moloney, *Westminster, Whitehall*, pp. 201–2.
70. Mathew to Flynn, 19 October 1941, Lnc.D.A., Flynn Papers.
71. Ibid.
72. For the history of this organization see, M. Braybrooke, *Children of One God: A History of the Council of Christians and Jews* (London: Valentine Mitchell, 1991).
73. Mathew to Temple, 1 November 1941 (copy), A.A.W., Mathew Papers, Correspondence with Canterbury and York 1938–41, File 1.
74. Quoted in Moloney, *Westminster, Whitehall*, p. 200.
75. The 'movement is in very great danger of becoming another ecclesiastical organization and missing the deeper things in which you have from the very first insisted': Bell to Christopher Dawson, 25 January 1942, L.P.L., Bell Papers 71, fo. 314.
76. Hinsley to Amigo, 13 November 1941, A.A.S., Amigo Papers, Cardinal Hinsley File
77. Notes of an Interview with Cardinal Hinsley, 14–15 October 1941, L.P.L., Bell Papers 223, fo. 253.
78. Ibid.
79. Moloney, *Westminster, Whitehall*, p. 202. It is interesting to note that it was Godfrey who suggested the 'silent prayer' solution to Williams as a way of giving 'a religious atmosphere at once', since he has been regarded as a strong critic of the Sword (Hastings, *English Christianity*, p. 396): Godfrey to Williams, 3 October 1941, B.A.A., Archbishops' Papers 1929–65. See also Notes of an Interview with Bishop Mathew, 30 July 1941, L.P.L., Bell Papers 71, fos. 137–9.
80. Mathew to Flynn, 13 November 1941, Lnc.D.A., Flynn Papers.
81. Flynn to Hinsley, 19 November 1941 (copy), ibid.
82. Mathew to Bell, 31 August 1941, L.P.L., Bell Papers 71, fo. 140.

83. Mathew to Flynn, 6 July 1942, Lnc.D.A., Flynn Papers.
84. Mathew to Flynn, 19 October 1941, ibid.
85. See also Mathew to Flynn, 25 September 1941, ibid.
86. Mathew to Flynn, 16 September 1941, ibid.
87. Mathew to Flynn, 12 October 1941, ibid.; also Mathew to Flynn, 25 September 1941, ibid.
88. See also Mathew to Flynn, 25 July 1941, ibid.
89. Hinsley to Flynn, 22 February 1942, ibid.
90. Quoted in Walsh, 'Ecumenism in War-Time Britain', I, p. 256.
91. Quoted in ibid.
92. Hinsley to Amigo, 4 February 1942, A.A.S., Amigo Papers, Cardinal Hinsley File.
93. Christopher Dawson to Bell, 31 January 1942, L.P.L., Bell Papers 71, fo. 319.
94. Mathew to Flynn, 6 March 1942, Lnc.D.A., Flynn Papers.
95. Christopher Dawson to Bell, 4 March 1942, L.P.L., Bell Papers 71, fo. 353.
96. Hinsley to Flynn, 28 February 1942, Lnc.D.A., Flynn Papers.
97. Notes for which had been prepared by the Fransiscan Fr Agnellus, who had been concerned that the cooperation question would be exploited by opponents of the Catholic social movement: Fr Agnellus to Marshall, 21 May 1942, Sal.D.A., Marshall Papers 181, fo. 199.
98. *Ad Clerum*, 2 July 1942, ibid., 204, fo. 302.
99. Bell to Amigo, 4 August 1942, A.A.S., Amigo Papers, Sword of the Spirit File.
100. *Ad Clerum*, 7 October, 1942, ibid.
101. Amigo to Bell, 17 August 1942 (copy), ibid.
102. Walsh, 'Ecumenism in War-Time Britain', II, pp. 383–4.
103. Flynn to Mathew, 29 June 1943, D.A.A., Mathew Papers, Correspondence 1943–58.
104. Mathew, *Catholicism in England* (1948 edn), p. 263.
105. Mathew to Flynn, 19 October 1941, Lnc.D.A., Flynn Papers.
106. A. Sisman, *A. J. P. Taylor: A Biography* (London: Sinclair-Stevenson, 1994), p. 150.
107. *Report of the Honorary Secretary of the First Annual General Meeting of the Sword of the Spirit held on 9 August 1941: Branch and Group Reports (Fylde)*, L.P.L., Bell Papers 71 (check), fos. 170–4.
108. *Lancashire Daily Post*, 22 September 1941.
109. Flynn to Mathew, 24 October 1941, D.A.A., Mathew Papers, Personal and Official 1939–42.
110. Fr Flanagan to Amigo, 12 August 1942, A.A.S., Sword of the Spirit File.
111. Flynn to Williams, 13 April 1940, B.A.A., Archbishops' Papers 1929–65, AP/C28/20.
112. C. Barnett, *The Audit of War: the Illusion and Reality of Britain as a Great Nation* (London: Macmillan, 1987 edn), ch. 1.
113. Meeting of the Bishops, 2–3 April 1940, A.A.W., *Acta*.

114. Meeting of the Bishops, 14–15 April 1942, ibid.
115. Fr T. S. Copsey to J. M. Cleary, 15 May 1961, C.S.G.A., J. M. Cleary correspondence, E22. Cleary was the CSG's historian.
116. *Blackfriars* (August 1942).
117. Williams to McNulty, 21 March 1940, B.A.A., CSG File.
118. Kent, *William Temple*, p. 156.
119. W. Temple, *Christianity and the Social Order* (London: SCM Press, 1950 edn), pp. 101–22.
120. Kent, *William Temple*, pp. 164–5.
121. *Catholics and the New World Order: A Joint Pastoral of the English Hierarchy* (London: CTS; Oxford: CSG, 1942), pp. 8–9.
122. Ibid., p. 9.
123. Machin, *Churches and Social Issues*, pp. 113–4.
124. Ibid., p. 116. 'We also recorded our disapproval of Tampax, but not by name. You *should* have been there!!': Flynn to Williams, 19 April 1940, B.A.A., Archbishops' Papers 1929–65, AP/C28/20.
125. Machin, *Churches and Social Issues*, pp. 118–9.
126. *Catholics and the New World Order*, pp. 9–10.
127. Ibid., p. 10.
128. Fr T. S. Copsey to J. M. Cleary, 15 May 1961, C.S.G.A., J. M. Cleary correspondence, E22. Archbishop Williams, speaking at the CSG summer school of 1943, said: 'We want the Beveridge Report carried into action as soon as possible ... The nation is ready for extension of social services and welcomes it; and we of the CSG, I think, also welcome it': quoted in Keating, *Roman Catholics, Christian Democracy*, p. 188.
129. Fr T. S. Copsey to J. M. Cleary, 15 May 1961, C.S.G.A., J. M. Cleary correspondence, E22
130. Dr F. M. R. Walshe to Williams, 16 August 1942, B.A.A., Archbishops' Papers 1929–65, AP/C28/64. Walshe also objected to the sections on contraception, repeating the comments of one 'indignant old gentleman' who had said to him, 'why must the clergy keep poking their noses into the marriage bed?' Walshe added: 'This of course is not quite reasonable, but is perhaps the natural response to pastoral comments that are themselves not wholly reasonable'.
131. Mathew to Flynn, 6 July 1942, Lnc.D.A., Flynn Papers.
132. Notes of an Interview with Bishop Mathew, 30 July 1941, L.P.L., Bell Papers 71, fos. 137–9.
133. Hinsley to Bell, 17 October 1941, ibid., fo. 264.
134. Flynn to Fr J. Murray, 31 July 1943 (copy); Fr J. Murray to Flynn, 12 August 1943, Lnc.D.A., Flynn Papers
135. A. C. F. Beales to Flynn, 18 November 1942, ibid.
136. Statement on Religious Freedom: Notanda, 19 August 1943 and Memorandum on Joint Statement on Religious Freedom (amended version), 5 June 1944, ibid.
137. Paton was the General Secretary of the International Missionary Council.

138. Memorandum on Joint Statement on Religious Freedom (amended version), 5 June 1944, Lnc.D.A., Flynn Papers.
139. Flynn to Fr J. Murray, 31 July 1943 (copy), ibid.
140. *Catholic Profiles* (London: Paternoster Publications, u/d), 56.
141. F. Kerr, 'David Mathew', *DNB*, 1971–80, pp. 552–4.
142. Quoted in Heenan, *Hinsley*, pp. 4–5; Moloney, *Westminster, Whitehall*, p. 243.
143. Fr Conrad Pepler to Bell, 22 March 1943, L.P.L., Bell Papers 103, fo. 8. Details of Pepler's life can be found in Gaine, *Obituary Notices of the English Dominicans*, pp. 97–8.
144. *Blackfriars* (May 1943).
145. Brown, *Through Windows of Memory*, p. 101.

7

Safety First 1943–1963

> We have just had my Bishop's Lenten Pastoral read out during lunch –
> a bewailing of the materialist influences entering Christian homes by
> means of radio, newspapers and periodicals, television and cinema; he
> suggests the erection of barricades of defence and withdrawal into an
> ivory tower. Most of the students thought it a good pastoral, but I
> thought it was a dead loss myself.
>
> An Ushaw student to Fr Vincent Wilkin, S.J., 1951

Writing of the Church of England in the post-war period, Alan
Wilkinson endorsed D. M. MacKinnon's view 'that the worst misfor-
tune to befall its leadership in the end of the war was less the
premature death of William Temple than his succession by Fisher of
London and not by Bell of Chichester'.[1] Historians of English
Catholicism have tended to see the succession of Bernard Griffin in
similar terms: as inaugurating a safe, conservative period after the
heady excitement and creativity of the Hinsley years.[2] In Adrian
Hastings's view, 'Griffin was the least important archbishop of
Westminster of the century, a nice, hard-working nonentity'.[3] But at
the time the expectation was not that a cautious administrator would
take over the reins. Godfrey, the Apostolic Delegate, informed
Archbishop Williams that the mood in Rome was that 'a young man
should be placed at Westminster to grapple with the after-war problems'.[4] The education question was one of the problems requiring
close attention; to reverse the drift which had so far characterized the
bishops' response to R. A. Butler's proposals was a major priority.
David Mathew, we have seen, was overlooked; it may have been that
he was too associated with dangerous innovations such as the Sword,
although in reality he was far more cautious than Hinsley; it is more
likely that he was seen as a rather eccentric, academic character ill-
equipped to handle effectively the minutiae of diocesan business. It
was a much more prosaic individual who was appointed to
Westminster on 18 December 1943, nine months after Hinsley's death.

Although Bernard Griffin (1899–1956) was very much the unknown quantity, his early career was a classic route to high ecclesiastical office. He was one of the brighter students of his generation at Oscott, and from there proceeded to the Gregorian University, Rome, where he took a higher degree. From Rome, Griffin went straight into the Birmingham Curia, where he was Private Secretary to the ailing Archbishop McIntyre: 'He was now on the lower rung of an almost inevitable climb up the ladder of ecclesiastical promotion for a priest of his stamp'.[5] As Diocesan Chancellor, Vicar-General, and from 1938 Auxiliary Bishop to Thomas Williams, Griffin was valued for his energy and assiduous attention to administrative detail. It was a very typical and unremarkable apprenticeship.

Once there, Griffin's first priority was to establish a coherent response to R. A. Butler's Education Bill. In the interregnum between Hinsley's death and Griffin's arrival at Westminster discussions between the Board of Education and the Catholic community had been largely unprofitable. There was little willingness on the part of the Catholic negotiating team, led by Downey, Amigo and Brown, to find a compromise that could have been acceptable to other parties. The mood in the country was for educational reconstruction and the continued existence of church schools, which formed half the schools in the country, was seen by many key interest groups as a drag on progress towards an equitable national system.[6] Certainly there was evidence which exposed the inefficient workings of the dual system; the recognition that material conditions in church schools had fallen well behind council schools was one of the reasons for William Temple's preparedness to see a modification of the dual system. Temple's delicate task was to wean his flock away 'from their distaste at the White Paper ... and the alleged threat to their schools'.[7] The preparedness of leading Anglicans to reach a compromise was to leave the Catholics altogether high-and-dry.

Butler's proposals, embodied in the White Memorandum, offered two alternatives for the denominational schools. The first (which was to be compulsory in single-school areas) was for the owners of non-provided schools to hand over their schools and all financial responsibility to the local authorities, the denominations still being entitled to use the premises on Sundays and weekdays when they were not required for educational purposes. This was never an option for Catholics. The second alternative was aimed at those who insisted on retaining the full denominational character of their schools. The proposed terms included a fifty per cent grant towards the capital costs of alteration and improvement; if managers were able to raise the remaining half they would retain the right of appointing and dismissing teachers – the central concern of the Church[8] – and the control of religious instruction. But for an expanding religious community the main concern was that the grant was not intended for the building of new schools. These were genuine worries, but still there was an excessive concentration on the negative aspects of the proposals on the part of the Catholic authorities: it seemed to Butler that the politics of the bishops had not moved on since 1902.[9] He found Downey particularly difficult to deal with.[10] Certainly there would be new official requirements and heavy financial burdens, yet, as Beales observed in 1950, there was insufficient stress 'in welcoming the *material* side of educational advance on which the country outside the Church set such increasing store'.[11] Butler went as far as he possibly could to meet Catholic concerns; the fifty per cent exchequer grant for the schools which chose 'aided' status was as much as he could offer without antagonizing other vital interests and thereby disrupting the entire settlement. Catholic agitations for a 100 per cent grant, organized through the recently launched Catholic Parents and Electors' Association, were unrealistic and unhelpful. The Education Bill, introduced on 15 December 1943, did allay some concerns. The grant of fifty per cent was to be extended to cover the cost of new schools in cases where a school had been transferred to a new site because the existing premises could not be adequately improved or as a result of movements of the population due to slum clearance or re-planning.[12] Butler established good relations with Griffin, who he found to be far more flexible in his approach than the old guard,[13] and successfully persuaded him to quell agitation against the bill in return for certain concessions. For the Catholics the schools question was still a live one throughout the late 1940s and 1950s as the community struggled with the new financial burdens of the 1944 Act. The Treasury calculations of 1943 had seriously underestimated the cost of a school place.[14] However, campaigns for extra state aid were conducted with far more restraint and realism than in the past. Here the stable and coherent leadership provided by a former headmaster George A. Beck (Bishop of Brentwood 1951–55; Bishop of Salford 1955–64; Archbishop of Liverpool 1964–76) was decisive.[15] The 1959 Education Act went a long way towards removing Catholic grievances by raising the capital grant from fifty to seventy-five per cent.

English Catholicism stood in uneasy relation to the post-war movement for social reconstruction. In one scathing assessment of the role of the churches in the education negotiations the Catholic Church emerged as the 'most constipating defender of a vested interest'.[16] The preservation of the Catholic subculture was of a higher priority than the good of the rest of society. Peter Coman has provided an authoritative study of the response of English Catholics to the establishment of the welfare state, which gives support to such a view. He found that in its reaction to the welfare measures in social security, education and health proposed and enacted in the 1940s and 1950s, the Catholic community simply 'reflected its modern historical development as a defensive, inward-looking minority community'.[17] The Catholic attitude to the welfare state, he argues, was cautious at best, occasionally hostile, and quite unlike the generally positive response of the 'increasingly secular wider society'.[18] How far did the bishops encourage such a negative response?

Although the Beveridge Report had been generally well received by Hinsley and Williams, with these more progressive influences off the scene (Williams died in 1946) a more hostile view of the extension of state welfare dominated the bench. The bishops would not have declared, as did one leading Methodist, 'I thank God for the Welfare State'.[19] Any understanding of social policy which seemed to undermine voluntary effort and parental rights was suspect. The link was made between totalitarian threats abroad and collectivism at home. Downey was acutely sensitive: sermon notes from this period declare that 'Many restrictions have been tolerated as necessary war measures but these should be removed at the first opportunity. We must resist Stateolatry in any shape or form and see that the sovereign will of the people is not overridden by bureauracy.'[20] He would have agreed with Heenan, appointed Bishop of Leeds in 1951, who stated in 1942 that 'This country is in danger of becoming National Socialist – too much is being handed over to the state – the state is looked upon by many as the source of all rights and the only legitimate provider of all man's needs'. Of the new education measures, Heenan declared: 'Mr Butler must have slept with a copy of *Mein Kampf* under his pillow to have devised such a Bill'.[21]

Griffin was less extreme than Downey (or Heenan), though no less wary of the pervasive influence of the state.[22] One reason was that he feared the erosion of local initiative. His father had been a councillor in Birmingham and from him he derived a high view of municipal politics.[23] As he put it on the occasion of the visit of the mayor of Finchley to St Alban's Church in 1945, 'I am a firm believer in local government because it seems to me that in it we have a true expression of democracy and liberty. The bond between those who are governing and those who are governed is much more intimate and local needs will be better understood and more easily dealt with by local authorities than by direction from Whitehall.'[24] 'Whatever their private politics', he told his flock in a pastoral letter of 1945, 'they should exert their influence in the public life of the towns in which they dwell.'[25] He feared that the extension of the state's responsibilities undermined independent initiative, insisting in an address to the Sword of the Spirit at Hull in June 1945, that 'Voluntary effort has a value which no State decrees can confer'.[26] The strong emphasis he placed on the family and parental rights[27] had a corollary in suspicion of the state, although he maintained that he was far from preaching unrestrained individualism.[28] Griffin almost made a cult of family life. His childhood had been intensely happy and until he went to Oscott in 1919 he had been rarely apart from his twin brother, Walter (who would also became a priest).[29] The Christian family was in Griffin's view the foundation of society. 'Unless all social reforms are directed to support and enhance the dignity and strength of the family they are, in the last analysis, irrelevant.'[30] The tendency of state intervention was to weaken parental control and responsibility and therefore to weaken home life and disunite children from parents.[31]

One area of social policy in which the Catholic authorities felt voluntary effort and parental rights to be threatened was health. Whereas the older, more variegated system was characterized by a considerable degree of local control, there was a concern that the establishment of a uniform National Health Service (NHS) under close central government control would result in the rapid spread of practices inimical to Catholic moral values, particularly artificial contraception ('those mechanical devices which prevent the procreation of children', as Griffin put it[32]). Previously, the diffusion of such practices had been more restrained.[33] Great emphasis was placed, therefore, on the existing Catholic voluntary hospitals (about sixty in all) as a safeguard of Catholic moral principles.

The key concern for the hierarchy was how to retain a 'Catholic character' in those voluntary hospitals which, under Aneurin Bevan's proposals, would be placed, along with the municipal hospitals, under regional hospital boards. The bishops sought an amendment to the 1946 Act to the effect that in those voluntary hospitals the management committees which were to be established by the regional hospital boards should remain under denominational control. Unless there was a Catholic management of at least a two-thirds majority, with absolute freedom to appoint its medical and nursing staff, the fear was, as Bishop Marshall of Salford put it, that 'it will only be a matter of time before the Catholic atmosphere will disappear'.[34] The most uncompromising of the bishops was Archbishop McGrath of Cardiff, a conservative who believed that most projects for social reform 'are not worth the paper on which they are written',[35] and who saw the Welfare State as proof that 'the country is being gradually sovietized'.

The proposal of the state to take over the voluntary hospitals was simply 'expropriation and pure robbery quite in line with J. Stalin's methods', the actions of a 'pink government'.[36] Bevan's unwillingness to give the kind of independence to the voluntary schools within the state system for which Griffin had lobbied led to the decision to withdraw the Catholic voluntary hospitals from the NHS, and these remained independent institutions, in straitened circumstances, serving just a small fraction of the community. Generally, Catholic opinion welcomed this as a heroic stand against the encroachments of the state.[37] But Michael de la Bedoyère, editor of *The Catholic Herald*, sounded a word of warning against the separatist tendencies which the ecclesiastical authorities were encouraging in the areas of health and education.

> Is it best in the long run that we should obtain at varyingly heavy prices and by the kind leave of the omnicompetent secularist state our own schools and our own hospitals, or that, having provided for the best spiritual and moral training in the parish and home, we should stand with the rest of the community as apostles and protagonists of the truth just there where in the long run the truth must prevail if it is to convert the world again.[38]

Whilst de la Bedoyère left the reader in no doubt which course he preferred, the Church leadership of the late 1940s and 1950s appeared rather less interested in forging those creative links with the wider society. Relations with other churches and religious groups, for instance, were distinctly chilly.

Griffin did not share his predecessor's interest in or enthusiasm for inter-church cooperation. Although he had had more contact with 'non-Catholics' than most of his contemporaries on the episcopal bench, his formative experiences encouraged a sense of apartness, not commonality. Recalling his schooldays at King Edward's, one of Birmingham's premier schools, where a condition was attached to his attendance that he need not be present at morning assembly, Griffin told the imperious Edward Ellis, who as Bishop of Nottingham prohibited even silent prayers with Protestants,[39] that 'In the midlands we have a magnificent tradition that neither Catholic teachers nor Catholic pupils attending non-Catholic schools take part, even remotely, in the prayers, scripture lessons, or religious instructions given in the school'.[40] Unlike Hinsley, Griffin did not develop close relations with the Archbishop of Canterbury. He had participated in initiatives under the auspices of the Joint Church Council with Geoffrey Fisher during and in the aftermath of the war in connection with reconstruction and the displaced persons,[41] and they had discussed the question of religious freedom in Spain over tea at Lambeth Palace in May 1946, but social and political issues did not trouble Fisher as they did Temple, and this absence of a common ground meant a distance between the two church leaders. Relations entered a frigid phase. Early into his archiepiscopate Griffin restated the Church's opposition to joint religious services.[42] Obstacles were placed in the way of cooperation on social questions after a constipated correspondence between Griffin and Fisher on the question of the protocol to be observed when issuing joint letters. Whilst Griffin and Fisher agreed that the Established Church should take precedence in any joint initiative, Griffin refused obdurately to recognize that one of the implications of this was that the name of the Archbishop of York should be above the Archbishop of Westminster. In a letter to Griffin in May 1947, Fisher stressed the 'real value in occasional letters signed jointly by Heads of the leading denominations and giving evidence that on some great matters touching our common Christian heritage (or on some simple points such as a welcome to Displaced Persons of many faiths) we can all speak with a common voice'. But Griffin's refusal to concede on the question of precedence meant there was to be no Catholic name attached to the letter welcoming the displaced persons of central and eastern Europe.[43]

Archbishop Fisher lamented the fact that the cooperation and better relations of wartime had not endured.[44] It was clear that he felt this was down to the rigidity of Catholics and not due to any absence of charity on his part. He would describe the attitude of the Catholic Church in a letter to Douglas Woodruff as 'ecclesiastical apartheid', and referred – ten years after the event – to his invitation to Griffin to tea and of the fact that this cordiality was not reciprocated: 'To be on visiting terms to each other's houses seems to me as simple an act of Christian courtesy and hospitality as can be found'.[45] But this comment is less evidence of Griffin's bad manners than it is of the huge social gulf which existed between the higher Anglican clergy and their Catholic counterparts: tea as a social event would not have been part of Griffin's culture.

More serious damage to inter-church relations was caused by the withdrawal of Catholics from the National Council of Christians and Jews (NCCJ) in 1954. Catholics had participated in the NCCJ ever since its formation in 1942 to combat anti-semitism. Hinsley became one of its presidents, but active on his behalf as ever was David Mathew, who was concerned about anti-semitic tendencies in English Catholicism.[46] Its leading Catholic members included the Conservative MP Sir Patrick Hannon, who 'had been touched by the miseries inflicted upon the Jews during the two World Wars' and felt the 'ostracism of the Jew because of his religion was intolerable';[47] Sir Desmond Morton, an old Etonian and former Private Secretary to Churchill; Lord Perth, former Secretary-General of the League of Nations and another Etonian convert; Frank Pakenham (later Earl of Longford), Oxford don, convert and socialist (he had been personal assistant to Beveridge between 1941 and 1944); Michael Derrick, author and assistant editor of *The Tablet*; Frs John Murray and Maurice Bévenot, scholarly Jesuits; and Thomas Fitzgerald, a priest from one of the toughest parishes in London, SS Mary and Michael's, Stepney – an area which had witnessed more than its share of anti-Jewish violence during the 1930s – who listed his interests in the *Catholic Who's Who* as 'Dishing the "Reds" and opposing Fascist Anti-Semites within and without the Church'. It was a cross-party and talented body of men.

The problems for the NCCJ began in Rome when its parent organisation, the International Council of Christians and Jews (ICCJ), fell under a papal prohibition. What concerned the Vatican authorities was that it had moved beyond the specific aim of fighting anti-semitism to a broader canvass of activity which included educative work in promoting the idea of religious toleration and respect for religious beliefs. Reasonable aims one might think. But in the late 1940s Pius XII was obsessed about the spread of 'religious indifferentism'; he believed that by admitting respect for other religious beliefs he would be encouraging the notion that one religion was as good as the next. On 20 December 1949 an instruction was issued by the Holy Office on the principles governing relations between Catholics and non-Catholics, warning bishops to be on their guard 'against those who under false pretexts stress the points on which we agree rather than those on which we disagree. Such an approach might give rise to a dangerous indifferentism ...'[48] Cyril Garbett, Archbishop of York, was moved to observe, 'that it would be difficult for a visitor from another world reading these carefully guarded permissions to understand that they concerned discussions not between Christians and militant atheists, but between those who believe in the same God and Saviour'.[49] If Pius XII was concerned to accentuate the differences between the churches then the definition in November 1950 of the doctrine of the Virgin Mary's bodily Assumption into heaven contributed emphatically to that aim: to its critics lacking in scriptural warrant and un-anchored in early Christian tradition – although overwhelmingly welcomed by Catholics – the definition was a hammer-blow to the movement for Christian reunion. This was the context for the condemnation of the ICCJ in October 1950.

It is perhaps surprising that the Holy See did not act more quickly against the NCCJ – it was not until 9 June 1954 that a plenary session of the Supreme Sacred Congregation issued a decree which stated: 'Having considered the dangers arising from the questionable ideas regarding religious toleration accepted by the Protestants and Jews of the National Council of Christians and Jews of England and the equivocations found in their ideas of education, it is not desirable that Catholics in England should have part in this aforesaid National Council'. It went on: 'As the matter is rather delicate it would be useful if the Catholic Press in England could publish an article showing that the Catholic Church has never been wanting in its mission of charity, nor in defending the rights of the human person, whether it be a question of the Jews or any other people or persons suffering persecution and violence'.[50] Godfrey, the Apostolic Delegate, instructed Griffin to resign his Vice Presidency, which he agreed to do 'diplomatically' albeit with some regret.[51]

The decree provoked feelings of consternation and despair amongst the Catholic members of the NCCJ. Maurice Bévenot spoke for most in what was the most forthright letter Griffin received: after dismissing the charge of indifferentism Bévenot stated that

> at a time when there is ... a mounting hostility to the Church because of her alleged intolerance, it is unfortunate that the Council should be banned as dangerous, when it is perhaps the only body which, by its constitution and practice, is prepared to listen to the Catholic side in a friendly way, and whose non-Catholic members will stand up for the Church when flagrant prejudice attacks it. There is a danger that the ban should be taken as a condemnation of all tolerance ...[52]

Griffin was sympathetic to Bévenot's appeal: he had already written a letter along similar lines to Cardinal Ottaviani, Prefect of the Supreme Sacred Congregation, before news of the decree spread to the NCCJ. He asked Ottaviani to recognize the NCCJ's efforts to raise awareness about the persecution of the Church in Eastern Europe; to recall its expressions of sympathy to the Holy Father after the arrest, in 1953, of Cardinal Wyszynski, primate of Poland; to see how participation in the NCCJ offered opportunities to clear up misconceptions about the Catholic religion; and if all that did not move him, to remember how the Council of the NCCJ had quietly shelved an embarrassing resolution deploring religious intolerance in Franco's Spain after private Catholic representations. But most of all Griffin spoke as the leader of a Church which had steadily consolidated its position in English society whilst causing minimal offence to Protestant sensibilities – to now raise the spectre of Catholic intolerance would threaten all this.

It is true to say that the Catholic teaching on Toleration is not generally understood by non-Catholics in this country. But on the whole the Catholic Church in England enjoys the respect and esteem of non-Catholics, save for a certain extremist section of non-Catholics. Our withdrawal from the Council on the ground of the views of some of its members on Toleration would undoubtedly be misconstrued and would achieve wide publicity such as would be gravely damaging to the esteem in which the Church is held in England today.

Griffin, more alert than most to any whiff of religious indifferentism, requested Ottaviani to keep the matter open to see whether there was some way of bringing a degree of Catholic 'supervision and control' to bear on certain of the NCCJ's activities – he was thinking of its publication, *Common Ground*, which regularly contained objectionable articles on religious liberty.[53]

The kindly General Secretary of the NCCJ, Revd W. W. Simpson, was sensitive to Griffin's difficulties and did his utmost to accommodate Catholic concerns about its educational programme by setting up a sub-committee to examine in this in the light of the Holy See's decree.[54] But conciliation was no easy task. From the other side he was harangued by Fisher, who wondered whether anti-Jewish feeling in the Vatican was behind the decree, and who could not understand why Simpson was delaying the business of the NCCJ in the vain hope of appeasing Rome's anxieties about indifferentism.[55] For Fisher the issue was simple: 'all it means is that the Romans are not Christian enough to be willing to take any further share in it'.[56] In spite of the decree lines of communication were kept open over the next few years between the NCCJ and the former Catholic members, led by Edmund Rothschild, with Simpson going the extra mile to allay Catholic anxieties. A change in the constitution of the NCCJ was mooted which would have substituted the words 'religious persecution' for 'religious intolerance', so that the aims of the organization would now read: 'To check and combat racial intolerance and religious persecution'. Fisher was scathing: 'Of course the Roman Catholics find the phrase "religious intolerance" difficult because they do not believe at all in religious tolerance, choosing stupidly to equate that with religious indifferentism which is a quite different thing'.[57] Despite these significant concessions the Holy See was unyielding: it was not until 1964 – when there was a very different pope and a very different religious climate – that Catholics could once more take their place on the NCCJ.

As the NCCJ episode demonstrated, the centralizing and authoritarian tendencies of the Roman authorities – which reached an apogee during the papacy of Pius XII – were reducing the scope for independent local initiative. The dead hand of Roman authority was increasingly making itself felt. The apostolic delegate had become, as the Holy See had envisaged, a more conspicuous figure on the English scene. The diffident Godfrey (now Archbishop of Liverpool) was replaced in June 1954 by a vigorous American and former Nuncio in Ireland, Gerald Patrick O'Hara (1895–1963). With the arrival of this outsider[58] to Parkside there appeared to be a greater degree of intrusiveness and watchfulness over the affairs of the English Church. No subject was allowed to pass O'Hara's attention: the state of biblical studies in England; the juridical and political situation of the Church in Great Britain; the general political situation and the education and discipline of the clergy (all of which the bishops were asked to comment on in a triennial report – an innovation); the efforts of the Church to fight communism; suspect inter-church activities; the Catholic Worker movement; questions of private morality such as divorce and homosexuality; offensive literature 'going under the name of sacred art'.[59]

Furthermore, whilst this Roman message-boy was becoming an increasingly significant figure in the English Church, it cannot be said that the episcopate of the 1950s yielded characters of sufficient stature to counterbalance papal power and continue the more independent tradition which had characterized previous generations of English bishops. The ecclesiastical hierarchy was more in the image of the papacy than at any time previously in the century – it had a conspicuously Roman look. 'The Venerabile seems to be more represented upon the Bench of Bishops, and for that at least I am glad', remarked Francis Grimshaw (1901–1965), a future Archbishop of Birmingham, to another alumnus, John King (1880–1965), Bishop of Portsmouth, in 1947. The Venerabile of Hinsley was a veritable breeding-ground for future bishops. One of Griffin's contemporaries and a close friend, Joseph Masterson (1899–1953), would later become Archbishop of Birmingham. John Heenan (1905–1975), Edward Ellis (1899–1979), Bishop of Nottingham between 1944 and 1974, Joseph Rudderham (1899–1979), Bishop of Clifton from 1949 to 1974, Cyril Restieaux (1910–1996), Bishop of Plymouth between 1955 and 1986, George Dwyer (1908–1987), Bishop of Leeds from 1957 to 1965 and Archbishop of Birmingham from 1965 to 1981, Thomas Pearson (1907–1987), Auxiliary Bishop of Lancaster between 1948 and 1987, and Joseph Halsall (1902–1958), Auxiliary Bishop of Liverpool between 1945 and 1958, all passed through the college during Hinsley's term of office, giving the episcopal bench of the period of this chapter a homogeneity it had not possessed previously. Such chumminess was unknown in earlier times.

Arguably the dominant figure on the episcopal bench was Hinsley's greatest acolyte, John Heenan. Attention was not directed to the same extent at Griffin or his successor, William Godfrey. Griffin was plagued with mental health problems during the second half of his archiepiscopate,[60] and the burden of work – the endless round of meetings, the drafting of sermons, speeches and pastoral letters – was taken on by his ambitious Private Secretary, Derek Worlock. Worlock went on to perform a similar role during Godfrey's period of office (1956–1963), such that the joke went round, 'Why is this man Godfrey signing Mgr Worlock's letters?'[61] But if any one was destined for high office it was Heenan. Heenan recalled an occasion when he was summoned to Westminster by Hinsley; on his arrival he found Hinsley trying on a new mitre, and 'in playful mood he put it on my head. It fitted perfectly. The Cardinal's face became serious: "One day . . . you will wear a mitre of your own and you will find it a crown of thorns"'.[62] As Bishop of Leeds (1951–1957), Heenan proved an indefatigable and zealous pastor, tough on layabout clergy, always in the public eye. He was the first bishop in England to adapt himself to the modern media and regularly appeared in television debates: 'Their ignorance of Catholic doctrine is so complete, it would be easy to make fools of them', he reassured the Jesuit Vincent Wilkin before an interview with Robin Day in February 1959.[63] In one *Panorama* interview Heenan famously said that he once had doubts, but these were so long ago he had forgotten what they were.[64]

On social and political questions there was no bishop blazing the reforming trail. Institutional priorities were absorbing energy. 'Material reconstruction is both urgent and necessary', Griffin had written in a pastoral letter of 1945, 'but it is far more important to make adequate provision for the spiritual needs of this diocese of Westminster.'[65] The mid-twentieth century saw a flood of immigration from Ireland; in the 1950s over 50,000 people were leaving the Irish Republic annually;[66] in 1955 Griffin stated that the Catholic population of England and Wales had increased by 750,000 in the ten years since the war.[67] This brought with it pressing pastoral demands, though the Irish and English hierarchies were brought ever closer together as a consequence,[68] a relationship helped by Griffin's outspoken public protests against the 'persecution' of Catholics in Northern Ireland.[69] The battalions were boosted further by refugees from central and eastern Europe[70] and, from the mid-1950s, by immigrants from the West Indies.[71] The concern that 'coloured workers' might drift from the Church into the arms of the communists[72] or a life of immorality,[73] was voiced in pastoral letters of the period. But this sharp numerical growth only served to heighten the mood of triumphalism and confidence within the Church, for in general the view was that the new arrivals, as Beck stated to the Bishop of Ferns (Ireland), 'would add greatly to the potential of the Church in this country'.[74] The Church was still attracting distinguished converts, such as the poet Edith Sitwell and the anthropologist Edward Evans-Pritchard who became a Roman Catholic in 1944.[75] There was a swagger about the Church in the 1950s. The year 1950, which marked the apogee of ultramontane fervour in England,[76] saw the celebrations of the centenary of the restoration of the hierarchy, an occasion for self-congratulation, although the volume of essays edited by Beck to commemorate the occasion struck a refreshingly reflective tone. 1954 was declared a Marian Year by Pius XII in commemoration of the centenary of the definition of the doctrine of Mary's Immaculate Conception, and the English celebrations culminated in a remarkable Rosary Sunday service (3 October) in honour of Our Lady of Willesden at Wembley Stadium, presided over by Griffin and attended by over 90,000 of the faithful.[77] If this recalled the great public demonstrations of strength of the past, the showing of the first Roman Catholic service on British television on 10 January 1954 pointed to the future.[78]

Throughout the 1950s the English bishops, following the Roman lead, were fixated on the decline in private moral standards and the communist threat. Bishops fulminated against the immorality of the present age: the high-rate of divorces especially in the aftermath of war troubled them and was the subject of many pastoral letters;[79] contraception; the growth of materialism and the salaciousness of modern novels and films were great bugbears.[80] Bishop John Murphy of Shrewsbury, who was partial to grandiloquent language and imagery, talked of the 'startling successes of Satan' in his Advent pastoral letter of 1953: not only was Satan at work in eastern Europe, 'in a less spectacular way he is just as active on this side of the Iron Curtain, softening up those pockets of resistance, which we call the Home, and preparing the ground for his harvest. With a whole romantic network of Film, Radio, Novel and Periodical, he has succeeded in stupefying virtue, and in glamourising sex.'[81]

With events in eastern Europe looming large in the Catholic mind due to the imprisonment and torture of prominent church leaders such as Cardinal Mindszenty of Hungary,[82] the episcopate intensified its opposition to communism and their political statements took a more conservative turn. The bishops gave financial support amounting to £5,000 to Italian Christian Democrats fighting the communists in the elections of 1948[83] and, following the papal lead,[84] Griffin declared in a Lenten pastoral letter of that year that Catholics in England were

free to vote for any political party but the communists.[85] He urged that
Catholic schools should adopt one of the countries behind the Iron
Curtain and pray regularly for its people.[86]

The Vatican throughout the 1950s was intensely fearful of any
movement which appeared to be fermenting 'class antagonism'. In
1953 it ordered the suppression of the Worker Priest movement in
France, a new form of evangelistic ministry given encouragement by
Cardinal Archbishop Suhard of Paris which sought to forge vital
connections between the Church and the alienated industrial prole-
tariat. In England, as a result of this hardening of papal attitudes, the
YCW, a far from radical movement, became the object of Cardinal
Ottaviani's suspicion. Griffin sought to re-assure the Apostolic
Delegate that they were under responsible leadership with the hierarchy's support,[87] although Archbishop Godfrey registered his concern
about the spread of 'rather extreme leftish views' and that some of the
things said in *The Catholic Worker* 'might well have been interpreted
as favourable to class war, against which the Holy See has spoken
strongly on more than one occasion'.[88] (The YCW avoided censure.)
The Association of Catholic Trade Unionists (ACTU), founded in
Hexham and Newcastle in 1943 to fight the secularist educational policies of the TUC,[89] became an organ of the hierarchy dedicated to
fighting communist infiltration in the workplace. They were seen by
their enemies as 'stooges of the bishops'.[90] Yet nationally they were
never a force and membership began to fall from the early 1950s.[91]
William Godfrey, Archbishop of Westminster from 1956, was more
suspicious of lay political action than Griffin. When in 1958 ACTU
decided to reprint the organization's prayer, which called on Our
Lady of Fatima to intercede for the conversion of Russia and all
communists, Godfrey refused because he thought some of the references 'might be misunderstood and taken as an expression of "class
war"'.[92] More importantly, the wider context had changed: the
communist threat to the Church was receding by the late 1950s,[93] and
Pope John XIII (1958–63) adopted a more constructive approach
towards communism; dialogue and understanding were urged instead
of panic and scare-tactics.[94] Organizations like ACTU had lost much
of its rasion d'être.[95] Bishop Beck described ACTU as 'moribund' in
a report to the Apostolic Delegate of 1957.[96]

Central to the social message of the Catholic hierarchy in this
period was the cult of Mary. Pius XII's intense devotion to the Virgin
Mary had an ideological dimension, focused on the cult of Our Lady
of Fatima. John Cornwell has written of the significance of this
cult for papal social thought; a key feature was its gnosticism – 'the
notion of dual realms of darkness and light beyond the mere "veil of

appearance", where reside the Godhead, the Virgin Mary, Michael and all the angels and the saints, opposed by the powers of the Prince of Darkness and his fallen angels ... What happens in this world of ours, according to this perspective, depends on Mary's intercession to so curb the power of Satan that war and discord will be vanquished.'[97] Since the dogma of Mary's Immaculate Conception was proclaimed on the Pope's sole authority, the magnification of Mary inevitably meant the magnification of papal authority. Pius XII's definition of the dogma of the Assumption in November 1950 intensified this link between the papacy and Mary. The idea of Mary's queenship of heaven was invoked in the Church's struggle against communism; only by 'miraculous interventions mediated by Mary and endorsed by the papacy' could human history be redeemed.[98] An intense statement of this world-view can be found in an Advent pastoral letter of Bishop Murphy of Shrewsbury from 1953, which addressed the persecution of the Church in eastern Europe.

> In this global war where Satan advances on all points and tramples underfoot the harvests of Christ, we have one certain hope, Mary the Mother of God. Her universal mediatorship is not merely horizontal, in the sense that she battles for each individual soul, but vertical in the sense that she battles for cities, states and empires. Continually throughout history, wherever her assistance has been invoked, her intervention has been at a high level. The Albigensian heresy, which threatened to be the scourge of Europe, was annihilated solely by invocation of Mary in the Rosary. The naval battle of Lepanto, which again saved Europe, was due to her intercession. And the famous battle of Vienna, which rolled back the infidels, and saved Christendom, was fought under the guardianship of Mary, the Mother of God. All three victories by Papal declaration have been attributed to the intercession of Mary. And now the present Holy Father, in this fateful age, has declared that this year should be dedicated to Mary, the Mother of God, as a Marian year.[99]

This emphasis on the miraculous tended inevitably to the denigration of human social endeavour.

Against this background, social peace rather than social justice was the dominant message of the Catholic hierarchy. Class hatred was the work of Satan, so social harmony was preached. It is significant that the lengthiest discussions of social questions by a Catholic bishop during this period, Bishop Murphy's *Employers and Employed*, was devoted to the question of cooperation and partnership in industry, a popular subject of Christian social comment in the more conservative 1950s.[100] Murphy's statement was intended initially to form the basis of a joint pastoral letter, but its strident and populist tone, heavy with purple passages, seemed undignified – although Grimshaw of Birmingham commended his ability to 'use the language that is most effective with the simple people' – whilst others thought it too vague in application.[101] The imperious Cowderoy of Southwark was at least grateful that 'no one will suspect me of being its author!'[102] It eventually appeared in 1959 as a pamphlet under Murphy's name alone; its title was *Employers and Employed*, which Godfrey and Worlock thought had a rather nice Gilbert and Sullivan ring about it.[103] Murphy called for more responsibility to be given to the individual workman in the larger and nationalized industries, 'so that he is not just a tool, but a human being with a mind which finds self-expression in work that is humanly satisfying'. There should be a measure of decentralization in these industries, and employers and employed should be seen as 'partners'. 'Better human relations', Murphy insisted, 'will not come from the legislation of government nor from industry as such, but from the efforts of individual persons; from managers and from individual workmen who, discarding class suspicion and human respect regard each other as brothers because they are the sons of God.' There was a feeling that, with 'extreme poverty banished'[104] the balance of power was tilting too far in favour of labour. Murphy urged that labour's 'newly-found power and organized strength be not used to coerce the management and the public unjustly', and warned workers to 'be on their guard against demagogues who think little of disrupting peace and order for selfish ends'.[105] Such views were voiced regularly by the bishops during this period. In a report to O'Hara of 1957, a year of sharply increased strike activity and economic crisis,[106] Bishop Beck stated that the 'duties of workmen concerning a fair day's work for a fair day's wage, are tending to be disregarded'.[107] As Archbishop of Liverpool, Heenan was conscious that his predecessors were never friends of the 'bosses',[108] but told the trade unionists gathered at the Metropolitan Cathedral that they must not 'live in the past. It is unrealistic to pretend that the nation is divided between exploiters and exploited. Beware of the agitators who talk as if workers are merely slaves ... Injustice is not only the sin of the employer.'[109] Godfrey made an uncharacteristic intervention into social questions in a pastoral letter of 1961 when, reflecting the impatience of middle England with unofficial strikes, he addressed the attitude of the Church to industrial action: strikes were to be the last resort after all negotiations had failed and at all times the 'idea of friendly partnership between employers and employed should be foremost in the minds of those who seek a remedy'.[110]

There was, therefore, no bishop blazing the reforming trail. Two of the leading figures, Godfrey of Westminster and Heenan of Liverpool, were conservative in their political instincts and with possibly one or two exceptions, namely Murphy in Shrewsbury and Beck of Salford through his educational work, few aspired to any public role. Bishop King of Portsmouth was perhaps an extreme example of a recognizable type. He had few interests outside the Church; the few passions he indulged included the history of recusancy, to which he frequently alluded in his pastoral letters, and a spot of gardening (naturally to beautify the Church grounds); he boasted that he had never cycled or driven a car, entered a cinema, participated in or watched any sport.[111]

William Godfrey, who succeeded Griffin in 1956, is probably the least known Archbishop of Westminster of the twentieth century. Unlike his predecessors he did not attract a biographer.[112] Heenan, in his obituary of Godfrey, remarked with great understatement that he was not a 'striking personality'.[113] The son of a haulage contractor, Godfrey came from a pious Liverpool home; his parish, St John's, claimed to have provided more priests than any other in the north of England.[114] His mother, widowed when William was young, sent him to Ushaw at the age of thirteen where he studied hard and was remembered as cheerful yet at the same time solitary. As his studies progressed in Rome, Godfrey became increasingly reserved and introspective. On his return from Rome he took up a curacy at St Michael's in his home town, where he was remembered as being shy and retiring. He had few interests outside the Church. After a period teaching philosophy and classics at Ushaw College (1919–28), Godfrey returned to Rome to replace Hinsley as Rector of the Venerabile. He was now less of the scholar and more of the organizer and administrator, and was not remembered with any great affection: the college discipline was more severe than it had ever been during Hinsley's Rectorship. Godfrey's approach to priestly formation, as expressed in a book he wrote whilst at Ushaw, *The Young Apostle* (1924), and applied first at the Venerabile then as Apostolic Visitor to the English seminaries in 1937, emphasized obedience to a raft of arbitrary rules and regulations the purpose of which was to 'instil obedience and discomfort to self', self-abnegation and detachment ('visits home were forbidden and holidays kept to a minimum ... particular friendships were discouraged').[115] Completely trusted by the Roman authorities, he became the first Apostolic Delegate to Great Britain in 1938, Archbishop of Liverpool in 1953, and finally Archbishop of Westminster in 1956 at the age of sixty-seven (he was created Cardinal in December 1958). His appearance, short, portly with a 'large, round face',[116] was reassuringly avuncular, but it was a rigid and austere moralist who led the Church into the 1960s, one who 'swam against the current of modern times with hefty strokes'.[117] He was a reticent public figure who spoke only after great deliberation: 'Dignified and at ease in his own Church, he was always a little uneasy a few yards away from it'.[118] But although he could appear grim and forbidding he was not without a lighter side: Derek Worlock, Godfrey's Private Secretary, recalled that he would often 'stagger a group of priests by capping some remark with a quotation from a 'pop' song of the moment. During the first Session of the Council he apparently delighted students in Rome by adapting the famous lines from *The Pirates of Penzance* to 'When Conciliar duty's to be done, to be done, A bishop's lot is not a happy one, happy one'.'[119] Very few of Godfrey's words would be remembered, although an exception was an address which became known as 'the poodle pastoral', in which he declared that 'a plump and pampered poodle might run all the more gaily after a reduced diet or simple fare'. Coinciding with the Crufts Show, his words aroused the ire of animal-lovers.[120] It is no surprise that wags referred to his years at Westminster as the 'safe period'. He was a moderate Englishman unruffled by ideas, politically conservative in his instincts though resistant to the more extreme manifestations of contemporary conservative Catholic social thinking. He did not, for instance, approve of Cardinal Ottaviani's ideas. A prominent member of the Vatican Curia, Ottaviani argued for the complete union of church and state in a statement later published as the *Duties of the Catholic State in Regard to Religion* (1954); it was an attempt to silence the American theologian John Courtney Murray, who had argued for the separation of church and state and religious liberty. Although Pius XII made a speech later in 1953 which was taken as a repudiation of this intransigent position, there were a number of English bishops, Godfrey admitted later, though he was not one of them, 'receptive to the Ottaviani ideas'.[121]

Godfrey's successor at Liverpool was John Heenan. Translated from Leeds in 1957, he appeared the antithesis of his predecessor – comfortable in his public role and entirely at home with the media, fluent in debate, an extrovert with a keen wit. His relentless energy and busyness – annoying to many of those on the receiving end[122] – found a focus in the building of a cathedral for Liverpool, a commitment which had taxed his predecessors for the best part of thirty years. Edwin Lutyen's grandiose design never rose above the crypt and a scaled-down version of this was rejected by Heenan as too costly; Frederick Hibberd's far more modest design was eventually accomplished in 1967, a testimony to Heenan's tough-minded pragmatism. Nor did this detract from an intense programme of school-building and church-building.[123] These were for Heenan the primary tasks of a bishop. 'Our greatest preoccupation is school build-ing' he told the *Osservatore Romano* on the eve of the Second Vatican Council.[124] In his report on the condition of the Church to the Apostolic Delegate in 1958, he stated that the 'normal anxiety of Bishops is to provide enough churches and chapels to meet the needs of our growing Catholic population'.[125] In the same report, Heenan commented on the fact that 'Catholics tend to regard politics and politicians exclusively in relation to the school problem'. Whilst understandable, this was to be regretted: 'As the Catholic body grows in strength it would be unfortunate if we were content to be vocal on matters of education'.[126] Yet Heenan's archiepiscopate was not char-acterized by any great encouragement to political commitment, and clerical political activity was discouraged. Political quietism was the order of the day.

*   *   *

Episcopal conservatism did not make for a vigorous Catholic social movement. However, the decline of the CSG from the mid-1950s was as much owing to intense internal disputes, although these tensions certainly reflected divisions in the wider Catholic commu-nity concerning the direction of social change. Writing recently, Michael Fogarty, a leading CSG figure in the mid-1950s, remembers the organization becoming a 'somewhat embarrassing battleground between supporters of the welfare state consensus and those (notably Paul Crane SJ) of the new wave of market thinking'.[127] Fr Crane, a Jesuit priest and a graduate of the London School of Economics (it was the LSE of F. A. Hayek and *The Road to Serfdom* (1944) which provided Crane's ideological compass), emerged as one of the leaders of a younger generation who assumed positions of leadership in the CSG from veterans like Fr McNabb (who died in 1943), Leslie Toke and Margaret Fletcher (who both died in 1944). Fogarty was another 'new blood' recruit: educated at Ampleforth and Oxford, where he chaired the Labour club and met Fr O'Hea who sparked his interest in Catholic social thought,[128] after his war service he worked as a researcher at the Institute of Statistics and Social Reconstruction Survey at Nuffield College, Oxford (becoming a Fellow in 1944); his early academic career culminated in his appointment as Montague Burton Professor of Industrial Relations at University College, Cardiff, in 1960.[129] O'Hea remarked to Archbishop Grimshaw of Birmingham that 'He is the only member of the Committee known to the outer world; a scholar of distinction . . .'[130] Crane and Fogarty represented opposite sides of the 'battleground'. Crane emerged as a vociferous opponent of the welfare state arguing that it was nothing but 'embryonic Communism'.[131] He believed the NHS undermined individual responsibility and the rights of the parent. Fogarty's complaint was that Catholics had not made enough of a positive contribution to the building of the new social order. Whilst Fr O'Hea remained on the scene these differences did not unduly rock the boat, but with the departure, in 1954, of this moderating influence to St Beuno's College, St Ataph, the strains became more apparent.

If Crane appeared to some to be leading the CSG up a blind alley of reaction he could easily counter that his fresh impetus was reaping material dividends. As the editor of *The Christian Democrat* from 1950, he was responsible for turning a flagging, little-read paper into a more attractive and lively format with a decent readership (it was selling 12,400 copies in 1952 compared to 8,000 before he took over).[132] The journal struck a populist tone focusing mainly on the threat of communism and totalitarianism. Surveying the decline in CSG membership in the early 1950s, Crane had some basis for the belief that a new approach here might also revive fortunes. Appointed Secretary of the CSG in June 1952, he set out to reconstitute the organization from one which had its basis in the study circle – an idea which he thought was played out[133] – to a 'Catholic Action' style cell structure devoted to rooting out communist influence in the workplace. However, Crane's irascible personal style was divisive: he could not accept that those who disagreed, particularly when they were laymen, might have a valid argument; in his determination to secure a new direction for the Guild he was not above using underhand methods. His attempt to manipulate the postal vote during the elections for the CSG Executive Committee in 1956 was exposed and brought simmering differences to the surface.[134]

Crane's most outspoken opponent was Fogarty. He objected to Crane's anti-Labour and anti-welfare state stance,[135] and the proposed shift away from social research to anti-communist agitation. He argued as a representative of the social sciences, insisting that the frequently amateurish quality of much previous CSG effort was inappropriate in an increasingly complex world, and that there should be a greater emphasis on rigorous social analysis and research.[136] At the 1956 AGM held at St Mary's College, Twickenham, he praised the Newman Association's Demographic Survey, which began in 1953 and published its first results in 1955,[137] as a model of pioneering religious sociology that the CSG would do well to imitate: 'We took no interest, played no part, and could not even be bothered to have an exhibition of the Newman Survey results at this school, though the question was raised ... In a rapidly changing world we must think before we spoke'.[138] It was a thinly-veiled attack on Crane's approach. Fogarty believed that much social Catholic literature had descended into polemic and that an opportunity was being missed to contribute meaningfully and from an informed perspective to public debate. To these ideological divisions was added no small amount of personal rancour.

Crane's attempt, in 1956, to pack the Executive Committee with those sympathetic to his approach sparked a dispute which precipitated the intervention of the bishops and a new constitution. With the 1957 AGM approaching there was talk of the Executive Committee using the occasion to force Crane's resignation. When an agenda was presented to Crane on 1 June 1957 it cited his growing overseas commitments as reason for relieving him of the burden of office. Crane responded by seeking to impress on members of the hierarchy the enormity of a situation in which a priest, as he put it in a phrase he never tired of repeating, could be 'put on the mat by a committee of laymen'.[139]

A key figure in the dispute was Archbishop Grimshaw of Birmingham, President of the CSG, who voiced his unease at events and brought the whole question of the future direction of the CSG before the hierarchy. He harboured mixed feelings about Crane, and these were in part bound up with mixed feelings about the direction of social change. In January 1959 the veteran convert Sir Henry Slesser, who had been Solicitor-General in the 1924 Labour government, wrote to Grimshaw expressing his dismay at Crane's constant attacks on the welfare state, questioning him on the hierarchy's position. Although insisting that 'I saw enough misery in a small country town when I was a boy to be glad that somebody did something', Grimshaw's reply illustrates well the ambivalence that characterized the episcopal response to the welfare state and social reform generally in this period:

> Inevitably there are aspects of the Welfare State which are disturbing to the Catholic mind. The family is the unit of society and ought to be allowed to make its own arrangements for such things as sickness and rainy days, with what help is necessary from the greater, civil society but with as little interference as possible. The Welfare State has tended to take responsibility out of the hands of the head of the family, or if he wants to keep it, to make him pay at least twice for it.
>
> On the other hand it is arguable that the circumstances made it at least very unlikely that the family unit would have sufficient sense of responsibility within itself to make its own arrangements. A period of education lasting for a whole generation might be needed to bring the

ordinary man in the street back to such a standard. There would always be some who would never reach it.[140]

But however much Grimshaw could sympathize with part of Crane's argument against the welfare state, he was not convinced that the CSG was being steered in the right direction; it was, he told the Father Provincial of the Jesuits, John Coventry, with some regret, 'a very different Guild from the Guild that Father Plater founded'.[141] Grimshaw's main concern, however, was not with the various views on the welfare state or the forms of social action, but rather with those questions raised by Crane concerning the relationship between clerical officers of the CSG and lay members of the Executive Committee. Grimshaw, echoing Crane, told Coventry that he 'objected strongly to a priest's being put on the mat by a committee of laymen'.[142] On 28 May 1957, he wrote to the Chairman of the CSG, Richard O'Sullivan, pointing to the 'weakness of the position of the Priest-secretary to the Guild'; the 'very fact of being a secretary makes him in some sense their servant. This position ought to be reviewed.'[143] The review of the constitution was announced by Grimshaw at the Manchester AGM of 1957, with Crane's position for the time secure.

Wider episcopal feeling towards the CSG ranged from the cold to the indifferent. In most dioceses the CSG, according to bishops who responded to Grimshaw's enquiries, were moribund or non-existent. 'Social studies never seem to prosper in this country', commented Bishop Dwyer of Leeds. Bishop Cowderoy of Southwark had the impression that it was 'somewhat "precious and exclusive" and caters for a few who regard themselves as intelligentsia. Very often it is concerned with what is abstract and theoretical without having any practical bearing on social problems.'[144] There was a general feeling, moreover, that lay members should be reined in.

A new constitution was announced on 31 October 1959. Its main intent was to bring the CSG under the control of the hierarchy. A diocesan framework was imposed with branches now under the direct responsibility of the bishops. The move to greater clerical control had been prepared a year earlier when the office of priest-secretary was replaced by a priest-director; his role, as the change in nomenclature indicates, was magnified – he was a leader, the representative of the hierarchy, and emphatically not a servant of the Executive Committee. The announcement of the new constitution at the AGM on 7 November 1959 at Belle Vue, Manchester, was accompanied by a rather stern message by Archbishop Grimshaw on the subject of obedience:

I want to say one thing seriously. I have tried to keep in mind the desire of the Church to entrust activity to Catholic laymen ... you must remember that work in this Guild is work you do for the Church and therefore under her guidance. Democracy, I am afraid, is not the Church's constitution. Government of the people by the people for the people is not the way Christ founded it. In these days when nobody reckons to obey until he is convinced that the order is a good one, it does not come too easily to accept on the direction of authority without question. As Catholics however we must![145]

Grimshaw reported to Worlock that the meeting 'passed off quite well'.[146]

There was, however, some unease, not so much about the assertion of hierarchical control[147] – indeed Fogarty claimed to welcome being tied 'more closely to the regular work of the Church and Dioceses'[148] – but about the more immediate threat of increasing clerical domination. Fogarty had written to Grimshaw on 4 May 1959 voicing his concern that the lay members would be reduced to 'lay advisers and auxiliaries' under Jesuit control; he had urged previously, along with other members of the Executive Committee, that the function of the priest should be that of a spiritual director rather than an officer in any administrative or business capacity.[149] He predicted a confusion of responsibility, and feared that the 'incentive for the lay element to use their full judgement and ability' would be 'greatly weakened'.[150]

Much would turn, therefore, on the relationship between the Executive Committee and the priest-director appointed in October 1958, Fr Henry Waterhouse, S.J. Would this 'expert' in marriage guidance[151] bring the warring sides together and inaugurate a new era of peace? Unfortunately Waterhouse was to prove as prickly and sensitive as Fr Crane, who had left his Guild employment in June 1959 to carry on his war against the welfare state in a new journalistic venture, *Christian Order*. Indeed, Waterhouse was close to Crane in political outlook: 'I cannot reconcile the supervision now exercized by the Government of this country with the ideas of the State's duties given in Quadragesimo Anno', he told Grimshaw soon after the appearance of one of Crane's articles.[152] He believed, with Crane, that the principle of subsidiarity had been neglected. But he regretted the controversy Crane had provoked and the tendency of writers like him to score cheap debating points – this had replaced the 'dispassionate discussion of a moral problem, such as might be carried on at a deanery conference or in a seminary classroom'.[153] He had a profound distrust of secular ideologies, believing in the continuing value of the Catholic Workers' College as a corrective against the 'theories of Rousseau, Hobbes, Locke, Marx and others ...'[154] (in short the canon of modern political theory), and tended to be wary of those who had been through the universities, foremost among them Fogarty. A passage on the last page of Fogarty's influential *Christian Democracy in Europe* (1957), which stated that 'Catholics for their part could have contributed little to Christian Democracy if they had not taken over from Protestantism its tradition of flexible adaptation to current trends and, in particular, its traditional emphasis on the role of the laity', gave Waterhouse particular cause for anxiety.[155] As a key figure in the drafting of the new constitution, with Grimshaw too preoccupied with the schools question to pay close attention, Waterhouse pushed for a firmer recognition of hierarchical control over the Guild. 'It is hard to get into the heads of the laymen who are prominent in the Guild the idea that all authority which they enjoy in directing operations comes from above – from the Hierarchy – and not from the members who have elected them to office', he told Grimshaw.[156] Such Lockean notions were anathema to Waterhouse.

The discussions concerning the amendment of the CSG's statutes in 1960 saw Waterhouse digging his heels in against any concessions to lay control – he threatened to resign if he did not get his way.[157] The introduction into his draft statutes of a category of 'privileged membership' for clerical members moved Worlock to protest against the provocative phraseology: 'I cannot help thinking that the document seems to be underlined with suspicion'.[158] Although Waterhouse withdrew this item, the statutes were in line with the Catholic Action model he favoured. 'Lay activity in the Guild shall be fostered and organised in accordance with the instructions of the Holy See on the lay apostolate', as the statute of 11 February 1960 put it.[159] As Waterhouse never tired of declaring, 'Nil sine episcopo' (nothing without the bishop).[160]

Talk of a revival in the fortunes of the CSG was to prove ill-founded. The internal disputes may have died down, however, falling membership, the financial difficulties facing the Catholic Workers' College, the ineffectiveness of the new diocesan structure,[161] and wider concerns about its lack of impact on public questions and the relevance of its approach in a complex society – what one report from the archdiocese of Birmingham described as its tendency to continue with the 1930s '"suet pudding" approach of first principles stated in a vacuum'[162] – all contributed to its eventual demise in 1967.

* * *

The reassertion of hierarchical and clerical authority over the Catholic social movement was one feature of the late 1950s, but it was not the entire story. Fogarty was one of a generation of graduates who could no longer be satisfied with the role of 'loyal subordinate'.[163] The Butler Act opened up educational opportunities, and with that the possibility of higher education was within the reach of many more school leavers, although it was still only a small percentage of that age group who went on to university. Nevertheless, by the late 1950s there was an emerging Catholic graduate presence who were articulate and questioning, less prepared to accept the word of a priest simply because he was a priest. The Newman Association, formed in 1942 as an organization for Catholic graduates to link the universities with the wider world, could claim 3,000 members by the mid-1960s, whereas in the mid-1940s its membership stood at around 1,000.[164] Several new university chaplaincies were established in the post-war period with the support of the Newman Association, and branches of the Union of Catholic Students flourished.[165] A dominant conception of the role of the chaplaincy as protecting the student from the dangers and pitfalls of university life was slowly falling away, and a new generation of younger chaplains was emerging with more positive views about higher education.

However, it was not until the mid–1960s that educated lay people began to speak with greater confidence on theological matters, through organs like *Search*, the *Herder Correspondence*, which first appeared in 1964, and the Cambridge-based Marxist-leaning *Slant* movement, which started in the same year.[166] The 1950s saw nothing similar. It seemed as though Catholic academics were content to keep their noses in their books. Writing in the late 1950s, John Lynch, Lecturer in Modern History at the University of Liverpool, delivered a trenchant critique of contemporary English Catholicism, highlighting its intellectual failings and its negligible public impact. Catholic academics should be leading the way, Lynch insisted, but whilst they were progressing in their specialist areas they were 'unknown to the general public'. The failure was not entirely theirs: they were under-utilized by the Catholic press and 'barely recognized by the Church authorities'.[167] Lynch may have had Liverpool in mind when he noted the lack of interest shown by the bishops in the universities. Heenan had little regard for the scholarly life; he did not move very far from the view he expressed in 1942, 'that the grim future is going to require missionaries with guts but not necessarily with degrees'.[168] Little wonder that the philosopher Anthony Kenny, as a young curate just down from Oxford in the late 1950s, found himself so out of sympathy with the ethos of Heenan's Liverpool. In an attempt to roughen up Kenny's smooth edges, Heenan dispatched him to one of the busiest, toughest parishes in the city, a thoroughly miserable, soul-destroying experience for the philosopher – one of his fellow clergy had been a seminary professor of theology, but his thoughts had long since turned to matters of the turf.[169] Heenan had very little interest in utilizing intellectual resources.[170] With alumni of the English College dominating the bench, there were fewer links with the universities than there had been during the Hinsley era. In 1959, the year in which Lynch's essay was published, only three on the episcopal bench had studied at an English university:[171] George Dwyer (1908–1987) of Leeds, who took a First in Modern Languages at Cambridge and remained throughout his life a dedicated supporter of St Edmund's House;[172] John Petit (1895–1973) of Menevia, another Cambridge graduate who was a successful Master of St Edmund's House between 1934 and 1946;[173] and the veteran Flynn of Lancaster. Lynch's essay had touched on an issue of some concern. His point about the lack of vigour in Catholic intellectual life was made by leading scholars such as Dom David Knowles, Regius Professor of Modern History at Cambridge,[174] and Abbot Christopher Butler, at the Catholic Conference on Higher Education held at Strawberry Hill in September 1958.[175]

There was one public issue, however, which saw a notable Catholic academic intervention. This was the issue of nuclear warfare. It was the quickening arms race in general and Britain's acquisition in 1957 of the hydrogen bomb in particular which raised the level of public concern about the nuclear threat. In January 1958 the Campaign for Nuclear Disarmament (CND) was founded and the Aldermaston march of that year put 'the bomb' firmly on the political agenda. A scattering of Catholics, including several academics, lent their support to the campaign. James Cameron, who was appointed to the Chair of philosophy at the University of Leeds in 1960, was nominated to the Executive Committee.[176] Cameron had been a regular at Spode House since its opening as a conference centre in 1949, which under the wardenship of the Dominican Conrad Pepler from 1953 became a vibrant and influential centre of Catholic peace activity 'out of all proportion to its size and facilities'.[177] Another Spode House regular, also based at the University of Leeds, was Walter Stein, a convert from Judaism, the most active of the younger Catholic academics in CND, and the founder of a Catholic nuclear disarmament group in September 1959.[178] It was Stein, moved by the absence of Catholic 'witness' on the subject of nuclear disarmament, who edited a collection of essays published as *Nuclear Weapons and Christian Conscience* in 1961.[179] The philosophers Elizabeth Anscombe and

Peter Geach were amongst those contributors who challenged the morality of nuclear deterrence and advanced arguments for resistance by non-violent means. The book's significance was rightly noted by Fr Herbert McCabe in *The Clergy Review*. Political and moral responsibility, he argued, went 'beyond merely accepting authoritative pronouncements', therefore it was a 'tribute to the maturity of the Church in England that this first most important treatise on the topic' should be the work of a new class of 'highly educated laymen whose interests are profoundly theological'.[180] Writing in 1967, Brian Wicker saw its appearance as a key moment in the development of the Catholic left in England.[181]

The bishops did not on the whole welcome these lay incursions into such a contentious area. Godfrey refused the *Nuclear Weapons and Christian Conscience* an *imprimatur* insisting that its publication by a Catholic firm would be 'inopportune'.[182] At the same time the bishops had not given any clear guidance on the subject, and papal statements could give encouragement to both sides of the debate. Canon Drinkwater, whose opposition to the H-bomb was long-standing,[183] described the attitude of the bishops in a letter to a lay person: 'their line at present is that every Catholic should use his own conscience and make up his own mind. This may seem rather feeble, still there is something to be said for it, at any rate it is rather a novelty for Catholics to be told to use their judgements in moral matters!'[184] In his Advent pastoral letter of 1961, Heenan stated: 'If your conscience tells you that the best way of avoiding nuclear war is to sit down on the public highway, you will do so'. Of course, Heenan reserved some withering comments for those who did take to the streets: 'The Pope has already given us a lead. He has asked us not, indeed, to sit down but to kneel down ... Prayer attracts no publicity but it is not for that reason less effective ... Those who have no belief in God, and think that death is the end of it all, are naturally stricken with panic ... The frenzy of recent demonstrations has its root in unbelief.'[185] There were several unsuccessful attempts to muzzle the most prominent Catholic pacifist in England, the maverick and fiercely independent Jesuit Thomas Roberts. Roberts, formerly Archbishop of Bombay, was a regular speaker at CND meetings and provided the foreword for Stein's book;[186] as Hasting's notes, he became 'an asker of awkward questions and a thorn in the side of the hierarchy' – furthermore, as he was not directly under their authority they could not get rid of him.[187] Other attempts to silence debate were more successful. Anthony Kenny wrote in support of unilateralism in the Liverpool diocesan newspaper, the *Catholic Pictorial*, but was ordered by Heenan to refrain from publishing any more on the grounds that it would leave the 'uneducated' and 'simple Catholic' with the impression that his 'opinion' was 'part of the teaching of the Church'.[188] (Kenny told Canon Drinkwater, who had sought to enlist his support for a joint letter, that he was getting in trouble with his Ordinary over the issue and 'I do not want to stick my neck out too often'.[189])

As much as the bishops saw Stein and his like as wrong-headed it was not possible to stifle all discussion. Since there had been no authoritative pronouncement there was space for argument, and in the late 1950s and early 1960s there were many articles on the subject from both sides of the debate in the Catholic press and periodicals. It was not so much the content of the arguments that was at issue – much as he disagreed with Kenny Heenan acknowledged that he had every right to hold his views[190] – rather it was the manner in which the arguments were delivered and the audience they were delivered to which concerned the bishops. It was best to keep such matter for *The Clergy Review* or *The Tablet*, or better still a deanery conference, rather than confuse the semi-literate average Catholic.[191] But there were signs of a less censorious approach to questions of morality in Bishop Beck's participation in a television debate in January 1962 on the issues raised by Stein's *Nuclear Weapons and Christian Conscience*. Beck was not himself university-educated but wanted to see the Church engage more with the universities, as was shown by his involvement in the Catholic Conference on Higher Education in 1958. His willingness to debate in public with lay experts with whom he differed, apparently untroubled by the earlier refusal of an *imprimatur* to Stein's book, was a sign of a less defensive mentality.[192]

* * *

Soon after his election to the papacy in October 1958, John XIII, who was seen very much as an elderly stop-gap,[193] surprised everyone with his calls for *aggiornamento* (a bringing up to date). In January 1959 he announced the decision to convoke the Second Vatican Council, and the antepreparatory phase began in earnest in May 1959. The President of the Antepreparatory Commission, Cardinal Tardini, called on around 2,500 bishops throughout the world to send to Rome the problems, suggestions and views they thought could be usefully discussed at the Council.[194] The replies (votum) of the English episcopate were unimaginative and narrow in their range of concerns, although this was not untypical.[195] As Fouilloux points out, the votum 'belonged to a well defined literary genre, that of a reply to Rome, and this fact must be carefully kept in mind for a correct interpretation of the considerable amount of material produced by the antepreparatory commission. On the whole, the responses were a rather conformist echo of an appeal, the new tone of which it was not easy to perceive.'[196] Sexual morality, birth control and mixed marriages were the major preoccupations of the English bishops; questions of internal Church discipline featured heavily, but the role of the Church in the surrounding world was largely ignored.[197] There was, however, a concern that any new Marian definitions – an obsession of many respondents[198] – would threaten dialogue between Christians,[199] a sign that ecumenical considerations were now being given weight. The momentous visit of Archbishop Fisher of Canterbury to Pope John XXIII in 1960 had clearly given an impetus to the idea of Christian reunion. But the contribution of the English bishops was emphatically not that of a Church full of insights derived from its experience of operating in a milieu of religious pluralism and liberal democratic politics.[200] As Clifford Longley's book on Worlock shows, the English bishops on the whole were mentally and psychologically unprepared for the storm that was about to break.[201] Poor Cardinal Godfrey was simply not there![202] Although from the late 1950s Heenan's boundless energy was directed to the cause of Christian reunion, there were few hints elsewhere that momentous changes were afoot.

Was there any need for a radical change of direction or major rethinking? The machine was running very smoothly. The Church was now in the mainstream of British society, and was represented at all levels. It attracted 13,735 converts in 1959 – a peak.[203] There was a growing graduate presence. Catholics now occupied university chairs, the latest of which was James Cameron in 1960; but they also maintained their strong presence at the higher levels of the trade union movement, with a Preston Catholic, George Woodcock, becoming General Secretary of the TUC in 1960. Throughout the 1960s Catholics could be seen moving into the 'moderate centre of national power'. As Hastings states, 'It was good to be an English Catholic bishop in 1960'.[204]

But at the same time, anticipating Mary Douglas's lament in 1970 that 'Now the English Catholics are like everyone else',[205] it seemed to some observers that with increasing social mobility and prosperity a distinctive Catholic sub-culture was under threat. In a pastoral letter of 1957 Heenan wondered whether 'We have become, perhaps, over-anxious to be regarded as respectable . . . Our actions often suggest that our standards are not really different from those of the rest of the world. Our ancestors never acted in this way.'[206] In a pastoral letter of 1955,

Griffin attributed the 'leakage' of young people from the faith to the 'growth of materialism'.[207] The decline in moral standards that went with prosperity and the banishment of poverty was the theme of a joint statement of the bishops issued in 1962.[208] Assimilation to the cultural values of the surrounding society had its price. Although by 1961 12.7 per cent of all marriages were in Catholic churches, the highest figure ever reached, there was concern about the growing proportion of mixed marriages in relation to all marriages involving Catholics – between the years 1960–64 these had risen to 58.9 per cent.[209] Mixed marriages were the main agent for the greater assimilation of Catholicism into English society, but it was also the belief of the Church that children out of mixed marriages were more likely to lapse.

Some began to question whether Catholics had anything distinctive to say on social and political questions. In parliament there were few Catholic politicians of the front-rank and they tended not to parade their faith, though they were loyal enough when Catholic interests, mostly relating to the schools or the family,[210] were at stake.[211] As I have shown, the CSG was floundering from the mid-1950s, although the appearance of a papal social encyclical, *Mater et Magistra* in 1961, did at least serve to stimulate fresh thinking. *The Christian Democrat* from 1963 became 'a much more varied paper concerned with a broad range of socio-economic issues but much less concerned with analysis of the British social structure in terms of the papal social encyclicals'.[212] Third World issues began to be discussed, in part a reflection of the emphasis *Mater et Magistra* placed on the question.[213] From the left, however, came a more critical questioning of the state of Catholic social witness. In an essay written in 1960, James Cameron reflected on the fact that the Church was present only on the margins of politics and commented that its social teaching was stated at a level of such generality as to have 'no political consequences whatsoever'. (He may have been more impressed by *Mater et Magistra* which, Beozzo notes, 'dropped the usual deductive method that rigified social doctrine by assimilating it to a code of abstract principles; instead it applied an inductive method, that is, it took current problems in their concreteness as its starting point'.[214]) Professor Cameron feared that Catholics had capitulated to mid-century capitalism and only seemed to stir when education and sexual morality were at issue.[215] It was a theme echoed by Fr Herbert McCabe two year later in a critique of the quietism in political matters encouraged by the English Church hierarchy, citing the recent 'Prayer not Protest' campaign held in the Salford diocese (and one can assume also Liverpool). 'It sometimes seems', McCabe observed, 'as though our modern Catholic culture provides very little alternative to the prevailing Western humanist outlook.'[216]

But these calls for political responsibility had too sharp an edge to move the English bishops. It would take *Gaudiam et Spes*, the Pastoral Constitution on the Church in the Modern World, promulgated by the Second Vatican Council in December 1965, to push themes like political participation, devotion to the common good, vocation in the political community into greater prominence.[217] The historian searches hard to find positive references to political life in pastoral letters of this period. There were signs, however, that some were beginning to grasp the significance of events and enter into the rhythm of the Council. In 1963, during the interregnum between Heenan's departure to Westminster and Beck's appointment as Archbishop of Liverpool, it fell to J. Bennett, Vicar Capitular of the diocese (not a bishop!) to deliver an Advent pastoral letter:

> Many years ago Father Martindale, S.J., remarked that the average Catholic is never more than fourteen years of age. What he meant was that while the average Catholic matured in every other respect, physically, socially, industrially, and so on, as a Catholic his growth was arrested when he left school. He tended to live in a vacuum, not equating it to the world in which he lived.
>
> Now he will be called to quit him like a man, to take a wider and more mature attitude to the world around him, to be an apostle to his neighbours ... and shed his ghetto mentality.[218]

Notes

1. Quoted in A. Wilkinson, *Dissent or Conform?: War, Peace and the English Churches 1900–1945* (London: SCM Press, 1986), p. 270.
2. Aidan Nichols has attempted to show that English Catholicism in the period was perhaps not as 'sclerotic and dull as it is sometimes alleged': Nichols, *Dominican Gallery*, p. 45. See also Hastings, *English Christianity*, pp. 485–7.
3. Ibid., p. 478.
4. Godfrey to Williams, 4 December 1943, B.A.A., Archbishops' Papers 1929–65, AP/A6.
5. M. de La Bedoyère, *Cardinal Bernard Griffin* (London: Rockliff, 1955), p. 27.
6. See Cruickshank, *Church and State in English Education*, ch. 7; P. H. J. H. Gosden, *Education in the Second World War: A Study in Policy and Administration* (London: Methuen and Co., 1976); P. Chadwick, *Shifting Alliances: Church and State in English Education* (London and Washington: Cassell, 1997), ch. 2. A detailed account of the Catholic negotiations is provided by J. Davies, "L'Art Du Possible", The Board of Education, the Catholic Church and Negotiations over the White Paper and the Education Bill, 1943–1944', *Recusant History*, 22 (May

1994), 231–50. For a balanced overview see Beales, 'Struggle for the Schools', pp. 393–403; P. Coman, *Catholics and the Welfare State* (London: Longman, 1977), pp. 56–9; Moloney, *Westminster, Whitehall*, pp. 161–7.

7. Cruickshank, *Church and State in English Education*, pp. 151–2, 156; quoted in Gosden, *Education in the Second World War*, p. 281.

8. Cruickshank, *Church and State in English Education*, pp. 157–8.

9. Moloney, *Westminster, Whitehall*, p. 164.

10. Davies, "L'Art Du Possible", pp. 242–4.

11. Beales, 'Struggle for the Schools', p. 405.

12. Gosden, *Education in the Second World War*, p. 321.

13. Davies, "L'Art Du Possible", p. 248.

14. Beales, 'Struggle for the Schools', p. 402.

15. Biographical details from S.D.A., Beck Papers, Box 096/001. For Beck the educationalist, see F. R. Phillips, *Bishop Beck and English Education 1949–1959* (Lewiston, Queenston, Lampeter: The Edwin Mellen Press, 1990).

16. Barnett, *Audit of War*, p. 281.

17. Coman, *Catholics and the Welfare State*, p. 67; cf. Norman, *Roman Catholicism in England*, p. 118.

18. Coman, *Catholics and the Welfare State*, p. 14.

19. Quoted in Hastings, *English Christianity*, p. 422.

20. Sermon notes in the possession of the author.

21. Quoted in Coman, *Catholics and the Welfare State*, p. 45.

22. *The Sunday Times*, 10 August 1947.

23. M. de La Bedoyère, *Griffin*, p. 70.

24. B. Griffin, 'Local Government' in *Seek Ye First: From the Addresses of His Eminence Cardinal Griffin* (London: Catholic Book Club, 1951).

25. Advent Pastoral Letter of 1945, A.A.W.

26. B. Griffin, 'Christian Responsibility' in *Seek Ye First*, p. 123.

27. See Lenten Pastoral Letter of 1951, A.A.W.

28. Griffin, 'Christian Responsibility', p. 122.

29. M. de La Bedoyère, *Griffin*, pp. 17, 22, 35.

30. B. Griffin, 'Rebuilding the Home', in *Seek Ye First*, p. 55. See also 'The Catholic Family' (his Advent pastoral letter of 1946), ibid., pp. 61–5

31. Griffin, 'Rebuilding the Home', p. 58; see also 'Christian Responsibility', p. 123.

32. Griffin, *Seek Ye First*, p. 5.

33. Coman, *Catholics and the Welfare State*, pp. 59–60.

34. Marshall to Griffin, 5 January 1947, A.A.W., Griffin Papers, Gr. 1/36; Griffin to Bevan, 8 December 1947 (copy), ibid.

35. From an Advent pastoral letter of 1941, quoted in T. O. Hughes, 'Archbishop Michael McGrath (1882–1961): A Twentieth-Century St David? The Irishman who came to Wales', in J. R. Guy and W. G. Neely (eds), *Contrasts and Comparisons: Studies in Irish and Welsh Church History* (Powys: Welsh Religious History Society; Keady, C.

Armagh, The Church of Ireland Historical Society, 1999), p. 145. I am grateful to Dr Hughes for this source. Quoted also in Hughes, *Winds of Change*, p. 168.

36. McGrath to Griffin, 31 December 1947, A.A.W., Griffin Papers, Gr. 1/36.
37. Coman, *Catholics and the Welfare State*, p. 61.
38. *The Catholic Herald*, 19 March 1948; quoted in Coman, *Catholics and the Welfare State*, p. 61. See also de la Bedoyère's comments in *Griffin*, p. 77.
39. Ellis to Griffin, 28 January 1946, A.A.W., Griffin Papers, Gr. 2/15.
40. Griffin to Ellis, 17 December 1946, *ibid.*
41. E. Carpenter, *Archbishop Fisher: His Life and Times* (Norwich: The Canterbury Press, 1991), pp. 111, 164.
42. Griffin to Ellis, 19 July 1945; *Ad Clerum*, 23 October 1946, A.A.W., *Acta*.
43. Fisher to Griffin, 7 May 1947, A.A.W., Gr. 2/86; Griffin to Fisher, 18 July 1947, ibid.
44. Carpenter, *Archbishop Fisher*, p. 712.
45. Fisher to Douglas Woodruff, 17 January 1956, L.P.L., Fisher Papers 180, fo. 4.
46. Mathew to Temple, 1 November 1941, A.A.W., Mathew Papers, Canterbury and York Correspondence.
47. Sir Patrick Hannon to Griffin, 5 November 1954, ibid., Griffin Papers, Gr. 2/76.
48. Quoted in B. and M. Pawley, *Rome and Canterbury Through Four Centuries* (Oxford: Alden Press, 1974), p. 311.
49. *York Diocesan Leaflet*, April 1950; copy held in A.A.W., Griffin Papers, Gr.2/86.
50. Godfrey to Griffin, 12 August 1954, ibid., Gr.2/76.
51. Griffin to Godfrey, 26 August 1954, A.A.L., Godfrey Papers, Series 1, I Documents, Apostolic Delegate Letters.
52. M. Bévenot to Griffin, 7 November 1954, A.A.W., Griffin Papers, Gr. 2/76.
53. Griffin to Cardinal Ottaviani, 13 September 1954, ibid.
54. W. W. Simpson to Griffin, 27 November 1954, ibid.
55. W. W. Simpson to Fisher, 12 November 1954, L.P.L., Fisher Papers 138, fos. 273–4; Fisher to W. W. Simpson, 11 November 1954, ibid., fo. 271
56. Fisher to the Bishop of Stepney, 16 November 1954, ibid., fo. 278.
57. W. W. Simpson to Fisher, 15 January 1955, ibid., fo. 6; Fisher to W. W. Simpson, 18 January 1955, ibid., fo. 6.
58. Despite his English father and Irish-sounding name the British Foreign Office described Gerald Patrick O'Hara as 'very American': D. Keogh, *Ireland and the Vatican: The Policy and Diplomacy of Church-State Relations, 1922–1960* (Cork: Cork University Press, 1995), p. 328.
59. See the correspondence in A.A.W., Griffin Papers, Gr. 2/38; A.A.L., Godfrey Papers, Series 1, I Documents. A Miscellany; S.D.A., Beck

Papers, Apostolic Delegate Correspondence; O'Hara to Grimshaw, 1 June 1956, B.A.A., Archbishops' Papers 1929–65, AP/A6.

60. M. de la Bedoyère, *Griffin*, pp. 87–8.
61. See C. Longley, *The Worlock Archive* (London: Geoffrey Chapman, 2000) for the Godfrey-Worlock relationship.
62. Heenan, *Crown of Thorns*, p. 10.
63. Fr Vincent Wilkin's hospital diary, 20 January 1959, E.P.S.J., 42/3/5/2.
64. G. Scott, *The RCs: a Report on Roman Catholics in Britain Today* (London: Hutchinson and Co: 1967), p. 5. There are interesting insights into Heenan's personality in B. Kent, *Undiscovered Ends: An Autobiography* (London: Fount Paperbacks, 1994 edn), pp. 96–107.
65. Trinity Sunday *Pastoral Letter of* 1945, A.A.W.
66. Delaney, 'Churches and Irish Emigration', p. 98.
67. Trinity Sunday *Pastoral Letter* of 1955, A.A.W.
68. *Acta*, Low Week Meeting of 27–8 April, ibid.; Delaney, 'Churches and Irish Emigration' p. 109.
69. See A.A.W, Griffin Papers, Gr. 1/37a.
70. J. L. Gula, 'The Roman Catholic Church in the History of the Polish Exiled Community in Britain 1939–1950' (unpublished Ph. D. dissertation, University of London, 1992).
71. Heenan, *Crown of Thorns*, ch. 12.
72. See e.g., ad clerum, 20 August 1955, A.A.S; Heenan to the Bishop of Kingston, 22 February 1956 (copy), S.D.A., Beck Papers, Box 096.
73. Heenan, *Crown of Thorns*, pp. 178–80. Heenan referred to the 'marriage shyness' of Jamaican men.
74. Beck to Bishop Staunton of Ferns, 18 March 1959, S.D.A., Beck Papers, Box 096.
75. Evans-Pritchard became Professor of Social Anthropology at Oxford in 1946.
76. S. Dayras, 'Les Voeux de L'Épiscopat Britannique: Reflets D'Une Église Minoritaire', in *Le Deuxieme Concile Du Vatican (1959–1965): Actes du colloque organisé par l'École française de Rome en collaboration avec l'Université de Lille III, l'Instituto per le scienze religiose de Bologne et le Dipartimento di studi storici del Medioevo e dell'età contemporanea de l'Università di Roma-La Sapienza* (Rome 28–30 mai 1986 (Palais Farnèse: École Française de Rome, 1989), 146; J. Champ, *The English Pilgrimage to Rome* (Leominster: Gracewing, 2000), p. 215.
77. *The Tablet*, 9 October 1954.
78. Ibid., 9 January 1954.
79. Whereas the divorce rate in 1938 had stood at 1.5 per cent per 10,000 of the population, by 1947 it had increased to 13.6 per 10,000: figures quoted in Machin, *Churches and Social Issues*, p. 149.
80. From a survey of Griffin's pastoral letters in A.A.W; Godfrey to Griffin, 2 April 1952, A.A.W., Griffin Papers, Gr. 2/38.
81. Bishop Murphy's Advent *Pastoral Letter* of 1953, ibid., Gr.2/44a.

82. D. J. Dunn, *The Catholic Church and the Soviet Government, 1939-1949* (New York: East European Quarterly, 1977), ch. 10; O. Chadwick, *The Christian Church in the Cold War* (London: Penguin Books, 1993 edn), part one; J. Luxmoore and J. Babisch, *The Vatican and the Red Flag: The Struggle for the Soul of Eastern Europe* (London: Geoffrey Chapman, 1999).
83. A.A.W., Griffin Papers, Gr. 2/139.
84. Duffy, *Saints and Sinners*, p. 266; Cornwell, *Hitler's Pope*, pp. 326–32.
85. Griffin's Lenten *Pastoral Letter* of 1948, A.A.W.
86. Griffin's Trinity Sunday *Pastoral Letter* of 1951, ibid.
87. O'Hara to Griffin, 13 August 1955; Griffin to O'Hara, 25 August and 22 September 1955, ibid., Griffin Papers, Gr.2/38.
88. Godfrey to O'Hara, 17 August 1955, A.A.L., Godfrey Papers, Series 1, I Documents. A Miscellany
89. Keating, 'Roman Catholics, Christian Democracy', p. 315.
90. Ibid., p. 338.
91. Ibid., pp. 335–6.
92. Quoted in ibid., p. 338.
93. Luxmoore and Babisch, *Vatican and the Red Flag*, p. 86.
94. J. Oscar Beozzo, 'The External Climate', in Alberigo (ed.), *History of Vatican II*, p. 401.
95. Pereiro, 'Who are the Laity?', p. 180.
96. Beck's report to the Apostolic Delegate (1957), S.D.A., Box 097.
97. Cornwell, *Hitler's Pope*, p. 273.
98. Ibid., p. 273.
99. Bishop Murphy's Advent *Pastoral Letter* of 1953, A.A.W., Griffin Papers, Gr. 2/44a.
100. Norman, *Church and Society*, pp. 390–1.
101. Murphy's original draft can be seen at S.D.A., Beck Papers, Box 097; see the responses of the bishops in A.A.W., Griffin Papers, G. 3/3/9.
102. Cowderoy to Godfrey, 27 September 1958, ibid.
103. Derek Worlock to Grimshaw, 19 January 1959, B.A.A., Archbishops' Papers 1929–65, AP/S8/5.
104. Joint Statement on Moral Standards, 31 May 1962, S.D.A., Beck Papers, Box 096.
105. J. Murphy, Bishop of Shrewsbury, *Employers and Employed: A Statement on the Social Question* (Oxford: CSG, 1959).
106. See the figures in A. H. Halsey (ed.), *British Social Trends since 1900: a Guide to the Changing Social Structure of Britain* (Basingstoke: Macmillan Press Ltd., 1988 edn), p. 195.
107. Beck's report to the Archbishop Delegate (1957), S.D.A., Box 097.
108. Heenan, *Crown of Thorns*, p. 336.
109. Address to Catholic Trade Unionists by the Most. Rev. J. C. Heenan, Metropolitan Cathedral, 1 May 1960, A.A.L., Heenan Papers, Series 1 I Documents, File of Sermons, Lectures and Broadcasts.
110. Cardinal Godfrey's Trinity Sunday *Pastoral Letter* of 1961, A.A.W.

111. Biographical information from Por.D.A, King Papers, 6.06.19, 6.06.23, 6.06.24.
112. Godfrey appears nowhere in Hornsby-Smith's *Catholics in England*.
113. *Guardian*, 23 January 1963.
114. Biographical details are drawn from the newspaper cuttings file on Godfrey (reference: Hq. 920. God) held in the Record Office, Liverpool Central Library.
115. M. E. Williams, 'Seminaries and Priestly Formation', in Hodgetts and McClelland (eds), *From Without the Flaminian Gate*, pp. 78–80.
116. Kent, *Undiscovered Ends*, p. 93.
117. *Daily Express* obituary quoted in *The Universe and Catholic Times*, 25 January 1963.
118. Ibid.
119. D. Worlock, 'Cardinal William Godfrey', *Wiseman Review*, 237 (Spring 1963), 5.
120. Ibid.; Kent, *Undiscovered Ends*, p. 74.
121. Quoted in Keogh, *Ireland and the Vatican*, p. 341.
122. Scott, *The RCs*, pp. 242–3.
123. Sheppard and Worlock, *Better Together*, p. 102.
124. Quoted in Norman, *Roman Catholicism in England*, p. 121.
125. Heenan to O'Hara (copy), 2 January 1958, A.A.L., Heenan Papers, Series 1 II Documents, Apostolic Delegate file.
126. Ibid.
127. M. P. Fogarty, 'Catholics and Public Policy', in Hornsby-Smith, *Catholics in England*, p. 132. See also Coman, *Catholics and the Welfare State*, pp. 80–4; McHugh, 'Changing Social Role', esp. ch. 2.; Buchanan, 'Great Britain', p. 272.
128. Fogarty, 'Catholics and Public Policy', p. 123.
129. Cleary, *Catholic Social Action*, pp. 186–7.
130. Fr O'Hea to Grimshaw, 26 May 1958, B.A.A., Archbishops' Papers 1929–65, AP/58/4.
131. From an article in *The Christian Democrat* (March 1950); quoted in Buchanan, 'Great Britain', p. 272.
132. Cleary, *Catholic Social Action*, p. 198.
133. Fr P. Crane to Grimshaw, 22 April 1957, B.A.A., Archbishops' Papers 1929–65, AP/58/4.
134. Memorandum on the Catholic Social Guild and Catholic Workers' College, Item No. 7 at the Low Week Meeting of 1958, A.A.L., Heenan Papers, Series 1 III Documents, A. Miscellany 1957–64.
135. Minutes of Executive Meeting, 22 January 1955, C.S.G.A, A1-6.
136. Confidential Memorandum on the Troubles in the CSG, 18 August 1957, B.A.A., Archbishops' Papers 1929–65, AP/58/4.
137. The Newman Demographic Survey is discussed in Cheverton, et al (eds), *A Use of Gifts: The Newman Association 1942-1992* (London: The Newman Association, 1992), pp. 34–7. I am grateful to the secretary of the Newman Association for providing me with a copy of this booklet.

138. Report of AGM: Held at St Mary's College, Twickenham, 5 August 1956, B.A.A., Archbishops' Papers 1929–65, AP/58/3.
139. Crane to Grimshaw, 23 May 1958, ibid., AP/58/4.
140. Sir Henry Slesser to Grimshaw, 5 January 1959; Grimshaw to Sir Henry Slesser, 8 January 1958 (copy); Sir Henry Slesser to Grimshaw, 10 January 1959, ibid., AP/58/5.
141. Grimshaw to Fr J. Coventry, 28 May 1957 (copy), ibid., AP/58/4. Grimshaw had himself directed a CSG study group as a parish priest: Cleary, *Catholic Social Action*, p. 221. See also Grimshaw to Godfrey, 11 July 1959 (copy), 11 July 1959, B.A.A., Archbishops' Papers 1929–65, AP/58/5.
142. Grimshaw to Fr J. Coventry, 28 May 1957 (copy), ibid., AP/58/4.
143. Grimshaw to R. O'Sullivan, 28 May 1957 (copy), ibid.
144. Cowderoy to Grimshaw, 3 July 1959; Murphy to Grimshaw, 1 July 1959; Heenan to Grimshaw, 2 July 1959; Godfrey to Grimshaw, 1 July 1959; Dwyer to Grimshaw, 7 July 1959; McGrath to Grimshaw, 30 June 1959; Restieaux to Grimshaw, 2 July 1959, ibid., AP/58/5.
145. Address to A.G.M., 7 November 1959., ibid.
146. Grimshaw to Worlock, 8 November 1959 (copy), ibid.
147. McHugh, 'Changing Social Role', p. 51.
148. Report of the AGM, 7 November 1959, B.A.A., Archbishops' Papers 1929–65, AP/58/5.
149. Michael Fogarty to Grimshaw, 4 May 1959, ibid.; Basil King to Grimshaw, 27 January 1958, ibid., AP/58/4; Memorandum on the Catholic Social Guild and Catholic Workers' College, Item No. 7 at the Low Week Meeting of 1958, A.A.L., Heenan Papers, Series 1 III Documents, A. Miscellany 1957–64.
150. Memorandum by M. Fogarty on 'The Future Constitution of the Catholic Social Guild', 7 December 1958, E.P.S.J., Fr Pridgeon Papers, 49/13/4.
151. Cleary, *Catholic Social Action*, p. 222.
152. P. Crane, 'The Moral Aspect of State Welfare', *The Christian Democrat* (January 1959); Fr Waterhouse to Grimshaw, 15 January 1959, B.A.A., Archbishops' Papers 1929–65, AP/58/5.
153. Ibid.
154. Fr Waterhouse to Grimshaw, 3 August 1959, ibid.
155. Fr Waterhouse to Grimshaw, 15 January 1959, ibid.
156. Fr Waterhouse to Grimshaw, 3 August 1959, ibid. Also Waterhouse to Grimshaw, 4 November 1959, ibid; Fr Waterhouse to Mr. Traynor, 9 May 1959, E.P.S.J., Fr Pridgeon Papers, 49/13/4.
157. Fr Waterhouse to Grimshaw, 13 March 1960, B.A.A., Archbishops' Papers 1929–65, AP/58/5.
158. Derek Worlock to Grimshaw, 17 March 1960, ibid.
159. Statutes of the Catholic Social Guild, 11 February 1960, E.P.S.J., Fr Pridgeon Papers, 49/13/4.
160. *The Christian Democrat* (January 1960), 13; see also Report of the

AGM held at Ampleforth, 31 July 1960, B.A.A., Archbishops' Papers 1929-65, AP/58/5.

161. Report of the AGM of the Catholic Social Guild by the Treasurer, Mr. G. B. King, August 1963; Catholic Workers' College Metropolitans' Report 1964; Catholic Workers' College: Memorandum on Policy and Prospects, 1 February 1966; Report to the AGM by the General Secretary, Mr R. P. Walsh, 11 August 1963; Background Papers for Members of the National Council of the C.S.G. for the Council Meeting on 8 February 1964, E.P.S.J., Fr Pridgeon Papers, 49/13/4.

162. Report on the Catholic Social Guild from the Archdiocese of Birmingham (April 1964?), ibid.

163. The phrase used by Fr Waterhouse in his 'Thoughts on the Catholic Social Guild', 27 January 1959, B.A.A., Archbishops' Papers 1929-65, AP/58/5.

164. B. Sharratt, 'English Roman Catholicism in the 1960s', in Hastings (ed.), *Bishops and Writers*, p. 132. For the history of the Newman Association see Cheverton (eds), *A Use of Gifts*.

165. The Union of Catholic Students and the Newman Association emerged out of the University Catholic Federation which was founded in 1920. In 1942 it was decided to divide the organisation into two parts: one for graduates, one for students.

166. Sharratt, 'English Roman Catholicism in the 1960s', p. 132. These initiatives are treated at length in P. McCaffery, 'Catholic Radicalism and Counter-Radicalism: a comparative study of England and the Netherlands' (unpublished D.Phil dissertation, Oxford, 1979). For Slant see B. Wicker, *First the Political Kingdom: A Personal Appraisal of the Catholic Left in Britain* (London and Melbourne: Sheed and Ward, 1967).

167. J. Lynch, 'England', in Hastings (ed.), *Church and the Nations*, p. 7.

168. Quoted in Walsh, *St Edmund's College*, p. 57.

169. Described in Kenny, *Path from Rome*, pp. 153-8.

170. Ibid., p. 121.

171. George Brunner (1899-1969), Bishop of Middlesbrough had a Classics degree from Durham but this was taken externally whilst at Ushaw. Before going to the English College, Rome, Bishop Rudderham of Clifton studied at Cambridge, but to the best of my knowledge did not take a degree.

172. Walsh, *St Edmund's College*, p. 65.

173. Ibid., p. 56. There are many references to Petit in Hughes, *Winds of Change*.

174. For Knowles's academic career see M. Cowling, *Religion and Public Doctrine in Modern England* (Cambridge: Cambridge University Press, 1980), pp. 130-55. Cowling states that Knowles gave Roman Catholicism 'a more massive role in the mainstream of English academic life than anyone else had given it in this century' (p. 131).

175. Sweeney, *St Edmund's House*, pp. 111-2.

176. R. Taylor, *Against the Bomb: The British Peace Movement 1958-1965* (Oxford: Clarendon Press, 1988), p. 21.

177. Gaine, *Obituary Notices of the English Dominicans*, p. 98; B. Wicker, 'Making Peace at Spode', *New Blackfriars*, 62 (July–August 1981), 311–20.

178. Flessati, 'Pax: The history of a Catholic peace society', pp. 305–10. This group was not part of the official CND structure although there was overlapping membership. Membership figures conflict in the secondary texts: Flessati puts it around 300 members, many of them young and university-educated; Peter McCaffery's dissertation puts the figure as high as 800.

179. W. Stein (ed.), *Nuclear Weapons and Christian Conscience* (London: Merlin Press, 1961). See Flessati, 'Pax: The history of a Catholic peace society', ch. 9, for a discussion of this influential text.

180. H. McCabe, 'Conscience and Nuclear War', *The Clergy Review* (March 1962), p. 131.

181. Wicker, *First the Political Kingdom*, p. 6

182. Ibid.; Flessati, 'Pax: The history of a Catholic peace society', p. 336.

183. See e.g., F. H. Drinkwater, *Conscience and War* (London: Watercross Press, 1950).

184. Drinkwater to Mrs Avery, 19 January 1962 (copy), B.A.A., Drinkwater Papers, Q9.

185. Heenan's Advent *Pastoral Letter* of 1961, A.A.L.

186. Kent, *Undiscovered Ends*, p. 91; B. Wall, 'Remembarance of Things Past', *New Blackfriars*, 61 (July–August 1980), 343.

187. Hastings, *English Christianity*, p. 485.

188. Heenan to Anthony Kenny, 30 April 1963 (copy), A.A.L., Heenan Papers, Series 1 II Documents A. Miscellany 1957–64. File 'Complaints'; Heenan to Anthony Kenny, 2 May 1963 (copy), ibid.

189. Anthony Kenny to Drinkwater, 10 December 1962, B.A.A., Drinkwater Papers, Q9.

190. Heenan to Anthony Kenny, 30 April 1963 (copy), A.A.L., Heenan Papers, Series 1 II Documents A. Miscellany 1957–64. File 'Complaints'.

191. Kenny, *Path from Rome*, pp. 184–5.

192. Wicker, *First the Political Kingdom*, p. 6; Flessati, 'Pax: The history of a Catholic peace society', pp. 336–7.

193. G. Alberigo, 'The Announcement of the Council', Alberigo (ed.), *History of Vatican II*, p. 9; Duffy, *Saints and Sinners*, pp. 268–9.

194. Étienne Fouilloux, 'The Antepreparatory Phase', in Alberigo (ed.), *History of Vatican II*, 93.

195. See P. Fortin, 'The American Hierarchy at the Eve of Vatican II', in *Le Deuxieme Concile Du Vatican*, pp. 155–64.

196. Fouilloux, 'The Antepreparatory Phase', pp. 108–9.

197. Bishop Dwyer of Leeds urged the Council to consider a statement clarifying the Church's position on the rights of man: Dayras, 'Les Voeux de L'Épiscopat Britannique', p. 150.

198. Fouilloux, 'The Antepreparatory Phase', p. 112.

199. Dayras, 'Les Voeux de L'Épiscopat Britannique', p. 146.

200. Cf. von Arx, 'Catholics and Politics', p. 267.
201. The first session of the Council opened on 11 October 1962.
202. Longley, *Worlock Archive*, chs. 2, 3. Godfrey died on 22 January 1963; he was succeeded by Heenan on 2 September 1963.
203. Hastings, *English Christianity*, p. 561.
204. Ibid., pp. 561–2.
205. Quoted in M. P. Hornsby-Smith, 'A Changing Church: facing the future', *Priests and People*, 14 (October 2000), 371.
206. Heenan's Lenten Pastoral Letter of 1959, A.A.L., Heenan Papers, Series 1 III Documents, A Miscellany 1957–1964.
207. Griffin's Advent *Pastoral Letter* of 1955, A.A.W.
208. Joint Statement on Moral Standards, copy held in S.D.A., Beck Papers, Box 096, Correspondence with Bishops 1956–64.
209. See Coman, *Catholics and the Welfare State*, p. 100–1.
210. The Matrimonial Causes and Reconciliation Bill of 1963 was a major preoccupation of the bishops and Catholic MP's, see Machin, *Churches and Social Issues*, p. 201.
211. Lynch, 'England', p. 6. There is an interesting discussion of the role of Catholic politicians in Scott, *The RC's*, ch. 3, though this was written in 1967. After the general election of October 1964 there was a more high-profile Catholic presence.
212. Coman, *Catholics and the Welfare State*, p. 81.
213. M. J. Schuck, *That They Be One: The Social Teaching of the Papal Encyclicals* (Washington D.C.: Georgetown University Press, 1991), pp. 123–4; Beozzo, 'The External Climate', p. 382; B. Davies, 'Opening the Windows: John XIII and the Second Vatican Council', in P. Vallely (ed.), *The New Politics: Catholic Social Teaching for the Twenty-First Century* (London: SCM Press, 1998), pp. 45–6.
214. Beozzo, 'The External Climate', p. 382.
215. J. M. Cameron, 'Catholicism and Political Mythology', in *The Night Battle* (London: Burns and Oates, 1962), pp. 2–3. See also Cameron's foreword to C. Amery, *Capitulation: an Analysis of Contemporary Catholicism* (London and Melbourne : Sheed & Ward, 1967).
216. H. McCabe, 'Conscience and Nuclear War', p. 130.
217. The translated text can be found in W. M. Abbott, *The Documents of Vatican II* (London: Geoffrey Chapman, 1967 edn), pp. 199–331.
218. The Archdiocesan Mission Fund: Pastoral Letter and Report, Advent 1963, A.A.L., Heenan Papers, Series 1 III Documents, A Miscellany 1957–1964.

Conclusion

This study will have left the impression that the contribution of the English Catholic bishops to public life in the period under consideration was not an especially distinguished one. Certainly the charge of parochialism and narrowness which has been directed at pre-conciliar English Catholicism is likely to linger.

It should be emphasized that as a study of the words and actions of bishops this is only a partial account of the story of English Catholicism's engagement with social and political questions. Alec Vidler commented in a foreword to Oliver's study of social concern in the Church of England between the wars: 'The principal lesson that I have learned since those days is that Christian social action is primarily a matter of lay people *doing* things in the various walks of life in which they hold responsibility and of which they have first-hand knowledge, and not of clerics and ecclesiastical assemblies *saying* things or passing well-intentioned resolutions about what other people might do'. Concentrating on the latter inevitably results in tales of 'inaction'.[1] Although this book has made a start in relatively uncharted territory, drawing on new archival sources and highlighting key issues and events, the history of English social Catholicism from the 'bottom-up' – which would, for instance, focus on the role of Catholics in trade unions – remains to be written.[2] More might possibly have been said in this book about Catholic parliamentary politicians, although the impression from the sources is not that of a particularly distinguished or distinctive contribution to national politics. Local studies may uncover traditions of political radicalism which have barely been hinted at in this book.[3] An interesting study could be written on the contribution of the religious Orders, notably the Dominicans, to Catholic social thinking. This being said, this is unapologetically a book about bishops and their contribution to political life; some attempt must be made, therefore, to assess the extent and value of their contribution.

The first point to make is that the episcopate did not throw up many individuals who aspired to any great public role. In general it was a conservative, insular group of men, who saw their primary tasks as those of providing schools, priests and churches. Their achievements in these areas lie outside the scope of the present study, but needless to say their labours were often heroic. Imagination and intellectual creativity were little valued; solid administrators and pastors were the guarantors of the Church's progress. Many bishops had come up through the diocesan administration, and whilst this provided continuity and stability it tended also to produce leaders with a narrow vision and a limited range of experience. Significantly, few Catholic bishops of this period had interests or friendships outside the Church.

But the picture is not quite as barren as this suggests. It is worth reflecting on a number of key episcopates which seem to epitomize certain tendencies and themes in the politics of English Catholicism at various stages of its development.

When historians describe the early twentieth-century bishops as 'men of efficiency, duty, and devotion'[4] rather than creativity or imagination it is probably Bourne above all others that they have in mind. He saw himself primarily as a diocesan pastor rather than a national Church leader, and although he found himself inevitably drawn into politics it was mainly as a defender of Church interests, whether it be protecting the Catholic schools – an issue which inevitably diverted attention away from all other public questions – or the right to hold religious processions. During the early part of his archiepiscopate he ventured out only rarely onto the national stage. It was the First World War which broadened Bourne's agenda. He began to recognize that the Church had a mission to the nation, and not just the Catholic community. Social and political questions were more readily discussed, and he even contemplated inter-church initiatives in these areas. But Bourne was ill-equipped to carry through a populist agenda with any great conviction. Partly this was due to his temperament and personality; he was somewhat remote and not a natural actor on the public stage.

There were other reasons why the shift towards greater sympathy for popular causes was restrained in Bourne's case. As he saw Roman Catholicism becoming an 'accepted part of religious pluralism', and as he surveyed the number of high-profile conversions in the post-war period, he could perhaps be forgiven for thinking of his Church as an alternative established religion. Conversion of England fantasies were becoming less fantastic. But one of the consequences of this was that a high premium was placed on political respectability. Irish radicalism and social radicalism at home had to be kept at an arm's-length.

It is striking that both during the Anglo-Irish War and the General Strike Bourne reflected Tory sentiment far more so than the Archbishop of Canterbury. But this was not a particularly far-sighted move on Bourne's part: he made far more political enemies than friends in the process. Any possibility that he might have become a popular public leader of the Catholic community was lost as a result of these interventions.

Turning from Westminster, it is worth considering two of the more political bishops, for they seem to epitomize two apparently conflicting tendencies in early twentieth-century English social Catholicism. Bishops Keating and Casartelli were key figures in the development of social and political Catholicism; their involvement in organisations like the CSG and the Catholic Federation went beyond mere figure-heading, and they bore a large responsibility for determining their respective courses. Before dwelling on the differences it is important to note that there were many similarities between the two men. Unusually for the times they both took a close interest in higher education for the clergy; they were convinced that lay people should take a more active and vigorous role in church life; they were interested to an unusual extent in social and political questions, and had distinct visions of a Christian social order; they shared anxieties about the rise of collectivism and class politics; they wanted the Church to take a more prominent role in public life; they recognized that the episcopate had to identify with the people and cut its links with privilege. At a personal level they got on well. Yet there were significant differences. Casartelli was less willing to see good in the Labour Party – it was socialist and that was the end of it. Catholic lay organizations were seen in defensive, negative terms as bastions against socialism and baleful secular influences. He was suspicious of inter-church movements, believing that the Church could learn nothing from the experience and should concentrate its energies on building up its own organisations and structures. Keating on the other hand could see that there were different kinds of socialism, not all of which were anti-God, anti-Church and anti-private property. He urged that Catholics should remain within the Labour Party and fight to ensure that this remained the case. He was prepared to look beyond the Catholic sub-culture and consider cooperating with other religious groups for social reform.

The direction which English social and political Catholicism took is generally thought to have been Keating's more 'open' approach.[5] Despite attempts by Catholic Tories to push the bishops into a more vigorously anti-socialist stance, the weight of episcopal opinion was emphatically against this course. Casartelli clearly lost the main battle in determining the direction of episcopal policy towards socialism and the Labour Party. But it would be more accurate to say that no one view of social and political questions ever achieved final ascendancy; there was no gradual movement in a progressive direction; that within English social Catholicism 'open' and 'closed' tendencies were always in tension with one another – indeed it is not unusual to find the tensions present in individual Catholics. What can be said with some certainty is that by the late 1920s the bishops of Bourne's generation had moved in a more 'closed' direction[6] – the sense of a mission to the nation had clearly receded in the course of a decade.

The more confrontational politics of the late 1930s was fertile ground for the development of exclusivist brands of social and political Catholicism. The papacy inculcated a vision of the Church locked in remorseless opposition to the surrounding society, and Catholic Action became the means by which the Church would counter these hostile forces. In England Catholic Action was given a faithful push by the bishops, although it was not as powerful a movement as some of its advocates might have hoped. The public impact of English Catholicism remained low, with the Spanish Civil War pushing progressive elements in the Church further to the margins.

It was the Second World War which enabled Hinsley to recover that sense of Catholicism's mission to the nation. His personal warmth, impulsiveness and plain speech; his patriotism and distaste for authoritarian politics; his willingness to pray with other Christians; these qualities which had been released after the inhibitions of the later 1930s made him a hugely popular figure within and outside the Church. Not since Manning had English Catholicism such a prominent leader. Yet this book is very much about the factors which inhibited these more challenging engagements.

There were structural factors which clearly militated against the bishops speaking with a united voice on social and political questions, the most fundamental of which was the weak sense of the bishops as a corporate body. Although it was appropriate that a bishop saw his primary duty as to the diocese, a certain myopia was always the danger: there was a tendency, as Bishop Dunn of Nottingham once put it, for each diocese or province to lead its own diocesan or provincial life.[7] (Interestingly, these concerns frequently arose in connection with the schools question, which of all public issues the bishops had to address is thought to have been the one that elicited something like a united and coordinated response.) Hinsley attempted to address this problem when he instituted a standing committee of the bishops, but throughout most of the period under consideration coordination was sporadic. Yet this weak corporate presence was not unusual amongst national ecclesiastical hierarchies – fragmentation was invariably the rule.[8] Indeed, the Holy See preferred to deal with bishops individually rather than entire hierarchies – it drove the point home that the Vatican was 'the summit of Catholicism and the pope the apex of the summit'.[9] The corollary of Roman centralization was a weak sense of collegiality: as Fouilloux puts it, 'any attempt at horizontal coordination within this kind of vertical or pyramidal structure was for a long time regarded by the Vatican as a potential threat'.[10]

Increasingly subordinated to Roman authority, yet within their own domain the bishops tended to see themselves as undisputed masters of all they surveyed. As we have seen, the bench of bishops contained a number of imperious mentalities who jealously guarded their prerogatives. It was impossible for a movement or organization to take root in a diocese without the permission of the bishop. Ambitious national projects such as Hinsley's Sword of the Spirit foundered precisely because of this. Independent initiatives were impossible.

Hinsley's legacy was not sustained. His reformist approach to social questions had been seen in the joint pastoral letter of 1942, *Catholics and the New World Order*, and in the welcome he gave to the Beveridge Report. In this he was supported by a key member of the episcopate, Archbishop Williams of Birmingham. But the reforming impetus was to fade with the passing of Hinsley and Williams. The result was a far from impressive contribution to the building of a new social order in post-war England. Whilst in the first half of the century the bishops, following the example of the papal social encyclicals, had, generally speaking, succeeded in maintaining a balance between attacking uncontrolled capitalism and individualism on the one hand and collectivism on the other, the emphasis now was very much on the dangers of the over-mighty state and the threats that the welfare state was supposed to present to the rights of the family and voluntary associations. Catholic bishops appeared from the outside more as defenders of their special institutional interests rather than as promoters of the common good. Of course, in practice the social composition of Catholicism was such that the social ameliorations promised by the Welfare State were largely welcome,[11] and most ordinary Catholics were indifferent to the theoretical debates which raged for the best part of fifteen years in the social Catholic pamphlets.

There was a complacency and confidence about the Church in the 1950s. Unlike the other major denominations it continued to grow after the war, and its strength was bolstered by immigration from Ireland, central and eastern Europe and the West Indies. Conversions reached a peak. At the same time the bishops were on the whole an anonymous bunch; certainly the Archbishops of Westminster – Griffin and Godfrey – made little public impression. They were concerned with the pastoral problems raised by immigration; the schools question (as ever); their pastoral letters expressed an anxiety about declining moral standards and the persecution of Catholics in communist countries. At least at episcopal level, with the exception of Heenan from the late 1950s, the interest in Christian reunion gathering apace in continental Catholicism was not a burning issue.

The last chapter describes a Church leadership that was static, rigid and unimaginative. It seems fair to say that there were fewer characters on the bench of bishops, and that they reflected a far narrower range of experience than previous generations – it was a homogenous group which had been socialized in the Venerabile. If Hinsley, a teacher to many of this generation, had suggested a more open approach to the involvement of lay people in the public witness of the Church, then his students showed few signs of following. If the term itself was less conspicuous by the 1950s, the 'Catholic Action' approach still dominated, with its emphasis on hierarchical direction, the subordinate position of lay people and the virtues of obedience and docility. There was plenty of scope for tension between this narrow conception of the lay apostolate and the more independent, 'cisalpine' strains that historians such as Hastings and Norman have discerned in English Catholicism's public, political face, though what is impressive in this period is the extent to which a balance, for the most part, was maintained. Nevertheless, there was no full flowering of independent lay initiative in this period: the lay apostolate was understood to be something hierarchically-driven.

It is ironic that the bishops were asserting and re-emphasizing their control over social Catholics organizations on the very eve of the Second Vatican Council. Although the CSG was still very much under clerical supervision and control, there was a growing number of lay members, many of them graduates, who were becoming impatient with the position of loyal subordinate. Questions about control and responsibility were now being aired within social Catholic circles, with the strains between two apparently irreconcilable views of the lay apostolate – one stressing lay action's direct dependence on the hierarchy, the other lay autonomy – becoming increasingly apparent. There was little or no awareness in England of contemporary continental Catholic theology on the lay apostolate (the key figure being the French Dominican Yves Congar), which might have enriched and raised the level of a debate too often conducted in an atmosphere of mutual suspicion, framed in the terms of these crude dichotomies.

The impressive network of organizations that sprang up in England under the influence of the papal social encyclicals at the beginning of the twentieth century passed away in the post-conciliar world. A distinct era in Catholic history had closed, and the conditions which had supported this network no longer obtained. The emergence of these organizations was in part related to the wider story of late-nineteenth and early twentieth-century Catholicism's response to social and political change; they formed a movement of defence, firmly under hierarchical control, to counter the advance of socialism and secularism. However, the English context out of which they emerged was less defensive; Catholicism was gaining a secure foothold in English life, and the Church looked out to the wider society with a considerable degree of confidence and optimism. Bishops inherited and negotiated the tensions thrown up by this paradoxical situation; but this study has shown that the tensions proved to be inhibiting rather than a source of creativity and vitality in political life.

Notes

1. A. Vidler's foreword in Oliver, *Church and Social Order*, p. vi. The italics are the author's.
2. Joan Keating's unpublished Ph.D. is the nearest we have to such a history. There is a useful discussion in Scott, *The RC's*, pp. 95–100.
3. Gilley, 'A Tradition and Culture Lost', p. 34.
4. E.g. Norman, *Roman Catholicism in England*, p. 109.
5. Whyte, *Catholics in Western Democracies*, p. 98; Von Arx, 'Catholics and Politics'.
6. Whyte comments that 'some movement towards a closed Catholicism occurred even in the Anglo-American world during the period covered by this chapter' [1920–60]: *Catholics in Western Democracies*, p. 96.
7. Dunn to Whiteside, 30 March 1920, Not.D.A., Dunn Papers, G.04.01.
8. See e.g.'s Fogarty, *Vatican and the American Hierarchy*, pp. 214–28; Callahan, *Catholic Church in Spain*, pp. 178–9; Fouilloux, 'The Antepreparatory Phase', p. 67.
9. Ibid., p. 66.
10. Ibid., p. 68.
11. Norman, *Roman Catholicism in England*, p. 118.

Appendix

Bishops of England and Wales 1903–63

Archdiocese of Westminster	Dates of tenure
Francis Bourne	1903–1935
Arthur Hinsley	1935–1943
Bernard Griffin	1943–1956
William Godfrey	1956–1963

Auxiliary Bishops

Charles Algernon Stanley, titular Bishop of *Emmaus*	1903–1928
Patrick Fenton, titular Bishop of *Amylca*	1904–1917*
William Johnon, titular Bishop of *Arindela*	1906–1909
Joseph Butt, titular Bishop of *Cambysopolis*	1911–1944
Bernard Ward, titular Bishop of *Lydda*	1917
John Manuel Bidwell, titular Bishop of *Miletopolis*	1917–1930
Edward Myers, titular Bishop of *Lamus*	1932–1956
David Mathew, titular Bishop of *Aeliae*	1938–1946
George Craven, titular Bishop of *Sebastopilis*	1947–1967
David John Cashman, titular Bishop of *Cantanus*	1958–1965

Archdiocese of Birmingham	
Edward Ilsley	1888–1921*
John McIntyre	1921–1929
Thomas Williams	1929–1946
Joseph Masterson	1947–1953
Francis Grimshaw	1954–1965

Auxiliary Bishops

John McIntyre, titular Bishop of *Oxyrynchus*	1917–1921
Michael Glancey, titular Bishop of *Flaviopolis*	1924–1925
John Barrett, titular Bishop of *Assus*	1927–1929
Bernard W. Griffin, titular Bishop of *Abya*	1938–1943
Humphrey Bright, titular Bishop of *Soli*	1944–1964

Archdiocese of Liverpool

Thomas Whiteside	1894–1921
Frederick Keating	1921–1928
Richard Downey	1928–1953
William Godfrey	1953–1956
John Heenan	1957–1963

Auxiliary Bishops

Robert Dobson, titular Bishop of *Cynopolis*	1922–1942
Joseph Halsall, titular Bishop of *Aabi*	1945–1958

Archdiocese of Cardiff

John Cuthbert Hedley	1881–1915
James Bilsborrow 1911, translated to Cardiff as Archbishop and Metropolitan	1916–1920
Francis Mostyn	1921–1939
Michael McGrath	1940–1961
John Murphy	1961–1983*

Diocese of Brentwood

Bernard Ward	1917–1920
Arthur Doubleday	1920–1951
George Andrew Beck	1951–1955
Bernard Patrick Wall	1956–1969*

Auxiliary Bishops

George Andrew Beck	1948–1951

Diocese of Clifton

George Ambrose Burton	1902–1931
William Lee	1932–1948
Joseph Rudderham	1949–1974*

Diocese of Hexham and Newcastle

Thomas Wilkinson	1889–1909
Richard Collins	1909–1924
Joseph Thorman	1925–1936
Joseph McCormack	1937–1958
James Cunningham	1958–1974*

Auxiliary Bishops

Richard Preston, titular Bishop of *Rhocea*	1900–1905
Richard Collins, titular Bishop of *Selinonte*	1905–1909
James Cunningham, titular Bishop of *Jos*	1957–1958

Diocese of Lancaster

Thomas Wulstan Pearson	1925–1938
Thomas Flynn	1939–1961
Brian Foley	1962–1985*

Diocese of Leeds

William Gordon	1890–1911
Joseph Cowgill	1911–1936
Henry Poskitt	1936–1950
John Heenan	1951–1957
George Patrick Dwyer	1957–1965

Auxiliary Bishops

Joseph Cowgill	1905–1911

Diocese of Menevia

Francis Mostyn	1898–1921, Apostolic-Administrator of Menevia till 1926
Francis Vaughan	1926–1935
Michael McGrath	1935–1940
Daniel Hannon	1941–1946
John Petit	1947–1972*

Diocese of Middlesbrough

Richard Lacey	1879–1929
Thomas Shine	1929–1955
George Brunner	1956–1967*

Auxiliary Bishops

Thomas Shine, titular Bishop of *Lamus*	1921–1929
George Brunner, titular Bishop of *Ellis*	1946–1956

Diocese of Northampton

Arthur Riddell	1880–1907
Frederick Keating	1908–1921
Dudley Charles Cary-Elwes	1921–1932
Laurence Youens	1933–1939
Thomas Leo Parker	1941–1967*

Diocese of Nottingham

Robert Brindle	1901–1915*
Thomas Dunn	1916–1931
John McNulty	1932–1943
Edward Ellis	1944–1974*

Diocese of Plymouth

Charles Graham	1902–1911
John Keily	1911–1928
John Barrett	1929–1946
Francis Grimshaw	1947–1954
Cyril Restieaux	1955–1986*

Diocese of Portsmouth

John Cahill	1900–1910
William Cotter	1910–1940
John Henry King	1941–1965

Auxiliary Bishops

William Cotter, titular Bishop of *Clazomenae*	1905–1910
John Henry King, titular Bishop of *Opus*	1938–1941
Thomas Holland, titular Bishop of *Etenna*	1960–1964

Diocese of Salford

John Bilsborrow	1892–1903
Louis Casartelli	1903–1925
Thomas Henshaw	1925–1938
Henry Marshall	1939–1955
George Andrew Beck	1955–1964

Auxiliary Bishops

John S. Vaughan, titular Bishop of *Sebastopolis*	1909–1925

Diocese of Shrewsbury

Samuel Allen	1897–1908
Hugh Singleton	1908–1934
John Ambrose Moriarty	1934–1949
John Murphy	1949–1961
William Grasar	1962–1980*

Auxiliary Bishops

John Ambrose Moriarty	1932–1934
John Murphy	1948–1949

Diocese of Southwark

Francis Bourne	1897–1903
Peter Amigo	1904–1949
Cyril Cowederoy	1949–1976

Auxiliary Bishops

William F. Brown, titular Bishop of *Pella*	1924–1951

Bishopric of the Forces

William Keatinge, titular Bishop of *Metellopolitano*	1917–1934
James Dey, titular Bishop of *Sebastopolis*	1935–1946
David Mathew, first Vicar of the Forces	1954–1963*

*Indicates retired

Bibliography

PRIMARY SOURCES

I Manuscript Sources

Government papers
London, Kew Gardens, Public Record Office (P.R.O.)
Cabinet Minutes (CAB 23/53)
Home Office papers (H.O. 045)
Foreign Office papers (F.O. 115)

Private papers
Armagh, Archives of the Archdiocese of Armagh (A.A.A.)
Cardinal Logue papers

Arundel, Arundel Castle Archives (A.C.A.)
Duke of Norfolk papers

Birkenhead, Diocesan Curial Offices, Shrewsbury Diocesan Archives (Shr.D.A.)
Bishop Singleton papers

Birmingham, Cathedral House, St Chad's, Birmingham Archdiocesan Archives (B.A.A.)
Archbishops' Papers 1929–1965
Canon Drinkwater papers

Brentwood, Cathedral House, Brentwood Diocesan Archives (B.D.A.)
Bishop Ward papers
Irish Emigrants File
Catholic Social Guild File

Bristol, St Ambrose, Clifton Diocesan Archives (C.D.A.)
Bishop Burton papers

Burnley, St Mary, Salford Diocesan Archives (Sal.D.A.)
Bishop Casartelli papers
Bishop Henshaw papers
Bishop Marshall papers
Bishop Beck papers
Catholic Federation papers
Catholic Social Guild Folder (9)
Catholic Societies (Box 181, 183)
Education 1935–6 (Box 066)
Vicar General Correspondence

Cambridge, Cambridge University Library (C.U.L.)
Stanley Baldwin papers

Cambridge, Churchill College Archives (C.C.A)
Virginia Mary Crawford papers

Cambridge, St Edmund's College Archives
College archives

Dartmouth, The Priest's House, Plymouth Diocesan Archives (Ply.D.A.)
Bishop of Plymouth's Acta

Dublin, Archives of the Archdiocesan of Dublin (A.A.D.)
Archbishop Byrne papers
Archbishop McQuaid papers
Archbishop Walsh papers

Dublin, National Library of Ireland (N.L.I.)
Shane Leslie papers

Durham, Ushaw College Archives
College archives

Hull, The University of Hull, Brynmor Jones Library (B.J.L.)
Mark Sykes papers

Leeds, Diocesan Curial Offices, Leeds Diocesan Archives
Acta of Bishop Gordon

Liverpool, Metropolitan Cathedral, Archives of the Archdiocese of Liverpool
    (A.A.L.)
Early Bishops' Correspondence
Archbishop Keating papers
Archbishop Downey papers
Archbishop Godfrey papers
Archbishop Heenan papers

London, Vauxhall Bridge Road, Archives of the Catholic Truth Society (A.C.T.S.)
Minute Books of the Executive of the CTS

London, Farm Street, English Province of the Society of Jesus Archives (E.P.S.J.)
Fr Francis Devas papers
Fr Leo O'Hea papers
Fr Joseph Keating papers
Fr Charles Plater papers
Fr Bernard Vaughan papers
Fr Vincent Wilkin papers

London, Guildhall University, Fawcett Library
Minute Books of the Catholic Women's Suffrage Society

London, House of Lords Record Office (H.L.R.O.)
Lloyd George papers
Patrick Hannon papers

London, Lambeth Palace Library (L.P.L.)
Bishop Bell papers
Archbishop Davidson papers
Archbishop Lang papers
Archbishop Fisher papers

London, Archbishop's House, Archives of the Archdiocese of Southwark (A.A.S.)
Bishop Amigo papers
Bishop Brown of Pella papers
Sword of the Spirit File

London, Abingdon Road, Archives of the Archdiocese of Westminster (A.A.W.)
Cardinal Bourne papers
Cardinal Hinsley papers
Cardinal Griffin papers
Cardinal Godfrey papers
Bishop David Mathew papers
Acta of the Bishop's Meetings

Middlesbrough, Diocesan Curial Offices, Middlesbrough Diocesan Archives (M.D.A.)
Bishop Lacy papers
Minute Book of the Hull Catholic Federation

Newcastle, Bishop's House, Hexham and Newcastle Diocesan Archives (H.N.D.A.)
Bishop of Hexham and Newcastle's Acta
Catholic Action File

Newcastle, Newcastle University Library
Walter Runciman papers

Northampton, Northamptonshire County Record Office
Elwes Family Papers

Northampton, Bishop's House, Northampton Diocesan Archives (Nrt.D.A.)
Bishop Keating papers

Nottingham, Diocesan Curial Offices, Nottingham Diocesan Archives (Not.D.A.)
Bishop Dunn papers
Bishop McNulty papers

Oxford, Bodleian Library
James Marchant papers
Gilbert Murray papers

Oxford, Plater College, Catholic Social Guild Archives (C.S.G.A.)
Catholic Social Guild papers
Drinkwater, F. H., *Notes on Fr Parkinson* (unpublished, 1959)
Ford, J., *Notes for the C.S.G. History: Manchester and Salford Area* (unpublished, 1960)

Portsmouth, St Edmund House, Portsmouth Diocesan Archives (Por.D.A.)
Bishop Cahill papers
Bishop Cotter papers

Preston, Lancashire County Record Office (L.C.R.O.)
Archives of the Roman Catholic Archdiocese of Liverpool
Francis Blundell papers

Preston, Talbot Library, Lancaster Diocesan Archives (Lnc.D.A.)
Bishop Flynn papers

Rome, Archives of the Sacred Congregation of Propaganda Fide (S.C.P.F.)

Rome, Vatican City State, Archivio Segreto Vaticano (A.S.V.)
Consistorial Congregation (*ad Limina* reports)

Stratton-on-the-Fosse, Downside Abbey Archives (D.A.A.)
Dom Bede Camm papers

Cardinal Gasquet papers
Bishop David Mathew papers

Sutton Coldfield, Oscott College, Oscott College Archives (O.C.A.)
Fr Henry Parkinson papers

Warwick, Warwickshire County Record Office
Feilden MSS (Minutes of the Executive of the Catholic Women's League)

II Printed Sources

Minutes
Hansard, Parliamentary Debates, Fifth Series

Newspapers
The Birmingham Post
The Catholic Herald
Catholic Times
Catholic World
Catholic Worker
Daily News
Dewsbury Reporter
Guardian
Jewish Chronicle
Leeds Mercury
Liverpool Daily Post
Liverpool Jewish Gazette
Liverpool Post and Mercury
Manchester Guardian
Northern Daily Telegraph
South London Press
The Tablet
The Times
The Universe
Weekly Herald
Western Daily Mercury
Yorkshire Daily Observer

Contemporary periodicals
Almanac for the Diocese of Salford
Birmingham and District Catholic Magazine
Catholic Social Guild Quarterly Bulletin
The Catholic Social Year Book
The Catholic Union Gazette
Christian Democrat
Clergy Review

The Cottonian
The Crucible
The Downside Review
Dublin Review
The Catholic Federationist
The Harvest; A Monthly Magazine in Aid of the Salford Catholic Protection and Rescue Society
The Messenger: Organ of the Apostleship of Prayer
The Month
Nineteenth Century
The Oscotian
Plymouth Diocesan Record
Southwark Record
St Chad's Magazine
Ushaw Magazine
The Venerabile
Westminster Cathedral Chronicle
Wiseman Review

Works of reference
Catholic Directory
Catholic Who's Who
Craig, F. W. S., *British Parliamentary Election Results 1918–1949* (Chichester, 1983 edn).
Currie, R., Gilbert, A., and Horsley, L. (eds), *Churches and Churchgoers: Patterns of Church Growth in the British Isles since 1700* (Oxford: Clarendon Press, 1977).
Dictionary of National Biography.
Fitzgerald-Lombard, C. (ed.), *English and Welsh Priests 1801–1914: A Working List* (Bath: Downside Abbey, 1993).
Gaine, S. F., *Obituary Notices of the English Dominicans from 1952 to 1996* (Oxford: Blackfriars Publications, 2000).
Gillow, J., *Bibliographical Dictionary of the English Catholics*, vol. V (London: Burns and Oates; New York: Benziger Books, 1902), pp. 87–8.
Gorman, W. Gordon, *Converts to Rome* (London: Sands and Co., 1910 edn).
Halsey, A. H. (ed.), *British Social Trends since 1900: a Guide to the Changing Social Structure of Britain* (Basingstoke: Macmillan Press Ltd., 1988 edn).
Plumb, B., *Arundel to Zabi: A Biographical Dictionary of the Catholic Bishops of England and Wales (Deceased) 1623–1987* (Warrington, 1987).
Who Was Who.
Who's Who.

Printed primary sources

Abbott, W. M., *The Documents of Vatican II* (London: Geoffrey Chapman, 1967 edn).

Anon. (almost certainly H. Somerville), 'The Confessions of a Catholic Socialist', *Dublin Review*, 115 (July 1914), 101–15.

Bagshawe, E. G., *Mercy and Justice to the Poor* (London: Kegan Paul and Co., 1885).

— *The Monstrous Evils of English Rule in Ireland: Especially since the Union* (Nottingham: Watchorn, 1886).

Bampton, S. J., Fr., *Christianity and Reconstruction: The Labour Question* (London and Edinburgh: Sands and Co.).

Barry, W., *The Layman in the Church* (London: CTS, 1905).

Belloc, H., *The Servile State* (London and Edinburgh: T. N. Foulis, 1913).

Belloc, H., and Chesterton, C., *The Party System* (London: Stephen Swift, 1911).

Bourne, F. Cardinal, *The Nation's Crisis* (London: CSG, 1918).

— *Ecclesiastical Training* (London: Burns Oates and Co., 1926).

— 'The Catholic Apostolic Roman Church', in J. Marchant (ed.), *The Reunion of Christendom: A Survey of the Present Position* (London: Cassell and Company, 1929).

— *Congress Addresses* (London: Burns Oates and Co., 1929).

Cameron, J. M., 'Catholicism and Political Mythology', in *The Night Battle* (London: Burns and Oates, 1962).

Casartelli, L., *Sketches in History* (New York, Cincinatti and Chicago: Benzinger Brothers, 1906).

The Catholic Church and Labour (London: CTS, 1908).

Catholics and the New World Order: A Joint Pastoral of the English Hierarchy (London: CTS; Oxford: CSG, 1942).

Carlen, C., *The Papal Encyclicals 1903–1939* (Washington: McGrath, 1981).

Carpenter, Fr Hilary, 'Catholics and European Political Development', in *Report of the 40th Annual Conference of Catholic Colleges and of the Annual Conference of the Convent Schools' Association* (London: Cole and Co., 1937), 81–98.

Catholic Social Guild Report of the 28th Annual Meeting held in Ruskin College, Oxford, on August 1, 1937, and Sixteenth Annual Report of the Catholic Workers' College (Oxford: CSG, 1937).

Catholic Studies in Social Reform (London: CSG, 1911).

Codex Iuris Canonica: Piu X Pontificis Maximi Iussu Digestus Benedicti Papae XV Auctoritate Promulgatus (Rome, 1918).

Crane, P., 'The Moral Aspect of State Welfare', *Christian Democrat* (January 1959), pp. 197–205.

Crofts, A. M., *Catholic Social Action: Principles, Purpose and Practice* (London: The Catholic Book Club, 1936).

Downey, R., 'Civic Virtue', in *Public and Platform Addresses* (London: Burns Oates, 1933), pp. 32–41.

— *Rebuilding the Church in England* (London: Burns Oates and Co., 1933).

Drinkwater, F. H., *Seven Addresses on Social Justice* (London: Burns, Oates and Co., 1937).

— *Conscience and War* (London: Watercross Press, 1950) .

Eighth National Catholic Congress: Official Report (Manchester: CTS, 1926).

Eppstein, J., *A Catholic Looks at the League* (Oxford: CSG, 1937).

Flee to the Fields: The Faith and Works of the Catholic Land Movement: A Symposium (London: Heath Cranton, 1934).

Fletcher, M., *Light for New Times* (London: Art and Book Company, 1903).

— *The School of the Heart* (London: Longmans and Co., 1904).

— *O, Call back Yesterday* (Oxford: Basil Blackwell, 1939).

Gill, E., *In a Strange Land* (London: Jonathan Cape, 1944).

Griffin, Bernard Cardinal, *The Catholic Church and Reunion* (London: CTS, 1950).

— *Seek Ye First . . .* (London, The Catholic Book Club, 1951).

Hedley, J. C., *The Public Spirit of the Catholic Laity* (London: CTS, 1900).

Heydon, J. K., *Wage-Slavery* (London: John Lane the Bodley Head, 1924).

— *Fascism and Providence* (London: Sheed and Ward, 1937).

Hinsley, A. Cardinal, *The Bond of Peace and other War-Time Addresses* (London: Burns and Oates, 1941 edn).

Keating, F. W., 'The Church and Social Reformers', *Publications of the C.T.S.*, 84 (London: CTS, 1911).

— 'The Catholic Episcopate', *The Messenger: Organ of the Apostleship of Prayer* (October, 1922).

Lattey, Fr C. (ed.), *The Church: Papers from the Summer School of Catholic Studies, held at Cambridge, August 6–15 1927* (Cambridge: Heffer and Sons, 1928).

— *Church and State: Papers Read at the Summer School of Catholic Studies, held at Cambridge, July 27th to August 6th 1935* (London: Burns Oates and Co., 1936).

— *Man and Eternity: Papers Read at the Summer School of Catholic Studies, held at Cambridge, July 25th to August 3rd 1936* (London: Burns Oates and Co., 1937).

Lilly, W. S., and Wallis, J. P., *A Manual of the Law Specially Affecting Catholics* (London: William Clowes, 1893).

de Lisle, E., *Pastoral Politics: A Reply to Dr. Bagshawe, Catholic Bishop of Nottingham* (London: Simpkin, Marshall and Co.; Loughbrough: H. Wills, 1885).

Liverpool Catholic Action Congress Report (Liverpool, 1937).

Lunn, A., *The Unpopular Front* (London: CTS, 1937).

McCabe, H., 'Conscience and Nuclear War', *Clergy Review* (March 1962), pp. 129–41.

McNabb, V., *Catholics and Nonconformists* (London: CTS, 1942 edn).

Mahoney, E. J., *Questions and Answers: Precepts* (London: Burns Oates and Co., 1949).

Manning, H. E., *The Vatican Decrees in their bearing on Civil Allegiance* (London: Longmans and Co., 1875).

Marinoff, I., *The Heresy of National Socialism* (London: Burns Oates and Washbourne, 1941).

Marshall, A., *The New Cambridge Curriculum in Economics and Appointed*

Branches of Political Science; its Purpose and Plan (London: Macmillan and Co., 1903).

Martindale, C. C., 'A Catholic Programme', in Fr C. Lattey, S.J. (ed.), *Church and State: Papers Read at the Summer School of Catholic Studies, Held at Cambridge, July 27ᵗʰ to August 6ᵗʰ 1935* (London: Burns Oates and Co., 1936).

Murphy, J., *Employers and Employed: A Statement on the Social Question* (Oxford: CSG, 1959).

Norris, J., *The Help of the Laity* (London: CTS, 1901).

Official Report of the First National Catholic Congress (Edinburgh and London: Sands and Co., 1910).

Parkinson, H. (ed.), *Pope Pius X on Social Reform* (London: CTS, 1910).

— *A Primer of Social Science* (London: P. S. King and Co; New York: Devin-Adair Co., 1913).

Plater, C., *Retreats for the People* (London: Sands and Co., 1912).

— *The Priest and Social Action* (London: Longmans, Green and Co., 1914).

The Pope and the People: Select Letters and Addresses on Social Questions (London: CTS, 1950 edn).

The Pope's Five Peace Points: Allocution to the College of Cardinals by His Holiness Pope Pius XII on December 24 1939 (London: CTS; Oxford: CSG, 1940).

Proceedings of C.O.P.E.C.: A Report of the Meetings of the Conference on Christian Politics, Economics and Citizenship (London, 1924).

Report of the 40ᵗʰ Annual Conference of Catholic Colleges and of the Annual Conference of the Convent Schools' Association (London: Cole and Co., 1937).

Reynolds, Sir J., 'Catholic Action in the Liverpool Archdiocese', *Liverpool Catholic Action Congress Report* (Liverpool, 1937).

Smith, P. (ed.), *The Bishop of Münster and the Nazis* (London: Burns Oates and Co., 1942).

Snowden, P., *Socialism and Syndicalism* (London and Glasgow: Collin's Clear Type Press, 1913).

Soderini, Count Edward, *Socialism and Catholicism* (London: Longman, Green and Co., 1896).

Stein, W. (ed.), *Nuclear Weapons and Christian Conscience* (London: Merlin Press, 1961).

Temple, W., *Christianity and the Social Order* (London: SCM Press, 1950 edn).

Vaughan, H., Bishop of Salford, *The True Basis of Catholic Politics* (Manchester: F. Walker, 1883).

— *The Work of the Catholic Laity in England* (London: CTS, 1900).

SECONDARY SOURCES

Adelson, R., *Mark Sykes: Portrait of an Amateur* (London: Jonathan Cape, 1975).

Alberigo, G. (ed.), *History of Vatican II: Vol. I Announcing and Preparing*

Vatican Council II Toward a new Era in Catholicism (Maryknoll: Orbis; Leuven: Peeters, 1995).

Altholz, L., 'The Political Behaviour of the English Catholics, 1850-1867', *Journal of British Studies*, 4 (November 1964), 89-103.

— 'Social Catholicism in England in the Age of the Devotional Revolution', in S. J. Brown and D. W. Miller, *Piety and Power in Ireland 1760-1960: Essays in Honour of Emmet Larkin* (Notre Dame, Indiana: University of Notre Dame Press, 2000), pp. 209-19.

Andrews, L., *The Education Act 1918* (London: Routledge and Kegan Paul, 1976).

Annan, N., *Our Age: The Generation that Made Postwar Britain* (London: Fontana, 1991 edn).

von Arx, J., 'Manning's Ultramontanism and the Catholic Church in British Politics', *Recusant History*, 19 (May 1989), 332-47.

— (ed.), *Varieties of Ultramontanism* (Washington, D.C.: Catholic University of America Press, 1998).

— 'Catholics and Politics', in V. A. McClelland, and M. Hodgetts (eds), *From Without the Flaminian Gate: 150 years of Roman Catholicism in England and Wales 1850-2000* (London: Darton, Longman and Todd, 1999), pp. 245-71.

Aspden, K., 'The English Roman Catholic Bishops and the Social Order, 1918-26', *Recusant History*, 25 (May 2001), 543-64.

Aspinwall, B., 'Before Manning: Some Aspects of British Social Concern before 1865', *New Blackfriars*, 61 (March 1980), 113-26.

— 'Broadfield Revisited: Some Scottish Catholic Responses to Wealth, 1918-40', in W. J. Sheils and D. Wood (eds), *The Church and Wealth* (Studies in Church History, 24; Oxford: Blackwell, 1987), 393-406.

— 'Rerum Novarum in the Transatlantic World', in P. Boury (ed.), *Rerum Novarum: Écriture, Contenu et Réception d'une Encyclique: Actes du Colloque International Organisé par L'École Française de Rome et le Greco N° 2 du CNRS, Rome, 18-20 Avril 1991* (École Française de Rome: Palais Farnèse, 1997), pp. 465-95.

— 'Towards an English Catholic Social Conscience, 1829-1920', *Recusant History*, 25 (May 2000), 106-19.

Bailey, C., *Francis Fortescue Urquhart* (London: Macmillan and Co., 1936).

Barlow, B., *'A Brother Knocking at the Door': The Malines Conversations 1921-1925* (Norwich: The Canterbury Press, 1996).

Barker, R., *Education and Politics 1900-1951: A Study of the Labour Party* (Oxford: Clarendon Press, 1972).

— *Political Ideas in Modern Britain: In and after the twentieth century* (London and New York: Routledge, 1997 edn).

Barnett, C., *The Audit of War: the Illusion and Reality of Britain as a Great Nation* (London: Macmillan, 1987 edn).

Beard, M., *Faith and Fortune* (Leominster: Gracewing, 1997).

Bebbington, D., *The Nonconformist Conscience: Chapel and Politics 1870-1914* (London: Allen and Unwin, 1982).

— *Evangelicism in Modern England: A History from the 1730s to the 1980s* (London: Unwin Hyman, 1989).

— 'The Decline and Resurgence of Evangelical Social Concern 1918-1980', in J. Wolffe (ed.), *Evangelical Faith and Public Zeal: Evangelicals and Society 1780-1980* (London: SPCK, 1995), pp. 175-97.

Beck, G. A. (ed.), *The English Catholics 1850-1950* (London: Burns Oates and Co., 1950).

Bedoyère, M. de La, *Cardinal Bernard Griffin* (London: Rockliff, 1955).

Bell, G. K. A., *Randall Davidson: Archbishop of Canterbury* (2 vols. London: Oxford University Press, 1935).

Bellenger, D. A., 'Cardinal Gasquet (1846-1929): An English Roman', *Recusant History*, 24 (October 1999), 552-60.

Bellenger, D. A., and Fletcher, S., *Princes of the Church: A History of the English Cardinals* (Stroud: Sutton Publishing, 2001).

Benkovitz, M. J., *Frederick Rolfe: Baron Corvo* (London: Hamilton, 1977).

Oscar Beozzo, J., 'The External Climate', in Alberigo, G. (ed.), *History of Vatican II: Vol. I Announcing and Preparing Vatican Council II Toward a new Era in Catholicism* (Maryknoll: Orbis, Leuven: Peeters, 1995), pp. 357-404.

Bernardi, P., 'Social Modernism: the case of the *Semaines Sociales*', in D. Jodock (ed.), *Catholicism Contending with Modernity: Roman Catholic Modernism and Anti-Modernism in Historical Context* (Cambridge: Cambridge University Press, 2000), pp. 277-307.

Biggs-Davison, J., and Chowdharay-Best, G., *The Cross of Saint Patrick: The Catholic Unionist Tradition in Ireland* (Bourne End: Kensal, 1984).

Birn, D. S., *The League of Nations Union 1918-1945* (Oxford: Clarendon Press, 1981).

Bolton, C.A., *Salford Diocese and its Catholic Past* (Manchester, 1950).

Bossy, J., *The English Catholic Community 1570-1850* (London: Darton, Longman and Todd, 1979 edn).

Boury, P. (ed.), *Rerum Novarum: Écriture, Contenu et Réception d'une Encyclique: Actes du Colloque International Organisé par L'École Française de Rome et le Greco N° 2 du CNRS, Rome, 18-20 Avril 1991* (École Française de Rome: Palais Farnèse, 1997).

Boyce, D. G., *Englishmen and Irish Troubles: British Public Opinion and the Making of Irish Policy 1918-22* (London: Jonathan Cape, 1972).

Braybrooke, M., *Children of One God: A History of the Council of Christians and Jews* (London: Valentine Mitchell, 1991).

Bromfield, J. F., *Souvenir of the Centenary of St Mary's Parish, Wednesbury 1850-1950* (Wednesbury, 1950).

Brown, W. F., *Through Windows of Memory* (London: Sands and Co., 1946).

Buchanan, T., and Conway, M. (eds), *Political Catholicism in Europe, 1918-1965* (Oxford: Clarendon Press, 1996).

Buchanan, T., *The Spanish Civil War and the British Labour Movement* (Cambridge: Cambridge University Press, 1991).

— 'Great Britain', in T. Buchanan and M. Conway (eds), *Political*

Catholicism in Europe, 1918–1965 (Oxford: Clarendon Press, 1996), pp. 248–74.

— *Britain and the Spanish Civil War* (Cambridge: Cambridge University Press, 1997).

Burke, T., *Catholic History of Liverpool* (Liverpool: C. Tinling and Co., 1910).

Burns, T., *The Use of Memory* (London: Sheed and Ward, 1993).

Buscot, W., *The History of Cotton College* (London: Burns Oates and Co., 1940).

Byrnes, T. A., *Catholic Bishops in American Politics* (Princeton: Princeton University Press, 1991).

Callahan, W. J., *The Catholic Church in Spain, 1875–1998* (Washington, D.C.: Catholic University of America Press, 2000).

Cameron, J. M., 'Catholicism and Political Mythology', in *The Night Battle* (London: Burns and Oates, 1962).

Cannadine, D., *The Decline and Fall of the British Aristocracy* (New Haven, Conn. and London: Yale University Press, 1990).

— *Class in Britain* (London and Basingstoke: Macmillan, 1996 edn).

Caraman, P., *C. C. Martindale* (London: Longman, Green and Co., 1966).

Carpenter, E., *Archbishop Fisher: His Life and Times* (Norwich: The Canterbury Press, 1991).

Carter, D., 'The Ecumenical Movement in its Early Years', *Journal of Ecclesiastical History*, 49 (July 1998), 465–85.

Cashman, J., 'The 1906 Education Bill: Catholic Peers and Irish Nationalists', *Recusant History*, 18 (October 1987), 422–39.

Catholic Profiles (London: Paternoster Publications, u/d).

Catterall, P., 'Morality and Politics: The Free Churches and the Labour Party between the Wars', *Historical Journal*, 36 (September 1993), 667–85.

Ceadel, M., *Pacifism in Britain 1914–1945: The Defining of a Faith* (Oxford: Clarendon Press, 1980).

— 'Christian Pacifism in the Era of the Two World Wars', in W. J. Sheils (ed.), *The Church and War* (Studies in Church History, 20; Oxford: Blackwell, 1983), pp. 391–408.

Chadwick, O., *Hensley Henson: A Study in the Friction between Church and State* (Oxford: Clarendon Press, 1983).

— *Britain and the Vatican during the Second World War* (Cambridge: Cambridge University Press, 1986).

— *The Christian Church in the Cold War* (London: Penguin Books, 1993 edn).

— *A History of the Popes 1830–1914* (Oxford: Clarendon Press, 1998).

Chadwick, P., *Shifting Alliances: Church and State in English Education* (London and Washington: Cassell, 1997).

Champ, J., *The English Pilgrimage to Rome* (Leominster: Gracewing, 2000).

Cheverton, et al (eds), *A Use of Gifts: The Newman Association 1942–1992* (London: The Newman Association, 1992).

Clarke, P. F., *Lancashire and the New Liberalism* (Cambridge: Cambridge University Press, 1971).

— *Hope and Glory: Britain, 1900–90* (London: Penguin, 1996).

Cleary, J. M., *Catholic Social Action in Britain, 1909–1959* (Oxford: CSG, 1961).

Clifton, M., *Amigo: Friend of the Poor* (Leominster: Fowler Wright, 1987).

Coates, D., *The Labour Party and the Struggle for Socialism* (London: Cambridge University Press, 1975).

Coman, P., *Catholics and the Welfare State* (London: Longman, 1977).

Connolly, G. P., 'The Transubstantiation of Myth: Towards a New Popular History of Nineteenth Century Catholicism in England', *Journal of Ecclesiastical History*, 35 (January 1984), 78–104.

Conway, M., 'Building the Christian City: Catholics and Politics in Inter-War Francophone Belgium', *Past and Present*, 128 (August 1990), 117–51.

— 'Introduction', in Buchanan, T., and Conway, M. (eds), *Political Catholicism in Europe, 1918–1965* (Oxford: Clarendon Press, 1996), pp. 5–33.

— *Catholic Politics in Europe 1918–1945* (London: Routledge, 1997).

Coppa, F. J., *The Modern Papacy since 1789* (London and New York, Addison Wesley Longman: 1998).

Cornwell, J., *Hitler's Pope: The Secret History of Pius XII* (London: Viking, 1999).

Corrin, J. P., 'Labour Unrest and the Development of Anti-Statist Thinking in Britain 1900–1914', *The Chesterton Review*, 8 (August 1982), 225–43.

Couve de Murville, M. N. L., and Jenkins, P., *Catholic Cambridge* (London: CTS, 1983).

Coventry, J., 'Roman Catholicism', in R. Davis (ed.), *The Testing of the Churches 1932–1982: A Symposium* (London: Epworth Press, 1982), pp. 3–31.

Cowling, M., *The Impact of Hitler: British Politics and British Policy 1933–1940* (Cambridge: Cambridge University Press, 1975).

— *Religion and Public Doctrine in Modern England* (Cambridge: Cambridge University Press, 1980).

Crichton, J. D., *The Secret Name: Selected Writings of Francis Harold Drinkwater* (Leominster: Fowler Wright, 1986).

Cruickshank, M., *Church and State in English Education* (London: Macmillan and Co., 1964).

Daly, G., 'Theological and Philosophical Modernism', in D. Jodock (ed.), *Catholicism Contending with Modernity: Roman Catholic Modernism and Anti-Modernism in Historical Context* (Cambridge: Cambridge University Press, 2000), pp. 88–112.

Daniel, C., 'Wales', in A. Hastings (ed.), *The Church and the Nations* (London and New York: Sheed and Ward, 1959), pp. 116–32.

Davies, A., and Fielding, S. (eds), *Worker's Worlds: Cultures and Communities in Manchester and Salford, 1880–1939* (Manchester: Manchester University Press, 1992).

Davies, B., 'Opening the Windows: John XIII and the Second Vatican

Council', in P. Vallely (ed), *The New Politics: Catholic Social Teaching for the Twenty-First Century* (London: SCM Press, 1998), pp. 42–59.

Davies, J., '"Rome on the Rates": Archbishop Richard Downey and the Catholic School Question, 1929–1939', *North West Catholic History*, 18 (1991), 16–32.

— 'The Liverpool Catholic Land Association', *North West Catholic History*, 19 (1992), 21–46.

— '"L'Art Du Possible", The Board of Education, the Catholic Church and Negotiations over the White Paper and the Education Bill, 1943–1944', *Recusant History*, 22 (May 1994), 231–50. .

— 'A Liverpool Priest and the Anglo-Irish Treaty of 1921', *North West Catholic History*, 24 (1997), 22–41.

— 'Bishop Henry Vincent Marshall: Relations with the Manchester Jewish Community and the Other Christian Churches', *North West Catholic History*, 26 (1999), 96–109.

— 'Bishop Ambrose Moriarty, Shrewsbury and World War Two', *Recusant History*, 25 (May 2000), 133–58.

Davies, S., *Liverpool Labour: Social and Political Influences on the Development of the Labour Party in Liverpool, 1900–39* (Keele: Keele University Press, 1996).

Dayras, S., 'Les Voeux de L'Épiscopat Britannique: Reflets D'Une Église Minoritaire', in *Le Deuxieme Concile Du Vatican (1959–1965): Actes du colloque organisé par l'École française de Rome en collaboration avec l'Université de Lille III, l'Instituto per le scienze religiose de Bologne et le Dipartimento di studi storici del Medioevo e dell'età contemporanea de l'Università di Roma-La Sapienza*, Rome 28–30 mai 1986 (Palais Farnèse: École Française de Rome, 1989), pp. 139–53.

Delaney, E., 'The churches and Irish emigration to Britain, 1921–60', *Archivium Hibernicum*, 52 (1998), 98–114.

Dick, J. A., *The Malines Conversations Revisited* (Leuven: Leuven University Press, 1989).

Doyle, P. J., 'Religion, Politics and the Catholic Working Class', *New Blackfriars*, 54 (May 1973), 218–25.

Doyle, Peter, 'The Catholic Federation 1906–1929', in W. J. Sheils and D. Wood (eds), *Voluntary Religion* (Studies in Church History, 23; Oxford: Blackwell, 1986), pp. 461–76.

— 'Charles Plater and the Origins of the Catholic Social Guild', *Recusant History*, 21 (1993), 401–17.

Duffy, E., '"Ecclesiastical Democracy Detected"': Part 1, *Recusant History*, 10 (January 1970), 193–209.

— '"Ecclesiastical Democracy Detected"': Part 2, *Recusant History*, 10 (October 1970), 309–31.

— *Saints and Sinners: A History of the Popes* (New Haven, Conn. and London: Yale University Press, 1997).

— 'The Thinking Church: a Recent History', *Priests and People*, 14 (October 2000), 374–9.

Dunn, D. J., *The Catholic Church and the Soviet Government, 1939–1949* (New York: East European Quarterly, 1977).

Dwyer, G., *Diocese of Portsmouth Past and Present* (Portsmouth, 1981).

Dwyer, J. J., 'The Catholic Press, 1850–1950', in G. A. Beck (ed.), *The English Catholics 1850–1950* (London: Burns Oates and Co., 1950), pp. 475–514.

Evennett, H. O., 'Catholics and the Universities 1850–1950', in G. A. Beck (ed.), *The English Catholics 1850–1950* (London: Burns Oates and Co., 1950), pp. 291–321.

Fielding, S. J., *Class and Ethnicity: Irish Catholics in England 1880–1939* (Buckingham and Philadelphia: Open University Press, 1993).

Finan, J., *Struggle for Justice: A Short History of the Catholic Teacher's Federation* (Nelson, 1975).

Fitzpatrick, D., 'A curious middle place: the Irish in Britain, 1871–1921', in R. Swift and S. Gilley (eds), *The Irish in Britain 1815–1939* (London: Pinter Publishers, 1989), pp. 10–59.

Flint, J., '"Must God go Fascist?": English Catholic Opinion and the Spanish Civil War', *Church History*, 56 (September 1987), 364–74.

Fogarty, G. P., *The Vatican and the American Hierarchy from 1870 to 1965* (Wilmington, Delaware: Michael Glazier, 1985 edn).

— 'Cardinal William O' Connell', in J. von Arx (ed.), *Varieties of Ultramontanism* (Washington, D.C.: Catholic University of America Press, 1998), pp. 118–46.

Fogarty, M. P., 'Catholics and Public Policy', in M. P. Hornsby-Smith, *Catholics in England 1950–2000* (London: Cassell, 2000), pp. 122–38.

Foster, R. F., *Modern Ireland 1600–1972* (London: Allen Lane, 1988).

Foster, S., 'A Bishop for Essex: Bernard Ward and the Diocese of Brentwood', *Recusant History*, 21 (October 1993), 556–71.

Fouilloux, E., 'The Antepreparatory Phase: The Slow Emergence from Inertia (January, 1959 – October, 1962)', in G. Alberigo (ed.), *History of Vatican II: Vol. I Announcing and Preparing Vatican Council II Toward a New Era in Catholicism* (Maryknoll: Orbis; Leuven: Peeters, 1995), pp. 55–166.

Fox, A., *A History of the National Union of Boot and Shoe Operatives 1874–1957* (Oxford: Basil Blackwell, 1958).

Furnival, J., and Knowles, A., *Archbishop Derek Worlock: His Personal Journey* (London: Geoffrey Chapman, 1998).

Gilley, S. W., 'Catholics and Socialists in Glasgow, 1906–1912', in K. Lunn (ed.), *Hosts, Immigrants and Minorities: Historical Responses to Newcomers in British Society 1870–1914* (Folkestone: Dawson, 1980), pp. 160–200.

— 'Catholics and Socialists in Scotland, 1900–30', in R. Swift and S. W. Gilley (eds), *The Irish in Britain, 1815–1939* (London: Pinter Publishers, 1989), pp. 212–38.

— 'The Roman Catholic Church, 1780–1940', in S. W. Gilley and W. J. Sheils (eds), *A History of Religion in Britain* (Oxford: Blackwells, 1994), pp. 346–62.

— 'The Years of Equipoise, 1892–1943', in V. A. McClelland, and M. Hodgetts (eds), *From Without the Flaminian Gate: 150 years of Roman Catholicism in England and Wales 1850–2000* (London: Darton, Longman and Todd, 1999) pp. 21–61.

— 'A Tradition and a Culture Lost, To be Regained?', in M. P. Hornsby-Smith (ed.), *Catholics in England 1950–2000* (London: Cassell, 2000), pp. 29–45.

Goldman, L., *Dons and Workers: Oxford and Adult Education* (Oxford: Clarendon Press, 1995).

Gooch, L., 'An Archbishop for Darlington?', *Northern Catholic History*, 39 (1998), 57–62.

Gosden, P. H. J. H., *Education in the Second World War: A Study in Policy and Administration* (London: Methuen and Co., 1976).

Gottlieb, J., *Feminine Fascism: Women in Britain's Fascist Movement 1923–1945* (London and New York: I. B. Tauris, 2000).

Green, Dom Bernard, 'David Knowles's First Book', *Downside Review*, 107 (April 1989), 79–85.

Green, D., *The Living of Maisie Ward* (Notre Dame and London: University of Notre Dame Press, 1997).

Greene, T. A., 'English Roman Catholics and the Irish Free State', *Éire-Ireland*, 19 (Spring 1984), 48–73.

Greene, T. R., 'Vichy France and the Catholic Press in England: Contrasting Attitudes to a Moral Problem', *Recusant History*, 21 (May 1992), 111–33.

Greenleaf, W. H., *The British Political Tradition: Volume Two The Ideological Heritage* (London and New York: Methuen, 1983).

Gregory-Jones, P., *A History of the Cambridge Catholic Chaplaincy 1895–1965* (Cagliari, 1986).

Gwynn, D., 'The Irish Immigration', in G. A. Beck, (ed.), *The English Catholics 1850–1950* (London: Burns Oates and Co., 1950), pp. 265–90.

— 'Manning and Ireland', in J. Fitzsimons (ed.), *Manning: Anglican and Catholic* (London: Burns and Oates, 1951), pp. 111–35.

Hachey, T., 'The Quarantine of Archbishop Mannix', *Irish University Review*, 1 (Autumn 1970), 111–30.

— (ed.), *Anglo-Vatican Relations, 1914–1939: Confidential Annual Reports of the British Ministers to the Holy See* (Boston, Mass.: G. K. Hall and Co., 1972).

Hagerty, J. M., 'The First National Catholic Congress', *Northern Catholic History*, 20 (1984), 21–30.

Harris, M., *The Catholic Church and the Foundation of the Northern Irish State* (Cork: Cork University Press, 1993).

Hart, P., '"Operations Abroad": The IRA in Britain, 1919–23', *English Historical Review*, 65 (February 2000), 71–102.

Hastings, A. (ed.), The *Church and the Nations* (London and New York: Sheed and Ward, 1959).

— 'Some Reflexions on the English Catholicism of the Late 1930s', in A.

Hastings (ed.), *Bishops and Writers: Aspects of the Evolution of Modern English Catholicism* (Wheathampstead: Anthony Clarke, 1977), pp. 107–125.

— *A History of English Christianity 1920–1985* (London: Collins; Fount Paperbacks, 1987 edn).

—'Catholic History from Vatican I to John Paul II', in A. Hastings (ed.), *Modern Catholicism: Vatican II and After* (London: SPCK, 1991), pp. 1–13.

— *Church and State: The English Experience* (Exeter: University of Exeter, 1991).

Heenan, J. C., *Cardinal Hinsley* (London: Burns, Oates and Washbourne, 1944).

— *A Crown of Thorns: An Autobiography 1951–1963* (London: Hodder and Stoughton, 1975 edn).

Heimann, M., *Catholic Devotion in Victorian England* (Oxford: Clarendon Press, 1995).

Henson, H., *Retrospect of an Unimportant Life* (3 vols. London: Oxford University Press, 1942–50).

Hickey, J., *Urban Catholics: Urban Catholicism in England and Wales from 1829 to the present day* (London: Geoffrey Chapman, 1967).

Hickman, M., *Religion, Class and Identity: The State, the Catholic Church and the Education of the Irish in Britain* (Guildford: Avebury, 1995).

Holmes, D., *More Roman than Rome: English Catholicism in the Nineteenth Century* (London: Burns and Oates; Sheperdstown: Patmos Press, 1978).

— *The Triumph of the Holy See: A Short History of the Papacy in the Nineteenth Century* (London: Burns and Oates; Sheperdstown Patmos Press, 1978).

— *The Papacy in the Modern World 1914–1978* (London: Burns and Oates, 1981).

Hornsby-Smith, M. P., *Roman Catholic Beliefs in England: Customary Catholicism and Transformations of Religious Authority* (Cambridge: Cambridge University Press, 1991).

— (ed.), *Catholics in England 1950–2000* (London: Cassell, 2000).

— 'A Changing Church: facing the future', *Priests and People*, 14 (October 2000), 369–73.

Horwood, T., 'Public Opinion and the 1908 Eucharistic Congress', *Recusant History*, 25 (May 2000), 120–32.

Hughes, P., 'The Bishops of the Century', in G. A. Beck (ed.), *The English Catholics 1850–1950* (London: Burns Oates and Co., 1950), pp. 187–222.

Hughes, T. O., *Winds of Change: the Roman Catholic Church and Society in Wales, 1918–62* (Cardiff: University of Wales Press, 1999).

— 'Archbishop Michael McGrath, 1882–1961: A 20th century St David? The Irishman who came to Wales', in J. R. Guy and W. G. Neely, *Contrasts and Comparisons: Studies in Irish and Welsh Church History* (Powys: Welsh Religious History Society; Keady, C. Armagh: The Church of Ireland Historical Society, 1999), pp. 135–53.

Hutton, A. W., *Cardinal Manning* (London: Methuen, 1892).

Inglis, K. S., *Churches and the Working Classes in Victorian England* (London: Routledge and Kegan Paul; Toronto: University of Toronto Press, 1963).

Iremonger, F. A., *William Temple, Archbishop of Canterbury, his Life and Letters* (London: Oxford University Press, 1949 edn).

Jasper, R. C. D., *George Bell: Bishop of Chichester* (London: Oxford University Press, 1968 edn).

Jedin, H., and Dolan. J. (eds), *History of the Church* (vols. 9-10, New York: The Crossroad Publishing Co., 1981).

Jodock, D. (ed.), *Catholicism Contending with Modernity: Roman Catholic Modernism and Anti-Modernism in Historical Context* (Cambridge: Cambridge University Press, 2000).

Johnstone, T., and Hagerty, J., *The Cross on the Sword: Catholic Chaplains in the Forces* (London: Geoffrey Chapman, 1996).

Jones, J., *Balliol College: A History* (Oxford: Oxford University Press, 1997 edn).

Keating, Joan, 'Discrediting the 'Catholic State': Britain and the Fall of France', in F. Tallett and N. Atkin (eds), *Catholicism in Britain and France since 1789* (London: Hambledon, 1996), pp. 27-42.

Kenny, A., *A Path From Rome* (Oxford: Oxford University Press, 1988 edn).

Kent, B., *Undiscovered Ends: An Autobiography* (London: Collins; Fount Paperbacks, 1994 edn).

Kent, J., 'Late-Nineteenth-Century Nonconformist Renaissance', in D. Baker (ed.), *Renaissance and Renewal in Christian History* (Studies in Church History, 14; Oxford: Blackwell, 1977), pp. 351-60.

— *William Temple: Church, State and Society in Britain*, 1880-1950 (Cambridge: Cambridge University Press, 1992).

Kent, P., *The Pope and the Duce* (New York: St Martin's Press, 1981).

Keogh, D., *The Vatican, The Bishops and Irish Politics 1919-1939* (Cambridge: Cambridge University Press, 1986).

— *Ireland and the Vatican: The Policy and Diplomacy of Church-State Relations, 1922-1960* (Cork: Cork University Press, 1995).

Keogh, D., and O'Driscoll, F., 'Ireland', in T. Buchanan and M. Conway (eds), *Political Catholicism in Europe, 1918-1965* (Oxford: Clarendon Press, 1996), pp. 275-300.

Kollar, R., *Westminster Cathedral: From Dream to Reality* (Edinburgh: Faith and Life Publications, 1987).

— 'The Reluctant Prior: Bishop Wulstan Pearson of Lancaster', *Recusant History*, 20 (May 1991), 412.

Kuhn, W. M., *Democratic Royalism: The Transformation of the British Monarchy, 1861-1914* (Basingstoke and London: Macmillan; New York, NY: St Martin's Press, 1996).

Lahey, R. J., 'Cardinal Bourne and the Malines Conversations', in A. Hastings (ed.), *Bishops and Writers: Aspects of the Evolution of Modern English Catholicism* (Wheathampstead: Anthony Clarke, 1977), pp. 81-105.

Lane, P., *The Catenian Association 1908–1983* (London: The Catenian Association, 1982).

Larkin, E., *The Roman Catholic Church and the Plan of Campaign 1886–1888* (Cork: Cork University Press, 1978).

— 'Socialism and Catholicism in Ireland', *Studies*, 74 (Spring 1985), 66–92.

Leonard, E. M., 'English Catholicism and Modernism', in D. Jodock (ed.), *Catholicism Contending with Modernity: Roman Catholic Modernism and Anti-Modernism in Historical Context* (Cambridge: Cambridge University Press, 2000), pp. 248–73.

Leslie, S., *The Passing Chapter* (London: Cassell, 1934).

— *Cardinal Gasquet* (London: Burns and Oates, 1953).

Lockhart, J. G., *Cosmo Gordon Lang* (London: Hodder and Stoughton, 1949 edn).

Longley, C., *The Worlock Archive* (London: Geoffrey Chapman, 2000).

Luxmoore, J., and Babisch, J., *The Vatican and the Red Flag: The Struggle for the Soul of Eastern Europe* (London: Geoffrey Chapman, 1999).

Lynch, J., 'England', in A. Hastings (ed.), *The Church and the Nations* (London and New York: Sheed and Ward, 1959), pp. 1–19.

Macentee, G. P., *The Social Catholic Movement in Great Britain* (New York: Macmillan Co., 1927).

McCarthy, J. P., *Hilaire Belloc: Edwardian Radical* (Indianapolis: Liberty Press, 1978).

McClelland, V. A., *Cardinal Manning: His Public Life and Influence* (London: Oxford University Press, 1962).

— *English Roman Catholics and Higher Education, 1830–1903* (Oxford: Clarendon Press, 1973).

— 'Bourne, Norfolk and the Irish Parliamentarians: Roman Catholics and the Education Bill of 1906', *Recusant History*, 23 (October 1996), 228–56.

— 'St. Edmund's College, Ware and St. Edmund's College, Cambridge; Historical Connections and Early Tribulations', *Recusant History*, 23 (May 1997), 470–82.

McClelland, V. A., and Hodgetts, M. (eds), *From Without the Flaminian Gate: 150 years of Roman Catholicism in England and Wales 1850–2000* (London: Darton, Longman and Todd, 1999).

McCleod, H., 'Building the "Catholic Ghetto": Catholic Organizations 1870–1914', in W. J. Sheils and D. Wood (eds), *Voluntary Religion* (Studies in Church History, 23; Oxford: Blackwell, 1986), pp. 411–442.

McCormack, A., *Cardinal Vaughan* (London: Burns and Oates, 1966).

McIntire, C. T., *England and the Papacy 1858–1861: Tories, Liberals and the Overthrow of Papal Temporal Power during the Italian Risorgimento* (Cambridge: Cambridge University Press, 1983).

McKenzie, R. T., *British Political Parties: The Distribution of Power Within the Conservative and Labour Parties* (London: Heinemann, 1963 edn).

McKibbin, R., *Classes and Cultures: England 1918–1951* (Oxford: Oxford University Press, 2000 edn).

McMillan, J. F., 'France', in T. Buchanan and M. Conway (eds), *Political*

Catholicism in Europe, 1918–1965 (Oxford: Clarendon Press, 1996), pp. 34–68.

McShane, J., *"Sufficiently Radical"*: *Catholicism, Progressivism, and the Bishops' Programme of 1919* (Washington, D. C.: Catholic University of America Press, 1986).

McSweeney, B., *Roman Catholicism: The Search for Relevance* (Oxford: Blackwell, 1980).

Machin, G. I. T., 'The Liberal Government and the Eucharistic Procession of 1908', *Journal of Ecclesiastical History*, 34 (October 1983), 559–83.

— *Churches and Social Issues in Twentieth-Century Britain* (Oxford: Clarendon Press, 1998).

Martindale, C. C., *Charles Dominic Plater S.J.* (London: Harding and More, 1922).

— *Bernard Vaughan, S. J.* (London: Longmans and Co., 1923).

Mason, F., 'The Newer Eve: The Catholic Women's Suffrage Society in England, 1911–1923', *Catholic Historical Review*, 72 (October 1986), 620–38.

Mathew, D., *Catholicism in England 1535–1935: Portrait of a Minority: Its Culture and Traditions* (London: Catholic Book Club, 1938 edn).

Mayall, D., 'Rescued from the Shadows of Exile: Nellie Driver, Autobiography and the British Union of Fascists', in T. Kushner and K. Lunn (eds), *The Politics of Marginality: Race, the Radical Right and the Minorities in Twentieth Century Britain* (London: Frank Cass, 1990), pp. 19–39.

Mews, S., 'The Churches', in M. Morris (ed.), *The General Strike* (London: Penguin, 1976), pp. 318–37.

— 'The Sword of the Spirit: A Catholic Cultural Crusade of 1940', in W. J. Sheils (ed.), *The Church and War* (Studies in Church History, 20; Oxford: Blackwell, 1983), pp. 409–30.

— 'The Hunger Strike of the Lord Mayor of Cork, 1920: Irish, English and Vatican Attitudes', in W. J. Sheils and D. Wood (eds), *The Churches, Ireland and the Irish*, (Studies in Church History, 25; Oxford: Blackwell, 1989), pp. 385–99.

Miller, D. W., *Church, State and Nation in Ireland 1898–1921* (Dublin: Gill and Macmillan, 1973).

Misner, P., *Social Catholicism in Europe* (London: Darton Longman and Todd, 1991).

— 'Catholic anti-Modernism: the ecclesial setting', in D. Jodock (ed.), *Catholicism Contending with Modernity: Roman Catholic Modernism and Anti-Modernism in Historical Context* (Cambridge: Cambridge University Press, 2000), pp. 56–87.

Moloney, T., *Westminster, Whitehall and the Vatican: The Role of Cardinal Hinsley 1935–43* (London: Burns and Oates, 1985).

Molony, J. N., *The Emergence of Political Catholicism in Italy: Partito Popolare 1919–1926* (London: Croom Helm, 1977).

Morey, Dom A., 'Benet House, Cambridge, Some Early Correspondence, 1895-1900', *Downside Review*, 103 (July 1985), 230–38.

Morris, K. L., 'Fascism and British Catholic Writers 1924–1939: Part One', *New Blackfriars*, 80 (January 1999), 32–45.

— 'Fascism and British Catholic Writers 1924–1939: Part Two', *New Blackfriars*, 80 (February 1999), 82–95.

Morris, M. (ed.), *The General Strike* (Harmondsworth: Penguin, 1976).

Mullins, D. J., 'The Catholic Church in Wales', in V. A. McClelland and M. Hodgetts (eds), *From Without the Flaminian Gate: 150 years of Roman Catholicism in England and Wales 1850–2000* (London: Darton, Longman and Todd, 1999), pp. 272–94.

Neville, G., *Radical Churchman: Edward Lee Hicks and the New Liberalism* (Oxford: Clarendon Press, 1998).

Nichols, A., *Dominican Gallery: Portrait of a Culture* (Leominster: Gracewing, 1997).

Nicholls, D., *The Lost Prime Minister: A Life of Sir Charles Dilke* (London: Hambledon, 1995).

Norman, E. R., *The Catholic Church and Ireland in the Age of Rebellion* (London: Longmans, Green and Co., 1965).

— *Anti-Catholicism in Victorian England* (London: George Allen and Unwin, 1968).

— *Church and Society in England 1770–1970* (Oxford: Clarendon Press, 1976).

— *The English Catholic Church in the Nineteenth Century* (Oxford: Clarendon Press, 1984).

— *Roman Catholicism in England from the Elizabethan Settlement to the Second Vatican Council* (Oxford: Oxford University Press, 1985).

O'Driscoll, F., 'In Search of a Christian Social Order: The Impact of Social Catholicism', in T. M. Devine and J. F. McMillan (eds), *Celebrating Columba: Irish-Scottish Connections 597–1997* (Edinburgh: John Donald, 1999), pp. 102–36.

Oldmeadow, E., *Francis Cardinal Bourne* (2 vols. London: Burns Oates and Co., 1944).

Oliver, J., *The Church and Social Order* (London: Alden and Mowbray, 1968).

Ombres, R., 'Strikes: Reformulating Catholic Thinking in Britain', *New Blackfriars*, 65 (Mar. 1984), pp. 120–3.

O'Neil, R., *Cardinal Herbert Vaughan* (London: Burns and Oates, 1995).

Osborne, M., '"The Second Spring": Roman Catholicism in Victorian Northamptonshire', *Northamptonshire Past and Present*, 9 (1994–5), 71–9.

The Oscottian: The Jubilee 1838–1888 *(Birmingham: St Mary's College, Oscott, 1888)*.

Pawley, B. and M., *Rome and Canterbury Through Four Centuries* (London and Oxford: Alden and Mowbray, 1974).

J. Pereiro, *Cardinal Manning: An Intellectual Biography* (Oxford: Clarendon Press, 1998).

— 'Who are the Laity', in V. A. McClelland and M. Hodgetts (eds), *From Without the Flaminian Gate: 150 years of Roman Catholicism in England and Wales 1850–2000* (London: Darton, Longman and Todd, 1999), pp. 245–71.

Pevsner, N., *The Buildings of England: Lancashire I The Industrial and Commercial South* (Harmondsworth: Penguin Books, 1979 edn).

Phillips, F. R., *Bishop Beck and English Education 1949-1959* (Lewiston, Queenston, Lampeter: The Edwin Mellen Press, 1990).

Plumb, B., 'The Founding Fathers of Lancaster Diocese', in J. A. Hilton (ed.), *Catholic Englishmen: Essays Presented to the Rt. Rev. B. C. Foley, Bishop of Lancaster* (Wigan: The North West Catholic History Society, 1984), pp. 53-8.

Pollard, J. F., *The Unknown Pope: Benedict XV (1914-1922) and the Pursuit of Peace* (London: Geoffrey Chapman, 1999).

Quinn, D., 'Manning as Politician', *Recusant History*, 21 (October 1992), 267-86.

— *Patronage and Piety: The Politics of English Roman Catholicism 1850-1900* (Stanford: Stanford University Press, 1993).

Rafferty, O. P., 'Nicholas Wiseman, Ecclesiastical Politics and Anglo-Irish Reflections in the Mid-Nineteenth Century', *Recusant History*, 21 (May 1993), 381-400.

— *Catholicism in Ulster 1603-1983* (London: Hurst and Co., 1994).

— *The Church, the State and the Fenian Threat 1861-75* (London: MacMillan, 1999).

Reynolds, E. B., *The Roman Catholic Church in England and Wales: A Short History* (Wheathampstead: Anthony Clarke, 1973).

Rhodes, A., *The Vatican in the Age of the Dictators 1922-1945* (London: Hodder and Stoughton, 1973).

— *The Power of Rome in the Twentieth Century: The Vatican in the Age of Liberal Democracies 1870-1922* (London: Sidgwick and Jackson, 1983).

Roberts, G., 'English Catholics and Politics in the Late Nineteenth Century', *Studies*, 74 (Winter 1985), 455-63.

Robbins, K., 'Britain, 1940 and 'Christian Civilization' ', in D. Beales and G. Best (eds), *History Society and the Churches: Essays in Honour of Owen Chadwick* (Cambridge: Cambridge University Press, 1985), pp. 279-99.

Robinson, G., *David Urquhart: Some Chapters in the Life of a Victorian Knight Errant of Justice and Liberty* (New York: Augustus M. Kelley, 1970 edn).

Santamaria, B. A., *Daniel Mannix* (Carlton. Ashford [Middx]: Melbourne University Press, 1984).

Schoenl, W. J., *The Intellectual Crisis in English Catholicism: Liberal Catholics, Modernists, and the Vatican in the Late Nineteenth and Early Twentieth Centuries* (New York and London: Garland Publishing, Inc., 1982).

Schuck, M. J., *That They Be One: The Social Teaching of the Papal Encyclicals* (Washington D.C.: Georgetown University Press, 1991).

Scott, C., *A Historian and his World: A Life of Christopher Dawson 1889-1970* (London: Sheed and Ward, 1984).

Scott, G., *The RCs: A Report on RCs in Britain Today* (London: Hutchinson, 1967).

Searle, G. R., *Corruption in British Politics 1895–1930* (Oxford: Clarendon Press, 1987).

Secrest, M., *Kenneth Clark: A Biography* (London: Wiedenfeld and Nicholson, 1984).

Segar, M., *Margaret Fletcher* (London: CTS, 1943).

Sharratt, B., 'English Roman Catholicism in the 1960s', in A. Hastings (ed.), *Bishops and Writers: Aspects of the Evolution of Modern English Catholicism* (Wheathampstead: Anthony Clarke, 1977), pp. 127–58.

Sheed, F., *The Church and I* (London: Sheed and Ward, 1975).

Sheppard, D., and Worlock, D., *Better Together: Christian partnership in a hurt city* (London: Hodder and Stoughton, 1988).

Sire, H. J. A., *Father Martin D'Arcy: Philosopher of Christian Love* (Leominster: Gracewing, 1997).

Sisman, A., *A. J. P. Taylor: A Biography* (London: Sinclair-Stevenson, 1994).

Skidelsky, R., *Politicians and the Slump: The Labour Government of 1929–1931* (London: Macmillan, 1967).

Smyth, C., *Cyril Forster Garbett: Archbishop of York* (London: Hodder and Stoughton, 1959).

Snead-Cox, J. G., *The Life of Cardinal Vaughan* (2 vols. London: Herbert and Daniel, 1912).

Speaight, R., *The Property Basket: Recollections of a Divided Life* (London: Collins and Harvill Press, 1970).

Steele, E. D., 'The Irish Presence in the North of England 1850–1914', *Northern History*, 12 (1976), 220–41.

Supple, J. F., 'The Role of the Catholic Laity in Yorkshire 1850–1900', *Recusant History*, 18 (May 1987), 304–17.

— 'The Catholic Church and the Yorkshire Poor, 1850–1900', in G. T. Bradley (ed.), *Yorkshire Catholics* (Leeds Diocesan Archives Occasional Papers, 1).

Supple-Green, J. F., *The Catholic Revival in Yorkshire 1850–1900* (Leeds: Leeds Philosophical and Literary Society, 1990).

Sweeney, G., 'The "wound in the right foot": unhealed?', in A. Hastings (ed.), *Bishops and Writers: Aspects of the Evolution of Modern English Catholicism* (Wheathampstead: Anthony Clarke, 1977), pp. 207–34.

— *St Edmund's House, Cambridge, The First Eighty Years: A History* (Cambridge: St Edmund's College, 1980).

Sweeney, M. V., 'Diocesan Organisation and Administration', in G. A. Beck (ed.), *The English Catholics 1850–1950* (London: Burns Oates and Co., 1950), pp. 116–150.

Symons, J., *The General Strike* (London: Cresset Press, 1959 edn).

Taylor, A. J. P., *English History 1914–1945* (Oxford: Clarendon Press, 1965).

Taylor, R., *Against the Bomb: The British Peace Movement 1958–1965* (Oxford: Clarendon Press, 1988).

Thompson, D. M., 'The Christian Socialist Revival in Britain: A Reappraisal', in J. Garnett and C. Matthew (eds), *Revival and Religion since 1700: Essays for John Walsh* (London: Hambledon, 1993), pp. 273–95.

— 'R. W. Dale and the 'Civic Gospel' ', in A. P. F. Sell, *Protestant Nonconformists and the West Midlands of England* (Keele: Keele University Press, 1996), pp. 99–118.

Thorpe, A., *The British General Election of 1931* (Oxford: Clarendon Press, 1991).

Thurlow, R., *Fascism in Britain: A History, 1918–1985* (Oxford: Blackwell, 1987).

Valentine, F., *Father Vincent McNabb, O.P.* (London: Burns and Oates, 1955).

Vidler, A., *A Variety of Catholic Modernists* (Cambridge: Cambridge University Press, 1970).

Vincent, M., 'Spain', in T. Buchanan and M. Conway (eds), *Political Catholicism in Europe, 1918–1965* (Oxford: Clarendon Press, 1996), pp. 97–128.

Waley, D., *British Public Opinion and the Abyssinian War 1935–6* (London: Maurice Temple Smith, 1975).

Wall, B., 'Remembrance of Things Past', *New Blackfriars*, 61 (July–August 1980), pp. 342–7.

Waller, P. J., *Democracy and Sectarianism: a Political and Social History of Liverpool 1868–1939* (Liverpool: Liverpool University Press, 1981).

Walker, W. M., 'Irish Immigrants in Scotland: Their Priests, Politics and Parochial Life', *Historical Journal*, 15 (December 1972), 649–67.

Walsh, M., *From Sword to Ploughshare: Sword of the Spirit to Catholic Institute for International Relations, 1940–80* (London: CIIR, 1980).

— 'Ecumenism in War-Time Britain: The Sword of the Spirit and Religion and Life, 1940–1945', pt. 1, *Heythrop Journal*, 23 (July 1982), 243–258.

— 'Ecumenism in War-Time Britain: The Sword of the Spirit and Religion and Life, 1940–1945', pt. 2, *Heythrop Journal*, 23 (October 1982), 377–94.

— *The Tablet: A Commemorative History 1840–1990* (London: The Tablet Publishing Company, 1990).

— 'Catholics, Society and Popular Culture', in V. A. McClelland and M. Hodgetts (eds), *From Without the Flaminian Gate: 150 years of Roman Catholicism in England and Wales 1850–2000* (London: Darton, Longman and Todd, 1999), pp. 346–70.

Ward, M., *Insurrection versus Resurrection* (London: Sheed and Ward, 1937).

— *Unfinished Business* (London: Sheed and Ward, 1964).

Waugh, E., *Monsignor Ronald Knox* (Boston and Toronto: Little, Brown and Co., 1959).

Weaver, M. J., 'George Tyrrell and the Joint Pastoral Letter', *Downside Review*, 99 (Jan. 1981), 18–39.

Wheeler, G., 'The Archdiocese of Westminster', in G. A. Beck (ed.), *The English Catholics 1850–1950* (London: Burns Oates and Co., 1950), pp. 151–186.

White, A., 'A History of *Blackfriars* and *New Blackfriars*', *New Blackfriars* (July/August 1996), pp. 320–33.

White, G., 'The Fall of France', in W. J. Sheils (ed.), *The Church and War* (Studies in Church History, 20; Oxford, 1983), pp. 431–41.

Whyte, J. H., *Church and State in Modern Ireland* (Dublin: Gill and Macmillan, 1980).

— *Catholics in Western Democracies* (Dublin: Gill and Macmillan, 1981).

Wicker, B., *First the Political Kingdom: A Personal Appraisal of the Catholic Left in Britain* (London and Melbourne: Sheed and Ward, 1967).

— 'Making Peace at Spode', *New Blackfriars*, 62 (July–August 1981), pp. 311–20.

Wilkinson, A., *The Church of England and the First World War* (London: SPCK, 1978).

— *Dissent or Conform? War, Peace and the English Churches 1900–1945* (London: SCM Press, 1986).

Williams, M. E., 'Seminaries and Priestly Formation', in V. A. McClelland and M. Hodgetts (eds), *From Without the Flaminian Gate: 150 years of Roman Catholicism in England and Wales 1850–2000* (London: Darton, Longman and Todd, 1999), pp. 62–83.

— *Oscott College in the Twentieth Century* (Leominster: Gracewing, 2001).

Williamson, P., *Stanley Baldwin: Conservative Leadership and National Values* (Cambridge: Cambridge University Press, 1999).

Wood, I. S., 'John Wheatley, the Irish and the Labour Movement in Scotland', *Historical Journal*, 31 (Autumn 1980), 71–85.

Wraith, B., 'A Pre-Modern Interpretation of the Modern: The English Catholic Church and the 'Social Question' in the Early Twentieth Century', in R. N. Swanson (ed.), *The Church Retrospective* (Studies in Church History, 33; Woodbridge: The Boydell Press, 1997), pp. 529–45.

Unpublished dissertations

Baxter, R., 'The Liverpool Labour Party, 1911–1963', unpublished D.Phil dissertation, University of Oxford (1969).

Bennett, B. S., 'The Archbishop of Canterbury in Politics, 1919–1939: selected case studies', unpublished Ph.D. dissertation, University of Cambridge (1992).

Broadley, M., 'The Episcopate of Thomas Henshaw, Bishop of Salford 1925–1938' unpublished M.Phil dissertation, University of Manchester (1998).

Brooke, M., 'Catholic Social Thought and Action in England', undergraduate dissertation, University of Cambridge (1994).

Butterworth, R. H., 'The Structure and Organisation of some Catholic Lay Organisations in Australia and Great Britain: A comparative study with special reference to the function of the organisations as social and political pressure groups', unpublished D.Phil. dissertation, University of Oxford (1959).

Fanning, M., 'The 1906 Liberal Education Bill and the Roman Catholic Reaction of the Salford Diocese', undergraduate dissertation, University of Oxford (1996).

Fielding, S. J., 'The Irish Catholics of Manchester and Salford: Aspects of their Religious and Political History, 1890–1939', unpublished Ph.D. dissertation, University of Warwick (1988).

Flessati, F., 'Pax: The history of a Catholic peace society 1936–1971', unpublished Ph.D. dissertation, University of Bradford (1991).

Gula, J. L., 'The Roman Catholic Church in the History of the Polish Exiled Community in Britain 1939–1950', unpublished Ph. D. dissertation, University of London (1992).

Keating, J., 'Roman Catholics, Christian Democracy and the British Labour Movement 1910–60', unpublished Ph.D. dissertation, Manchester University (1992).

McHugh, F. P., 'The Changing Social Role of the Roman Catholic Church in England, 1958–1982', unpublished Ph.D. dissertation, University of Cambridge (1982).

Mews, S. P., 'Religion and English Society in the First World War', unpublished Ph.D. dissertation, University of Cambridge (1973).

Index